KERRY JAMES MARSHALL
RYTHM MASTR

THE TIME HAS COME SO IT BEGINS[1]

THE SUPERHERO-CENTRED COMIC BOOK IS A VERY POPULAR ART FORM THAT HAS RARELY FEATURED BLACK CHARACTERS IN THE LEAD ROLE—YET MORE INVISIBILITY. AND OF THE FEW BLACK CHARACTERS THAT HAVE APPEARED, NONE OF THEM IS THE PRODUCT OF A BLACK ARTISTIC IMAGINATION, AND NONE HAS ACHIEVED THE STATUS OF SUPERMAN, BATMAN, SPIDER-MAN, OR THE FANTASTIC FOUR. SO THAT PRESENTS YET ANOTHER CHALLENGE . . . WITHOUT A PARADIGMATIC HERO FIGURE, AND NO HEROIC FANTASIES TO SPEAK OF THAT CAN BE TRANSMITTED OVER GENERATIONS, BLACK YOUTH ARE AS TRAPPED AS BLACK ADULTS ARE IN AN IMAGE WORLD THAT PRIVILEGES WHITE PERSONS AS BOTH HEROIC IDEALS AND IDEALS OF BEAUTY. SO I DEVELOPED THE *RYTHM MASTR* COMIC PROJECT STARTING IN 1999 BECAUSE THERE WAS JUST TOO LITTLE OUT THERE FEATURING BLACK PEOPLE AT THE CENTER OF IT ALL.[2]

KERRY JAMES MARSHALL

WHEN Kerry James Marshall made the decision to create a superhero comic series on the occasion of the 53rd Carnegie International 1999/2000 at the Carnegie Museum of Art in Pittsburgh, it marked a significant moment in his professional trajectory. What very few people anticipated was just how important in both the history of contemporary art and that of superhero comics Marshall's creation—titled *Rythm Mastr* (1999–)—would turn out to be. Up until that point, in a career that had spanned almost two decades, Marshall had been busy building a discourse where historical and sociopolitical subjects were addressed through an oblique and provocative approach, effectively revolutionizing the way in which the Black figure had been represented in American painting up until that moment. His intention was to resolve a fundamental historical inadequacy: the number of Black painters within the canonical history of painting as presented by Western institutions. He also wished to address how Black people are often portrayed with a political symbology attached to them and rarely as an ideal representation of grace and elegance. He gradually developed a body of work that investigated these ideas while referring to the great tradition of picture-making initiated by the Old Masters, from Flemish Painting to the Renaissance. Adopting historical styles and genres left little to chance. In Marshall's view, he needed a format that he could adapt at will in order to construct, control, and calibrate it.

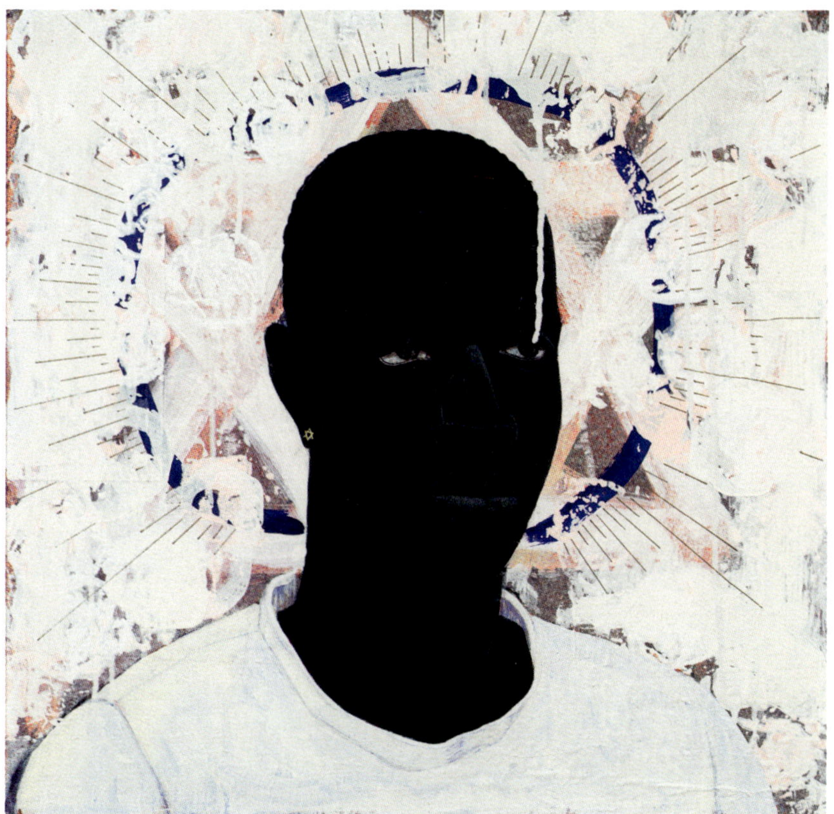

FIG. 1 **KERRY JAMES MARSHALL,** *Lost Boys: AKA Black Johnny*, 1995. Acrylic and collage on canvas, 24×24 in. (61×61 cm).

In the late 1990s, Marshall's two primary artistic concerns were to give the Black figure a central role and make sure that this could happen under the umbrella of art's most celebrated historical styles and genres. This developed into what can retrospectively be described as a trilogy of works that was to play a pivotal role in his art-making—"Lost Boys" (1993); "Garden Project" (1994), and "Mementos" (1998). "The Lost Boys," a group of paintings inspired by the misfortunes encountered by his brother and the death of their father **[FIG. 1]**, constituted, up to that point, a rarity in the artist's practice. Seldom before had Marshall operated within the parameters of a series, and scarcely ever had he let biographical elements play a role in his work, which he considered to be many things, but never a tool for plain "self-expression." With that in mind, he expanded the premise and turned "The Lost Boys" into a series embodying the concept of innocence and loss. The children portrayed never had the chance to grow up, as indicated by the inclusion of their birth and death dates in the background.

2 "An Argument for Something Else: Kerry James Marshall in conversation with Dieter Roelstraete," in Nav Haq (ed.), *Kerry James Marshall: Painting and Other Stuff* (Brussels: Ludion, 2013), 29.

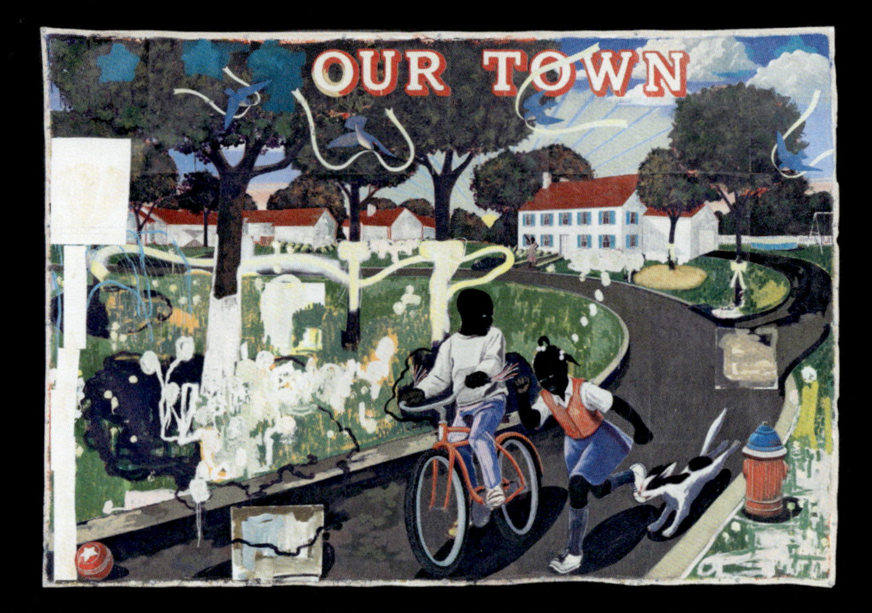

FIG. 2 **KERRY JAMES MARSHALL**, *Our Town*, 1995. Acrylic and collage on canvas, 101×143 in. (256.5×363.2 cm). Crystal Bridges Museum of American Art, Bentonville, Arkansas.

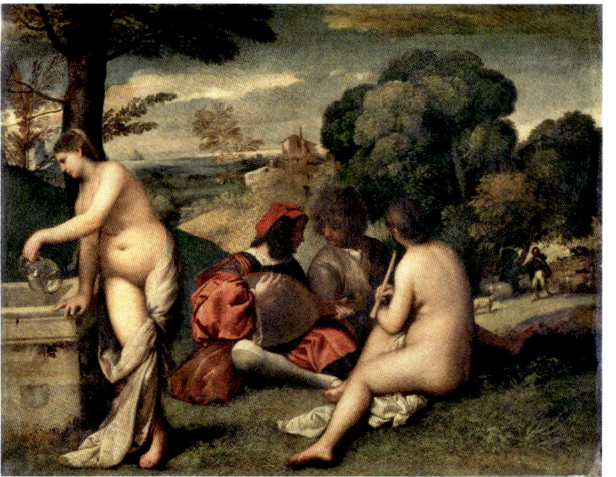

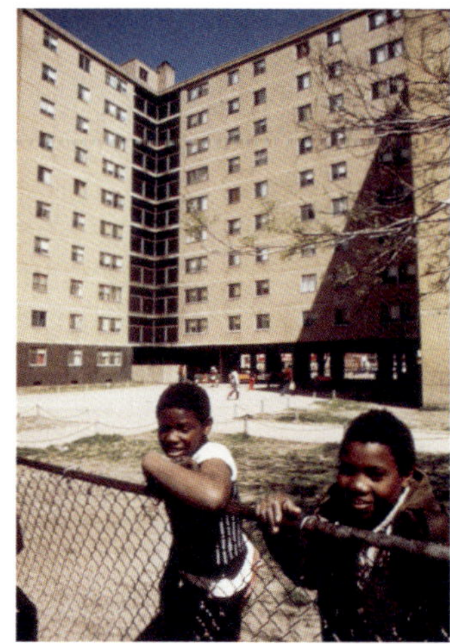

FIG. 3 **GIORGIONE OR TITIAN**, *Concerto Campestre*, c. 1509–25. Oil on canvas, 41 ¾×54 in. (105×137 cm). Louvre Museum, Paris.

↗ FIG. 4 Children outside the Stateway Gardens on Chicago's South Side. The complex had eight buildings with 1,633 two- and three-bedroom apartments housing 6,825 people in total. They were built under the US Housing Acts of 1949 and 1968 and were managed by the Chicago Housing Authority which was responsible for 41,500 public housing dwellings. Photograph by John H. White, May 1973.

"The Lost Boys" was followed by a series of bucolic representations of people engaged in leisure activities such as picnicking, playing street games, or listening to music. The paintings, collectively known as the "Garden Project," that would later spawn offspring in the form of *Our Town* (1995; **[FIG. 2]**), are a self-declared attempt to paint with a collage sensibility. In their allegorical depiction of conviviality, they provided a line of continuity from Giorgione's *Concerto Campestre* (c. 1509–25; **[FIG. 3]**)[3] and Édouard Manet's *Le déjeuner sur l'herbe* (1863), but with one significant difference: in Marshall's work, the rural European setting has been replaced by the Garden Projects in Chicago.[4]

When built in the mid-1950s, Chicago's Stateway Gardens **[FIG. 4]** was a classic example of the over-ambitious grand architectural schemes that marred the twentieth century. By the 1980s, the promise to residents of providing a comfortable and idyllic place to live had fallen short, and the buildings were ridden with structural complications, crime, and poverty. A report by the Roosevelt University published in the February 1995 issue of *Jet* ranked Stateway Gardens as the poorest housing development in the US.[5] The City of Chicago's short-term solution was to plan their demolition, and high-rise public houses were torn down, as if this would automatically erase the problem, thereby generating a massive wave of displaced people and a spike in violence.

Typically, Marshall decided to address the issue without resorting to a rhetorical representation of this reality or compromising his dignification of the Black cultural body. Instead he concentrated on the gardens' original premise and their failed utopia while flagging the complexity of the people who inhabit them and their stories. As he recalled years later, "What matters is a place where you can project new reality. I see it as a necessity. By the mid-1990s, all the people in [Stateway Gardens] were literally at the mercy of the state. Once again, a trauma ensued. There was violent/misogynist rap music blasted all the time. How can children do their homework in that context? Everybody in the building was scared to tell them to turn it down."[6]

The third and final part in the trilogy that followed "Garden Project" is actually made up of two cohesive groups of paintings, together "Mementos," the title under which they were exhibited at the Renaissance Society in

Chicago in 1998. As with most people born in the first postwar years, Marshall's early sociopolitical ideas had begun to form at a decisive time. At eight years of age, he had seen the assassination of a president—something impactful enough if read about in a history book, but much more shocking when experienced in real time. When Dr. King and Senator Kennedy met equally violent ends within two months of each other in 1968, the whole nation entered a state of grieving and soul-searching. Banners portraying the Kennedy brothers and King with the words "We Mourn Our Loss" became a ubiquitous presence in American homes and institutions **[FIGS. 5–7]**.

Twenty-five years later, the sight of one of these placards—now desirable vintage items—hanging on the wall in a Flag & Banner store on South Chicago Avenue inspired Marshall to revisit that particular moment in history and create images that would define the decade, while giving viewers both a space of commemoration and contemplation. It was a complex subject to come to terms with, and Marshall did so in a complex way, repositioning the banner in the interiors of homes belonging to a very specific generation of owners—those who, like his parents, witnessed the events in the prime of their lives.

---

3 It should be noted that the attribution and dating of the painting are to this day uncertain. André Chastel identifies Giorgione as the author of *Concerto Campestre*, although he concedes that Giorgione's most talented pupil, Titian, might have played a role in finishing it after his master's death. Other art historians, including Giorgio Vasari and David Rosand, give Titian a much bigger role. As Giorgione passed away in 1510, the painting is placed within a temporal frame that oscillates between 1509 and 1525, but the issue over its authorship and actual date of execution will never be satisfactorily resolved.
4 One of the paintings in the series, called *Watts 1963* (1995), features Nickerson Gardens in Los Angeles, where Marshall lived for two years after moving from Birmingham, Alabama.
5 "Nation's Poorest Citizens Living in Chicago Housing Developments: Study," *Jet*, February 13, 1995, 19. To give an example of the gravity of the situation in Stateway Gardens, the infamous Cabrini-Green housing project was ranked eighth.
6 Kerry James Marshall in conversation with the author, October 26, 2020. Unless otherwise stated, all Marshall's quotes are from conversations with the author.

FIG. 5 **KERRY JAMES MARSHALL**, *Souvenir III*, 1998. Acrylic, collage, and glitter on unstretched canvas, 108×161 in. (274.3×409 cm). San Francisco Museum of Modern Art/Gift of Shawn and Brook Byers, Collectors' Forum, Emily Carroll and Thomas Weisel, Doris and Donald Fisher, Susan and Robert Green, Diane and Scott Heldfond, Patricia and Raoul Kennedy, Elaine McKeon, Elle Stephens, and Phyllis C. Wattis.

FIG. 6 **KERRY JAMES MARSHALL**, *Souvenir I*, 1997. Acrylic, collage, and glitter on canvas, 108×157 in. (274.3×398.8 cm). Museum of Contemporary Art Chicago. Bernice and Kenneth Newberger Fund.

FIG. 7 **KERRY JAMES MARSHALL**, *Untitled (Mementos)*, 1998. Chromogenic print, 24×20 in. (61×50.8 cm).

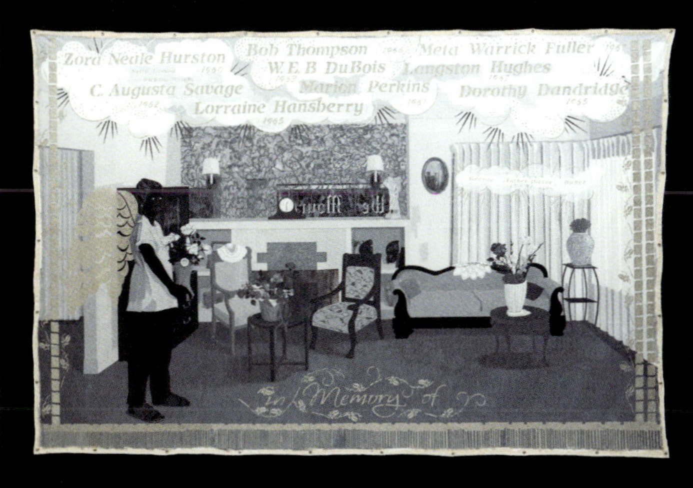

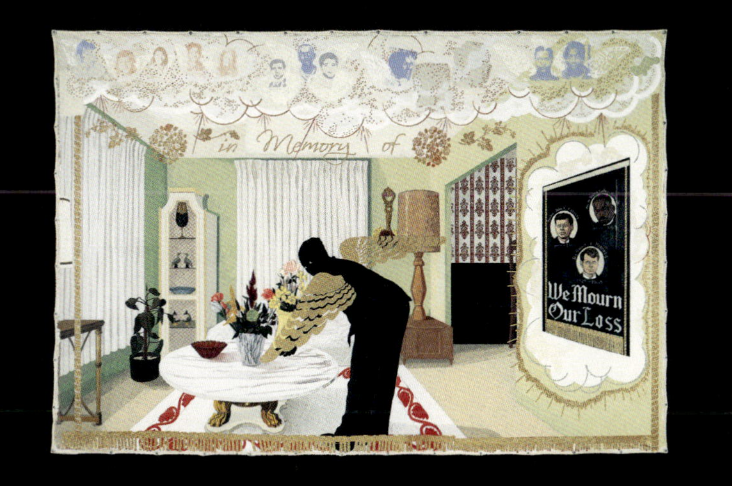

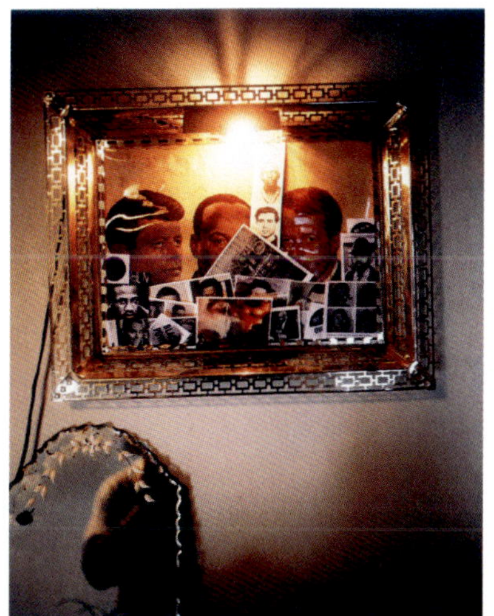

The first group of paintings within "Mementos"—"Souvenirs"—depicts four middle-class homes, each inhabited by a woman with golden wings. These are actually the real living rooms of Marshall's relatives and close acquaintances—Ruth and Albert Glover, Bertha Mae and Clifford Clark, his mother-in-law, Thelma Bruce, and her best friend Lois Ricks. The women's roles as guardian angels are emphasized by them welcoming us in to honor the crowd of ethereal figures floating amidst clouds near the ceiling, their heads framed by the line "In Memory of." The faces of people who made a great contribution to the cause of social justice, with little recognition, and who paid with their lives, are honored here—Jesse Belvin, Medgar Evers, Lorraine Hansberry, Viola Liuzzo, Jimmie Lee Jackson, and Mark Clark, among others. The placards featuring the Kennedy brothers and King visible in each home in "Souvenirs," were developed further to create "We Mourn Our Loss"—the second group of paintings in the show.

Marshall stated that the scope of "Mementos" was to function "as some kind of requiem for the Civil Rights Movement and the Black Liberation Struggle."[7] The fact that, together with "Who's Afraid of Red, Black and Green" (2012),[8] a series first exhibited in a solo show of the same title at the Secession in Vienna in 2012, "Mementos" is possibly the most openly political episode in Marshall's career is supported by the exhibition catalogue for the Austrian show. "By any means necessary," the words popularized by Malcolm X during his speech at the founding rally of the Organization of African-American Unity (OAAU) in 1964, opens the book. They are followed by a black and white photograph of the Black Panthers, Bobby Rush and Fred Hampton, showing the door to the group's Chicago compound after it was raided by the FBI in 1969. Save for the preface by Susanne Ghez, director at the time of The Renaissance Society, Chicago, the publication doesn't feature any conventional art contributions, relying instead on essays and poems by luminaries such as Will Alexander, Cheryl I. Harris, and Richard J. Powell. Although well-balanced in their aspiration to celebrate such an important chapter in American history, the two series significantly differ in tone. "We Mourn Our Loss" is somber, somehow conventional, and funereal. Conversely, "Souvenirs" comes across as elusive, mystical, and hopeful—qualities that seem to imply that the characters lurking in the background of the room have left behind an equally powerful and lasting legacy despite their perceived lack of visibility or popularity when compared to the ones in "We Mourn Our Loss."

In light of the almost two decades spent carefully assembling a cohesive oeuvre that would defiantly stand the test of time, Marshall's sudden recourse to the low art of comics—just when the 53rd Carnegie International, the oldest international exhibition of contemporary art in North America, knocked on his door—appears to be a perplexing move. As time has proven, however, *Rythm Mastr* was anything but a false step. It turned out to be an opportunity for Marshall to reconcile his art with his feelings about the lack of a strong Black presence within the comics industry that he had internalized over the course of his life. With time, *Rythm Mastr* has emerged as possibly one of Marshall's most stylish, multilayered, and enduring projects to date. Its relevance has grown exponentially, making it a keystone of his practice, as well as one of the most significant creative endeavors dating to the turn of the millennium. But in order to achieve a better understanding of the genesis of *Rythm Mastr* and the motivations behind it, it is necessary to take a step back and analyze the history of superhero comics, and how they ended up carving out a special place in North American culture, as well as in Marshall's own life and work.

INFINITY OR OBLIVION

One of the many strands within an industry that covers multiple genres, American superhero comics established themselves as a dominant force in the first two postwar decades. The history of the genre, like that of civilization, is traditionally divided into a trilogy of distinct time periods—with one significant difference. Whereas the model for civilization is structured around progress, with the Stone Age leading to Bronze, which evolves into Iron, the metallic tripartition employed for superhero comics instead follows Olympic criteria, but in reverse order, with Gold (1938–56), Silver (1956–70), and Bronze (1970–84). It's admittedly an odd structure, but perhaps to be expected if one considers that unlike the original three-age system, which was conceived with the benefit of a passage of time across twenty centuries and by an archaeologist of great distinction—Christian Jürgensen Thomsen—the one for comics was devised within a much smaller temporal window by its fans and collectors. Discordant narratives have emerged around the attribution of responsibility for this methodology, with the credit at times given to people such as sci-fi author and editor Richard A. Lupoff, or readers like one Scott Taylor from Westport, CT.[9]

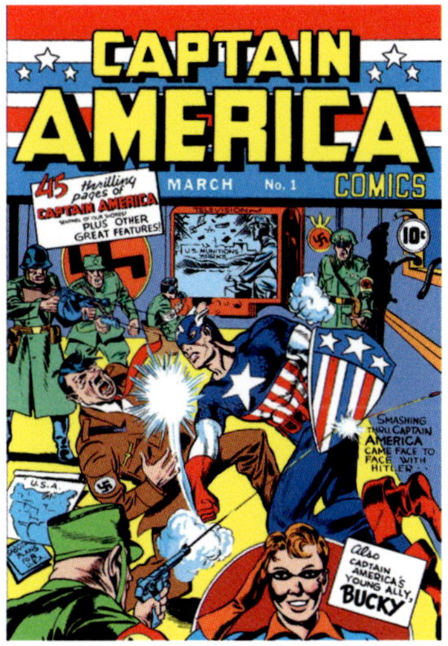

FIG. 8 Cover of first issue, *Captain America*, December 1940. (Cover dated March 1941). Art: Jack Kirby and Joe Simon. Published by Timely Comics, New York.

Most importantly, the competition-based model of the three-age system goes some way to account for the consistent lack of critical credibility given to superhero comics in art and literature circles over the course of their existence. The very term "Golden Age" implies that everything that comes after will be somehow inferior. Following the Gold–Silver–Bronze logic, even in its finest moment, a creative effort will never be able to match the quality or relevance of its predecessors. Supporters of the system argue that the moment of inception when techniques are invented is inevitably the "Golden Age," but there are plenty of examples from the history of creative disciplines that testify to derivation and inspiration being far from the same thing. A generation of artists might deserve credit for opening the door, but it's often the job of those who follow to deliver.

In the particular case of superhero comics, it is no coincidence that their so-called golden moment in America coincides with the outbreak of World War Two, when the notion of extraordinary stock characters sporting red, white, and blue proved extremely popular with a readership that needed to be entertained, reassured, and inspired in equal measure. One of the earliest specimens in this particular category was *The Shield*, the brainchild of artist Irv Novick and writer Harry Shorten. Originally published in 1940 by MJL Comics, *The Shield* revolved around the story of Joe Higgins, a US army lieutenant who develops extra-human powers through a scientific experiment designed to form an army of "Super Soldiers." The Shield was joined by a sidekick called Dusty the Spectacular Boy Detective, a borrowing of the Sherlock Holmes/Watson dynamic. This idea was successful enough to be almost immediately co-opted by Bob Kane and Bill Finger, with the invention of Robin to augment their 1939 creation, Batman,[10] and soon grew into a stable feature in most superhero ventures. The ginger-haired Shield also set the yardstick for other similarly tailored and motivated characters, including Fawcett Comics' short-lived and overly patriotic *Minute-Man* (1941–44), and the Shield's most famous epigone, and to a certain extent direct descendent, Timely Comics' *Captain America* (dated March 1941, released December 1940) **[FIG. 8]**.

7 Roelstraete, "An Argument," 16.

8 Based on Barnett Newman's series of paintings, "Who's Afraid of Red, Yellow and Blue" (1966–70), Marshall created a series of works focused on the three colors of the Pan-African flag designed by Marcus Garvey in 1920 as an emblem for his Universal Negro Improvement Association (UNIA). See András Pálffy, Rael Jero Salley, and Annette Südbeck, *Kerry James Marshall: Who's Afraid of Red, Black and Green* (Vienna: Secession, 2012).

9 Taylor was allegedly the first to coin the term "Silver Age of Comics" in the letters page of an issue of Gardner Fox's *Justice League of America* in 1966. "If you guys keep bringing back the heroes from the Golden Age," Taylor stated in his letter, "people twenty years from now will be calling this decade the Silver Sixties!" in "JLA Mailroom," *Justice League of America*, no. 42 (February 1966): 98.

10 Up until April 1940, Batman was a vigilante gunning down his opponents in a style similar to antecedent series like Walter B. Gibson and Vernon Greene's *The Shadow* (1930). The arrival of Robin had the twofold effect of toning down the level of violence and instilling doubts about the two heroes' sexual orientation—a tricky subject in the 1950s. Psychiatrist Fredric Wertham speculated in his controversial 1954 book *Seduction of the Innocent* that Batman and Robin were gay partners. This was enough to elicit DC to counteract the argument by introducing the character of Batwoman in 1956 as a potential female love interest. The repercussions of Wertham's moral crusade also resulted in the formation of the infamous regulatory organization Comics Code Authority the same year his book was published. One of the most damning moments in the life of this organization, which only ceased to exist in 2011, was its request to alter the racial identity of a Black astronaut in *Judgment Day*, a story about a planet inhabited by bigoted robots created by Al Feldstein and Joe Orlando, and published in issue 33 of EC Comics' *Incredible Science Fiction* (1956). EC's publisher, William Gaines, defied the order and although the story ran uncensored, *Incredible Science Fiction* ceased publication thereafter.

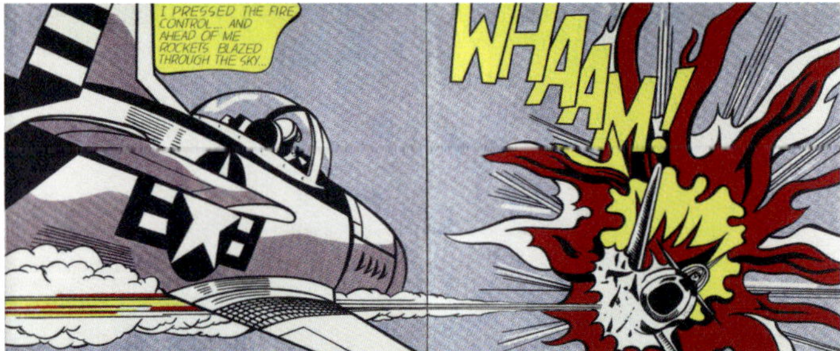

FIG. 9 **ROY LICHTENSTEIN,** *Whaam!*, 1963. Acrylic and oil on canvas, 68×160 in. (172.7×406.4 cm). Tate, London.

FIG. 10 **RUSS HEATH,** *Hero in Action: Bottle of Wine*, 2014. Color and lettering: Darwyn Cooke.

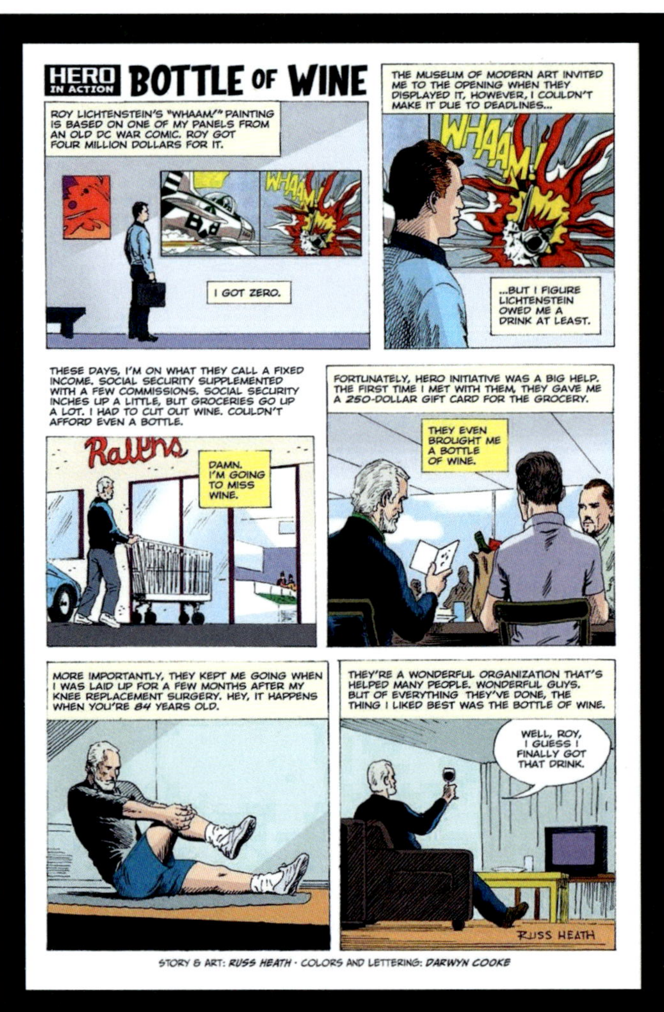

With "Captain" replacing the by then trite "Super," and "America" providing unconditional identification, the creation of artist Jack Kirby and writer Joe Simon essentially used the same blueprint as *The Shield*. The corporally frail aspiring soldier Steve Rogers undergoes a scientific experiment with similar consequences to Higgins. Having received his superpowers, Rogers and his partner Bucky Jones are enlisted to fight the Nazis in Europe, even going as far as to confront Adolf Hitler in person. Kirby, who later in life would be the victim of a much-publicized miscarriage of justice when he saw his hard-earned royalties for the character he had cocreated denied, acknowledged the debt of *Captain America* to *The Shield* at every turn, from making a buckler the Captain's favorite weapon, to naming the fictional espionage agency aiding him in his assignments S.H.I.E.L.D (Supreme Headquarters, International Espionage and Law-Enforcement Division).

By the end of World War Two, the topical nature of these early superheroes relegated them to secondary roles, if not outright anonymity. This made room for a new generation of characters more attuned to the postwar climate and the potential readership looming on the horizon—the newly identified demographic of teenagers. Detective Comics, also known as DC, was quick to spot the necessity of overhauling its characters, and did so thanks to a formidable group of editors, writers, and artists who included John Broome, Irwin Donenfeld, Joe Giella, Robert Kanigher, and Carmine Infantino. Series like *Superman*, *Batman*, *Aquaman*, *The Flash*, and *Wonder Woman*[11] all performed well on the newsstands, either as individual publications or in collections of stories. The latter instituted a shared continuity, inaugurating what fans would later refer to as the "DC Universe."

As for war heroes, *Captain America* fell into the hands of DC's main competitor, Marvel Comics, and became a textbook case of adapting to adverse circumstances. The foundational changes the captain went through to stand the test of time started in the 1960s, when he acted as a reminder of America's good-natured fighting spirit at a time when the Vietnam War had established a voluminous gray zone in the black and white chart of evil versus good. In the 1970s, he rode the glassy-eyed wave of 1950s nostalgia that gave birth to *American Graffiti* (1973), *Happy Days* (1974–84), and *Grease* (1978).[12]

Gaining critical credibility proved to be a formidable challenge, even for battle-hardy comic creators. As has been widely acknowledged, the mass production and distribution of superhero books diluted the overall idea of comics as a legitimate art form. This was best expressed in recent times in

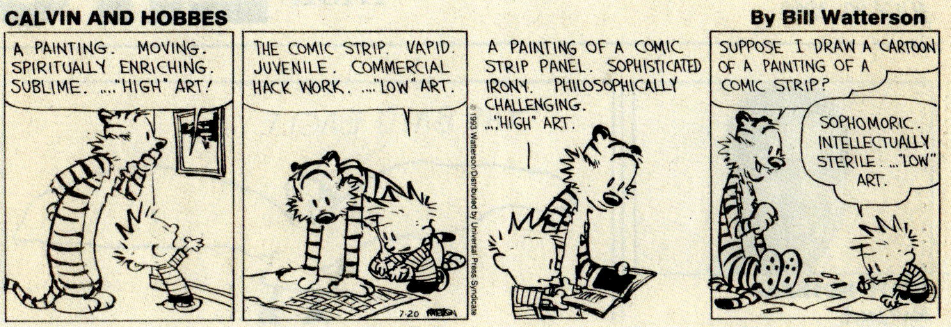

FIG. 11 **BILL WATTERSON,** *Calvin and Hobbes*, July 20, 1993.

2014, when American comic-book artist Russ Heath made a caustic strip about Roy Lichtenstein's appropriation of one of his panels for the iconic painting *Whaam!* (1963; **[FIG. 9]**), currently in the collection of Tate Modern, London. "Roy got four million dollars for it. I got zero," states a young Heath in the strip while standing in front of a larger-than-life replica of his own drawing. By reappropriating Lichtenstein's appropriation, he casts a shadow on the American Pop artist's merits, as well as contemporary art's procedures in general. "I figured Lichtenstein owed me a drink at least," concludes Heath, pointing out that his current fixed income is barely enough to survive and that he can't afford to buy a bottle of wine **[FIG. 10]**.[13]

Lichtenstein's painting didn't sell for four million dollars—that's the contemporary value—and Lichtenstein, without doubt, didn't see that amount of money. *Whaam!* was originally exhibited in the artist's second solo show at Castelli Gallery in New York in 1963. Tate, in London, eventually purchased it three years later for £3,940 (about $130,000 in 2024) after a lengthy negotiation with Castelli's then-wife, Ileana Sonnabend. Of this money, Lichtenstein most likely saw half. Still, the basic principle remains and Heath's bitterness is understandable. His determination to publicly vent his frustration fifty years after the fact laid bare in no uncertain terms the complex relationship that contemporary art and mass-produced comics have enjoyed for the best part of their parallel existence.

The intricacies of this subject and the contextual nature of an image's value was to be explored in a lighter but nevertheless effective manner by Bill Watterson in one of his *Calvin and Hobbes* on July 20, 1993. In the four-panel storyline, the two protagonists—the mischievous kid Calvin and his pet tiger Hobbes—flip through an array of art and comic books, noting how a painting of a comic strip is regarded as "sophisticated" and "challenging" and a cartoon of a painting of a comic strip "sophomoric" and "intellectually sterile." To complicate the matter even further, in the name of appropriation, Joseph Kosuth would add another layer to the debate in the years to come by incorporating Watterson's strip into a number of his works **[FIG. 11]**.[14]

11 Wertham didn't content himself with his bigoted study of Batman and Robin, extending his doubts to the social grace of Wonder Woman too. In his book, he laments her excessive emancipation and love of bondage, implying that she too is gay. Wertham's nefarious theories regrettably left a deep mark. It took almost forty years for there to be a U-turn, first with Robin coming out in *Nightwing* no. 81 (1996)—a special issue designed to support LGBTQIA+ rights—and later with the creation of Ragneron, the first Black queer superhero (2019). Creator Milan Christopher has stated that the idea for Ragneron—a fitness instructor who acquired magic powers after he came into contact with galactic debris—came to him when he learned about the suicide of teenager Nigel Shelby, who was bullied at school in Huntsville, Alabama. In most recent times, Wertham's psychosis was the subject of both study and scorn in Angela Robinson's film *Professor Marston and the Wonder Women* (2017) and in Darieck Scott's book *Keeping It Unreal: Black Queer Fantasy and Superhero Comics* (New York: New York University Press, 2022).

12 Stan Lee: "I always loved [*Captain America*], so I decided to bring it back. And I tried to write a story where he had been frozen in a glacier for years, and they found him and he came back to life, and so forth. And I tried to give him a personality where he was an anachronism. He was living in our day, but yet he had the values of twenty or thirty years ago." "The Stan Lee Deposition on The Origins of the Marvel Universe for Kirby Family vs. Marvel Lawsuit," *Bleeding Cool*, March 9, 2011.

13 Russ Heath, "Hero in Action: Bottle of Wine," *Hero Initiative*, November 7, 2014. *Hero Initiative* is a Los Angeles–based nonprofit organization established in 2000 with the purpose of aiding comic-book creators in need.

14 See *Amnesia: Various, Luminous*, Kosuth's exhibition at Sprüth Magers, London in 2014.

In many ways, the rivalry between art and mainstream comics seems to narrow down to the old idea of the grass being greener on the other side. Naturally situated in a middle-of-the-road position between literature and visual art, superhero comics face a struggle for critical credibility that runs parallel to art's desire for a larger popular acceptance that transcends the cloistered world of museums and galleries. The few instances where the two have intertwined have been dismissed as minor episodes by luminaries in their respective camps.[15] Examples of this would be when an artist dabbled in both activities with the same degree of integrity and authority—such as Ad Reinhardt's cartoons for many media outlets in New York—or when the inherent eccentricities of the cartoonist's work justifies its inclusion in an art context, such as the work of Robert Crumb. As Swiss curator Fabrice Stroun observed when he organized an exhibition of work by the cartoonist Gary Panter at Le Magasin in Grenoble, France, in 2000:

> *Comics are a narrative medium. Comics are meant to be read at a pace of your own choosing. Whether you focus on a single drawing, or follow a sequence from one panel to the next, their unique attributes are best experienced flipping through the pages of a book. It's nearly impossible to recreate such a focused solitary experience by looking at a comic book page hung on a wall, in a physical, public space devoted to contemporary art. But the main issue might be one of audience expectation. Comics are made for comic readers, who are generally very knowledgeable of their idiosyncratic history. It's a highly specialized, erudite field. Contemporary art, on the other hand, aims to cast a much wider net. In that sense, the Gary Panter show I organized failed to find its audience.*[16]

The notion of superhero comics as a lowbrow medium mostly satisfying people with an interest in violence and titillation is still hard to shake off. Ironically, the theory that comics fans are obsessed with superheroes due to their inability to relate to reality and their consequent desire to seek shelter in an alternative one, has a long history, and it is surprisingly resonant with the objectives of film, literature, and contemporary art itself.

Lichtenstein's resolve to focus on comics might have made him a fortune in the long term but early on, the reception was lukewarm. A few months after *Whaam!* was first exhibited in New York, *Life* magazine published a piece by its arts editor Dorothy Seiberling on Lichtenstein's work with the headline "Is He the Worst Artist in the US?"[17] This was somewhat baffling, since Lichtenstein was ultimately a formalist and by far and away one of Pop art's most technically proficient artists. The way in which he took the processes and techniques of comics and exploited them for art purposes was both masterful and unique. However, the article wasn't as mean-spirited as its sensational title might suggest. Seiberling's view of Lichtenstein's talent was sympathetic overall. What she was dubious about was why an artist of that caliber would bother glorifying comics and cartoons in his art—something the editors of *Life* clearly bracketed in the lowest echelons of popular culture.

Pop art, in its aspiration to represent mass culture, was well prepared to be challenged in this respect. Canned-soup and soft-drink manufacturers had no intellectual pretenses for their products and certainly no objection to the free advertising derived from their association with Andy Warhol and his peers. The disapproval, however, from the comics establishment was something relatively unexpected and more arduous to deal with. The Silver Age was witnessing artists and writers engaging in a delicate maturation process in their work. Their readership was no longer made up of kids wondering if the Flash was faster than the Whizzer, but competent, opinionated young adults who, on a regular basis, discussed artistry, plot developments, and occasional visual and conceptual inconsistencies. Having taken exception to Lichtenstein's territorial invasion, the comics industry (which, contrary to art, was and still is labeled an "industry" rather than a "world") developed a resentfulness that was not soothed by Lichtenstein's insistence that his work was a tribute and not a swipe. Five decades later, as Heath's stance proves, the fracture that ensued was yet to heal.

To add fuel to the fire, in the intervening time came the controversially titled exhibition *High and Low: Modern Art and Popular Culture* at the Museum of Modern Art in New York (1990). The show's premise, according to the curators Kirk Varnedoe and Adam Gopnik, was to articulate how "The story of the interplay between modern art and popular culture is one of the most important aspects of the history of art in our epoch. It was central to what made modern art modern at the start of this century, and it has continued to be crucial to the work of many younger artists in the last decade."[18] Despite the organizers' best intentions, the exhibition ended up building a wall instead of a bridge. Lichtenstein was praised once more for making panels from facile comic books like *Young Romance* and *G.I. Combat* more powerful; Joan Miró was lauded for refining the simplicity of George Herriman's visual vocabulary in *Krazy Kat*; Philip Guston was hailed as a true innovator for his ability to infuse a sense of personal drama into cartoon imagery; and there was more such admiration along the same lines. But the comic strips and books that served as the jumping-off point for this great art were relegated to a subservient role and generally so poorly installed that visitors were left in no doubt as to where the threshold between High and Low art was located.

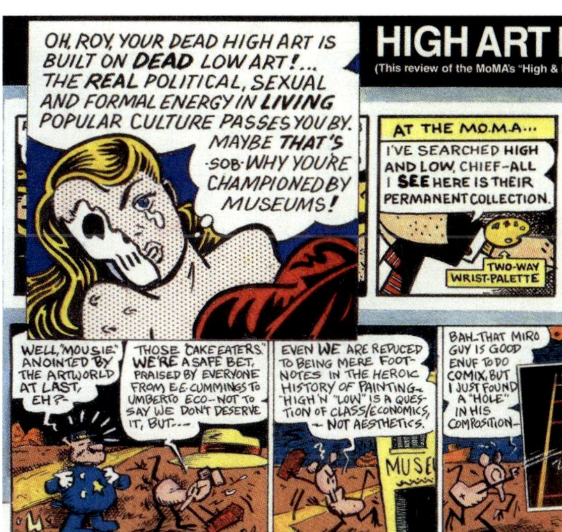

FIG. 12 **ART SPIEGELMAN,** *High Art Lowdown*, *Artforum*, December 1990.

One visitor, Art Spiegelman, was particularly incensed—both about the way in which comics were represented as mere footnotes in the history of painting and by the ignorance of the curators. In his view, they couldn't tell the difference between "serious" comic artists like himself—a proud protagonist of the 1970s underground "comix"[19] scene—and second-rate illustrators like Heath. Spiegelman found a vector to express his anger in the pages of *Artforum*, where he submitted a scorching review in his favorite format: the comic strip. Needless to say, one of his main targets was Lichtenstein. "Oh, Roy, your dead high art is built on *dead* low art!... The *real* political, sexual, and formal energy in *living* popular culture passes you by. Maybe *that's*—sob—why you're championed by museums!" cries a young lady in a Lichtenstein-like painting **[FIG. 12]**.[20]

15 This doesn't apply to the pre-superhero generation of comics artists who were active at the turn of the nineteenth century during the so-called Platinum Age. Similarly, artists like George Grosz and Giuseppe Novello were able to operate in both camps with equal credibility, their satires and grotesque caricatures providing a welcome distraction, or in some cases a much-needed proxy to the official narrative during the first global conflict. See also Eberhard Demm, "Propaganda and Caricature in the First World War," *Journal of Contemporary History*, January 1993, 163–92.

16 Stroun elaborated further: "The many artists I appreciate who use comic book tropes (Ad Reinhardt, Öyvind Fahlström, Mike Kelley, Jim Shaw, Steven Parrino, Julien Ceccaldi, etc.) interest me first and foremost as 'fine' artists. Their appeal to comic book readers is best compared to that which Cindy Sherman's 'Film Stills' series might hold for cinephiles. It's rather limited," in conversation with the author, February 15, 2021.

17 Dorothy Seiberling, "Is He the Worst Artist in the US?" *Life* magazine, January 5, 1964, 79–83. Fifty years later, the debate around the legitimacy of Lichtenstein's actions is still a matter of dispute. Artist Dave Gibbons seems to echo Heath's opinion: "We have a term in the business called swiping. When you are stuck for an idea, you riffle through your comics, and you trace what somebody else has done. A lot of Lichtenstein's stuff is so close to the original that it actually owes a huge debt to the work of the original artist. But in music, for instance, you can't just whistle somebody else's tune no matter how badly without crediting or getting payment to the original artist." Alastair Sooke, "Is Lichtenstein a Great Modern Artist or a Copycat?" BBC, October 21, 2014, https://www.bbc.com/culture/article/20130717-pop-artist-or-copy-cat.

18 Press release for *High and Low: Modern Art and Popular Culture*: https://www.moma.org/momaorg/shared/pdfs/docs/press_archives/6826/releases/MOMA_1990_0077_80.pdf.

19 A term coined in the late 1960s to mark the distinction between underground and mainstream comics. The "X" was used to emphasize the X-rated content of those publications. Spiegelman has been associated with the scene together with other artists such as Robert Crumb, Trina Robbins, Manuel 'Spain' Rodriguez, and Gilbert Shelton.

20 Art Spiegelman, "High Art Lowdown,' *Artforum*, December 1990, 115. Spiegelman is only one of the many comic authors who is deeply unimpressed with Lichtenstein's work. "Lichtenstein did no more or less for comics than Andy Warhol did for soup," Peter Sanderson, "Spiegelman Goes to College," *PW Comics Week*, April 24, 2007.

Until then, *Artforum* had rarely, if at all, discussed sequential art in its pages. Spiegelman was an exception. His serialized anthropomorphic tale *Maus* (1980–91), a biographical account of his father—a Holocaust survivor—in Europe during World War Two, had captured unprecedented media attention, changing forever the public perception of comics as implausible stories about implausible characters for an acritical audience. In 1991, when the *New York Times* included *Maus* in its bestsellers list, the author successfully requested it to be in the nonfiction category—an unprecedented event in the history of the medium.[21] Spiegelman found in *Artforum* the ideal ally in his refusal for the world of comics and cartoons to be perceived as a monolithic entity. In short, it was felt that the line between "High" and "Low" shouldn't have been drawn between art and comics, but between Spiegelman, along with the cartoonists who made a genuine effort to improve the format, and the easy, unpretentious, teen-friendly material that figures like Heath produced, and from which Lichtenstein had drawn inspiration.

This openness to cartoons took a further step forward fourteen years later, when *Artforum* published an issue focused on the relationship between art and animation. The cover, created by Canadian comic artist and author Julien Ceccaldi, was a four-panel story entitled "I Am My Goals," in which two girlfriends discuss objectives and expectations **[FIG. 13]**. Both women leave this existentialist conversation feeling contrite—one upset for trying too hard to maintain appearances, the other one for trying too hard to bring her friend down. Whether Ceccaldi's work was intended as an allegory of the relationship between comics and art, a dig at the urban, over-educated, New York–centric demographic that many perceive as the core readership of a magazine like *Artforum*, or neither of the above, the cover signaled an important moment all the same since it had been specially commissioned by the editors—a very rare occurrence in the history of the publication up until then.[22]

Even more strikingly, in December 2016, *Artforum*'s online diary reported on Comic-Con in San Diego. In its fifty-five-year history, the magazine had never covered any of the forty-six editions of the convention, implicitly dismissing it as a subcultural event. To treat it now with the degree of attention normally reserved for art-market events like the Armory Show or Art Basel was a sudden change of direction in the magazine's policy. The *Artforum* editors were evidently aware of this, and practiced a form of damage control by commissioning the article from comics scholar and associate professor at the University of Chicago, Hillary Chute, who also provided a rare and welcome female perspective on the subject. In her report, Chute did her best to reconcile her area of interest with the expectations of a readership unaccustomed to comics by running with the hare and hunting with the hounds. Comic-Con attendees are derided as nerds, while artists are celebrated. One telling hint that might explain the magazine's refreshed attitude toward Comic-Con could be found at the end of Chute's review, where she stated that the convention was "not about the comics anymore."[23] Indeed it was not. Films, video games, and television shows had begun to dominate.

FIG. 13 **JULIEN CECCALDI,** *I Am My Goals*, *Artforum*, summer 2014.

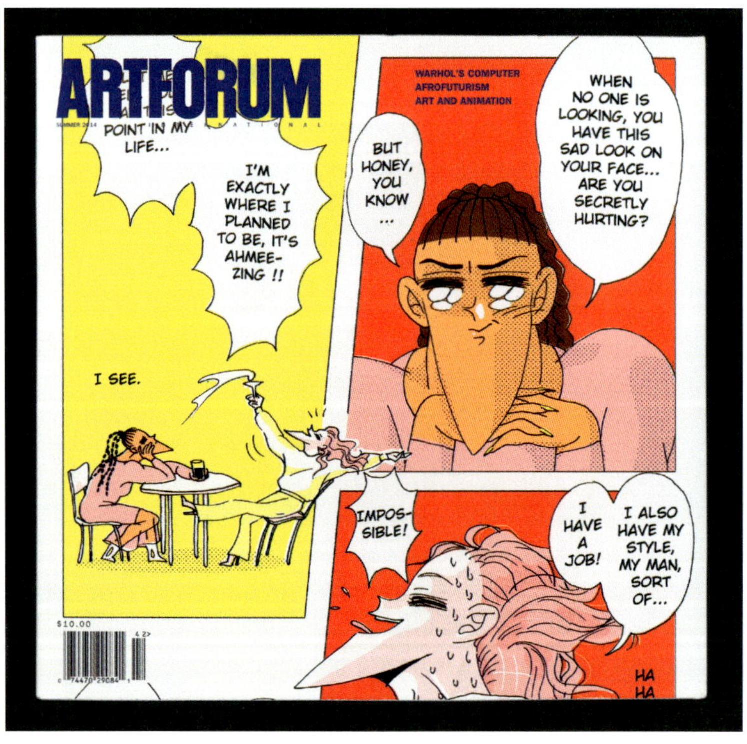

THIS JUST CAN'T BE REAL

Up until the late 1980s, Marvel had regularly lagged behind DC on the road to Hollywood. This was irritating for Marvel, since at the dawn of the Silver Age, the company had brought about one of the biggest paradigmatic shifts in the field when its leading creative force, Stan Lee, had the bright idea of furnishing his superheroes with a set of super problems. Power, in Lee's mind, came with pressure and responsibility. Done were the days of Bruce Wayne, the flawless, genial, athletic playboy billionaire who turns into Batman at night and lives his two lives with no apparent discomfort. Extracurricular adventures of this kind had to extort a psychological price on their protagonists. *Spider-Man* (first appearing in August 1962), created with artist Steve Ditko, and one of Lee's most successful creations, introduced a tangible explanation for the hero's inhuman powers: he was bitten by a radioactive spider while attending a science exhibition. Crucially, Spider-Man's superpower didn't exempt his alter ego—the part-time photographer and university student Peter Parker—from the burden of an ordinary existence. When he is not wearing his Spider-Man outfit, he has rent to pay, an old aunt to help, jealous girlfriends to juggle, and a short-tempered boss to deal with. *The Hulk* (May 1962), the fruit of Lee and Jack Kirby's fertile imaginations, pushed the concept even further. The Hulk's powers, which were earned when his alter ego, the scientist Robert Bruce Banner, was hit by a nuclear blast during an experiment in the desert, are more of a curse than a blessing. The Hulk and Banner can only exist on alternate shifts, generating a personality conflict not dissimilar to the one explored in Robert Louis Stevenson's gothic literary masterpiece *The Strange Case of Dr. Jekyll and Mr. Hyde* (1886). The absence of a costume—a staple in the superhero world until then—in favor of a simple permutation in skin color and size, helped accentuate The Hulk's humanity.[24] The moral dilemma of having power, and as such feeling the duty to put it into use for the sake of humankind, would plague the vast majority of Marvel's characters from then on. They didn't inhabit the fictional, semi-futuristic world of Metropolis or Gotham City, but the colorful and occasionally harsh reality of New York City's boroughs.[25]

The different approach to their subjects taken by Marvel and DC was summarized by comics historian and researcher Peter Sanderson in a column written in 2003:

> *DC was the equivalent of the big Hollywood studios: after the brilliance of DC's reinvention of the superhero genre in the late 1950s and early 1960s, it had run into a creative drought by the decade's end... The Marvel of the 1960s was in its own way the counterpart of the French New Wave and the foreign innovators in film: Marvel was pioneering new methods of comics storytelling and characterization, addressing more serious themes, and in the process keeping and attracting readers in their teens and beyond.*[26]

---

21 Art Spiegelman, "A Problem of Taxonomy," *New York Times*, December 29, 1991.

22 Ida Applebroog, Cory Arcangel, Stephanie Burt, Julien Ceccaldi, Ian Cheng, Hillary Chute, Kerry James Marshall, Jim Shaw, Art Spiegelman, Fabrice Stroun, Jordan Wolfson, and Douglas Wolk, "Graphic Content: Art and Animation," *Artforum*, summer 2014, 294–337.

23 Hillary Chute, "Unkenny Valley," *Artforum Diary*, July 29, 2016, https://www.artforum.com/diary/hillary-chute-at-the-47th-comic-con-in-san-diego-62445. According to comics author Gino Udina, this trend started with the period of crisis the comics industry encountered in the 1990s. "By 1999 the fair was already more about films, TV shows, and video games. The comics angle felt like cheese on a mousetrap," in conversation with the author, January 25, 2021.

24 The Hulk was originally supposed to be gray. A coloring issue made him green. Lee liked it and it stuck.

25 Interestingly, Marvel editors were a little more cautious about placing their superheroes in real locations when off US soil. Two prime examples are the Fantastic Four's most celebrated villain, Doctor Doom, who is from the fictional Baltic country of "Latveria"; and Wolverine's adventures in Southeast Asia in the city-state "Madripoor."

26 Peter Sanderson, "Comics in Context #14: Continuity/Discontinuity," *IGN*, October 11, 2003, updated June 17, 2012, https://www.ign.com/articles/2003/10/11/comics-in-context-14-continuitydiscontinuity. Some technical considerations have to be made in order to better understand DC's dominance until the 1960s and the rivalry between DC and Marvel. Up until the mid-1950s, it was standard practice for comic publishers to distribute their own titles. In 1956 Martin Goodman, the owner of Atlas Comics (Marvel's previous incarnation), made the ill-fated decision to get his products distributed by American News Company, a large organization with a monopolistic approach to business. Following an unfavorable verdict in a Justice Department Lawsuit, ANC went out of business just one year later, and Goodman had to ask DC to carry his titles, which DC, sensing the power of its position, agreed to do on very constrained terms. (Atlas could only issue eight titles a month versus DC's fifty.) In the 1970s, book agent David Obst, of *All the President's Men* fame, brokered a deal that saw Marvel and DC agree on a package of crossover titles that went on with mixed results from 1976 through 1981.

The new humanity and realism of Marvel's characters reached its peak in 1972 with the introduction of Luke Cage, aka Power Man, created by Archie Goodwin, John Romita Sr., George Tuska, and Roy Thomas—the first Afro-American superhero to have his own series **[FIG. 14]**.[27] Cage's origins mirror those of many of his predecessors (a scientific experiment gone wrong) and result in a tale of redemption and empowerment—from juvenile delinquent to hero for hire and eventually *pro bono* streetfighter. Whereas the Fantastic Four or The Avengers would travel to mysterious exotic islands and distant planets to fight their foes, Cage's playground was his New York City neighborhood. Mr. Fantastic, Iron Man, and Co. would fight super villains, aliens, and even gods. And while Cage would have his share of super villains, he would also chase drug dealers, corrupt cops, and mobsters.

A June 1979 *X-Men* story written by John Byrne and Chris Claremont illustrated how Cage, in his dealings with ordinary thugs, was by no means less extraordinary than his more celebrated colleagues. In it, *X-Men*'s Ororo "Storm" Monroe, a half-Kenyan, half-American heroine whose power to control the weather made her a deity in the eyes of her compatriots, goes on a trip down memory lane to find the house in Harlem where her parents first met.[28] When she discovers that the place is now a crack house, her feelings toward the occupants are ambivalent, as she can't help but see them as victims of a discriminating society. Her consequent reluctance to use her powers would have cost her dearly had the streetwise Cage not come to her rescue.[29]

To legitimize the Luke Cage franchise, Marvel took the unprecedented decision to hire a Black author. This was William Henderson Graham, known as Billy Graham, a New York–born artist who had learned his ropes at Warren Publishing as art director in the 1960s. Deeply conversant with the Harlem Renaissance scene so masterfully illustrated in cartoon form by Elmer Simms Campbell in the 1930s,[30] Graham had an affinity with his subject, and his input grew over the course of a handful of issues from ink artist to penciller and co-plotter. When Graham moved to new pastures and started working on *Black Panther* with Don McGregor, Cage was paired with private investigator and martial arts expert Mercedes "Misty" Knight—a classic blaxploitation character created by Tony Isabella, of *Black Lightning* fame,[31] and Arvell Jones.[32] When blaxploitation began to lose mainstream momentum toward the end of the 1970s, Cage struggled for survival.[33] The template within which his adventures took place, however, still resonated, and ended up playing a decisive part in the reinvention of another Marvel character who had hit hard times: Daredevil.

Originally penned by Lee and Bill Everett in 1964, Daredevil was a lawyer who survived an accident from which he emerged without his sight, but with all his other sensorial faculties incredibly amplified. The originality of his backstory, however, didn't conceal the fact that narratively he had little new to offer. Artist and writer Frank Miller came on board with the idea of turning the superhero into a neighborhood watcher. Thanks to a couple of team-ups—with Marvel's other official household vigilante, Vietnam-veteran The Punisher, and the ever-present Spider-Man—*Daredevil: The Man Without Fear* turned into one of Marvel's most successful series. It reached its peak in Miller/David Mazzucchelli's wonderful seven-part story *Born Again* (1986)—a tale of fall and redemption infused with Roman Catholic symbolism that would continue to guide and inspire many authors of the series in the years to come.[34]

Even before *Born Again*, DC, having taken note of Marvel's business model, had elected to respond in style. Karen Berger, one of DC's most talented editors and the future founder of the Vertigo imprint,[35] astutely looked for ideas across the ocean, where a different type of sensibility was in place. Northampton-based writer Alan Moore, who had been responsible with David Lloyd and Tony Weare for one of the UK's most successful comics series, *V for Vendetta* (1982–89), was invited to collaborate

FIG. 14 Cover of first issue, *Luke Cage: Hero for Hire*, June 1972. Art: John Romita, Sr. Published by Marvel Comics, New York.

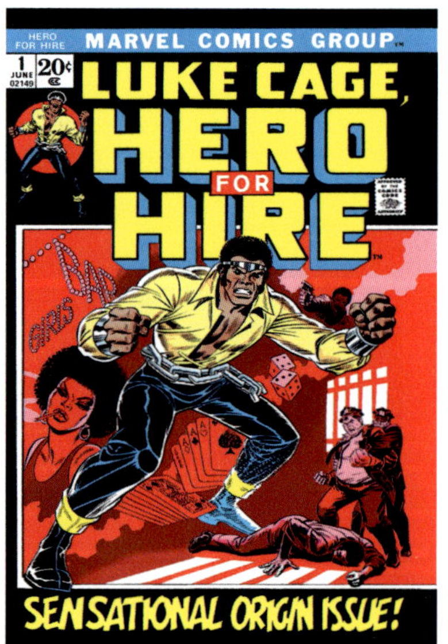

along with artist Dave Gibbons. The result was *Watchmen* (1986–87), a twelve-issue maxi-series in which superheroes are portrayed as a gang of misfits in a dystopian society that has moved on from their Golden Age antics. Humanized to a degree that makes Marvel's 1960s' "superheroes with super problems" revolution pale in comparison, the key characters in Moore's vision of 1980s America are pretty much the equivalent of the Jedi Knights in the original film from the *Star Wars* franchise—an anachronism. Such a deconstructive process, however, did not happen at the expense of the format, making *Watchmen* a masterpiece in the institutional critique of superhero comics. Blessed with astonishingly detailed panels, multiple narrative threads, and even a story within a story about a pirate crew called *Tales of the Black Freighter*, *Watchmen* took the possibilities of sequential art to an unparalleled level, departing at once from the preconception that superhero comics are about escapism, and claiming a place as one of the most important books of this genre ever to be made.[36]

27 Some historians think this title belongs to Dell Comics' *Lobo*, a gunslinger created by Don J. Arneson and Tony Tallarico in 1965. The series lasted only two issues and its scarce visibility doesn't seem to qualify it as a proper exponent of mainstream comics. Arvell Jones: "I never saw the [Lobo] book. Most people didn't" in Cornelius Fortune, "Comic Creator Arvell Jones Talks Black Panther's Impact and Detroit Connection," BLAC *Magazine*, February 1, 2018, https://www.blac.media/news-features/comic-creator-arvell-jones-talks-black-panthers-impact-and-detroit-connection.

28 Storm's predecessor and probable source of inspiration, DC Comics's Nubia, was created by Robert Kanigher and Don Heck as the Amazonian counterpart of Wonder Woman in 1973. The character was later controversially clad in more austere clothing before undergoing a satisfactory redevelopment with a slight change in name (nu'Bia') at the hands of Doselle Young in the mid-1980s. Marvel's first Black female superhero, contrary to popular belief, wasn't Storm but Valerie, a librarian who briefly takes the role of Spider-Woman in a story by Jean Thomas and Winslow Mortimer in the June 1974 issue of *Spidey Super Stories*.

29 John Byrne, Chris Claremont, and Terry Austin, "Cry for the Children," *The X-Men*, no. 122, June 1979.

30 Campbell was the first Afro-American cartoonist ever published in a national magazine when his drawings made it into *Life* in the late 1920s, and this paved the way for Chester Commodore and Jackie Ormes. Campbell devised his "A-Night-Club Map of 1930s Harlem" (1932) as a humorous tribute to the vitality of the city's music scene. In 2017 the *National Geographic* named it (together with Saul Steinberg's "View of the World from 9th Avenue" [1976]), one of the most unique cartographic representations of New York City.

31 *Black Lightning* only lasted eleven issues before becoming a casualty of the infamous 1978 DC Implosion (the company's sudden cancellation and revamp of a number of series to halt poor sales). The character was subsequently absorbed by other titles until it found new fortunes thanks to the eponymous CW drama television series in 2016.

32 Byrne and Claremont would later make Misty Knight and Iron Fist the protagonists of the first interracial kiss in mainstream comics in the *Marvel Team-Up* "If Death Be My Destiny," no. 64, December 1977.

33 The sartorial and haircut changes Cage was put through in the following decades to keep him real are a textbook case of the limits a character encounters when its authors confound historical significance with fashion. Other reinventions, however, were more successful and eventually contributed to restoring Cage's popularity. In 2008, a poll conducted by *Wizard Magazine* saw him ranked as the 34th greatest comic-book character of all time, beating the likes of Iron Man, Thor, The Punisher, and Silver Surfer.

34 The most notable example in this sense is Joe Quesada, Kevin Smith, and Jimmy Palmiotti's eight-issue story *Guardian Devil* (1999)—almost a remake of *Born Again*. The visuals and literary quality of *Born Again* was such that even visual arts publications traditionally not inclined to take superhero comics too seriously paid their respects. See, for example, Michael Fitzgerald and Justen Ladda, "Narratives Strategies in Everyday Myths," *Parkett*, no. 10, 1986, 91–99.

35 A DC subdivision aimed at an adult audience, granting artists and authors a degree of freedom seldom experienced before. Following Berger's departure in 2013, Vertigo underwent a series of structural changes, before being reintegrated into DC in 2020.

36 Moore was so adamant in his vision of *Watchmen* as a liminal venture that could only exist as a comic book that he categorically refused to be associated with film adaptations of this and any other of his works. When the *Watchmen* film came out in 2009, Moore demanded to be uncredited and gave all his percentage points to Gibbons. "There is something about the quality of comics that makes things possible that you couldn't do in any other medium…Things that we did in *Watchmen* on paper could be frankly horrible or sensationalist or unpleasant if you were to interpret them literally through the medium of cinema. When it's just lines on paper, the reader is in control of the experience—it's a tableau vivant. And that gives it the necessary distance. It's not the same when you're being dragged through it at 24 frames per second." Steve Moore, "Alan Moore: An Extraordinary Gentleman," *The Guardian*, March 16, 2009, https://www.theguardian.com/books/2009/mar/16/alan-moore-watchmen-lost-girls. This view is echoed by Art Spiegelman, who always turned down offers to make an animation film of *Maus*. And also by John Byrne, who on the cinematic treatment of his and Chris Claremont's X-Men *Dark Phoenix Saga*, stated: "I don't know how they can even pretend to take a story that took us four years to tell and do it in two hours…The movies always feel like Hollywood is trying to show us how to do it right…and not succeeding," Mike Avila, "John Byrne Reacts to *Dark Phoenix* and Looks Back at His X-Men Run," *SyFy*, April 4, 2019, https://www.syfy.com/syfywire/john-byrne-on-dark-phoenix-and-his-x-men-run.

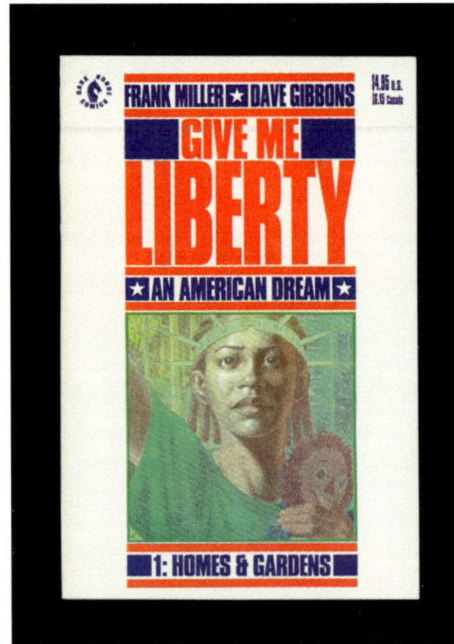

FIG. 15 Cover of first issue, *Give Me Liberty*, June 1990. Art: Dave Gibbons. Published by Dark Horse Comics, New York.

DC's second move to lure talent away from Marvel with the promise of extra-generous financial rewards, was more obvious, but no less effective. In 1986, Miller jumped ship and created, with Klaus Janson, *Batman: The Dark Knight* (1986), a four-book series in which the aging hero returns after years of retirement to fight organized crime one last time. Regrettably DC's higher pay wasn't accompanied by creative control, and in 1990 Miller changed publisher again, his taste for controversial political satire and apocalyptic scenarios finding more latitude with a new company keen on breaking the DC/Marvel duopoly,[37] and appropriately called Dark Horse Comics. The Gibbons-penciled miniseries *Give Me Liberty* (1990) is one of Miller's finest works and possibly the first comic book to feature an Afro-American superheroine as protagonist **[FIG. 15]**.[38] This is Martha Washington, a precocious teenager who turns into a galactic superhero after fighting poverty and discrimination in a public-housing project called The Green—a none too subtle reference to Chicago's infamously violent Cabrini-Green Homes.[39] *Give Me Liberty* confirmed Miller's moment in the sun and put Dark Horse on the map, but the cultural footprint of *Watchmen* and *Batman: The Dark Knight* went beyond every superhero tale that was published until the 1980s and for many more years to come. Marvel's subversion of the modern superhero archetype was revolutionary, but it was DC that invented it and, ultimately, took it to a new level.

DIRECT HIT: MISSION ACCOMPLISHED

If DC, as Sanderson pointed out, was the superhero comics equivalent of the big Hollywood Studios, it was only a matter of time before Hollywood itself would start paying attention. Richard Donner's film *Superman* (1978), starring Marlon Brando, Gene Hackman, and Christopher Reeve, with a script by Mario Puzo, or Tim Burton's *Batman* (1989), featuring Jack Nicholson, Kim Basinger, and Michael Keaton, eclipsed all the efforts Marvel had made up to that point to bring its most successful characters to life on the big screen. Marvel fared slightly better on the small screen, but even there, the five-year run of Kenneth Johnson's television series *The Incredible Hulk* (1977–82) on CBS was overshadowed by the cult status of Lorenzo Semple Jr.'s hyper-camp *Batman* during the two years it aired on ABC (1966–68),[40] or Stanley Ralph Ross's *Wonder Woman* (1975–79), starring former Miss World, Lynda Carter.[41]

Things changed again in 2000 thanks to the cinematic transposition of *X-Men*, first conceived in 1963 by Lee and Kirby. Tired of the radioactive-accident-leading-to-super-powers formula, they focused instead on a group of natural-born superpowered individuals in their early twenties gathered around a wheelchair-bound luminary called Professor Charles "X" Xavier. Their prodigious capabilities implied that the X-Men had to be educated on the meaning of their powers, their ethical implications, and especially their use. Their mutant status came with a fascinating scientific explanation—the "X" factor, a genetic alteration that made them "Homo Superiors"—a new step in human evolution after "Homo Erectus" and "Homo Sapiens." With the adroit Xavier on a perpetual mission to discover and mentor new mutants, the X-Men's Connecticut mansion soon turned into the superhero equivalent of the New York High School for Performing Arts—a center for the extra-talented, offering a shelter to generations of kids rejected by their families and society as a whole for being "different." Under Xavier's guidance, the institute works simultaneously as a power-training ground and a school for self-acceptance, fostering mutants until they are ready to live in the actual world.

This facet was elevated in 1982 by Claremont and artist Brent Anderson in the graphic novel *X-Men: God Loves, Man Kills*. Here, the X-Men do not have to battle a super villain, but the very human Reverend William Stryker, an evangelist engaged in a moral crusade against them as aberrations of humanity. All, needless to say, in the name of God. The story's abrupt opening, with the lynching of two mutant children by the Purifiers, a killing squad secretly affiliated to Stryker, introduced the issue of racism in a way that the world of superheroes had rarely, if at all, employed until then. To leave no doubt about their message, the authors chose to make the two kids Black, and to let them be found by the X-Men's nemesis, Magneto, hanging from a tree with signs reading "Mutie" around their necks **[FIG. 16]**. Magneto—himself a Holocaust survivor—sourly reflects, "Once more, genocide in the name of God. A story as old as the race," before vowing to fight the enemy and make them pay with their lives for their crime.[42]

Although armed with noble intentions, the references in *X-Men: God Loves, Man Kills* to actual forms of racism occasionally provokes feelings of irritation rather than identification—perhaps unavoidable given the complexity of the subject and the background of its creators. Claremont depicts the rub between Xavier's desire for acceptance and peaceful coexistence and Magneto's take-no-prisoners stance as being comparable to that between Dr. Martin Luther King, Jr. and Malcolm X over the Civil Rights Movement, but he does so in superficial terms, somehow reducing methodological and philosophical

FIG. 16 Panel from *God Loves, Man Kills*, November 1992. Art: Brent Anderson; color: Steve Oliff; text: Chris Claremont. Published by Marvel Comics, New York.

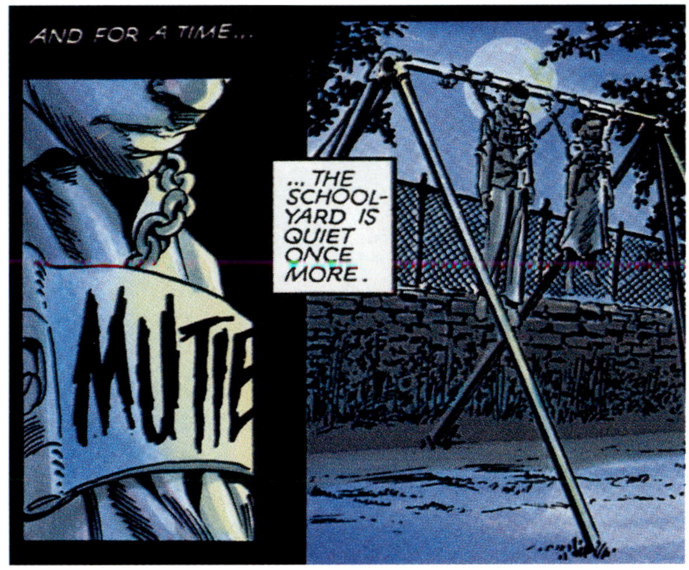

37 The term "superhero," in use since 1917, was jointly copyrighted by DC and Marvel in 1979. Dark Horse and other unaffiliated publishers are free to use "super" and "hero", but not the two together.

38 Although Marvel and DC had introduced black superheroines before, these characters weren't honored with an eponymous miniseries or graphic novel for a long time. *Give Me Liberty* anticipated by several years Carlo Barberi and Marc Sumerak's *Ororo: Before the Storm* (2005); G. Willow Wilson's *Vixen: Return of the Lion* (2009); and Stefano Caselli's and Brian Michael Bendis's *Ironheart: Riri Williams* (2015).

39 The state of social and architectural degrade of the Cabrini-Green Homes was made even more pronounced by their proximity to affluent areas such as Lincoln Park and the Gold Coast. They were finally demolished between 1995 and 2011 after making international news headlines. As was true of the fictional character Martha Washington, the Cabrini-Green Homes were openly referred to in the origins of Amanda Waller, a character created by John Byrne, John Ostrander, and Len Wein in 1986 as the leader of DC's *Suicide Squad*.

40 According to Bob Kane, the success of the *Batman* TV series saved the comics from cancellation. Interestingly, the producers replaced Julie Newmar, the actress who played Catwoman, with Eartha Kitt for the show's final season, making Kitt the first Black woman to portray a DC character on screen. Although this was hailed as a groundbreaking move at the time, it had consequences. The sexual tension between Batman and Catwoman, until then a leitmotif in the interplay between the two characters, was written out for the whole time Kitt was on the show.

41 Despite the significant progress made in various social areas, the representation of women in superhero comics is still problematic at the time of writing. If the Golden Age relied exclusively on "Hunks and Babes," the Silver Age's policy of introducing not particularly good-looking yet interesting men—see *Fantastic Four*'s Ben "The Thing" Grimm or X-Man Henry "The Beast" McCoy—was not extended to superheroines or superheroes' girlfriends, who invariably continued to be beauties. A typical example is The Hulk's female equivalent, She-Hulk, who in contrast with her male counterpart's monstrous image is portrayed as a stunning, carefree Amazonian. The only exception to the rule seems to be Charles Xavier's skeletal and charmless twin sister Cassandra Nova who, as a manifestation of Xavier's brain, doesn't actually exist.

42 Brent Anderson and Chris Claremont, *X-Men: God Loves, Man Kills* (New York: Marvel Comics, 1982). Claremont, who originated Magneto's backstory twenty-five years after the character's inception, said he was inspired by Israeli politician Menachem Begin.

differences to an anodyne confrontation of good versus evil. In another panel, Black dance teacher Stevie Hunter is subjected to an abusive verbal attack from her star pupil, Kitty Pryde, when she fails to appreciate the Mutant's predicament. While well-intended, the exchange is problematic. As graphic novelist John Jennings remarked in his review:

> *[Most] of the classic X-Men team [can] easily pass for "human" and are phenotypically white. Because they aren't perceived as different, that analogy doesn't map well onto how racism is constructed. Stevie states that while Kitty is right to feel as she does, she, a white teen, will never experience the trauma of racism that Stevie has endured and will continue to endure until we end systemic racism* **[FIG. 17]**.[43]

Shortcomings notwithstanding, the thinly disguised representation of violent white supremacy in *X-Men: God Loves, Man Kills* covered uncharted territory in the superhero comics industry. Claremont, together with artist John Byrne, had already taken the notion of Mutant segregation to new heights during their tenure at the helm of *X-Men* between 1977 and 1980.[44] *X-Men: God Loves, Man Kills*, however, sent out a message that twenty years later was still as resonant as when it was first emitted. It also had the advantage of being made into a complete stand-alone book, in the form of one of Marvel's early graphic novels. In 2003, the plot of *X-Men: God Loves, Man Kills* laid the foundation for the second film in the franchise, Bryan Singer's sanitized treatment *X2*, which finally projected Marvel into the Olympus of Hollywood. Although the film betrayed some of the fundamental propositions on which it was built, and privileged an imagery-based rather than dialogue-driven trajectory, it netted $214,949,694 in North America alone, becoming the sixth-highest-grossing film in 2003.[45]

The production team behind *The Avengers*, having taken note of the cinematic success of *X-Men*,[46] fully exploited the idea of the group made of strong, easily recognizable individuals, building anticipation with a series of solo presentations for *The Hulk* (2003 and 2008); *Iron Man* (2008 and 2010); *Captain America* (2011); and *Thor* (2011), eventually leading to a much-awaited, star-studded ensemble piece, Joss Whedon's *The Avengers* (2012).[47] The film became the connective tissue between its prequels and a series of spin-offs about characters who were already part of, or could potentially be added to, the

FIG. 17 Panel from *God Loves, Man Kills*, November 1992. Art: Brent Anderson; color: Steve Oliff; text: Chris Claremont. Published by Marvel Comics, New York.

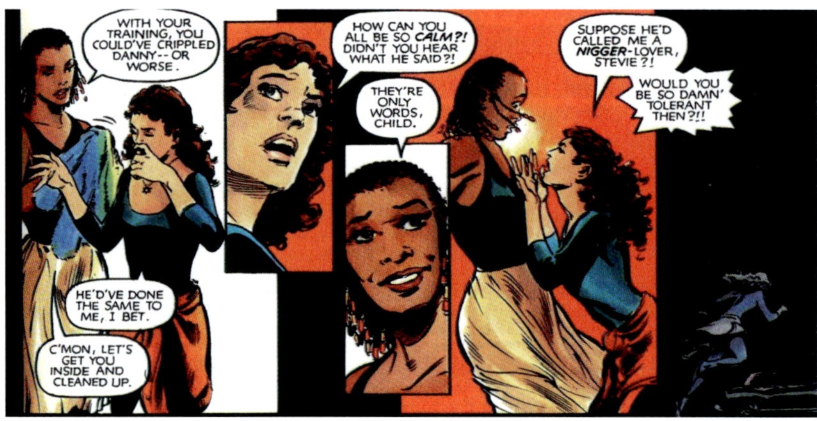

FIG. 18 Cover of *Black Panther*, April 2016. Art: Brian Stelfreeze; text: Ta-Nehisi Coates. Published by Marvel Comics, New York.

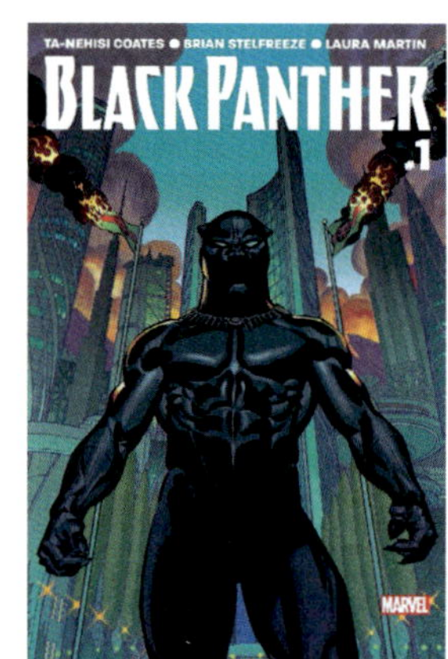

FIG. 19 Cover of *Dark Reign: Black Panther*, May 2009. Art: Ken Lashley; text: Reginald Hudlin. Published by Marvel Comics, New York.

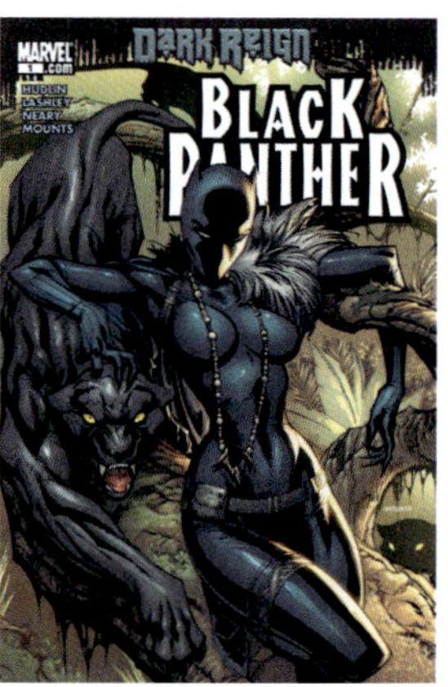

cinematic version of the group in the future. Among these were Peyton Reed's film *Ant-Man* (2015) and Ryan Coogler's *Black Panther* (2018).[48] The latter featured the first prominent Black superhero in the Marvel universe[49] and turned out to be the most popular Marvel film for a long time, reaching sections of the public ordinarily uninterested in superhero comics or even cinema.

After years of conjecture and speculation (early conversations about the film started as far back as 1992 when Wesley Snipes expressed an interest in playing the role), *Black Panther* was finally confirmed to be in the works in 2016. The venue for the announcement was the *Artforum*-reviewed 47th edition of Comic-Con in San Diego in 2016. Three months earlier, the magazine had devoted a column to the last installment in the *Black Panther* book series. The artist and writer of the graphic novel were Brian Stelfreeze and famed journalist and nonfiction writer, Ta-Nehisi Coates. Marvel's strategy of hiring well-known names outside the comics industry with the ambition of being taken more seriously worked, but it didn't automatically translate into a memorable product. Writing comics and writing fiction present different challenges, as Lee, Claremont, and Byrne discovered during their brief spell as sci-fi or horror authors.[50] Still, the presence of Coates gave *Black Panther* unprecedented agency outside the comics community. Many critics also pointed out that the Coates/Stelfreeze *Black Panther* was the first book authored by an all-Black team in the fifty-year history of the publication **[FIG. 18]**. This wasn't true. "That distinction goes to [Reginald] Hudlin and Ken Lashley on the fabulous *Dark Reign* series in 2009 (probably the best-executed *Panther* story arc since artist Billy Graham drew the Don McGregor–scripted stories in the mid-1970s)"[51]—authoritatively stated by the author of the *Artforum* review, Kerry James Marshall **[FIG. 19]**.

---

43 John Jennings, "Solving for X: *God Loves, Man Kills* Through the Lens of Now," Marvel.com, July 8, 2020, https://www.marvel.com/articles/comics/solving-for-x-god-loves-man-kills-through-the-lens-of-now.

44 Although Byrne and Claremont are largely responsible for *X-Men*'s most fortunate run, artist Dave Cockrum and writer Len Wein deserve credit for co-inventing some of the material for the series. In contrast with the original All-American group, the second generation of X-Men introduced by Wein and Cockrum in 1975 featured members from Austria, Canada, Kenya, Ireland, Russia, and, for a brief period of time, even an Arizona Apache, John "Thunderbird" Proudstar. This internationalist twist successfully strengthened the notion of genetically mutated individuals as a global phenomenon.

45 Chris Claremont: "I liked the idea of [mutants] being outcasts. That was the whole point of evolving Magneto's state until he could make a choice to live his life a better way, a newer way. That was the exemplification of *God Loves, Man Kills*—Magneto starts out by looking at the death of two innocents and vowing vengeance. At the end, he approaches the conflict at Madison Square Garden, standing with the X-Men and erring on the side of justice rather than vengeance. The actual act of justice comes not from a mutant, not from a super being, but from a New York cop, defending a kid who's about to be killed by William Stryker." Alex Abad-Santos, "God Loves, Man Kills: The Creators of the Legendary X-Men Story Reflect on its 35-Year Legacy," Vox.com, May 3, 2017, https://www.vox.com/culture/2017/5/3/15341432/god-loves-man-kills-claremont-anderson-interview.

46 Over twelve box-office hits and counting, as per 2024, including solo vehicles for characters such as Deadpool, the Dark Phoenix, and Wolverine.

47 The Avengers, Lee and Kirby's version of a super group, were molded in 1963 in a bid to compete with DC's *Justice League of America*. Their first incarnation, comprising Thor, Iron Man, The Hulk, The Wasp, and Ant-Man, didn't last long. The Hulk, a difficult character to write for in a team context, was soon replaced by the resurrected Captain America, giving way to numerous lineup changes in the years to come. On top of the aforementioned Scarlett and Quicksilver—the first two new recruits—The Avengers would then be joined, betrayed, abandoned, and rejoined by a broad gallery of characters that included The Vision, Hawkeye, Hercules, The Black Widow, Wonder Man, Yellow Jacket (Ant-Man under a different guise), Swordman, X-Men's refugee The Beast, Tigra, She-Hulk, Giant-Man (Ant-Man under yet another guise), Hellcat, Moondragon, Namor, Warbird, Goliath (Ant-Man again), and the Black Panther.

48 At the time of writing, all four films from *The Avengers* franchise are in the top twelve highest-grossing-films-of-all-time pantheon, together with the likes of *Avatar*, *Titanic*, *Star Wars*, *The Lion King*, and *Harry Potter*.

49 Kirby and Lee introduced T'Challa Prince of Wakanda, also known as the Black Panther, in the July 1966 issue of *Fantastic Four*.

50 There are, of course, exceptions to the rule. Nancy A. Collins, Neil Gaiman, Joe Hill, Charles R. Johnson, Jonathan Maberry, Joe R. Lansdale, and Alan Moore are some of the authors who managed to accomplish good results in both fields.

51 Kerry James Marshall, "Marvel's *Black Panther*," *Artforum*, September 2016, 103–04.

ALL THIS CAIN'T EXIST WITHOUT THERE BEING SOME KIND OF PURPOSE

Kerry James Marshall was born in Birmingham, Alabama, in 1955. About seven years later, his family relocated to Nickerson Gardens, Watts, and then to South Central Los Angeles, where he would live until his mid-twenties. The local Black Panthers headquarters, established in 1967, was at 41 and Central, only a few blocks away, and would be the target of many police raids at that time. In the mid-1980s, as artist-in-residence at the Studio Museum in Harlem, Marshall often visited Una Mulzac's Liberation Bookstore between Lenox Avenue and 131st in New York. He eventually settled in the South Side of Chicago in 1987, when the city's first Afro-American mayor, Harold Washington, had just been re-elected after his inaugural term. Even discounting the big political events that marked the 1960s and the 1970s, such biographical circumstances inevitably contributed to instill in Marshall a strong sense of social responsibility.

A series of episodes that took place in his childhood and early teens proved to be momentous in steering Marshall toward the visual arts. First, there was his kindergarten teacher at the Holy Family School in Birmingham, Ms. Hill, the only non-white member of staff, as well the only one who wasn't a nun. Ms. Hill's scrapbook—a panoply of cards and images cut from magazines—was only made available to kids who behaved. The moment Marshall set eyes on it, an epiphany occurred. Picture-making, he thought, was exactly what he wanted to do. Then there was another teacher, Ms. Foley, who was in charge of the holiday art decorations. Having enlisted Marshall's aid, she would ask him to stay after school and instruct him on how to hold the brushes so he could assist her in painting flower petals.

Less close to home, but equally important, was art instructor Jon Gnagy, known for his NBC TV show, *You Are an Artist* (1946–50). A self-taught painter and draftsman with a democratic, almost-Beuysian sense of art as a career path accessible to everyone, Gnagy's second TV show, *Learn to Draw* (1950–55), developed a group of assiduous followers, among them a young Andy Warhol. Through syndication, the Saturday morning reruns in the 1960s were watched by millions of people across the US, appealing to a new generation of viewers, including Marvel's Joe Quesada, Disney animator Ron Husband, and Marshall, who went on to put Gnagy's advice into practice.

Marshall's third-grade teacher took note of his pupil's enthusiasm and directed him to the local library. There, propelled by a natural curiosity about art and history, Marshall got his hands on all the publications he could find. One book that particularly stood out was a recently published encyclopedia by Russell L. Adams, a young professor of political science at Durham University, UK, called *Great Negroes Past and Present* (1963; **[FIG. 20]**).[52] The book was illustrated with portraits of all the politicians, inventors, and scientists it profiled. This was due to the involvement of Eugene Winslow, artist and cofounder of one of the first Afro-American publishing ventures, Chicago's Afro-Am, which put the book out. Flipping through it, already precociously alert to the dangers of a codified education, Marshall learned about the existence of a figure who would cast an enormous influence over his visual upbringing: Charles Wilbert White **[FIG. 21]**.

White, a native of the Chicago South Side, had felt driven to be an artist since his early years. At the age of fifteen, he started showing his remarkably executed drawings at every given opportunity—in empty stores, parking lots, churches, and any other venue where people would look at them. The experience proved to be formative—White's early exposure to a casual audience would guide his social-realist depictions of the everyday experience of Afro-American people for the rest of his life. After graduating from The Art Institute of Chicago, he went on to enjoy a commercially and critically successful career,

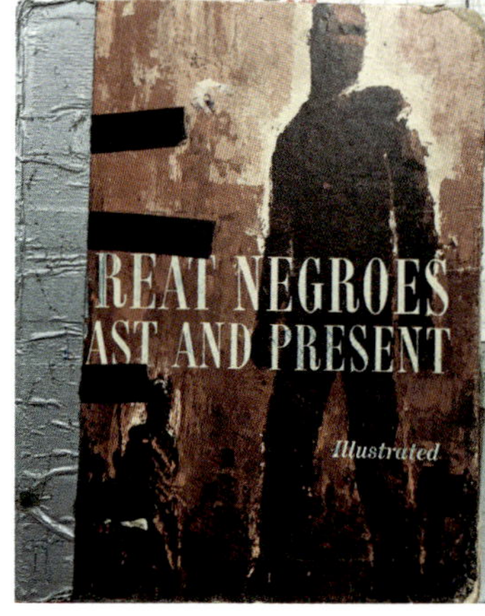

FIG. 20 Kerry James Marshall's copy of Russell L. Adams's *Great Negroes Past and Present* (Chicago: Afro-Am, 1963). Cover by Eugene Winslow.

FIG. 21 **CHARLES WHITE,** *Black Sorrow*, 1946. Lithograph, 24 3/8×19 3/4 in. (framed), (62×50 cm). Philadelphia Museum of Art.

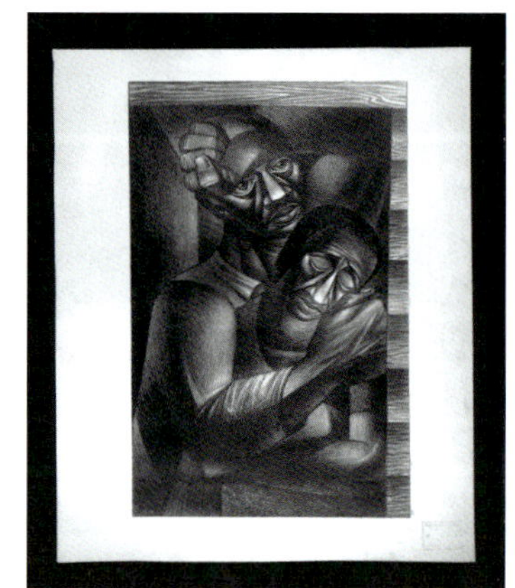

with his virtuoso representations of humanity even transcending the canvas to directly grace some of the walls in his murals at Hampton and Harvard universities, among other locations.

Marshall was extremely impressed by White. He was particularly taken by the skill and expertise White showcased in drawing Black people in his book *Images of Dignity: The Drawings of Charles White* and picked him for his school project for Negro History Week. Possibly due to White's proximity to pioneers such as Edmonia Lewis, Robert S. Duncanson, Edward Mitchell Bannister, Marion Perkins, and Malvin Gray Johnson in the pantheon of *Great Negroes: Past and Present*, Marshall assumed that White was no longer around. However, as he discovered during a presentation given by his seventh-grade teacher George De Groat, not only was the great artist alive and well, but was teaching at Otis College of Art and Design in Los Angeles, a few miles away from where Marshall lived. Marshall couldn't attend White's evening classes—nobody in his family could drive him there—but he was nonetheless able to meet with him and followed his teachings whenever he could. White became a mentor, showing Marshall the craft and importance of having a personal relationship with your subject. His presence also led to another realization: Marshall's work, in order to be successful, had to make the same impact on other artists as White's had made on him. "What's the point of making artwork—of making anything," reflected Marshall years later, "if it doesn't in some way become influential or meaningful to the progress of somebody else?"[53]

Marshall turned down a scholarship at Chouinard Art Institute—a commercial art school in Los Angeles—and enrolled instead in a Saturday class at Otis while in high school, where he was taught by Sam Clayberger, an animator with an instrumental sense of color derived from his work experience at Hanna-Barbera. "His approach to color looked arbitrary but it wasn't," recalled Marshall in 2016. "[Clayberger] said you could substitute any kind of color to function as a shadow as long as it had a relationship to the other colors that were near it. And so I learned to start building shadows using purple, green, and blue from him."[54] When Marshall finally went to study full-time at Otis in January 1977, he met a teacher who would provide another piece in the mosaic of his education: scenic artist, activist, and one-time victim of McCarthy's Witch Hunt, Arnold Mesches. Mesches's paintings might have been flawed in many respects but they had structure. Otis's methodology, like most art institutions in North America at the end of the 1970s, was increasingly oriented toward conversation and concept, and Marshall was invited early on to develop his own.

52 *Great Negroes: Past and Present* is out of print but it can in a way be considered the forerunner of educational publications like Bertram A. Fitzgerald Jr.'s *Golden Legacy* comics—a series of illustrated books celebrating figures like Frederick Douglass, Harriet Tubman, and Walter Francis White between 1966 and 1976.
53 Sam Worley, "This Modern Master Spent His Life Bringing Black Faces to Classic Art," *Chicago Magazine*, March 29, 2016, https://www.chicagomag.com/Chicago-Magazine/April-2016/Kerry-James-Marshall/.
54 Kerry James Marshall in conversation with Charles Gaines, in Charles Gaines, Greg Tate, and Laurence Rassel, *Kerry James Marshall* (London: Phaidon, 2017), 22.

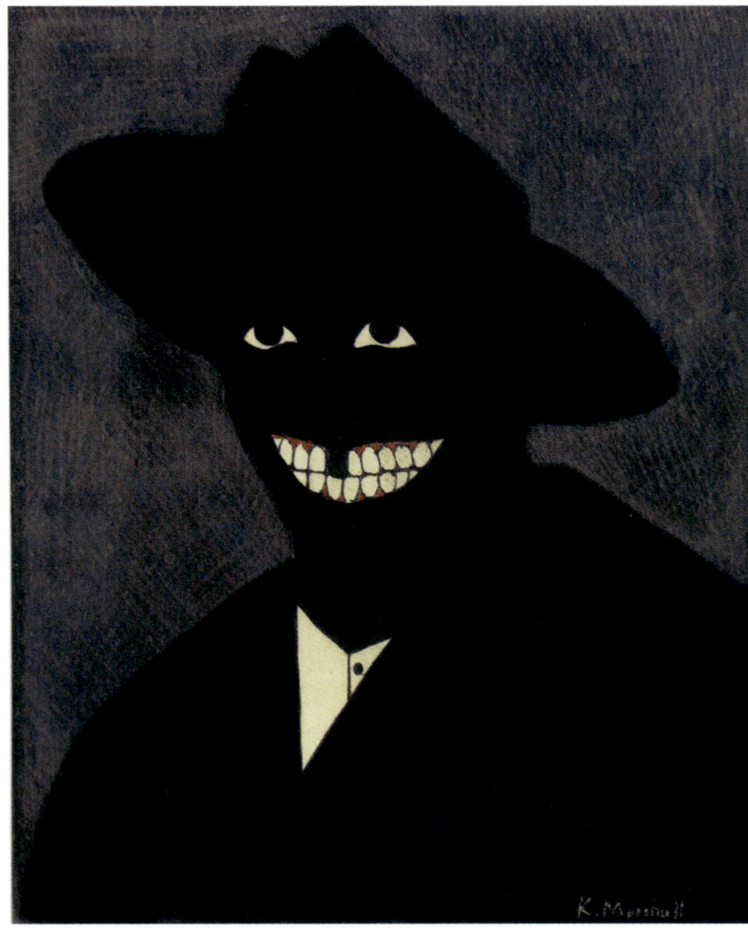

FIG. 22 **KERRY JAMES MARSHALL,** *Portrait of the Artist as a Shadow of His Former Self*, 1980. Egg tempera on paper, 8×6 ½ in. (20.3×16.5 cm). Los Angeles County Museum of Art.

Marshall's initial response, after having obtained his MFA in 1978, was to go against the grain of his education. After spending a few years working on politically charged, Romare Bearden–inspired collages, he turned decisively to painting, and produced what would turn out to be his seminal work, *Portrait of the Artist as a Shadow of His Former Self* (1980; **[FIG. 22]**). Made with egg tempera on paper, the 8 × 6 ½-in. (20.3 × 16.5 cm) painting depicted a Black male rendered almost completely invisible by the background, save for his eyes, the white collar of his undershirt, and his gap-toothed smile. Flat-looking and schematic, the work was built on everything Marshall had learned from an analytical approach to picture-making. An attentive examination reveals it to be very carefully constructed with the three detectable elements perfectly aligned. It was inspired by Ralph Ellison's *Invisible Man* (1952)—a take on H. G. Wells's sci-fi tale *The Invisible Man* (1897). But whereas the invisibility of the lead in Wells's novel was the result of an experiment, Ellison's was first and foremost psychological. "I am invisible, understand, simply because people refuse to see me,"[55] states the unnamed protagonist in the prologue. Published in the 1950s, Ellison's book had sociopolitical implications that transcended the story of an individual, and hit hard at a time when America was belatedly coming to terms with the idea that a racially segregated society had no future.[56] As Marshall recalled years later, "[Ellison's *Invisible Man*] has the paradoxical quality of being present and absent at the same time. That was the key. The problem to be solved was: How could I have a figure and no figure simultaneously? I hit upon the device—it's a Minimalist painting strategy, in a way—of putting a black image against a black background. But in order to effect a perceptual change between the image and the ground, I would change the color temperature of the paint: I would paint a warm black figure against a cool black background, or vice versa. Sometimes, even if the values weren't all that different, that shift in color temperature was enough to effect a shift in perception, so that you could see the figure at certain angles while at other angles it faded into the background."[57]

Ray Bradbury's novel *Fahrenheit 451* (1953), the tale of "fireman" Guy Montag's undertaking to burn down every building containing books, was another important title in Marshall's education. The novel features a group of intellectuals called the Drifters, who memorize books and whose motto is "Stuff your eyes with wonder." This concept of taking in all the amazing facts that can be learned from a book resonated with Marshall. Equally powerful was a biographical detail in Bradbury's life relating to how he came to be a sci-fi writer. In 1932, at the age of twelve, Bradbury went to a carnival in his hometown in Illinois

FIG. 23 Cover of *Fantastic Four*, July 1966. Art: Jack Kirby; text: Stan Lee. Published by Marvel Comics, New York.

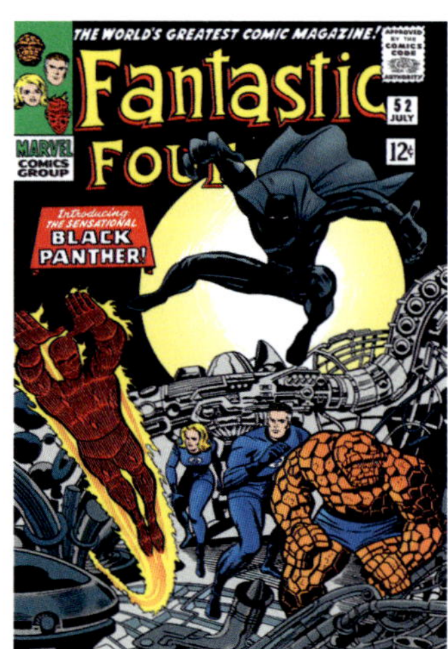

where an entertainer, Mr. Electrico, touched his head with an electric sword and shouted "Live Forever!" "I felt that something strange and wonderful had happened to me because of my encounter with Mr. Electrico," recalled Bradbury years later. "[He] gave me a future… I began to write full-time."[58] The author's epiphany is significant for Marshall, whose craving to investigate the inner workings of everything that interests him would play a big part in his art.

Marshall's excursion into the world of sci-fi literature was by no means accidental. The early 1960s, the years of his coming-of-age, coincided with the Silver Age of comics. Marshall, like many of his peers, was an avid reader of works featuring the Fantastic Four, Spider-Man, and the other characters in the Marvel universe. He was so determined in his passion for comics that when he and his brother Wayne discovered a second-hand magazine store in Huntington Park, he skipped class one morning and walked all the way there and back—some eight miles—to buy comic books. A school trip to the Los Angeles County Museum of Art during fifth grade (the very same year he learned about Charles White's work) had put him in front of Paolo Veronese's masterpiece *Allegory of Navigation with an Astrolabe* (1555–60), featuring a very big, muscular figure—a historical antecedent of the representation of superheroes. The other piece in the museum that stood out in Marshall's memory was a wooden sculpture of a tribal figure from the Ivory Coast—a feather-headed, stick-armed Senufo executioner that he found "scary" and that, as will be seen later, was to play a key role in the creation of *Rythm Mastr*. The visit to the museum, needless to say, was the first of many more to come **[FIG. 24]**.[59]

In the process of consuming all the comics he could find, and producing his early experiments in tracing and copying, Marshall became acutely conscious of the absence of Black action heroes in mainstream comics.[60] This was unsurprising in the Golden Age—after all, in the first part of the twentieth century, America was still racially segregated. The Silver and Bronze Ages, however, were a different story. With the Civil Rights Movement gaining momentum and the 1965 Watts Riots in Los Angeles taking place (a few blocks from Marshall's home)—all of which was heavily televised—even the entertainment industry was slowly coming to the conclusion that a more substantial representation of the diversity in American society was in order. In his maiden apparition in 1966, the Black Panther, Marvel's first Black superhero, successfully challenges the Fantastic Four, only to reveal that he was testing their attributes as potential allies and friends. Having taken measure of the group, the Panther recruits them to go to his native land, The Kingdom of Wakanda, to help him defeat the villainous Klaw, who is after his royal mantle. Marshall was ten at the time **[FIG. 23]**.[61]

FIG. 24 **ANONYMOUS ARTIST,** *Oracle Figure* (*kafigeledjo*), 20th century. Wood with coarse cloth and feathers, 8 ¼×7 ⅞×7 ⅞ in. (21×20×20 cm). Los Angeles County Museum of Art. Gift of Mr. and Mrs. Herbert Baker.

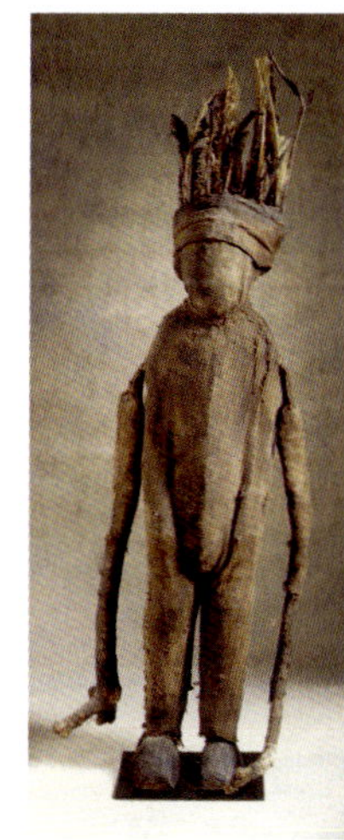

55 Ralph Ellison, *Invisible Man* (New York: Random House, 1952), 3.
56 Marshall's first solo show took place at the Los Angeles Southwest College in 1981, and featured a presentation by his former fellow Otis graduate, Greg Pitts. About three years later, Culver City dealer Marti Koplin offered Marshall official gallery representation. The same year Koplin sold *Portrait of the Artist as a Shadow of His Former Self* to the collector Stephen Lebowitz for $850. The painting is now in the collection of the Los Angeles County Museum of Art.
57 Kerry James Marshall, "Notes on Career and Work," in *Kerry James Marshall* (New York: Harry N. Abrams, 2000), 117.
58 Ray Bradbury, "In His Words," raybradbury.com, December 2001.
59 Among the museum exhibitions that impressed Marshall, there were two in particular at LACMA: *Three Graphic Artists* (1971), in which Timothy Washington, fellow Otis alumni, David Hammons, and Marshall's hero Charles White offered three distinct but equally strong perspectives on the representation of the Black body; and David Driskell's *Two Centuries of Black American Art* (1976), a show acknowledged as the first truly extensive survey of the Black contribution to American visual culture. A final mention goes to the Brockman Gallery, a private venture founded by artists and brothers Alonzo and Dale Davis in 1967 to promote Afro-American art.
60 The first known all-Black publications, *All-Negro Comics*, was authored and published by John Terrell and George J. Evans Jr. in 1947. Motivated by good intentions, the two protagonists—detective Ace Harlem and the very tribal Lion Man—were meant to build a bridge between the Black American community and its African heritage, but it nonetheless looks depressingly stereotyped and there was only one issue. According to Terrel and Evans Jr., this was due to the distributors' prejudice and competition from other publishers. *All-Negro Comics* became a prized rarity among collectors until it was independently reprinted in 2013.
61 Marvel's first Afro-American superhero is considered to be The Falcon (aka Samuel Thomas Wilson). Introduced by Gene Colan and Lee in an issue of *Captain America* in 1969, the Falcon is, according to some, predated by Bill Foster, Ant-Man's lab assistant in *The Avengers* #32, September 1966. Created by Don Heck and Lee, Foster will later become the Black Goliath (*Luke Cage, Power Man* #24, April 1975). Marv Wolfman and Gene Colan's *Blade* (1973) and DC's John Stewart, a character introduced by Dennis O'Neil and Neal Adams as part of the *Green Lantern* franchise in 1972, also deserve a brief mention.

Following a few more guest spots in *Fantastic Four* and *Captain America*, the Black Panther subsequently found a semi-temporary home in *The Avengers* in 1968. He wormed his way into *The Avengers*'s fan base by successfully fighting foes while quietly taking stock of the strange world he had chosen to live in, often acting as the voice of reason next to his capricious teammates.[62] By then, the authors of *The Avengers* (Sal Buscema, Roy Thomas, and Frank Giacoia) had set up a dichotomy in their characters where physical strength and psychological fragility walked hand in hand. Once secluded in the privacy of their headquarters, the same people who were responsible for saving the planet in the public eye would turn into a bunch of loners who had found in one another the family they had never had. But the Panther and Mighty Thor were the two exceptions. The African Prince and the Scandinavian god couldn't have been further apart in terms of cultural background. What they had in common, however, were obligations to relatives, friends, and love interests in a faraway kingdom—a conundrum that created an inner turmoil driven by the question as to whether their services would be put to better use if oriented toward collective rather than personal priorities.

The concomitant presence of Thor and the Panther in *The Avengers* raised an issue that Marshall was quick to spot. Thor, just like his fellow Avengers, Hercules and Namor the Sub-Mariner, was a transposition of classical European mythology into the world of comics. But similar and equally ancient sacred narratives from Africa, although prominently represented in the colonial wings of most Western museums, never enjoyed the same currency on a broader stage. Within contemporary culture, the pantheon of African gods, when compared to their Scandinavian, Roman, and Greek counterparts, were made to look hopelessly inert, if not obsolete. Marshall took notice, and another important piece in the jigsaw puzzle that twenty years later would lead to the creation of *Rythm Mastr* was semi-consciously laid.[63]

The advent of *Black Panther*, rather than filling a gap, made the absence of Black super heroes even more palpable. Having played his part in shaping Luke Cage, Billy Graham was considered a natural choice for the *Jungle Action* series in 1973, an embarrassing remnant from the company's 1950s catalogue that its authors McGregor, Rich Buckler, and Gil Kane were only too eager to revamp. Following a trial issue that reproposed an old episode of *The Avengers* in which the Panther had a starring role, Graham and McGregor were given carte blanche and they saw in *Jungle Action* an opportunity to give the character more context—something Graham had only partially been able to achieve with Luke Cage.

In the early 1970s, a large part of America was intellectually unequipped for, if not openly hostile to, the notion of an empowered Black hero in an emancipated society alien to the traumas of enslavement and ghettoization. As an African Prince, and not a domestic hero, the Panther wasn't inhibited by these limitations, and that gave Graham and McGregor the perfect vehicle to realize their ideas. Wakanda, the Panther's homeland, was transported from the periphery of the story to its center. The move is a tribute to the duo's creative temerity, and it did not go unnoticed by the most conservative and cautious executives at Marvel, who occasionally voiced anxiety about the novelty of a white-free series.

But *Jungle Action* is also notable as an early attempt to create a cohesive story arc across multiple issues. It laid a cornerstone for the foundation of the graphic-novel format that would become popular a few years later, giving superhero comics the aura of respectability that they had lacked up until then. As it emerged, Graham's talent was too big for the comics industry

FIG. 25 Panel from *Justice League of America*, no. 26, December 2008. Art: Ed Benes; text: Dwayne McDuffie. Published by DC Comics, New York.

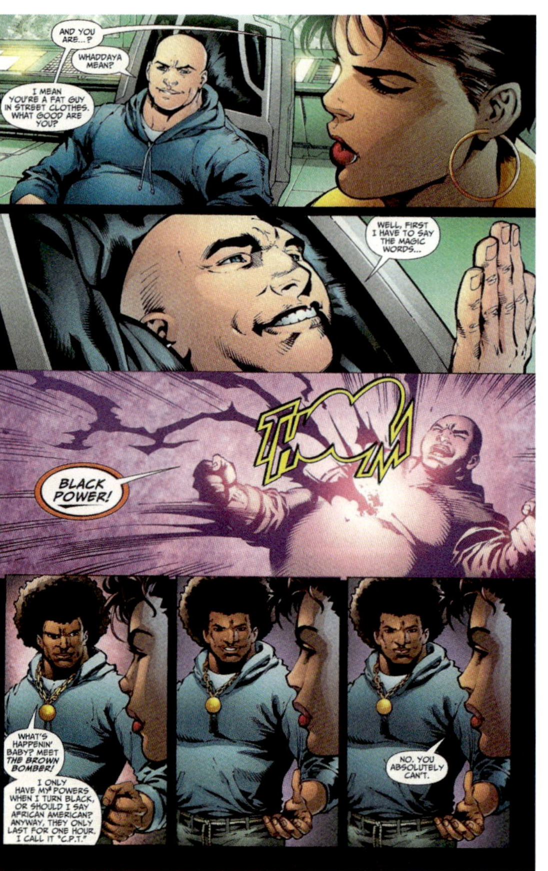

alone. In the late 1980s he embraced a successful career as a playwright and set designer. By 2018, his contribution to the comics world had become so marginalized that at a matinee of Ryan Coogler's high-grossing, Academy Awards–nominated (and *Artforum*-reviewed) *Black Panther* film, Graham's granddaughter Shawnna rallied her family to show up sporting custom-made shirts with a picture of her illustrious grandfather and the superhero he had played such a big hand in defining.[64]

If the road to the creation and establishment of a Black superhero franchise was bumpy for Marvel, the one taken by DC turned out to be decidedly treacherous. The origins of the company's first serious but failed attempt to add a Black superhero to its roster go back to 1976 and are rather hazy. Borrowing from two of their rival's most popular creations, *The Hulk* and *Captain America*, the DC editors came up with the *Black Bomber*—an ironic case of *nomen est omen*. The little information available indicates that the basic concept of the Bomber was about a white bigot who, having been subjected to an experimental chemical camouflage drug devised to disguise US troops in the Asian jungle, transformed himself into a Black superhero in times of duress. Comics historian and *Toonopedia* creator Don Markstein described the idea as "an insult to anybody with any point of view at all" **[FIG. 25]**.[65] DC called on Tony Isabella to doctor the existing scripts. Isabella judged them unsalvageable, and went on to heavily rework the material with artist Trevor Von Eeden. The Black Bomber character was permanently shelved, giving way to Black Lightning—a city-based schoolteacher named Jefferson Pierce who acquires his power from a hyper-technological belt.[66]

The events that took place over the following two decades, however, seem to suggest that DC didn't quite learn its lesson. One of the company's reboots, Geoff Johns's and Phil Jimenez's celebrated seven-issue crossover comic book series *Infinite Crisis* (2005–06) featured only three Black superheroes out of hundreds—Black Lightning, Firestorm (who in his original incarnation had been white), and John Stewart (who temporarily replaced Guy Gardner, a white character, as the Green Lantern, only to be kicked back into obscurity when Gardner decided to have a second go at the job).[67]

---

62 "One of my jobs [at Marvel] was to read all the reprint titles. One of those was *Jungle Action*, a collection of jungle genre comics from the 1950s, mostly detailing white men and women saving Africans or being threatened by them. I voiced a lament that I thought it was a shame that in 1973 Marvel was printing these stories, and couldn't we have a Black African hero?…Now, it was one of those unwritten rules that if you worked in editorial, you would be given things to write. It was at such a meeting that I learned I would be given *Jungle Action*, with the *Black Panther* to write." Don McGregor, "Panther's Chronicles," in Don McGregor and Rich Buckler, *Marvel Masterworks: The Black Panther Volume 1* (New York: Marvel Worldwide, 2010), 7.

63 In the intervening period between the Panther's birth and *Jungle Action*, a social event of seismic proportions had also taken place: the birth of the Black Panther Party for Self Defense organization in Oakland, California, in October 1966. The chronological progeniture of the character over the movement and vice versa have been disputed for a long time. In all probability, their simultaneous emergence, as Arvell Jones observed a few years later, was the result of a cultural ripple. The Black Panther movement and the Black Panther character did not directly influence each other, but their coming to life was inspired by similar concerns and aspirations. John Hulett's Lowndes County Freedom Organization, a political party formed in Alabama in 1965, and the 761st Tank Battalion, a unit of predominantly Afro American soldiers stationed in France during World War Two, both sported black panthers as their logo. The situation was viewed as sensitive enough to prompt Marvel to address the issue in *Fantastic Four* #119 (February 1972), where the Panther temporarily changes to Black Leopard, since he feels the name now has "political connotations" in America. According to author Roy Thomas: "Stan [Lee] directed me to try calling [the Black Panther] the Black Leopard, which I didn't care for, but I did as I was told." See Aaron Couch, "'Black Panther' Flashback: When T'Challa (Briefly) Became the Black Leopard," *Hollywood Reporter*, February 14, 2019, https://www.hollywoodreporter.com/heat-vision/black-panther-flashback-tchalla-became-black-leopard-1185811. In January 2021 the story of the Black Panther Party became the subject of a comic book adaptation—see David F. Walker and Marcus Kwame Anderson, *The Black Panther Party: A Graphic Novel* (Berkeley, CA: Ten Speed Press, 2021).

64 Sean Howe, "Black Panther, Luke Cage, and the first Black Artist to Draw Both," *New York Times*, March 7, 2018, https://www.nytimes.com/2018/03/07/movies/black-panther-luke-cage-artist-billy-graham.html. To get an exhaustive view of the Afro-American authors and artists who played a big (and often unrecognized) role in shaping the American comics industry, see Ken Quattro, *Invisible Men: The Trailblazing Black Artists of Comic Books* (New York: IDW Publishing, 2020).

65 Don Markstein, "Black Lightning," http://www.toonopedia.com/b_lightn.htm.

66 "In each of the two completed *Black Bomber* scripts, the white bigot risks his own life to save another person whom he can't see clearly (in one case, a baby in a stroller) and then reacts in racial slur disgust when he discovers that he risked his life to save a Black person. He wasn't aware that he had two identities, but each identity had a girlfriend, and the ladies were aware of the change. To add final insult, the Bomber's costume was little more than a glorified basketball uniform. DC had wanted me to take over writing the book with the third issue. I convinced them to eat the two scripts and let me start over. To paraphrase my arguments…'Do you *really* want DC's first Black superhero to be a white bigot?,'" Tony Isabella, http://worldofblackheroes.com/2010/06/17/brown-bomber/.

67 One of the most insightful critiques on the shortcomings of *Infinite Earths* and the importance of superheroes comic books came from screenplay writer John Ridley in the pages of *Filter* magazine. "There's like a billion heroes from all over these multi-verses, outer space, and other dimensions and, like, three of these billions of heroes are Black…So one might think, what's the big deal anyway? It's all some made-up crap kids shouldn't be reading. Not true. Kids need to learn to imagine; they need to get some life lessons that are more wondrous than mundane. And if they are reading comics, they are reading. Tell me how that's a bad thing." John Ridley, "Feng Shui and the American Way," *Filter*, Fall 2006, 110.

SO WE MIGHT KNOW OURSELVES NOW

Marshall's first-known professional foray into the world of superhero comics and his decision to address the absence of prominent Black characters within it can possibly be traced to *X-Man*, the large mixed-media composition on canvas he made in 1989 that is now permanently housed in the Rennie Museum in Vancouver **[FIG. 26]**. What became even more evident at that particular juncture was that Marshall's proposed reading of the work was increasingly oscillating between plain figuration and enigmatic symbolism. As he later stated, *X-Man* was not inspired by the Marvel comic book series but rather "the way Nation of Islam [leaders] dropped their slave name and adopted the X as an unknown quantity."[68] This is supported by the portraits of some of these same leaders sketched on the left-hand side of the painting. Yet, the central figure, surrounded by magic rings and armed with a phallic sword, has an undeniable superhero quality. His head partially covers the title of the painting (a technique Marvel frequently adopted for its cover design) which is assembled from fonts openly referencing the ones used in the eponymous comic book.

In his formative years, Marshall and other kids often tried to copy the imagery of Marvel Comics. But by his own admission, Marshall wasn't the most talented of his lot. "My images tended to get overworked really fast, and had a lot of lines, erasures, and scratches."[69] This technique, which would later serve him well in terms of developing an understanding of process as an integral part of the image, is very much detectable in its nascent form on the rough canvas of *X-Man*. The painting, however, cannot be dismissed as a minor episode in Marshall's early career. The year it was made—1989—was the year he moved to Chicago's Hyde Park neighborhood after marrying his partner, the actor Cheryl Lynn Bruce. Thanks to a grant from the National Endowment for the Arts, he was able to get a proper studio space—a welcome novelty that finally enabled him to create larger paintings. Despite its roughness, *X-Man* builds a bridge between works like *A Portrait of the Artist as a Shadow of His Former Self* and *When Frustration Threatens Desire* (1990)—a visual rendition of a quote from Paul Garon about magic as a way to attain the impossible—and the first hint of a representational form that in the years to come would be refined and amplified to become one of the most recognizable features of Marshall's work **[FIG. 27]**.

The beginning of the 1990s, on top of being an important time for Marshall both professionally and personally, marked a seismic change in the world of superhero comics too. Following the end of the Bronze Age, the industry entered what many have labeled a period of crisis. The competition from other entertainment enterprises, starting with television and ending with the popular use of the Internet, had over time had a dramatic impact on potential readers. When a whole pool of early teenagers tuned in to the new Disney Channel and Cartoon Network, and gradually lost interest in the adventures of heroic individuals on paper, publishers found themselves cut off from their primary target audience. As a consequence, the core readership of superhero comics became mostly composed of collectors or people who had formed their passion during the previous years and continued to enjoy the format out of either habit, loyalty, or affection.

68 Hadani Ditmars, "Kerry James Marshall on Painting, Politics, and P Diddy's Record-Breaking Purchase of His Work," *The Art Newspaper*, June 3, 2018, https://www.theartnewspaper.com/2018/06/03/kerry-james-marshall-on-painting-politics-and-p-diddys-record-breaking-purchase-of-his-work.
69 Calvin Reid, "Interview with Kerry James Marshall," *Bomb*, winter, 1998.

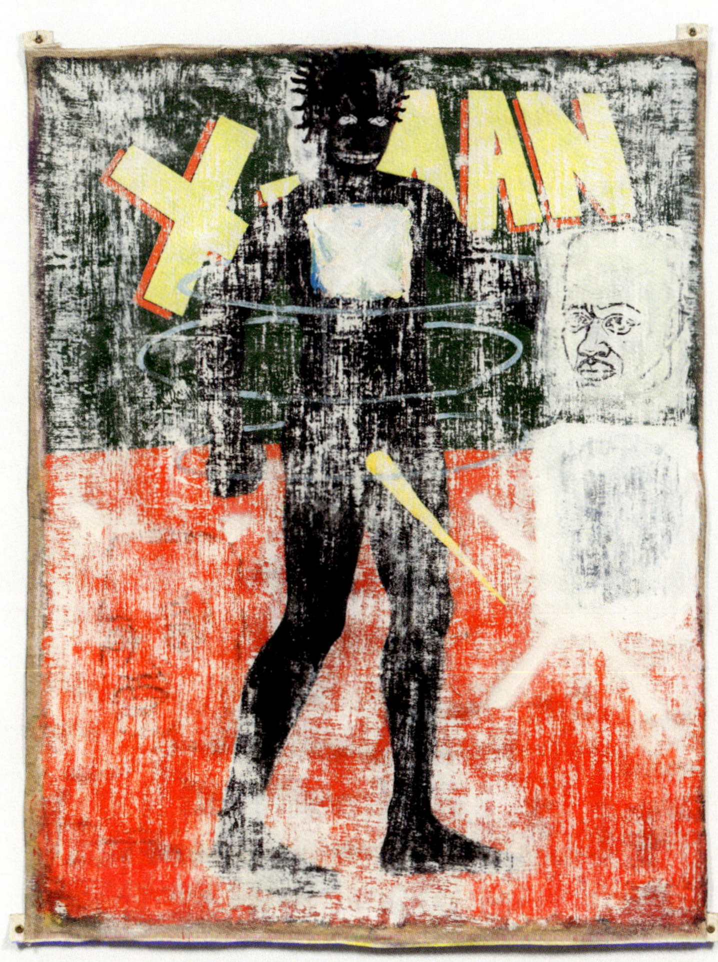

FIG. 26 **KERRY JAMES MARSHALL,** *X-Man*, 1989. Mixed media on canvas, 54×41 in. (137×104 cm). Rennie Museum, Vancouver.

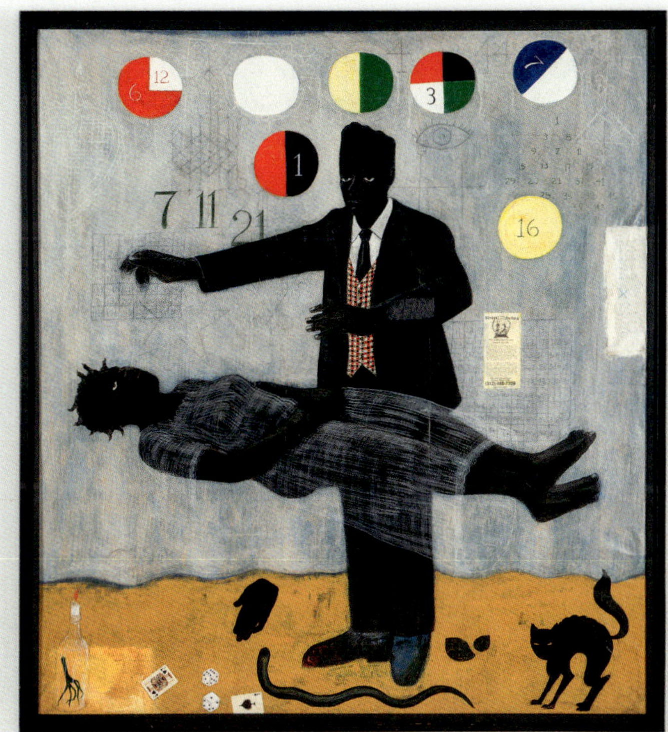

FIG. 27 **KERRY JAMES MARSHALL,** *When Frustration Threatens Desire*, 1990. Acrylic and collage on canvas, 80×72 in. (203.2×182.9 cm). Collection of April Sheldon and John Casado.

Anxious to cater to the appetite of this adult audience, the industry went on to release expensively packaged products, often darker in tone and laced with self-referential artistry, and to adopt questionable marketing strategies like issuing an exaggerated number of collectable items, or creating stories as publicity stunts, such as DC's *The Death of Superman* (1993). Or, alternatively, in an attempt to imitate their on-screen competitors, it jumped on the new technology available, employing not particularly accomplished authors whose sloppy imagery could be made to look good with rotoscoped panels and excessive coloration.[70] Graphic novels blatantly affected by a cinematic aesthetic were also produced in an attempt to increase their appeal to potential investors and attract lucrative movie and television deals.[71]

In DC's case, their 1989 merger with Time Warner had made this an unavoidable occurrence, inaugurating a trend of superhero comics adapted from their screen counterparts rather than the other way around. As for Marvel, the company suffered a serious setback in 1992 when seven of its main artists (Erik Larsen, Jim Lee, Rob Liefeld, Todd McFarlane, Whilce Portacio, Marc Silvestri, and Jim Valentino) staged a group walkout to form a rival enterprise, Image Comics. On the brink of bankruptcy, Marvel was saved by a takeover from Toys Biz five years later. Disenchanted by what they regarded as a corporate world, with toy manufacturers and film studios now running the show, some of the remaining major players like Miller, Moore, and Mazzucchelli left to either start independent companies or pursue other creative adventures.

Faced with a landscape where the two giants that had carried the North American superhero comics industry on their backs for decades were now on life support, and the exodus of a generation of artists and authors, the future of superheroes on paper looked bleak.[72] Yet some of the biggest sociocultural innovations take place in challenging times, and the 1990s went down in history as a moment that registered vital changes. One of those was the first serious attempt by Afro-American comics authors to regain control of the way the Black body was depicted and narrated.

The circumstances in which Black Panther, Luke Cage, and the Falcon came to life coincided with a chaotic time in African-American history. For the Black community in South Central Los Angeles, the spring of 1992 turned out to be a terrible reminder of 1965, and a marker of how little progress had been made in the intervening years. Following the acquittal of four LA Police Department officers charged with using unnecessary force during the arrest of Rodney King, the city experienced dramatic unrest. King's beating had been taped by an amateur video operator, George Holliday. This had the twofold effect of suggesting that police brutality was a regular occurrence, and that it often went unpunished even when documented. The flagrant discrepancy between the evidence and the verdict ignited riots. But there were other catalysts already in place: poverty, unemployment, and social inequality were rife in the area. Furthermore, there were other controversial incidents, chief among them the killing of teenager Latasha Harlins by a shopkeeper only two weeks after King's beating.

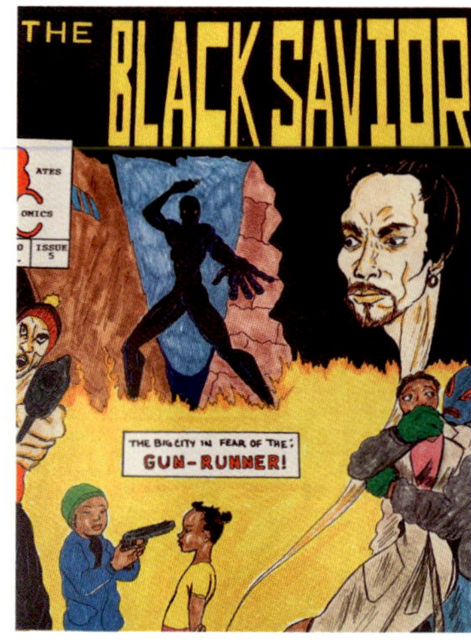

FIG. 28 Cover of *The Black Savior*, July 1992. Art: Roger Bates. Published by Oakland Comics Entertainment, Oakland.

The uprising was ended by the intervention of the National Guard after six long days, but its cultural resonance lasted much longer. It was addressed in film (Spike Lee's *Malcolm X* [1992]); music (Rage Against the Machine's album *The Battle of Los Angeles* [1999]); and literature (Adaeze Nkechi Nwosu's *Heal the Hood* [2020]). One of the earliest responses, however, was *The Black Savior*, a comics series originated by Roger Bates and Cedric Shabazz's Oakland Comics Entertainment in 1991, about a district attorney turned superhero who fights gangsters and drug dealers in his community **[FIG. 28]**. The intention was to create a series made by Black authors and publishers for a Black audience—until then an almost unprecedented step—that would appeal to hip-hop fans. When the third issue of *The Black Savior* featured a cover illustration unmistakably referencing King's battering, the magazine doubled its sales. This unexpected success did not elevate the series to mainstream status (indeed it would close within three years after a very intermittent shelf life), but it signaled the beginning of a new consciousness among the Black comics community that was to have a tidal effect.

In 1993, artist, author, and designer Turtel Onli, already a founding member of BAG (Black Artists Guild), after years of independent publishing coauthored with Cassandra Washington the graphic novel *Sustah Girl: Queen of the Black Age*.[73] In February of the same year, Onli inaugurated the first Black Age Comics Convention at the Southside Community Arts Center in Chicago—a moment of enlightened self-determination that acted as a launching pad for what he himself called the "Black Age of Comics Movement." Fifteen exhibitors showed up to display their creations.[74] This was enough to thrust the editors of *TCJ*, one of the oldest critical comics publications, to put out an issue entirely focused on "Black American Comics Artists" for the first time in its twenty-five-year history.[75]

Finally, a New York–based collective of artists and writers composed of Denys Cowan, Michael Davis, Derek T. Dingle, Dwayne McDuffie and, for a brief period, Christopher Priest,[76] founded Milestone Media, a company with close ties to DC. Their most notable accomplishment was the creation of *Hardware*, the story of a prodigious Black inventor named Curtis Metcalf with no superpowers but exceptional skills in martial arts and a brilliant mind dedicated to building ingenious gadgets to fight criminals. Written by McDuffie and penciled by Cowan, the early issues of *Hardware* tell the story of Metcalf's decision to take down his boss, Edwin Alva Sr., after the latter's refusal to acknowledge his work—a story that, according to some, aimed to shine a light on McDuffie's own experience at Marvel a few years earlier **[FIG. 29]**.

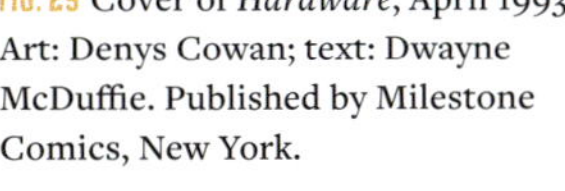

FIG. 29 Cover of *Hardware*, April 1993. Art: Denys Cowan; text: Dwayne McDuffie. Published by Milestone Comics, New York.

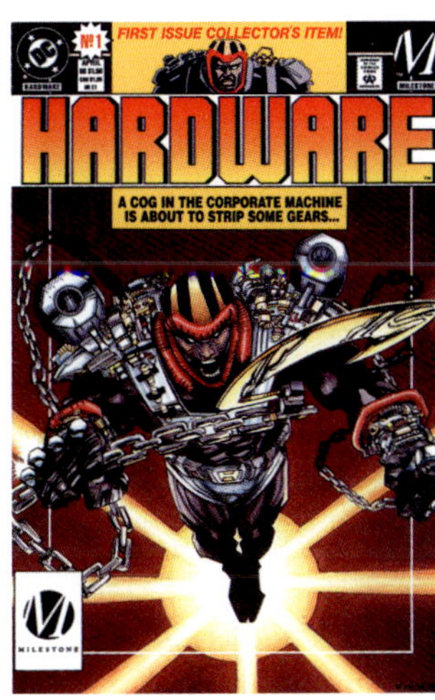

Critically and commercially well-received, *Hardware* made a name for its publisher. Milestone's robust program would continue with McDuffie's and Mark D. Bright's *Icon* (an alien who assumes human form and is aided in his inner-city missions by a single mother called Rocket); the collectively created *Static* (a teenager who earned prodigious electro-magnetic powers during a chemical experiment); and Milestone's version of the Justice League of America, the *Blood Syndicate*, which saw McDuffie and Cowan aided by cartoonist Ivan Velez Jr. "The Black Age of Comics," announced by Onli, had officially begun.[77]

Milestone's successful introduction of independent Black superheroes captured the imagination of many young readers and its ability to sustain such a model became a shining light for a generation of authors and artists. Yet it encountered objections from both sides of the social spectrum. Prejudices about producing "Comics for Blacks" were difficult to shake off, and in defiance of DC's support, many retailers shied away from carrying the company's titles.

---

70 Artist Greg Land's limited visual vocabulary is often used as an example of this trend. Known for repeatedly using photographic references or, in some cases, even lifting his colleagues' ideas in their entirety, Land has been accused on multiple occasions of damaging the comics industry by editors, publishers, and even his peers.

71 Kevin Eastman's and Peter Laird's *Teenage Mutant Ninja Turtles* provides an example of the profitability of the merchandising business in the 1990s. This comic book was put out by Mirage in 1984, and after being picked up and turned into a child-friendly animated series by Playmates Toys and CBS, it had racked up between $400 and $500 million a year in licensing alone by 1993.

72 Just like the "Death of Painting" idea that has plagued the art world for decades, the forecasts regarding the end of comics superheroes turned out to be largely unfounded pessimism. Garth Ennis's, Gregg Hurwitz's, and Laurence Campbell's *The Punisher* (2004), and John Romita Jr.'s, Reginald Hudlin's, and Klaus Janson's *Black Panther* (2005) are universally considered some of the best story arcs Marvel has ever put out.

73 A Chicago native, Onli was the creator of, among other things, the sci-fi series *NOG: Protectors of the Pyramids* in 1981.

74 "Nobody was talking about the fact that the *Sun-Times* and the *Tribune* for years didn't carry any Black cartoon strips, and neither did the *Defender*. The *Defender* had Mickey Mouse and Donald Duck and Henry and Hazel in there. We couldn't get work with anybody…A lot of people were visually hung up on creative interpretations of how Black people look. If you have image problems with yourself, then you're not that comfortable with creative interpretations of yourself," Turtel Onli in interview with Rebecca Zorach, *Never the Same*, November 2014, https://never-the-same.org/interviews/turtel-onli/.

75 Carole Sobocinski (ed.), "Building the Issue: Black Comics Artists," *The Comics Journal*, no. 160 (June 1993): 33–106. The issue included interviews with Stan Shaw, Nabile P. Hage, Seitu Hayden, Ho Che Anderson, the Sims Brothers, and the staff at Milestone as well as essays by Trina Robbins and Jeff Winbush.

76 Priest, together with Sheena Howard, would later edit the 2017 seminal *Encyclopedia of Black Comics* for Chicago Review Press.

77 Also worth mentioning is *Brotherman: Dictator of Discipline*, a comic book series starring lawyer-turned-vigilante, Antonio Valor. Authored and published by brothers Dawud Anyabwile (born David Sims), Guy A. Sims, and Jason E. Sims between 1989 and 1996 through their own Philadelphia-based imprint Big City Comics, *Brotherman* was sold almost exclusively in Black-owned bookstores. Despite its avoidance of the mainstream market, the series sold about 750,000 copies before being discontinued. To better illustrate the extent to which Black artists and authors were overlooked in the superhero comics industry, it wasn't until the mid-1990s that Universal Zulu Nation's prominent members Afrika Bambaataa & The Soul Sonic Force opted to be portrayed as a group of fictional superheroes on the cover of their empowering 1983 single *Renegades of Funk*, and Emmy-award-winning artist and animator Bob Camp was commissioned to do the cover art.

At the opposite end of the spectrum, a more ideologically oriented criticism came from a rival consortium of publishers called ANIA (Swahili for "Serve and Protect"), who accused Milestone of not doing enough to perpetuate the Black Cause.[78] Led by Atlanta's Dark Zulu Lies president, Nabile P. Hage,[79] the ANIA associates (Dark Zulu Lies; San José's Africa Rising; Greensboro's UP Comics; and New York's Afro Centric Comics Books) made no bones about their contempt for Milestone's involvement with DC. Fearing a perpetuation of the ethnic, attitudinal, and verbal inaccuracies of Black characters in mainstream comics due to them being written from a white perspective (or, in this case, creatively controlled and distributed from a white perspective), ANIA put out products like *The Motorbike Puppies*, *Purge*, and their own take on *Black Panther*, *Zwanna, Son of Zulu* **[FIG. 30]**.

The rivalry that ensued between Milestone and ANIA, coupled with Onli's expanding business (editions of his conventions took place in Detroit, Atlanta, and New York) contributed to the assessment that the "Black Age of Comics" was a reality. By fostering an impressive amount of talent during their tenure, Milestone and ANIA, along with other relatively short-lived initiatives such as Ghettosake and Big City,[80] gave a generation of Black comics authors the opportunity to express themselves on their own terms for the first time in history. Yet, like Milestone, even ANIA wasn't immune from criticism. Its flagship series, *Zwanna, Son of Zulu*, occasionally slipped into the exoticizing combination of glamour and tribalism that fosters misconceptions about African culture.

FIG. 30 Cover of *Zwanna Son of Zulu*, April–May 1993. Art: John Ruiz; text: Nabile P. Hage. Published by ANIA, Chicago.

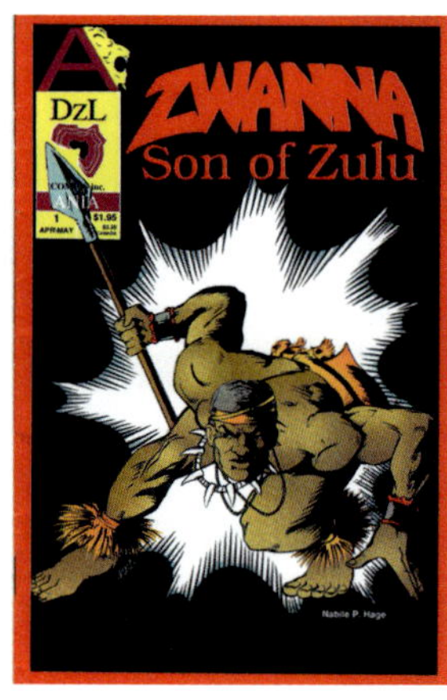

Twenty years later, Coogler's *Black Panther* film did very little to correct such an approach. The film, though enjoyable, is rife with inconsistencies. Wakanda is introduced as one of the most technologically advanced places on the planet and yet its inhabitants are using spears and shields. The nation has Vibranium—a metal capable of absorbing, storing, and releasing large amounts of kinetic energy—but no one is adopting technology apart from Shuri, T'Challa's sister, and the country's powers that be are resistant to the idea of sharing their knowledge with neighboring countries. Marshall himself wasn't impressed with what he saw: "You can tell how much confidence people have in the power of the images they produce by how long they let you look at them. Wakanda should have been absolutely fantastic-looking but they don't let you look at it long at all. The first thing you get to see is skyscrapers with sticks and straws on their roofs. Street vendors are selling old African-looking baskets like you would see in the 1970s."[81]

Marshall also has mixed feelings about the one-dimensionality of the characters and the way they are represented:

> *All superhero movies have a love story. There's nothing like a love story in Black Panther. We don't know anything about T'Challa, we don't care about him. There's no reason to—he's a symbol. He cares about Black people all over the world but not about the Black girl who's supposed to be his girlfriend. The way she was killed—that was wrong in any way you can think about it. Why do you have Black people who care so little about each other but care so much about liberation vs. white supremacy? Everybody is supposed to perform an ideal Black self. One is the modern victim and the other is the resistance hero. That movie shows how desperate Black people are for recognition. It just puts you in a position where you can be easily exploited.*[82]

Both ANIA's and Milestone's strategy of revisiting existing blueprints in the creation of their characters produced relatively conventional superheroes too anchored to previous models to effectively imagine a way forward. As Marshall pointed out, "Even before Milestone came out with *Hardware*, I didn't like a lot of the characters. It seemed clear all they were doing was trying to do a multicultural version of *X-Men* and *The Fantastic Four*. That's not enough. I don't need to see a Black Green Lantern or Iron Man. That's not progress. At some point Black folk have to demonstrate they have the same capacity to invent their own characters."[83]

EVERY BEAT OF MY HEART

> *Origin: The new phoneme recalls the standard, rhythm, and the patois, riddim, or riddum. Its meaning is derived from the third definition of "rhythm" found in the 1996 pocket Oxford Dictionary: "3: a pattern of successive strong and weak movements. This is combined with the noun, Mastr, or Master; 4: prevailing person; 11: a boy too young to be called Mr. "Rythm Mastr" is meant to avoid the implied dominance associated with the term Master, while retaining a link to history and culture.*[84]

When Marshall learned that his designated space at the Carnegie International 1999/2000 was the museum's Treasure Room—a recessed section designed to display decorative art—his reaction was to think of a creative way to challenge the status of the room itself. In his words, he wanted to "throw back a stone at a large glasshouse."[85] He did so by emphasizing how the intrinsic value of the exact same object can mutate depending on its positioning. His solution was to fold newspapers to form paper hats and ships that would be installed inside the museum's vitrines, but perceptible only through the shadow they projected onto the glass.

Vitrines, as artists like Jeff Koons and Damien Hirst have shown, reek of institutionally assigned merit, and everything that goes into them is automatically assessed as precious. Conversely, Marshall figured, newspapers have no value. They are mass-produced, dispensable, and far from unique. Their official lifespan is the day of their release, but their second life consists of being recycled for a disparate array of activities, from packaging items to protecting surfaces. This play on the shift in value depending on which side of the vitrine the paper finds itself, along with the notion of the shadow, would also act as a powerful metaphor for the "absence with a capital A"[86] that had kept Black culture on the margins for centuries.

Marshall also chose to use some of the newspapers as screens, by taping them to the inside of the vitrines, in a fashion not dissimilar to that of shops and stores undergoing refurbishment. Although the papers were positioned upside down or sideways to further emphasize the casualness of the situation, Marshall wasn't oblivious to the fact that some of them would be legible, and as such potentially distracting. Some form of visual information that resonated with the project had to be printed on them. And what kind of images are normally printed on cheap, pulp paper? Marshall had the answer: comics. But existing comics wouldn't have worked as there was nothing available that would have fitted with his concept. The only solution was to conceive, create, and print a brand-new series of comics himself.

78 In 2008, Milestone's characters and universe were officially absorbed by DC Comics and revived in different existing series. Following a few aborted attempts and a lawsuit from the McDuffie estate over their exclusion from the proceedings, Milestone was relaunched in August 2020 with the seventeen-page sampler *Milestone Returns #0*, written by Reginald Hudlin and Greg Pak with art from Denys Cowan, Chris Sotomayor, Jim Lee, Ryan Benjamin, Khoi Pham, Scott Hanna, Bill Sienkiewicz, Don Ho, Alex Sinclair, and Deron Bennett.

79 A multifaceted artist, Hage made headlines in Atlanta in 1992 for a performative action in which, dressed as a Zulu Warrior, he climbed onto a third-floor ledge of the State Capitol and tossed comic books around.

80 Founded by brothers Robert, Jeremy, and Maurice Love, Ghettosake is remembered for publishing *Chocolate Thunder* (1998), an interesting but hardly innovative series that according to many epitomized this generation of authors' lack of imagination when it came to creating new characters.

81 Kerry James Marshall in conversation with the author, 2020.

82 Marshall with author, 2020.

83 Marshall with author, 2020. An interesting case of a character's color mutation in this sense is S.H.I.E.L.D.'s leader and Captain America's ally Nick Fury. Samuel L. Jackson portrayed Fury in the late-2000s *Iron Man* films, his towering performance leading Marvel to retire the original character and have him replaced by one modeled on Jackson in its comic books from then on.

84 Kerry James Marshall, *Dailies: Origin*, 2010, screenprint printed in black and buff on Rives BFK paper.

85 Marshall with author, 2020.

86 Kyle MacMillan, "Kerry James Marshall Changing the Narrative of Art History," *Chicago Sun Times*, April 20, 2016.

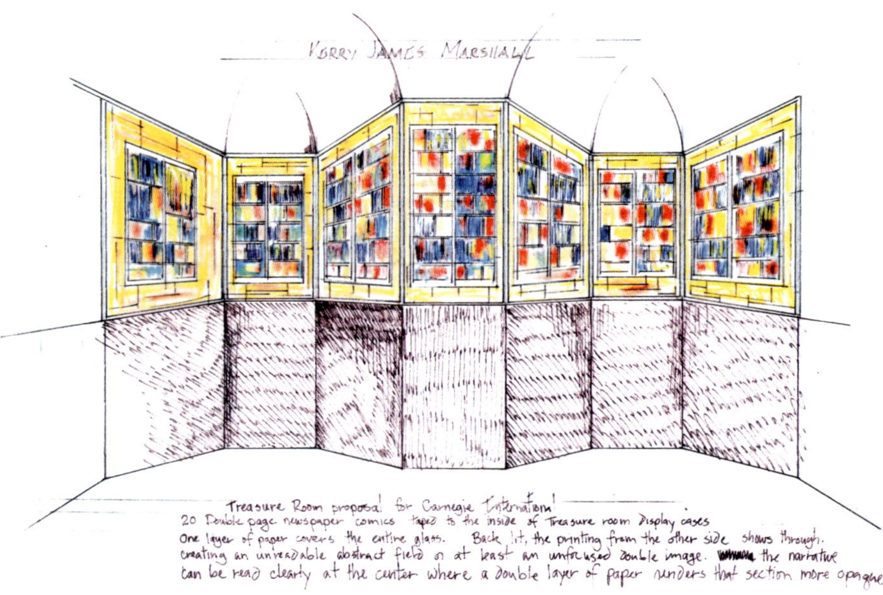

FIG. 31 Study for *Rythm Mastr* installation at the Carnegie International, 1999. Ink, pencil, and color pencil on tracing paper, 14 ½×22 in. (36.8×55.9 cm).

Marshall outlined his proposal in a preparatory sketch that was submitted to the board of the Carnegie International, where a drawing of the obscured Treasure Room was accompanied by the following text: "Twenty double-page newspaper comics taped to the inside of the Treasure Room display cases. One layer of papers covers the entire glass. Backlit, the printing from the other side shows through, creating an unreadable abstract field or at least an unfocused double image. The narrative can be read clearly at the center where a double layer of paper renders that section more opaque **[FIG. 31]**."[87]

Marshall had years of experience as a consumer, but he had never seriously ventured into the world of comics before as an artist. Creating a fresh series with interesting characters and a convincing story arc was not a matter of just a few months—especially given that he would be assuming the roles of writer, penciler, editor, inker, and colorist all himself.[88] This was a very unusual way of working within this industry, but important for maintaining control of the process and the appearance of the artwork.

Looking back to the comic books he had enjoyed as a child helped him clarify what he *didn't* intend to do. For starters, his heroes wouldn't be ordinary people who have accidentally bumped into something radioactive and now have power; they would acquire their astounding capabilities in an original way that would make African culture the focus, stressing the conflict between tradition and modernity and the underlying concern of the "struggle of Black folks" sapiently articulated by W. E. B. Du Bois. Their adventures would take place in a social context with which the Afro-American community could identify, without slipping into the narrative trap associated with Luke Cage and Misty Knight thirty years before, where supernaturally gifted Black heroes end up fighting petty crime. Marshall would weave into his project all the dynamics of the community that surrounded him on his own terms, with an overlap of the impoverished and the astonishing. In line with the superhero comics tradition, powers would come from authentic trauma, but the protagonists' appearance wouldn't be that of muscular, chiseled bodies, mantles, and capes—they would look like "real" people living in a "real" place where extraordinary things nevertheless happen. Lastly, the hero's name wouldn't be attached to adjectives like "spectacular," "amazing," "fantastic," or "incredible." What Marshall was looking for in his characters' names was something that could achieve the same effect of magnificence while staying truthful to the context in which his characters were conceived and would operate.

The solution he found was to conjure an individual who starts an action that soon inspires others to follow or imitate him, building an ideal bridge across different moments in history—the Rythm Master. However, in order to remove the negative connotation of the word "master" in Afro-American history, it would be spelled so as to reflect the vernacular language that Marshall was to use in the dialogue. In classic comics style, the title *Rythm Mastr* would feature like a logo at the top of each page, blending urban tagging and traditional African typefaces **[FIG. 33]**.

The duality that characterizes *Rythm Mastr* is detectable from the opening stages of the first story, "Every Beat of My Heart," with a mug-shot-style introduction of the two main protagonists—computer whiz Stasha and her boyfriend Farrell—along with a group of five African art-inspired superheroes—Boli, Ibeji, Nkisi, Oba, and Senufo[89]—and the title character, the Rythm Mastr **[FIG. 32]**. In the upper part of the panel, we get a glimpse of the construct in which the story is going to take place. "The long-dreamed-of capital of the Black World,"[90] later known as Black Metropolis, is a faraway city, but realistic enough to let readers know that everything that happens there could be happening in any American urban conglomerate.

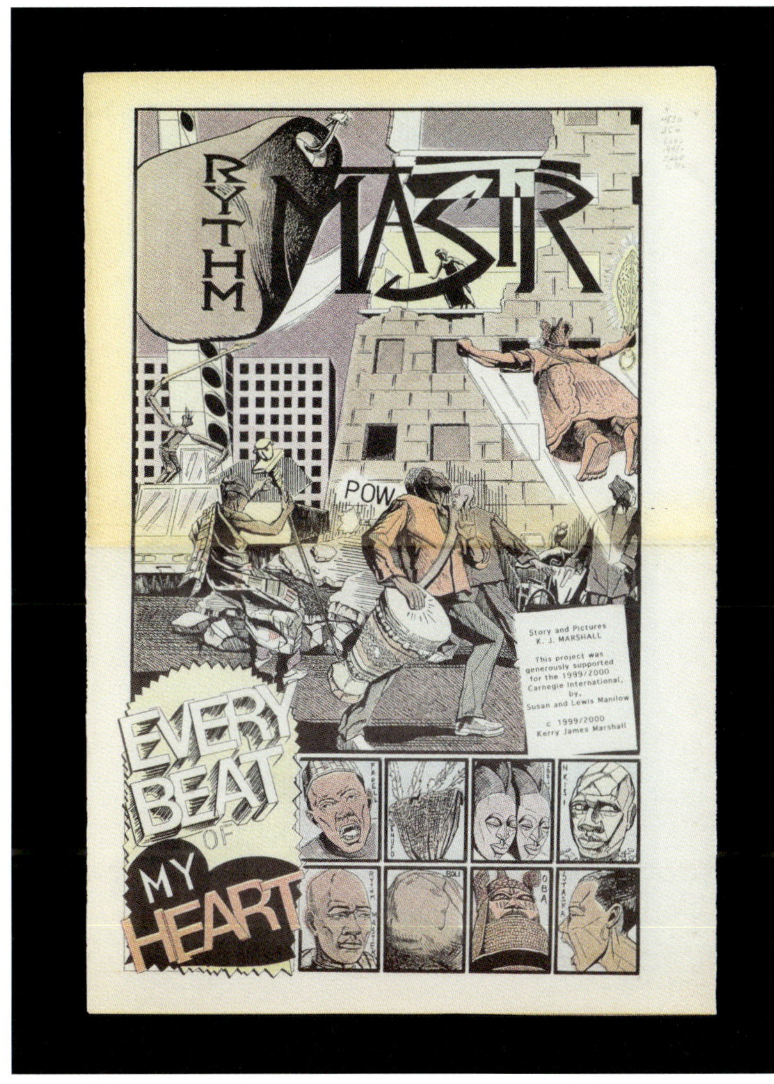

FIG. 32 Cover of Kerry James Marshall's *Rythm Mastr: Every Beat of My Heart*, 1999–2000. Published by Carnegie Museum of Art, Pittsburgh. See p. 65.

FIG. 33 **KERRY JAMES MARSHALL**, Rythm Mastr logo, 1999–.

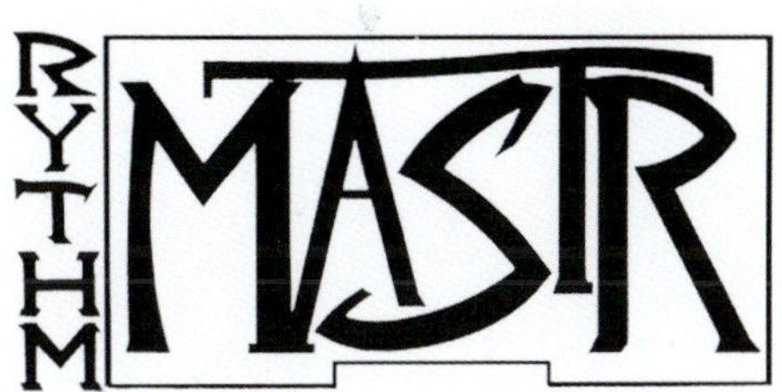

87 David S. Frankel (ed.), *Carnegie International 1999/2000*, vol. 1 (Pittsburgh: Carnegie Museum of Art, 1999), 54.

88 New York graphic artist and animator Tim Fielder aided Marshall with coloring. Fielder, the founder of multimedia company Dieselfunk Studios, in 2015 put out one of his most famous creations, *Matty's Rocket*, with an Afrofuturist heroine.

89 The five cult figures reference various regions of West and Central Africa. Boli is a Malian zoomorphic creature used to communicate with the afterlife; Ibeji is an Orisha twinned-figure originally from Nigeria and later embraced by the Latin American African diaspora; Nkisi is a spirit-inhabited object from Congo; Oba is a Trans-African ruler who exists in different manifestations in Benin and Nigeria; and Senufo is an Ivory Coast feathered oracle.

90 Kerry James Marshall, "Artist's Project," *Esopus*, no. 14, spring 2010. The name is both a nod to the set of Superman's adventures and an expression coined by St. Clair Drake and Horace R. Cayton to describe Chicago following the first big migration in their book *Black Metropolis: A Study of Negro Life in a Northern City* (San Diego: Harcourt, Brace & Company, 1945).

In the prologue, the two main protagonists, Stasha and Farrell are talking to their friend Grant on the street when a group of gang members drives by and attacks them with fire **[FIG. 34A]**. In the chaos that ensues, the fate of the two main characters will be sealed forever, drawing a line of physical and spiritual separation between them that will account for their future actions and set the binary tone of *Rythm Mastr*. Stasha gets shot and sustains life-changing injuries. Once out of danger, her retaliatory feelings and technological knowledge are channeled into devising remote-controlled cars capable of committing vengeful drive-bys, and a device that enables her to walk again and even fly out of windows. Her parents worry about the amount of time she spends in front of her computer, and suspicions are raised about her involvement in the strange events that are sending shockwaves through the neighborhood. The inexplicable sight of monstrous flying creatures, unexpected earthquakes (the phenomenon in the final segment of "Every Beat of My Heart," whereby the highway asphalt becomes sentient, is a visual and narrative masterpiece), vehicles crashing and burning with no one inside, are all reported with great sensationalism by the journalists April and Ebony Jones, and the anchorwoman Valerie, for the fictional KMET television station **[FIG. 34B]**.[91]

In the second part of the story, "Tower of Power,"[92] these accidents are followed by the mysterious destruction of water tanks—at the time a vanishing feature of the Chicago cityscape. On the final page, bystanders express their wonder on realizing once the smoke from the explosion dissipates that the water tank in question is still intact. "Unbelievable! How is that possible?" asks a crowd member. In a masterful cinematic sequence, the final panel substitutes the group of observers looking up with the five superheroes mirroring their pose. "That was close. The sonic field held this time, but they'll most certainly increase the explosive field," comments Nkisi, revealing that the water tank is somehow connected with their activities. "Soon there will be few of these structures left," concludes Ibeji. "We must move quickly now. Our time grows shorter" **[FIG. 34C]**.

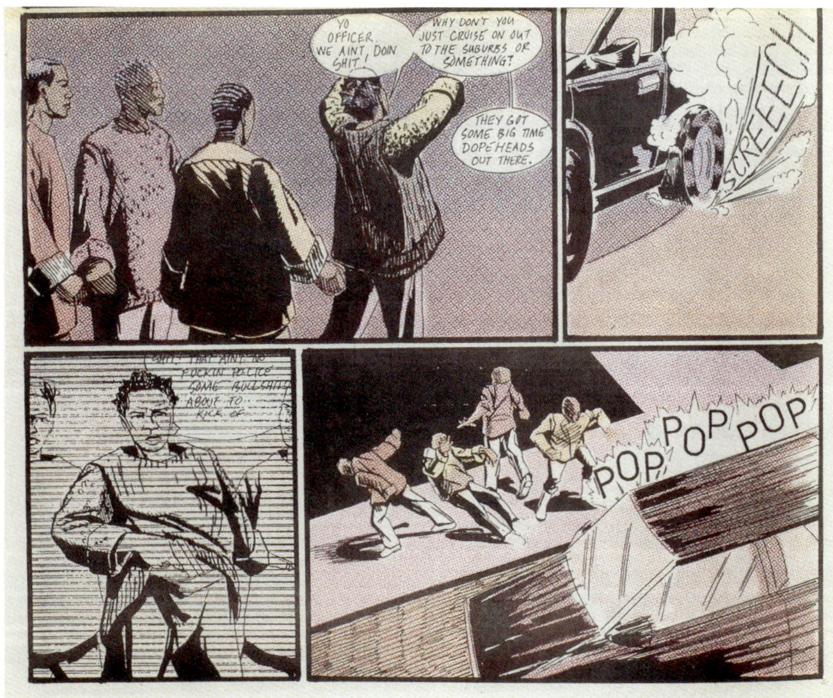

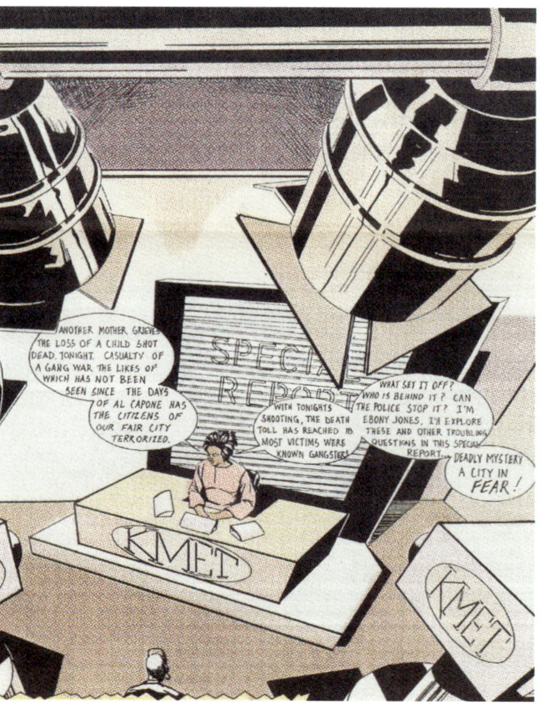

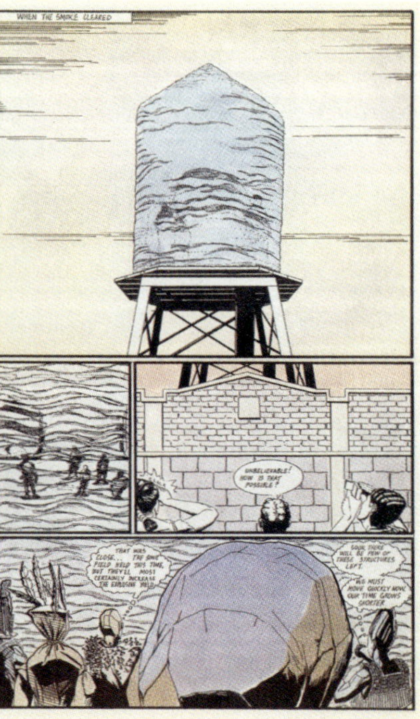

FIGS. 34A–C Details from Kerry James Marshall's *Rythm Mastr* newsprint comics (1999–2000). Published by Carnegie Museum of Art, Pittsburgh. See pp. 65–79.

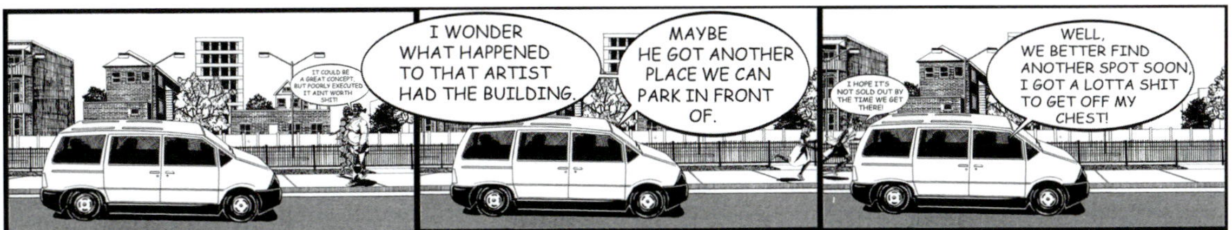

FIG. 41 Detail from Kerry James Marshall, *Rythm Mastr Daily Strip*, 2017. See p. 197.

years earlier, Marshall had all the qualities in place to take the form, process, and technique of a comic strip and exploit it for art. Hence, the third manifestation of *Rythm Mastr*—the "Dailies"—was born.

TOWER OF POWER

On the occasion of *One True Thing: Meditations on Black Aesthetics* at the Museum of Contemporary Art in Chicago in 2003—a highly-anticipated solo show following a gap of five years and his first at the city's venerable institution—Marshall introduced a new body of work conceived with the idea of significantly expanding the boundaries of *Rythm Mastr*. The "Dailies," named after the newspaper practice of comic strips covering multiple story arcs through a series of daily installments during the course of a week, were presented as a group of framed panels mounted on lightboxes—an idea probably fueled by the desire to maintain a formal link with the paper-on-glass technique adopted at the Carnegie. To reinforce the concept of the newspaper format, Marshall positioned a "Times" header at the top left of each page **[FIG. 39]**.[101]

Characterized by ample white space, the "Dailies" offer a more open-ended, but at the same time less esoteric, narrative than their predecessors. Aerial views of the buildings and the streets of Black Metropolis now made more open references to the Bronzeville neighborhood of Chicago. A long road—35th Street—cutting across public high-rises and the Ludwig Mies van der Rohe–designed campus for the Illinois Institute of Technology was used to introduce two characters living in the same area but separated by a profound social divide—a young boy living in the projects and a student learning robotics. New lead characters and narratives, such as P-Van—A Discursive Vehicle—and Ho's Stroll (later to be reintroduced as "On the Stroll"—a group of women loosely based on streetwalkers who used to frequent Marshall's neighborhood) gained prominence, with their philosophical observations evolving into narratives and spin-off cartoons. The dialogue, at once witty and touching, often revolved around philosophy and art but debated in the conversational style of Chicago's South Side barbershops. As Greg Tate once noted, while discussing Marshall's 1993 painting *De Style* **[FIG. 40]**, "Nothing is more unassailably Black an experience than Black hair care and the arenas constituted and committed to its routine weekly maintenance."[102] The inscription of such esoteric themes into popular parlance gives them a slightly farcical dimension, but this doesn't affect their power. "I gave them conversations to have, but conversations that you wouldn't expect to hear from them," explained Marshall.[103] Some might say that putting these high-brow topics within the context of street-talking characters in a comic strip is somehow cheapening, but there is no denying the implicit suggestion that these ideas are relevant to society.

In a particularly riveting panel, Marshall indirectly introduces himself as a background character when P-Van drives by the location of the artist's former studio only to discover that the building is gone. "I wonder what happened to that artist who had the building." "Maybe he got another place we can park in front of," observe the occupants of P-Van. (Marshall's inspiration for P-Van's "Discursive Vehicle" came from a group of people who used to sit in a white truck in front of his studio seven days a week, from morning to night, just hanging out. **[FIG. 41]**)

---

99 Katy Siegel, "1,000 Words: Kerry James Marshall," *Artforum*, summer 2000, 149.

100 Marshall with author, 2020.

101 In all probability, the chosen typeface is a reference to the *New York Times* and the paper's policy of not running cartoon strips.

102 Greg Tate, "The Marvellous Black Familiars of Kerry James Marshall," in Charles Gaines, Greg Tate, and Laurence Rassel, *Kerry James Marshall* (London: Phaidon, 2017), 92.

103 Ann Binlot, "Kerry James Marshall Created Comic Strip with Black Characters to Show 'It Can Be Done,'" *Document Journal*, October 15, 2018, https://www.documentjournal.com/2018/10/kerry-james-marshall-created-comic-strip-with-black-characters-to-show-it-can-be-done/.

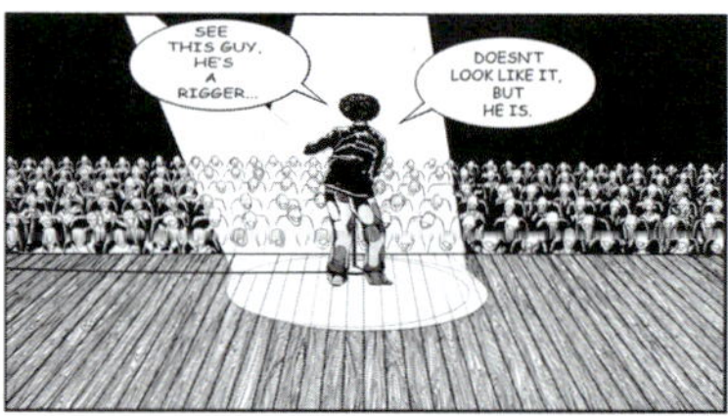

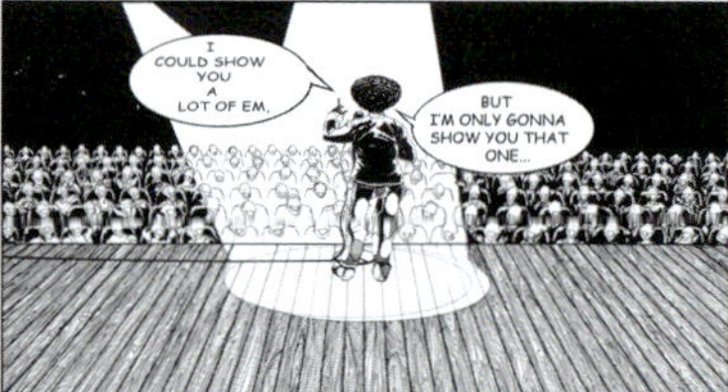

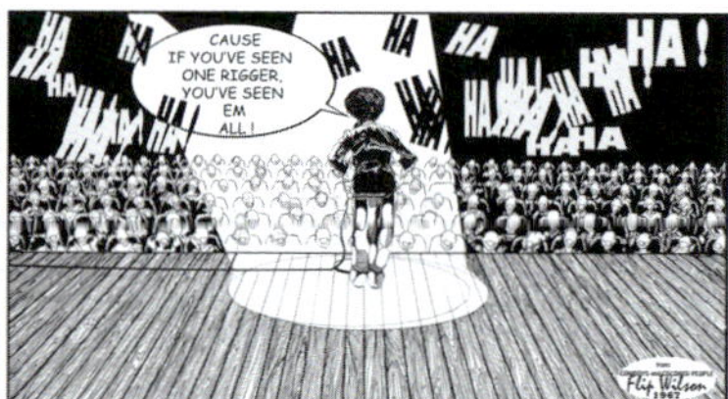

FIG. 42 Detail from Kerry James Marshall, *Rythm Mastr* (*Dailies*), 1999–.

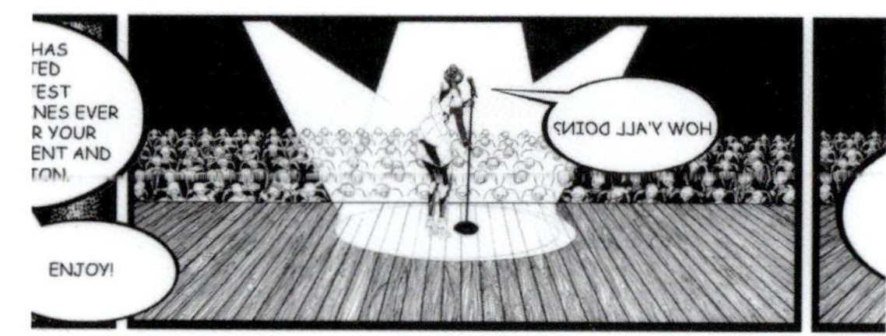

FIG. 43 Detail from Kerry James Marshall, *Rythm Mastr Daily Strip* (*Runners*), 2018. See p. 199.

In a panel from the subplot "Classic Comedy Comics," we meet another group of central characters—the Comedian. Conceived in the line of blue material acts such as Redd Foxx, counterculture stand-up star Richard Pryor, and the whole generation of entertainers who followed in his footsteps (perhaps also with a nod to the eponymous character featured in *Watchmen*), the comedians are shown performing a stand-up routine in a theater, their backs to the viewer. In front of a full house, one of them can be seen talking about his manager's advice to rig (i.e. manipulate) the audience. He goes on to suggest that two doormen are "riggers," and concludes his monologue with the line "Once you've seen one rigger, you've seen them all," to an audience that roars with laughter **[FIG. 42]**. In time, the comedians, collectively named "The Classic Comedy Comic Troupe," take to the stage, each bringing a different routine, somehow shifting the focus from the individual to the whole scene. In some versions, Marshall takes the liberty of highlighting the unusual perspective from which each comedian is seen, by flipping their balloon horizontally, as if this is an active element within the scene and not just a representation of the dialogue **[FIG. 43]**. (Years later, a similar occurrence will take place in one of Marshall's most celebrated tableaux, the empowering *School of Beauty, School of Culture* (2012; **[FIG. 44]**), in which a toddler seems to be the only one to notice the floating, anamorphic specter of a white sleeping beauty at the center of the composition in a room full of people busy with their everyday lives.)

The "Dailies" partly reprise Lichtenstein's idea of extrapolating a fraction of sequential art and converting it into a stand-alone image. But while most of Lichtenstein's Ben-Day dots paintings are taken directly from existing material (save for the exception of a few slightly altered panels in which he features his comic alter-ego, Brad),[104] Marshall prefers to create rather than appropriate. This establishes a connection to the author that is further substantiated by the expanded psychological profile of the *Rythm Mastr* characters. Apart from the aforementioned Brad, none of Lichtenstein's characters is recurrent or developed. There is no possibility of having feelings of antipathy or sympathy toward them—they just serve a function. By contrast, the treatment to which the characters in the Classic Comedy Comics Troupe, P-Van, On the Stroll, and the fictional TV talk show "Platform" are subjected in the "Dailies," makes them relatable—the addition of volume to their personalities and surroundings further confirming Marshall's long-term investment in his project.[105]

FIG. 44 **KERRY JAMES MARSHALL,** *School of Beauty, School of Culture*, 2012. Acrylic on canvas, 108×158 in. (274×401 cm). Birmingham Museum of Art, Alabama. Purchased with funds provided by Elizabeth (Bibby) Smith, the Collectors Circle for Contemporary Art, Jane Comer, the Sankofa Society, and general acquisition funds.

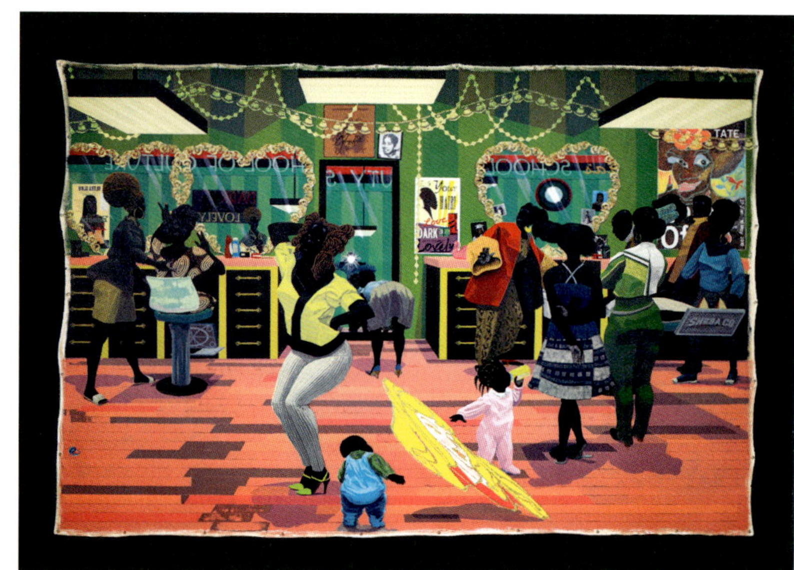

From a visual standpoint, the "Dailies" are conspicuous for perpetuating the use of the monochromatic aesthetic as seen with the NICC installation in Antwerp, and for the strong illumination provided by the lightboxes—a solution Marshall would later withdraw in favor of plain India ink drawings on paper. This latter choice reaffirms in unequivocal terms the images' autonomous status from the rest of Marshall's production. It is somewhat ironic that by referring to their monochromatic nature—a formal solution associated with classic films and greatness in cinema but instead with the cheapest production techniques in superhero comics—Marshall would find the tools to restore the status of his creation as a conceptual art project. His love of paper—a support he favors over canvas—did the rest.

In a review of the Chicago exhibition published in *Art Papers*, art critic Matthew Biro observed how Marshall's drawings resulted in "haunting images [that] would make great murals."[106] These words proved to be prophetic when, in June 2015, Marshall made a large-scale wall painting on the High Line in New York. Fittingly called *Above the Line*, it reproposed elements from *Rythm Mastr* such as space vehicles and water tanks—the latter converted into luxury homes **[FIG. 45]**.

On the occasion of the strip's third appearance in printed format, when Marshall agreed to an artist's project for Tod Lippy's now defunct magazine *Esopus* in 2014, the evolutionary steps taken from *Rythm Mastr* in the "Dailies" become even more vivid. The characters' skin tone is now closer to the complex, highly recognizable black in many of Marshall's paintings. The background is minimally hatched but serves its purpose extremely well in rendering the atmosphere in which the dialogue takes place, while the use of "Black speech" inflections to discuss history and philosophy results in a contrast that challenges anti-intellectual assumptions.

104 Famously, Lichtenstein's first comics-inspired work, *Look Mickey* (1961), was made after a bet with his children who challenged their father to prove he could be as good as Bob Grant and Bob Totten, the authors of the 1960 original cartoon panel "Donald Duck Lost and Found."

105 To further enhance the accessibility of the "Dailies," Marshall opted to have them translated into different languages when they were exhibited internationally. Portions of dialogue in Chinese, Dutch, or Korean are occasionally inserted in place, or next to the original English. This intervention is also used in those panels where two characters break the fourth wall to sell T-shirts reading "Nat Turner: A Real Freedom Fighter," "Enemy of the State," or "Enemy of the Police State" priced at "only 12.99." It should be noted that Nat Turner (1800–1831), an enslaved carpenter who led a four-day rebellion in Virginia in 1831, was the subject of Marshall's 2011 painting *Portrait of Nat Turner with the Head of His Master*.

106 Matthew Biro, "Representing Blackness: Kerry James Marshall's Recent Work Re-Thinks the Meaning of 'Black Art,'" *Art Paper*, March–April 2004, 34–39.

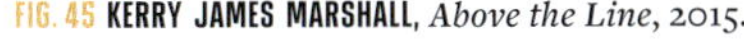
FIG. 45 **KERRY JAMES MARSHALL**, *Above the Line*, 2015.

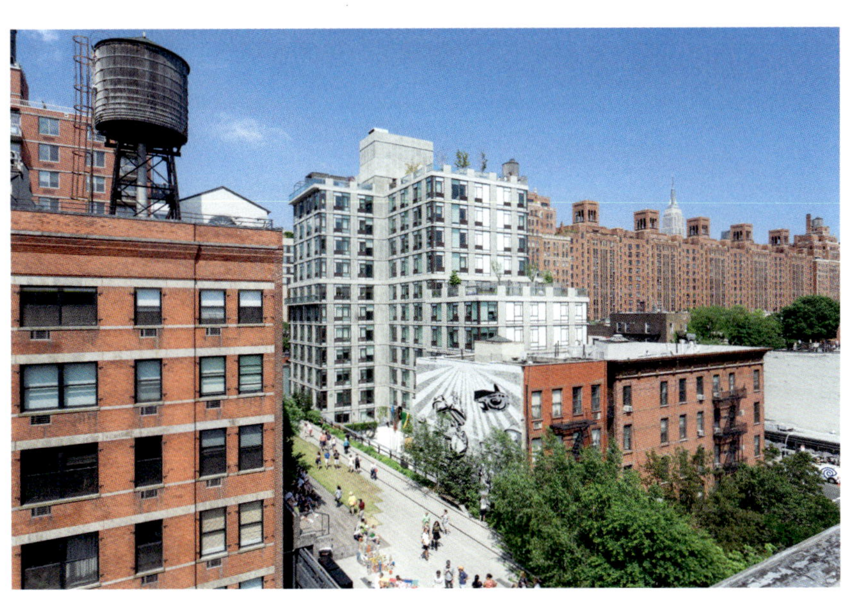

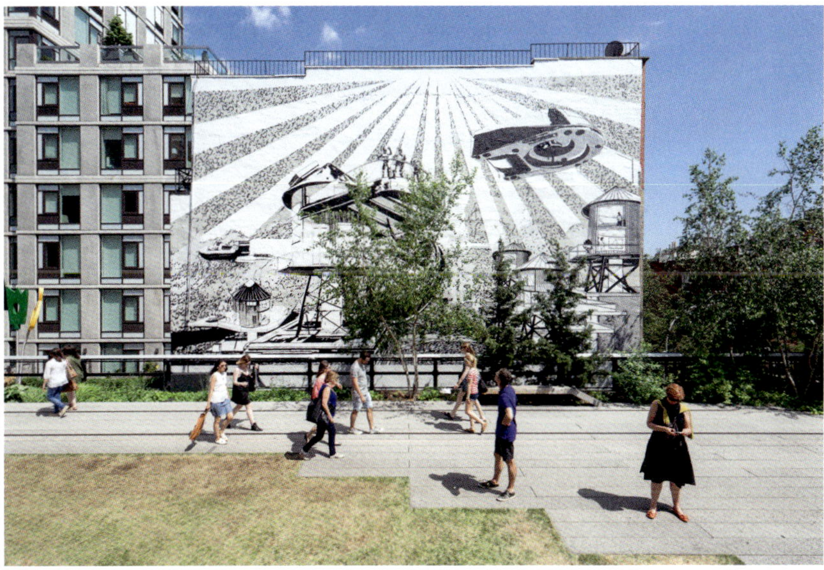

The first part of the six-page spread, titled "It's so Hard to Say Goodbye," opens on a street view of Black Metropolis with two men discussing Afrocentrism and how this has been impacting metropolitan areas. The conversation verges on the philosophical. Are these *dashiki*-wearing people filling their houses with Ndops and Chiwaras and giving their children African names the cultural equivalent of born-again Christians? Or does their Afrocentrism derive from the odd pleasure stemming from "pursuing the unobtainable"? They are interrupted by the arrival of two beautiful women, whom the men catcall **[FIG. 46]**.

The second segment, titled "Naps and Knots" (cue a beautifully stylized Afro comb), opens with the two men being scolded by the ladies for their advances. It then picks up on the women's conversation. What troubles them, it emerges, is not "Black folks who embrace a particular socio-political, cultural, or even essentialist identity..." but that those who "believe they've 'transcended' don't seem to know what the game is about," succumbing to an assimilationist logic. The story closes with the warning, disguised as a classic comics line: "To be continued, for sure." This leads to a final panel listing an array of fictional companies (Baobab Inc., Nubian Network, Gongotronix) and the two men, distinguishable by their silhouettes, who have forgotten what they were talking about in the first place.

Here is where the power of *Rythm Mastr* and the "Dailies" lies. The men and the women are representatives of two views of the world—the mainstream, accepted notion portrayed in the *Black Panther* movie that sees Afrofuturism as a safe way to imagine a present that transcends the Black experience versus the idea that the passive acceptance of this mix of fact and fabulism is ultimately delusional and that real change can only happen when such craving for recognition is overwritten by a genuine process of emancipation.

Marshall's decision to tap into the narrative and visual arc of *Rythm Mastr* for the *Esopus* commission, while quite natural in light of the printed format, highlights how the series is an ideal resource for limited editions. After the first apparition of the "Dailies" in Chicago, a few variations, including the powerful set of three inkjet prints *Everything Will Be Alright, I Just Know It Will* (2004), and the similarly titled woodcut *Everything Will Be Alright* from

FIG. 46 Details from Kerry James Marshall, artist project for *Esopus* 14 (spring 2010). See pp. 178–183.

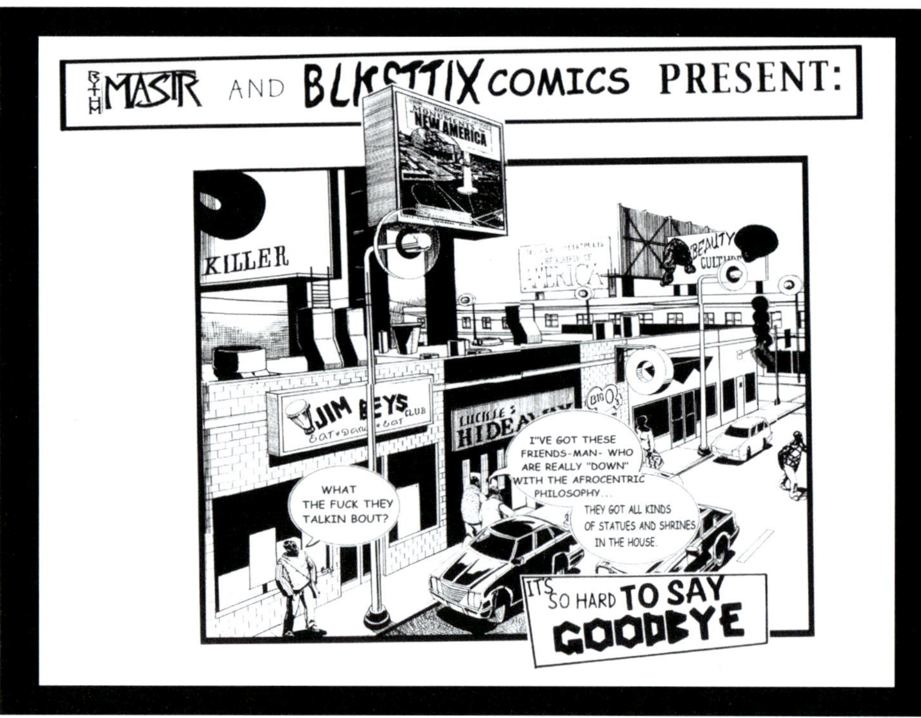

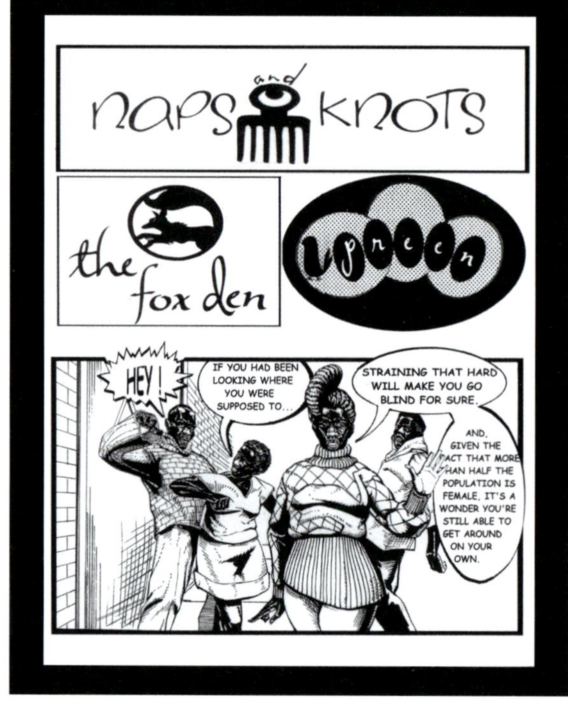

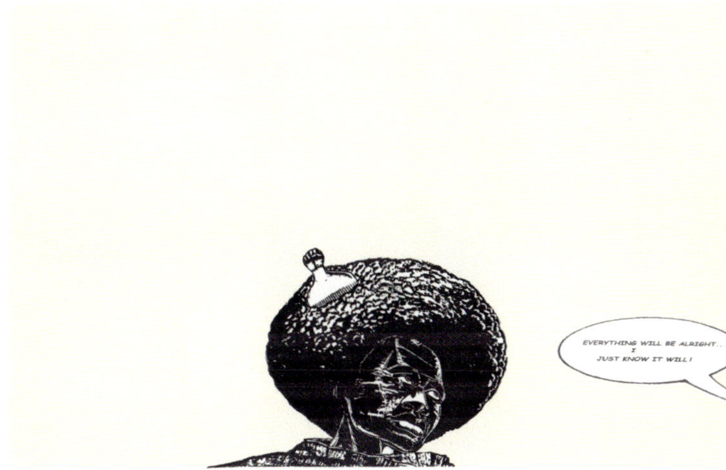

FIG. 47 **KERRY JAMES MARSHALL**, *Everything Will Be Alright*, 2004. See p. 155.

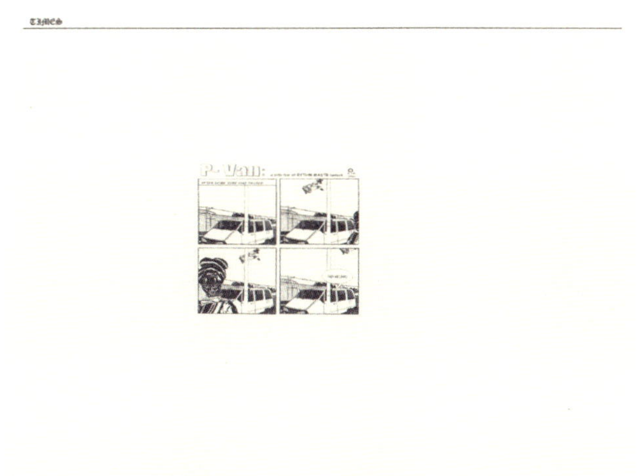

FIG. 48 **KERRY JAMES MARSHALL**, *They Are Liars!*, 2005. See p. 156.

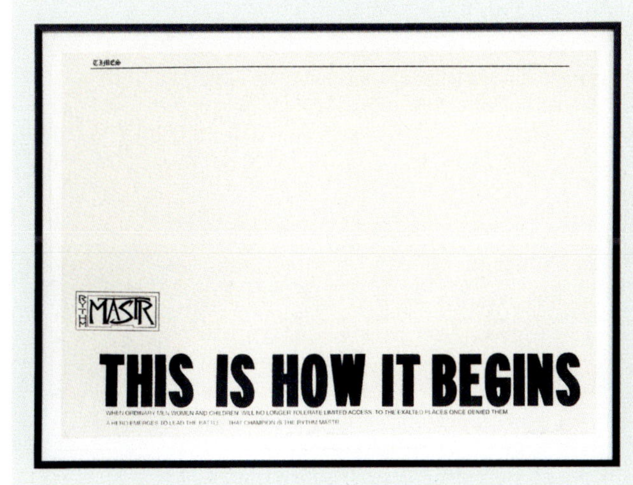

FIG. 49 **KERRY JAMES MARSHALL**, first screenprint of *Dailies*, 2010. See p. 169.

the same year, will lead the way to numerous editions where the visual and conceptual language deployed in *Rythm Mastr* is duly explored and expanded. The very sentence "Everything will be alright" **[FIG. 47]**, a classic sample of superhero lingo, when partially isolated from its original context, assumes a broader meaning, conveying a universal message of optimism and reassurance in the most straightforward way. Similarly, screen prints like *They Are Liars!* (2005) **[FIG. 48]**, made in conjunction with Marshall's solo show at the Camden Art Centre in London in 2005, or the ones related to the "Dailies" produced in 2010 in collaboration with Thomas Lucas, borrow some components from the original *Rythm Mastr* in their attempt to recreate a newspaper feel by introducing a sepia-toned background. This latter set of nine is perhaps the one in which the state of intent of *Rythm Mastr* is most successfully reiterated. The first two prints show no images—the *Rythm Mastr* logo supporting a large block-lettered title proclaiming "This Is How It Begins" and two opening texts **[FIG. 49]**. Although epic in tone, they do not offer a recapitulation of the events leading to the story, but rather, a philosophical explanation of the context in which it takes place. "When ordinary men, women, and children will no longer tolerate limited access to the exalted places once denied them," recites the first panel, "a hero emerges to lead the battle. That champion is the Rythm Mastr."[107]

107 Kerry James Marshall, "This is How It Begins," from the "Dailies" (2010). Over the following years, Marshall would go on to produce numerous iterations of *Everything Will Be Alright*, including single, diptych, and triptych panels made with digital UV-cured printing equipment installed in his studio in 2017. A comprehensive read of Marshall's limited editions can be found in Susan Tallman's book *Kerry James Marshall: The Complete Prints* (Brussels: Ludion, 2023).

FIG. 50 **KERRY JAMES MARSHALL**, *Two Invisible Men Naked*, 1985. Acrylic on paper on wood panel, two parts, each 60×41 in. (152.4×104.2 cm).

The episodic nature and continuous reworking of *Rythm Mastr* in different forms over the two decades that have passed since its creation have convincingly demonstrated the central role it occupies within Marshall's practice. Its legacy, as testified to by words of praise coming from a new generation of authors and artists like Jiba Molei Anderson and Ashley A. Woods, is firmly established. With so many different embodiments in place, it is not difficult to understand why *Rythm Mastr* has a special status within Marshall's oeuvre. Although he had occasionally made references to his previous work in his own paintings (as, for example, the diptych from 1985, *Two Invisible Men Naked* in reference to *A Portrait of the Artist as a Shadow of His Former Self* **[FIG. 50]**), never before had he created something that could only be fully comprehended if seen in close relationship with its precedents.

At the same time, it is interesting to note how *Rythm Mastr* influenced many projects yet to come. This is the case, for example, with *Every Beat of My Heart* at the Wexner Center for the Arts in Columbus, Ohio, in 2008, where a combination of futuristic and traditional accoutrements for Stasha and Farrell was adapted into a Japanese Bunraku puppet theater performance with the involvement of local teenagers, transforming a solitary activity into a collaborative project in which every participant was necessary to its realization **[FIG. 52]**.[108] Or with Marshall's *A Monumental Journey* (2018), a commissioned memorial in Des Moines, Iowa, celebrating Gertrude Rush and the pioneering Afro-American lawyers who, in 1925, helped establish the National Bar Association (originally the Negro Bar Association) **[FIG. 51]**. Taking the form of two oversize West African talking drums, one balanced precariously on top of the other, the piece is about communication, but it also presents clear analogies with the drums used by Farrell to invoke the Rythm Mastr. It also seems to offer a variant on a 2008 segment from the "Dailies" called "A Monument for New America," originally featured in the February 15, 2008 edition of the *Washington Post*, outlining a proposal to build a monument to celebrate enslaved preacher Nat Turner's August 1831 rebellion in Southampton County, Virginia.[109] The four panels illustrate how three of the main characters respond to the idea. The women in "On the Stroll" typically consider the philosophical and historical implications; the occupants of P-Van practically decide to go and have a look for themselves; and the Rythm Mastr, after receiving a replica of the monument, puts it on his mantlepiece declaring that whatever they have done is good but not enough. "I still wanna see Nat's face on a postage stamp!" he concludes.[110]

FIG. 51 **KERRY JAMES MARSHALL**, *A Monumental Journey*, 2018. Manganese ironspot brick, steel, and granite. Height: 30 ft. (9.14 m). Hansen Triangle Park, Des Moines, Ohio. Commissioned by Greater Des Moines Public Art Foundation.

FIG. 52 **KERRY JAMES MARSHALL**, *Every Beat of My Heart*, 2008. Japanese Bunraku live performance with 23 students from 14 Central Ohio High Schools in Columbus. Music: Kahil El'Zabar; producer: Shelly Casto. Wexner Center for the Arts at The Ohio State University.

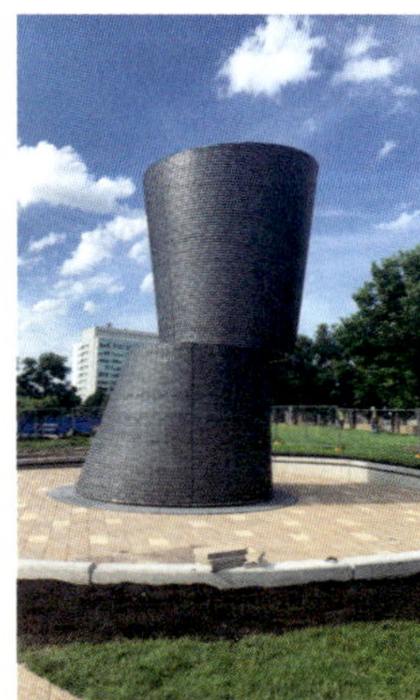

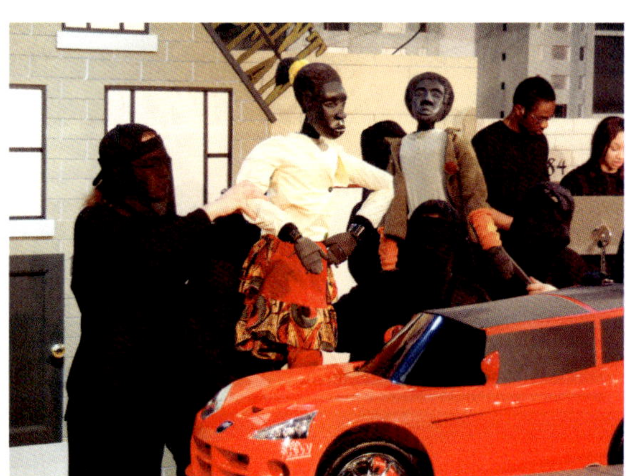

THE WALLS COME TUMBLING DOWN

The Carnegie installation and the one at the NICC, the comic books, the New York mural, the theater performance in Columbus, the *Esopus* magazine spread, and the ongoing series of *Dailies* all manage to function autonomously. But to fully understand them—and to see how, through them, Marshall accomplished that phenomenological value he had been seeking ever since the beginning of his artistic career—one needs to grasp the red thread running through them.

Rythm Mastr's aesthetic affiliation with comics may be treated with skepticism by those who look down on the genre, but there is no doubt that if viewed in its entirety, the series possesses just as much existential authority as Marshall's most celebrated works. It is defined by integrity, force, and complexity, major themes are not diffracted but tackled head-on. The Black figure normalizes its presence within the dominant culture; the characters fulfill the uncompromising posture typical of their forerunners in the paintings, and, just as the paintings have contributed to diversifying the art canon, they add another layer to an existent platform. This may be an ambitious target, but as Marshall stated in his "Letter to a Young Artist" six years after the inception of *Rythm Mastr*, "You should have grandiose ideas about your future success. No one with small ambitions and vague goals ever amounted to much in this game."[111]

In April 2016, exactly thirteen years after the introduction of the *Dailies*, the Museum of Contemporary Art in Chicago inaugurated the first leg of a major retrospective of Marshall's work, which traveled to the Metropolitan Museum of Art in New York and the Museum of Contemporary Art, Los Angeles. Given the size and scope of the project, which aimed to cover thirty-five years of practice, only a small section of the exhibition was dedicated to the *Dailies*, but the fact that the title of the show was *Mastry*—although also a nod to the Old Masters—left no doubt about the status Marshall affords *Rythm Mastr* within his oeuvre. To further underline this point, the accompanying catalogue, edited by Helen Molesworth, features a few panels strategically positioned to create their own independent narrative within the publication. The first image we encounter is a traditional comics splash page titled "Rythm Mastr: The time has come so it begins." It features two museum night guards at a loss as to what has happened in one of the rooms they are invigilating, where all the vitrines have been broken and strange noises can be heard in the background. Halfway through the book there is a plate showing the exterior view of a building, thereby revealing that the institution in which the incident has taken place is The Ancient Egyptian Museum. The catalogue closes with excerpts from the *Rythm Mastr* comics.[112] A six-page extract from the "On the Stroll" segment starts off with a debate over who was the first to coin the term "Post Black" **[FIG. 53]**.[113]

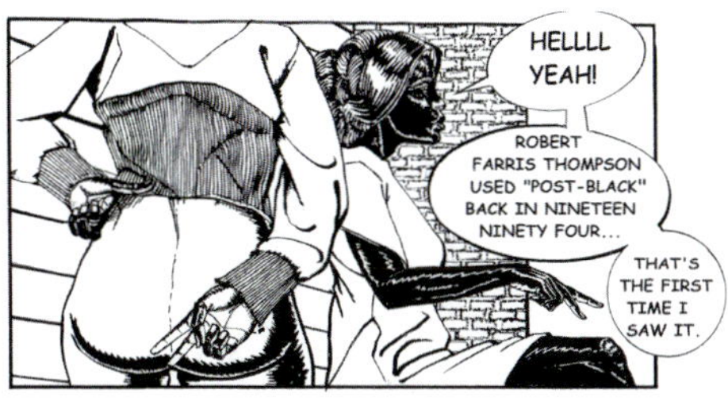

FIG. 53 **Detail from Kerry James Marshall,** *On the Stroll*, 2017. See p. 186.

108 A comprehensive account of the experience can be found in Rebecca Wanzo, "Black Nationalism, Bunraku, and Beyond: Articulating Black Heroism through Cultural Fusion and Comics," in Frederick Luis Aldama (ed.), *Multicultural Comics: From Zap to Blue Beetle* (Austin: University of Texas Press, 2010), 93–104.

109 Rather than building a brand-new memorial, the document advances the idea of augmenting the Washington obelisk in DC with a gargoyle-style statue of Turner. In 2017 Marshall reiterated the concept of modification rather than removal on the occasion of the controversy surrounding the monument to Italian fascist aviator Italo Balbo in Burnham Park, Chicago. See Blake Gopnik, "Monumental Man," the *Washington Post*, February 15, 2008; Kerry James Marshall, in "Graphic Content: Art and Animation," *Artforum*, summer 2014, 294–337; and Kim Janssen, "Add Statue of Mussolini's Mutilated Body to Balbo Monument: Kerry James Marshall," *Chicago Tribune*, August 29, 2017.

110 The final and fourth panel was eventually published in the Spring 2010 issue of the College Art Association's *Art Journal*. In an alternative illustration of "Monuments for a New America" Marshall makes an open reference to the Liberty Bell in Philadelphia.

111 Kerry James Marshall in Peter Nesbett, Sarah Andress, Shelly Bancroft (eds.), *Letters to a Young Artist* (New York: Darte Publishing, 2006), 25.

112 See Ian Alteveer, Helen Molesworth, Dieter Roelstraete, and Abigail Winograd, *Kerry James Marshall: Mastry* (New York: Skira Rizzoli, 2016).

113 It was in fact art critic Robert Farris Thompson in a 1991 issue of *Artforum* who coined the term first, although many attribute it to curator Thelma Golden and artist Glenn Ligon, who contributed to popularize it for Golden's *Freestyle* exhibition at the Studio Museum in Harlem, New York, in 2001. This is another case of revisionism or "historical amnesia," as Marshall put it, where merit is reassigned in order for the system to be able to play a role. See Robert Farris Thompson, "Afro-Modernism," *Artforum*, September 1991, 91–94; and Thelma Golden and Hamza Walker, *Freestyle* (New York: Studio Museum in Harlem, 2001), 14.

The story then progresses with a visit to the run-down looking Ancient Egyptian Museum, where a group of visitors receive the disappointing news that the new African wing won't open for six months. Is this a veiled reference to the Art Institute of Chicago's belated move to create an African Gallery (which eventually opened at the end of 2018)? Or, to stay within the *Rythm Mastr* story, does it suggest that the museum is still coming to terms with the mysterious escape of the African artifacts following Farrell's ritual? This is followed by a single panel from the *Dailies*, featuring a visibly upset Farrell consoled by a woman who tries to reassure him with the by now well-established line within the series: "Everything Will Be Alright, I Just Know It Will." Such optimism, however, is challenged by what is featured in the endpapers: an illustration of the conflict between past and future embodied by the two main protagonists of the series. "No Farrell. I cain't go back. Not Now!" says Stasha to a drum-carrying Farrell, each of them standing on a piece of separating debris floating in outer space **[FIG. 54]**. Art historian Ellen Y. Tani, then a postdoctoral curatorial fellow at Bowdoin College Museum of Art in Brunswick, Maine, was one of the journalists who interviewed Marshall at the time.[114] During her visit to his studio, she was able to see some of the drawings and archival material that informed *Rythm Mastr* and hear from Marshall himself about the different narratives threading through the work, which she immediately recognized as critical and powerful from an art-historical perspective. As she would recall years later:

> *It became clear to me that [Marshall's Rythm Mastr drawings] were extremely important to his working process, his painting practice, his past, and his worldview. And because comics are a more "pedestrian" or "low" art form, nothing art historical had been written about them; people either didn't know how to deal with them or they weren't taken seriously. This intrigued and bothered me. Kerry's tone was different when talking about them vs. talking about his paintings, maybe because that's the nature of the comics experience, both in reading them and making them—you can realize and control a narrative, which is*

FIG. 54 **KERRY JAMES MARSHALL**, *Rythm Mastr* (*Dailies*), 1999–. Inkjet prints on Plexiglas mounted on five lightboxes, each 14 1/8×72 in. (36×183 cm). Installation view, Museum of Contemporary Art Chicago, 2016.

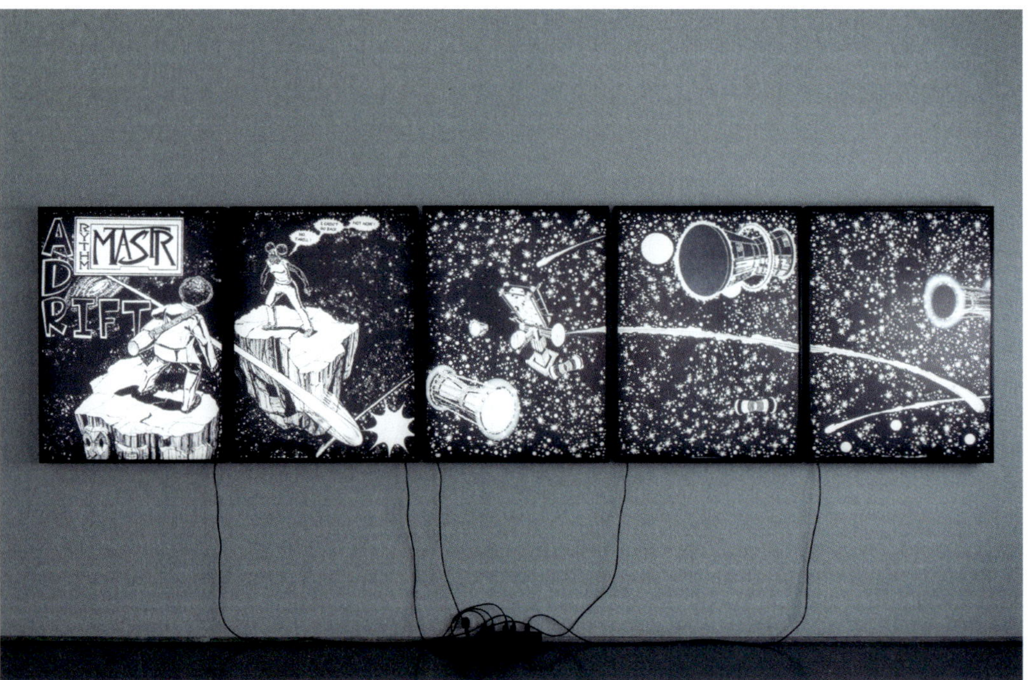

FIG. 55 **KERRY JAMES MARSHALL**, *Rythm Mastr Daily Strip*, 2018. Installation view, Carnegie International, Pittsburgh, 2018.

so energizing. The ink on paper method, too, is a commitment. It's unforgiving in its certitude—you can't hide anything if you mess it up, which I really respected. Even though materially they seem quite provisional, formally they are quite confident. And funny. And dark. And much more coded than the paintings in their use of dialogue.[115]

In 2018, things came full circle when Marshall received an invitation to participate in the 57th edition of the Carnegie International, in the same venue where almost two decades earlier *Rythm Mastr* had made its debut **[FIG. 55]**. The opportunity for a comparative analysis of where *Rythm Mastr* started, and where it was now, proved to be irresistible. Marshall responded with a seventy-foot black and white strip running along the walls of the museum's lobby, using the narratives and characters he had developed over the intervening years, and in doing so outlined the difference between the original images and the new ones. In one panel, two characters attending an opening at an art space, comment: "I saw the painting he made from this drawing in a show at the Carnegie last year" in front of Marshall's 2016 *Untitled (Gallery)*, creating a Droste effect **[FIG. 56]**.[116] In another panel, the occupants of P-Van declare to have seen "a man made out of iron flying through the air," while said man indeed hovers over a corner of the neighborhood, which encompasses most of the venues featured so far, including the Classic Comedy Place and the Naps and Knots hair salon.

114 Ellen Y. Tani, "The World of Groundbreaking Artist Kerry James Marshall," *Artsy*, April 20, 2016, https://www.artsy.net/article/artsy-editorial-how-kerry-james-marshall-became-a-superhero-for-chicago-s-housing-projects.

115 Ellen Y. Tani in conversation with the author, April 4, 2020. Tani wrote an in-depth study of *Rythm Mastr* for a conference on Black portraiture at the University of the Witwatersrand in Johannesburg, November 19, 2016.

116 On December 2016, the Carnegie Museum announced the acquisition of Marshall's *Untitled (Gallery)*. It was later exhibited in *20/20: The Studio Museum in Harlem/Carnegie Museum of Art*, Carnegie Museum of Art, Pittsburgh (July 22–December 31, 2017).

FIG. 56 **KERRY JAMES MARSHALL**, *Untitled (Gallery)*, 2016. Acrylic on PVC panel, 60 ½×48 ½ in. (153.7×123.2 cm). Carnegie Museum of Art, Pittsburgh.

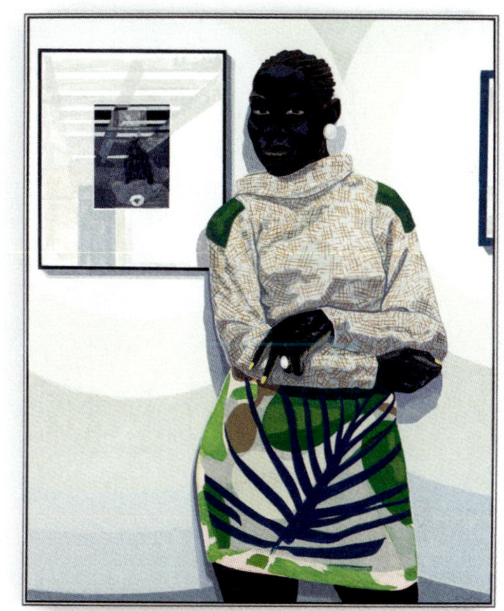

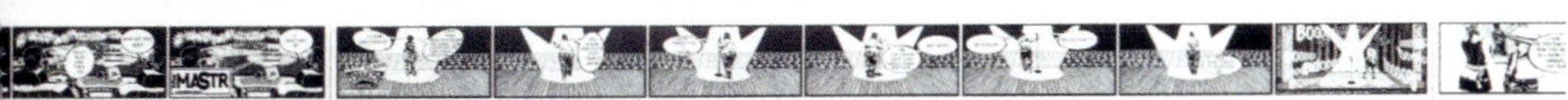

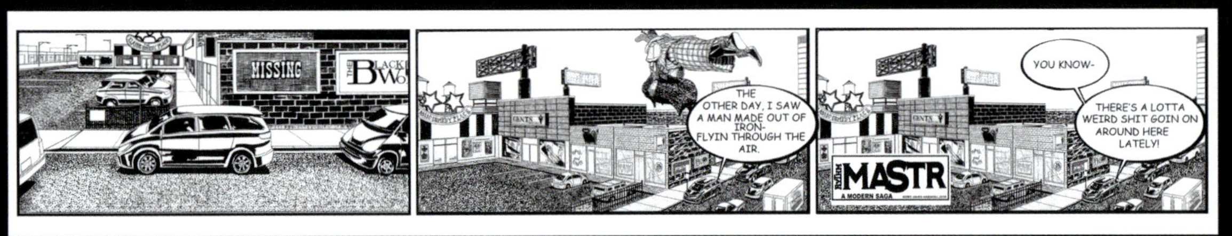

FIG. 57 Detail from Kerry James Marshall, *Rythm Mastr Daily Strip* (*Runners*), 2018. See pp. 209–210.

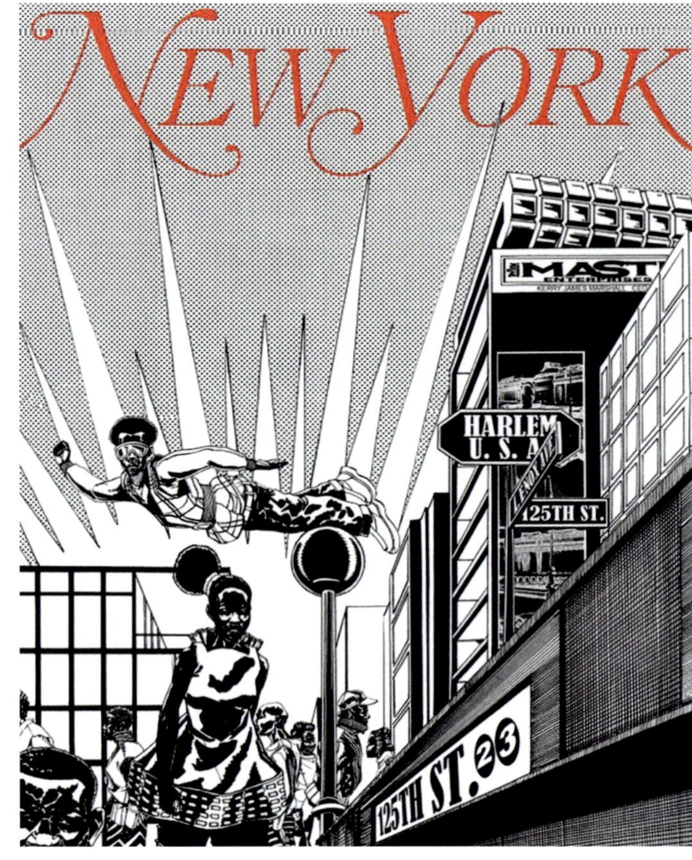

FIG. 58 Cover of *New York* magazine, February 27, 2018. Art: Kerry James Marshall. An 8×12 ft (2.4×3.7 m) poster was installed inside the main entrance of the Port Authority Bus Terminal at 40th Street and 8th Avenue as part of the "50 New York Covers: A Public Art Project" in New York, 2018.

The first installation of *Rythm Mastr* had used comics to question the notion of value, while this later version, enhanced by the subtitle "A Modern Saga," unapologetically gave comics center stage, showcasing a degree of visual maturity, attention to detail, and sophistication that its predecessor hadn't had **[FIG. 57]**.

Later in 2018, an invitation from *New York* to create a cover to celebrate the magazine's fiftieth anniversary, furnished Marshall with an opportunity to add another installment to the *Rythm Mastr* saga, celebrate an important period of his life, and at the same time contribute his view at a time when the country was still immersed in the hype surrounding the *Black Panther* movie **[FIG. 58]**. The single-panel image offers a view of the crossing point of 125th Street and Lenox Avenue in New York. The choice is not random. This is the same place where, almost thirty years before, he would hang out while on a residency at the Studio Museum in Harlem, and where he met his future wife. Such a picture of mundane urbanity is disrupted by the passage of a flying man dressed in attire loosely designed to highlight his status while paying tribute to the neighborhood's first superhero, Marvel's Luke Cage. The crowd does not appear to mind him in the slightest. Everyone carries on as if such an occurrence is nothing out of the ordinary, and the work incorporates this very real fragment of New York's landscape into the fantastical world in which *Rythm Mastr* takes place. To leave no doubt regarding the framework in which this scene takes place, the *Rythm Mastr* logo dominates the image in the form of a billboard on top of a building reproducing an image in negative of a museum building. The piece itself would later have its share of street life when the magazine chose to display it in a 6 × 8-foot format inside the Manhattan Port Authority Bus Terminal at the 40th Street and Eighth Avenue entrance. Wakanda, Marshall seemed to suggest, is not the only place where supernatural events and technological wonders have a home. New Yorkers were invited to look up at the sky over Harlem and perhaps experience some of the same.[117]

MONUMENTS FOR A NEW AMERICA

With the aesthetic of *Rythm Mastr* now satisfactorily in place, the time seemed ripe for a revisitation of the storyline. Not being entirely satisfied with some of the fundamental traits that defined his characters in the initial stages, Marshall decided to draw a brand-new graphic novel that could lay the foundation for an animated feature film. Panels were redrawn, characters revisited both sartorially and physically, and some elements expanded. For the most academic minds familiar with the original *Rythm Mastr* comics, this move felt mildly confusing. Who was the "real" Farrell, the clean-cut kid with styled hair seen in the 1999/2000 edition of the Carnegie? Or the one now sporting a big afro **[FIG. 59]**? In truth, this is an argument without legs in the world of superhero comics, where characters, due to their extraordinary longevity, have to constantly be subjected to updates in order to make them more resonant with the times they live in. And, to a certain extent, it doesn't have legs in the art world too. If Giorgio de Chirico spent most of the postwar years repainting his work from the 1930s (and in so doing, giving legions of art historians and dealers a serious headache), why shouldn't Marshall do the same for a body of work that had been created in a restricted period of time in order to establish a critical dialogue with a venerable institution? He had put on the table a large number of issues, from rediscovering a lifelong passion to rectifying a cultural oversight, and finding a way to incorporate it into his artistic practice. The versatility of *Rythm Mastr* was further enriched

117 On the occasion of the launch of Marshall's cover, *New York* distributed a handful of free prints reproducing the cover image.

FIG. 59 Original art for the "Tower of Power" segment and the same pages reworked in c. 2001. The switch from color to black and white introduced changes to some of the figures, including a different look and the use of Marshall's distinctive ebony-black to depict their skin complexion.

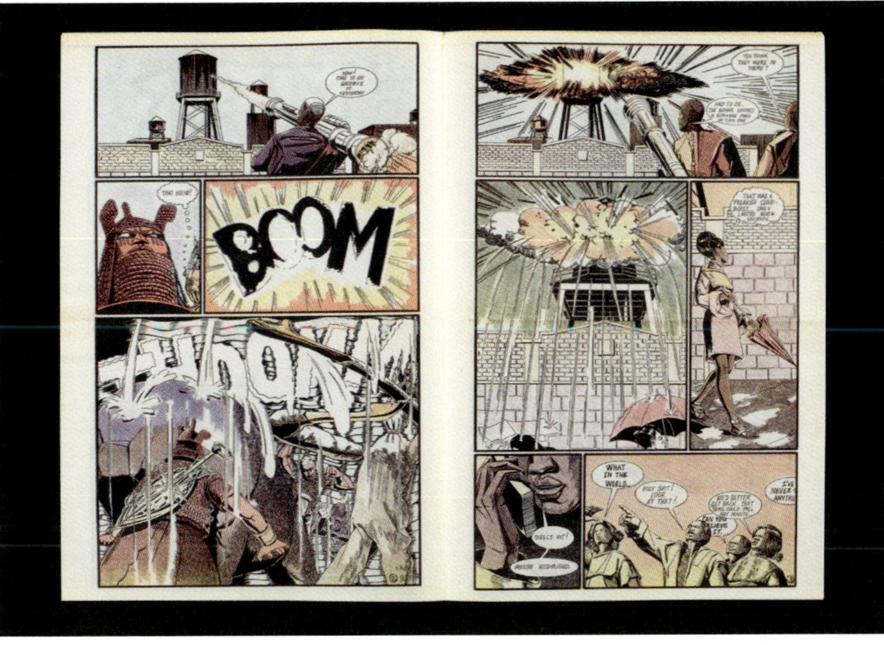

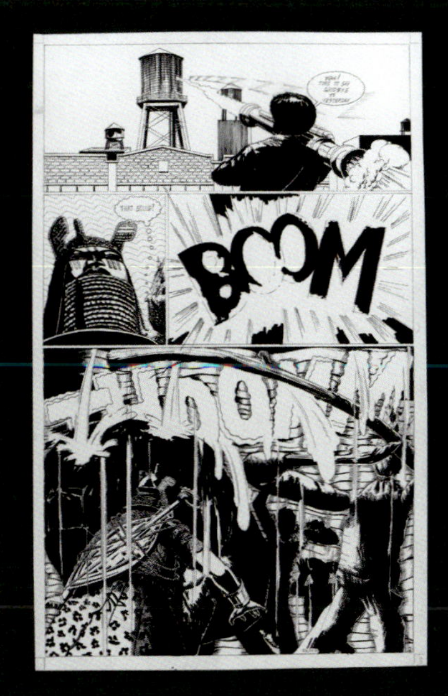

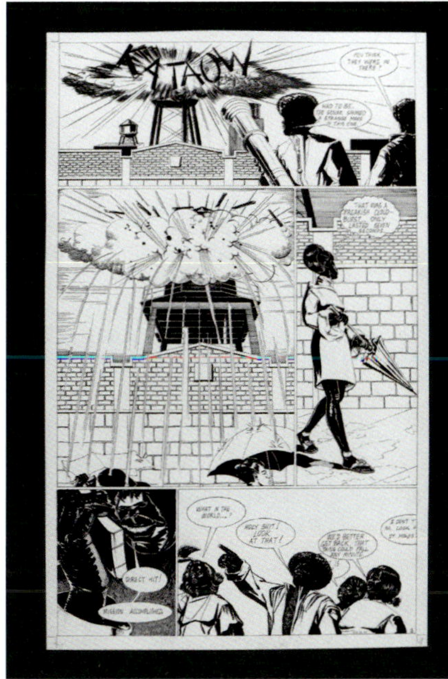

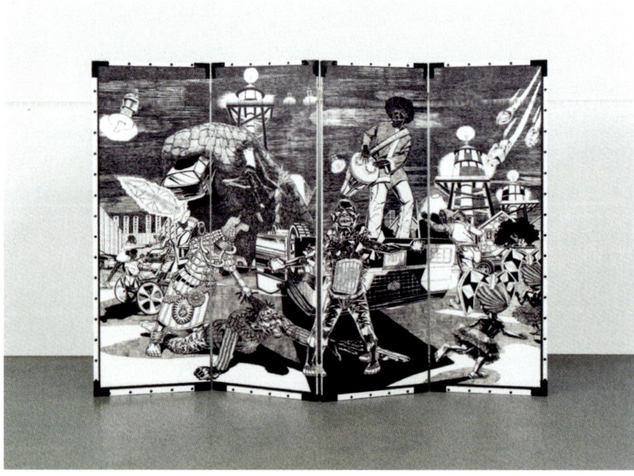

FIG. 60 **KERRY JAMES MARSHALL**, *"Untitled" Rythm Mastr Splash*, 2023. Inkjet print on PVC panel, four parts, overall dimensions 65×90 ½ in. (165.1×229.9 cm). Installation view, Fondazione Prada, Milan, 2023.

FIG. 61 **KERRY JAMES MARSHALL**, *Rythm Mastr Daily Strip* (*Drum Solo*), 2021. Installation views, Museum of Contemporary Art, Chicago, 2021. See pp. 214–219.

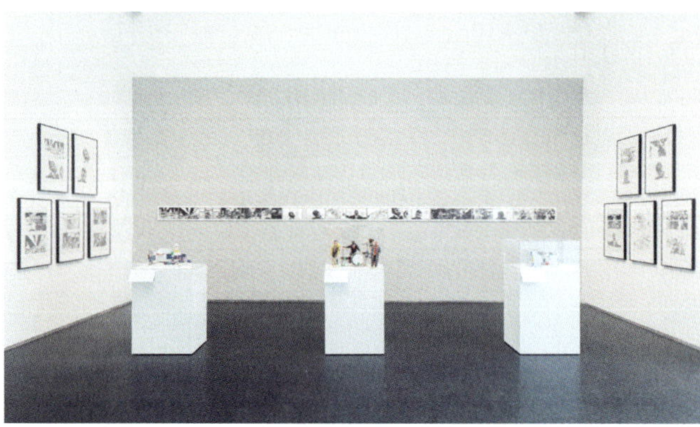

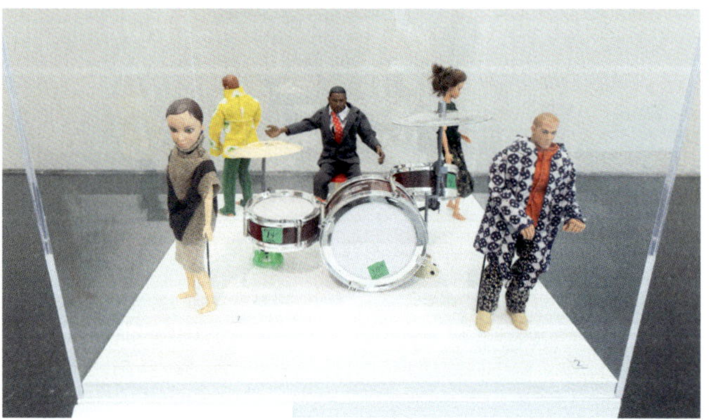

in 2023, when Marshall contributed another large panel for the exhibition *Paraventi: Folding Screens from the 17th to 21st Centuries* organized by Nicholas Cullinan at Fondazione Prada in Milan. Placed in a context that sought to investigate the relationship between Eastern and Western culture, art, and design, *Rythm Mastr* reveals itself to be exceptionally fluid. The project can be collaged or inscribed within a given setting that relates to something seemingly beyond its concerns without running the risk of distortion **[FIG. 60]**.

When *Rythm Mastr* started, Marshall's investment in every production detail, from designing the clothes of the protagonists to building miniature sets of the locations, implied that even the most casual-looking image was the result of a long, laborious process. This was made evident at the Dan Nadel–curated exhibition *Chicago Comics: 1960 to Now* at the Museum of Contemporary Art in Chicago in 2021—one of the rare occasions when Marshall agreed to publicly show elements of his process as well as the final product. Taking the cue from some basic questions that the show posed, such as "How do cartoonists work?," "How do they collaborate?," and "What tools do they use to build rich worlds and characters?," Marshall displayed some of the models he created in his studio of both interiors and aerial views of the city as well as some of the characters' clothing **[FIG. 61]**. From an art perspective, the idea of letting the audience see what led to the realization of a particular artwork or series is often seen as a magic-spoiler. The world of superhero comics, however, operates under different rules. Marshall himself, an ardent collector of comics, jumped on the 2013 edition of *Watchmen* featuring sketches and other previously unpublished materials. "I just love that stuff. I love to learn how things get done."[118]

118 Marshall with author, 2020.
119 Marshall's work, in the form of a design-specific colored panel reproducing a KMET announcer (the fictional TV station that exclusively scooped some of the events chronicled in *Rythm Mastr*) graces the cover of the exhibition catalogue. See Nadel (ed.), *It's Life as I See it.*
120 Marshall with author, 2020.
121 This segment made its official debut in panel form in the exhibition *Chicago Comics: 1960 to Now.*

The relevance of Marshall's inclusion in an exhibition celebrating the rich and varied heritage of the Windy City comics scene can hardly be underestimated.[119] It officially sanctioned *Rythm Mastr* as a creative effort that successfully transcends the art world to earn itself a place within the superhero comics community. In his quest to give center stage to something underrepresented by relying on an undervalued creative form, and always careful not to slip into the easy sensationalism that can make an image impactful but ultimately shallow, Marshall managed to create a superhero comics imagery that is at once true to the entertaining principles demanded by the format and capable of making viewers think deeply. For the graphic novel he started developing, an analogous procedural mode had to be activated. This was achieved by redrawing the full story within a fixed, cinematic frame of 9 × 17 inches from newly made, concise models, creating something cohesive both in terms of narrative and style. "I've started building sets for all the players, locations. I'm making the technology that needs to be done. I'll have Black people flying around too, but they're inventing their own thing. It's going to be original. Everything is organized systematically," explained Marshall.[120]

The *Rythm Mastr* graphic novel opens in a nightclub called Jim Bey (a pun on "djembe," the rope-tuned goblet drum from West Africa), where the Rythm Mastr himself is listening to a drum solo that resonates with his own heartbeat.[121] At the same time, a group of high-school pupils emerge from a field trip to the African wing of The Art Institute of Chicago. On the way home, they become the victims of an episode of gang violence that leaves Stasha seriously wounded. While recovering in the hospital, she plots her revenge and talks her friends into forming their own posse and gangs (now known as the Minutemen and the Sweaters) aided by highly technological drones. Later in the story, Farrell temporarily separates from Stasha to make a pilgrimage to South Carolina with the Rythm Mastr to find his own evoking drum. To do so, he has to descend into an abandoned mine shaft—an occurrence that mirrors Odysseus's journey into the underworld in Homer's epic. It also hints at the historical practice of hiding drums underground during the time of slavery in North America, since their use was forbidden for fear that they could convey secret communication codes.

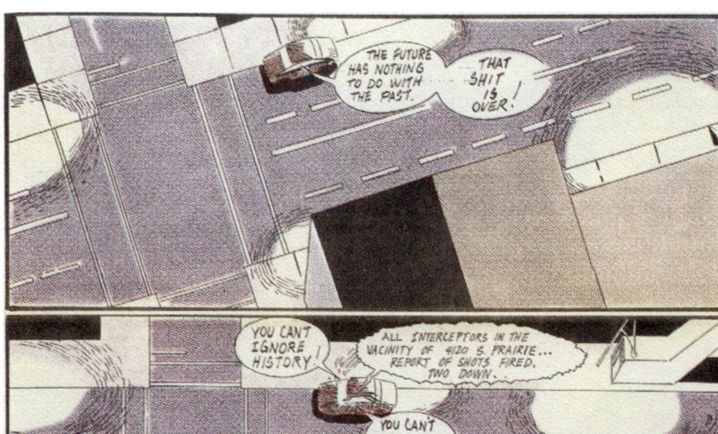

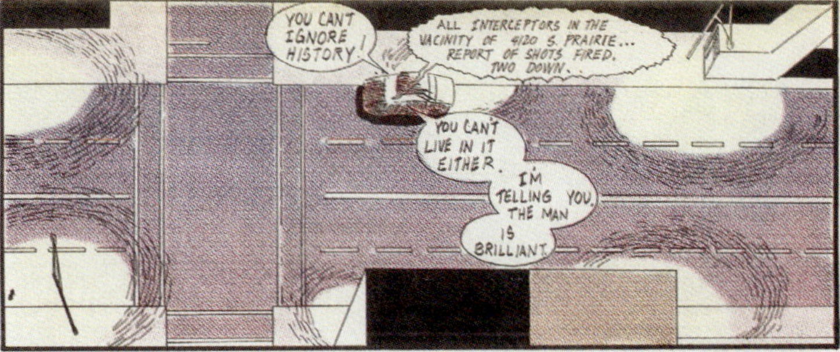

FIG. 62 Detail of Kerry James Marshall, *Rythm Mastr: Every Beat of My Heart*, 1999–2000. Published by Carnegie Museum of Art, Pittsburgh. See p. 68.

The quandary between past and future, technology and tradition, estrangement and connection live on, and the tale continues to be told in grandiose, epic terms. The Afro-American notion that to elucidate a commentary on identity means to think about how things were prior to the time of slavery and colonization is subverted and rewritten in contemporary tones. The salvation of a people through the arrival of a hero is merged with the equally powerful statement that the past can never win in the present nor be our future. It seems that by deciding to rework his 1999 creation into the new millennium, Marshall is adhering to one of his character's most cogent quotes about how you can't relive the past but you can't also ignore it **[FIG. 62]**. The mission has been accomplished and we are left with a sense of eager anticipation for what will come next in the *Rythm Mastr* universe. Cue drum roll.

KERRY JAMES MARSHALL'S RYTHM MASTR

RYTHM MASTR PRINCIPAL CHARACTERS

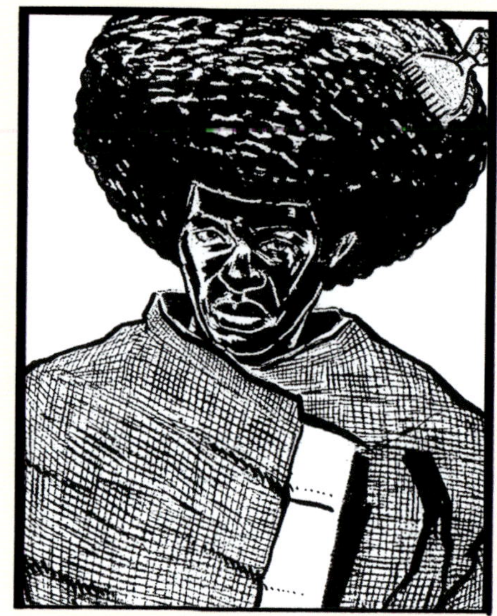

FARRELL

Co-protagonist of the series along with his girlfriend Stasha, Farrell is a young man who takes the mantle of the Rythm Mastr after a chance meeting with him in The Ancient Egyptian Museum. Farrell's newly acquired power—an evoking drum that enables him to summon the five Yoruba-inspired superheroes—creates a rift with Stasha over their fighting methodology and motivations. Of all the *Rythm Mastr* characters, Farrell is the one who undergoes the most tangible physical changes from the original comics through to the "Dailies," where he develops a more aggressive and distinguished look.

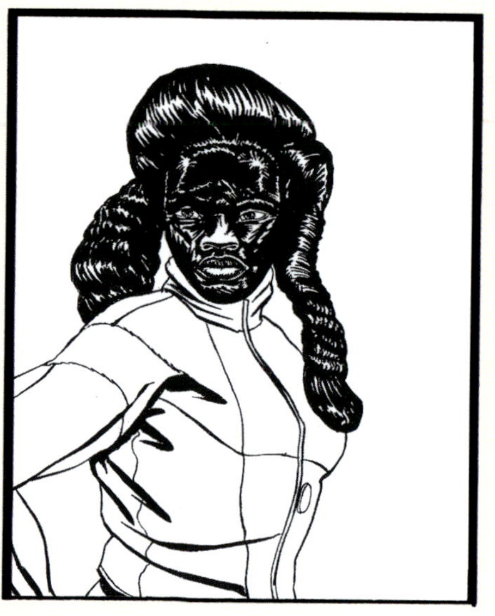

STASHA

Stasha is Farrell's girlfriend. An altercation with a group of street gang members, who shot her after she rejected their advances, leaves her confined to a wheelchair. Stasha, however, is a genius behind the desk and a robotics expert—a combination that allows her to build an outfit that enables her to walk and fly. Stasha's disagreements with Farrell are a leitmotif of the story, their contrasting attitudes and occasional reconciliatory exchanges ("Everything will be alright. I just know it will") marking different episodes within the entire arc of the series. Stasha is also responsible for coming up with an incident-generating device that prevents cars from running on the road.

1999–2000

RYTHM MASTR: EVERY BEAT OF MY HEART

Three issues of *Rythm Mastr* comics, each consisting of five double-sided color photo-offset lithographs on folded newsprint

Sheets: 17×11 ¼ in. (43×28.5 cm) folded; 17×22 ½ in. (43×57 cm) unfolded

Edition: unknown, c. 1,500

Published by Carnegie Museum of Art, Pittsburgh

The first issue of *Rythm Mastr* introduces the principal characters and setting: an African American urban neighborhood where superhuman intervention is required in order to address an alarming rise in crime and lawlessness. A group of teenagers who fall foul of a drive-by shooting includes Stasha and her boyfriend Farrell, who will later be initiated into the secret of unlocking the power of a group of African sculptures by the titular character. The presence of superheroes Senufo, Ibeji, Nkisi, Oba, and Boli brings to the fore a central theme of *Rythm Mastr*—the way in which ancient African deities have been ignored and marginalized by museums and Western institutions. This trivialization has resulted in the colonial narrative of the African continent as a savage land that needs to be civilized. Forced migration and slavery subsequently spread Yoruba beliefs across the Ocean, resulting in different permutations of the same stories and legends across the Caribbean and Latin America.

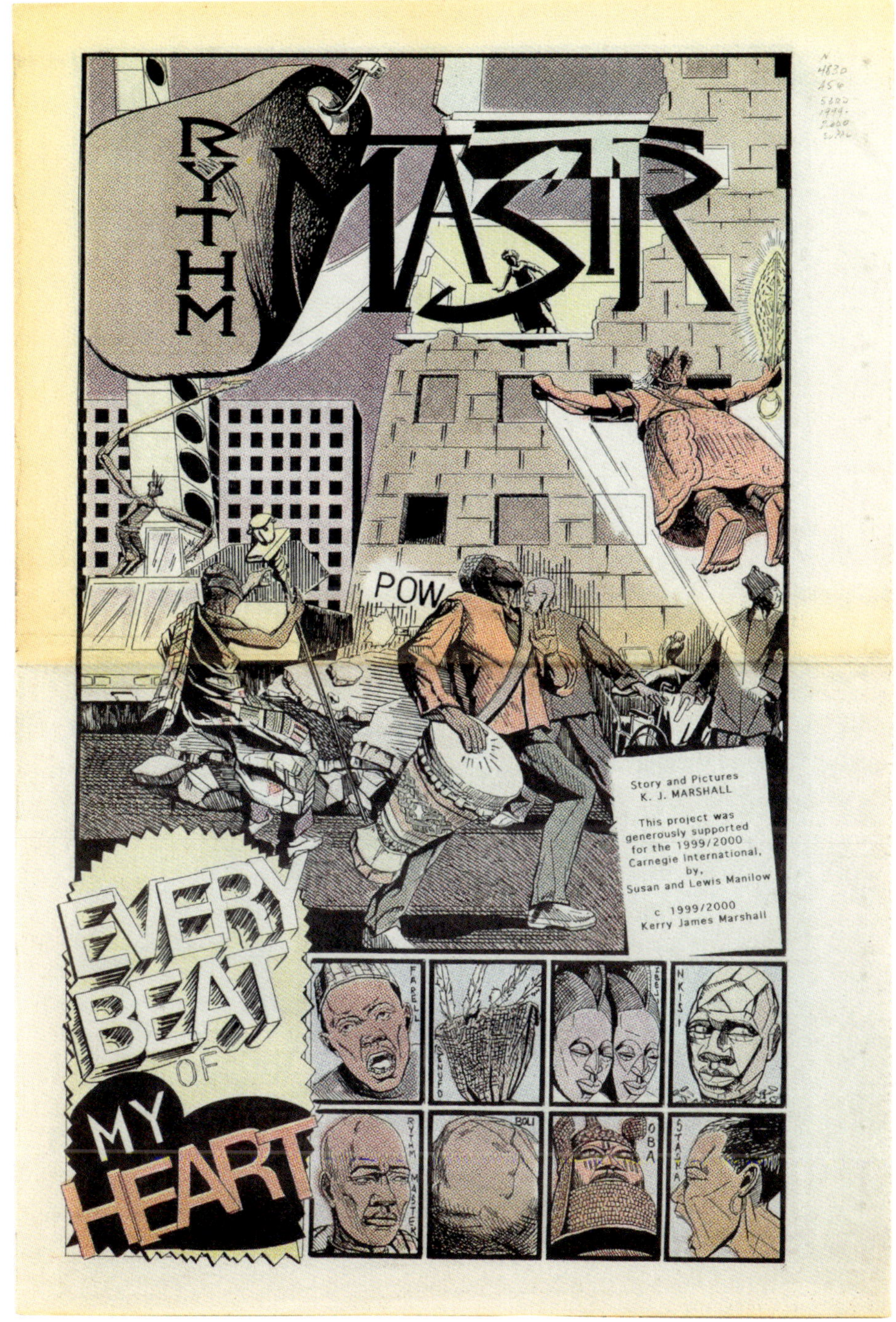

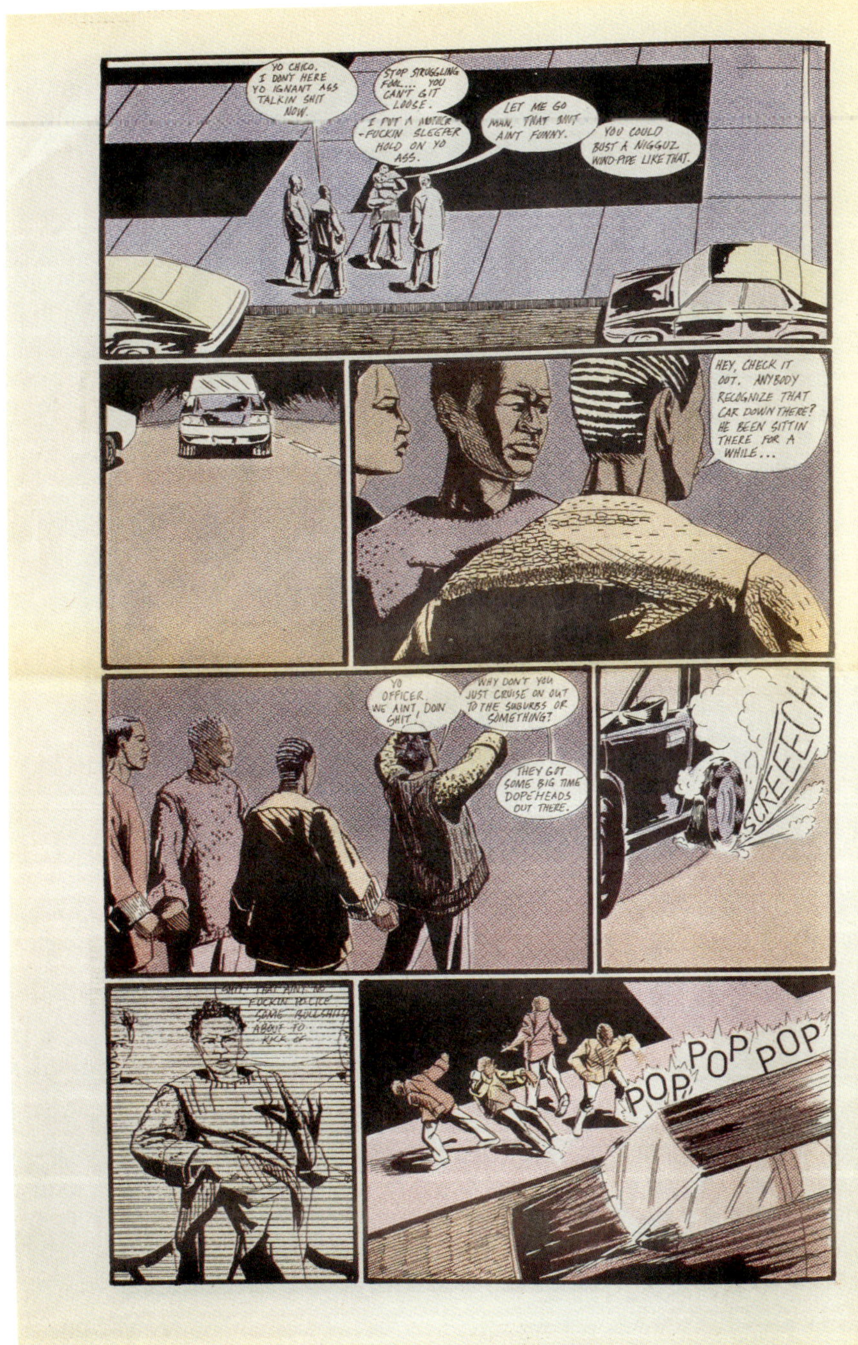
YO CHICO. I DONT HERE YO IGNANT ASS TALKIN SHIT NOW.
STOP STRUGGLING FOOL... YOU CAN'T GIT LOOSE.
I PUT A MOTHER-FUCKIN SLEEPER HOLD ON YO ASS.
LET ME GO MAN, THAT SHIT AINT FUNNY.
YOU COULD BUST A NIGGUZ WIND-PIPE LIKE THAT.
HEY, CHECK IT OUT. ANYBODY RECOGNIZE THAT CAR DOWN THERE? HE BEEN SITTIN THERE FOR A WHILE...
YO OFFICER. WE AINT DOIN SHIT!
WHY DON'T YOU JUST CRUISE ON OUT TO THE SUBURBS OR SOMETHING?
THEY GOT SOME BIG TIME DOPEHEADS OUT THERE.
SCREEECH
POP POP POP

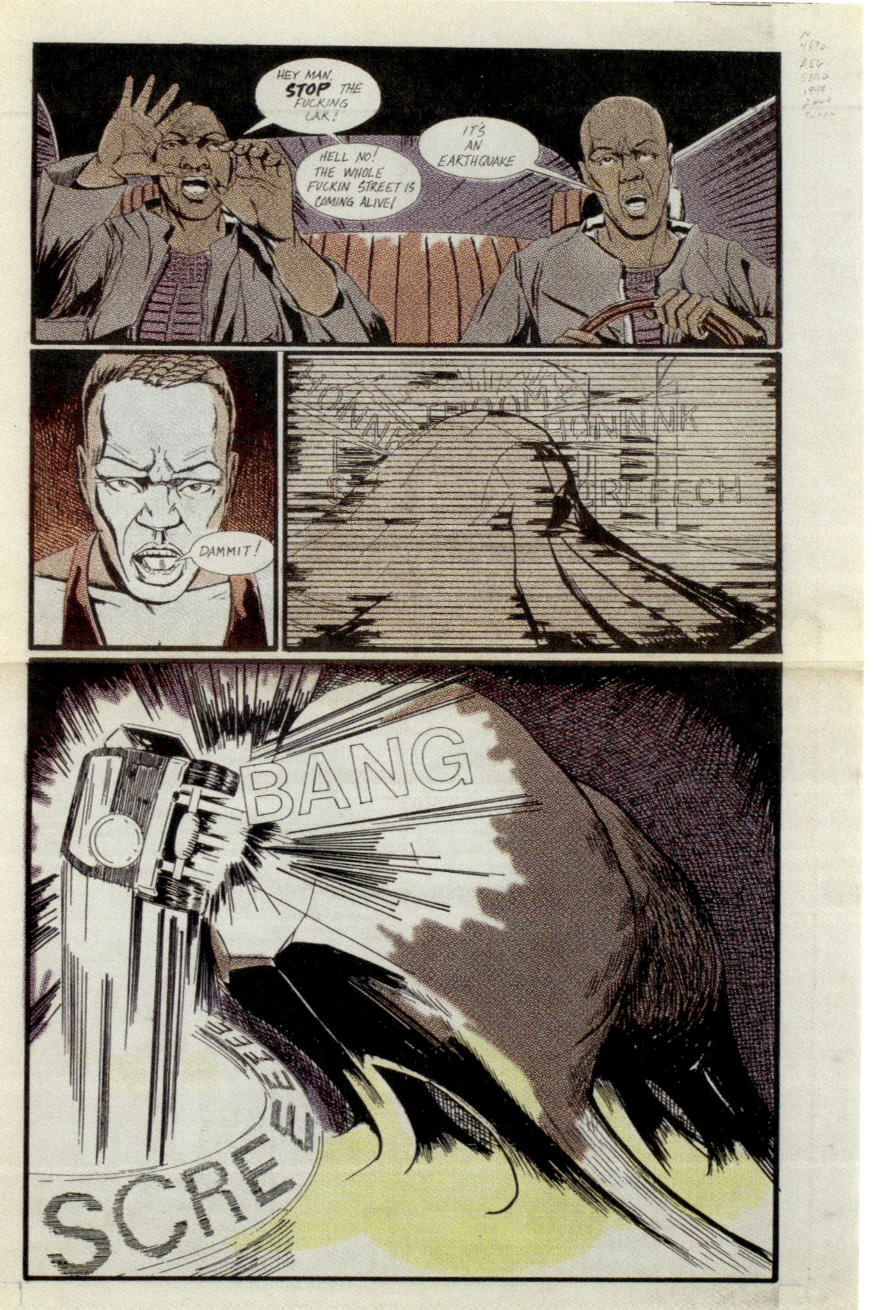
HEY MAN, STOP THE FUCKING CAR!
HELL NO! THE WHOLE FUCKIN STREET IS COMING ALIVE!
IT'S AN EARTHQUAKE
DAMMIT!
BANG
SCRE

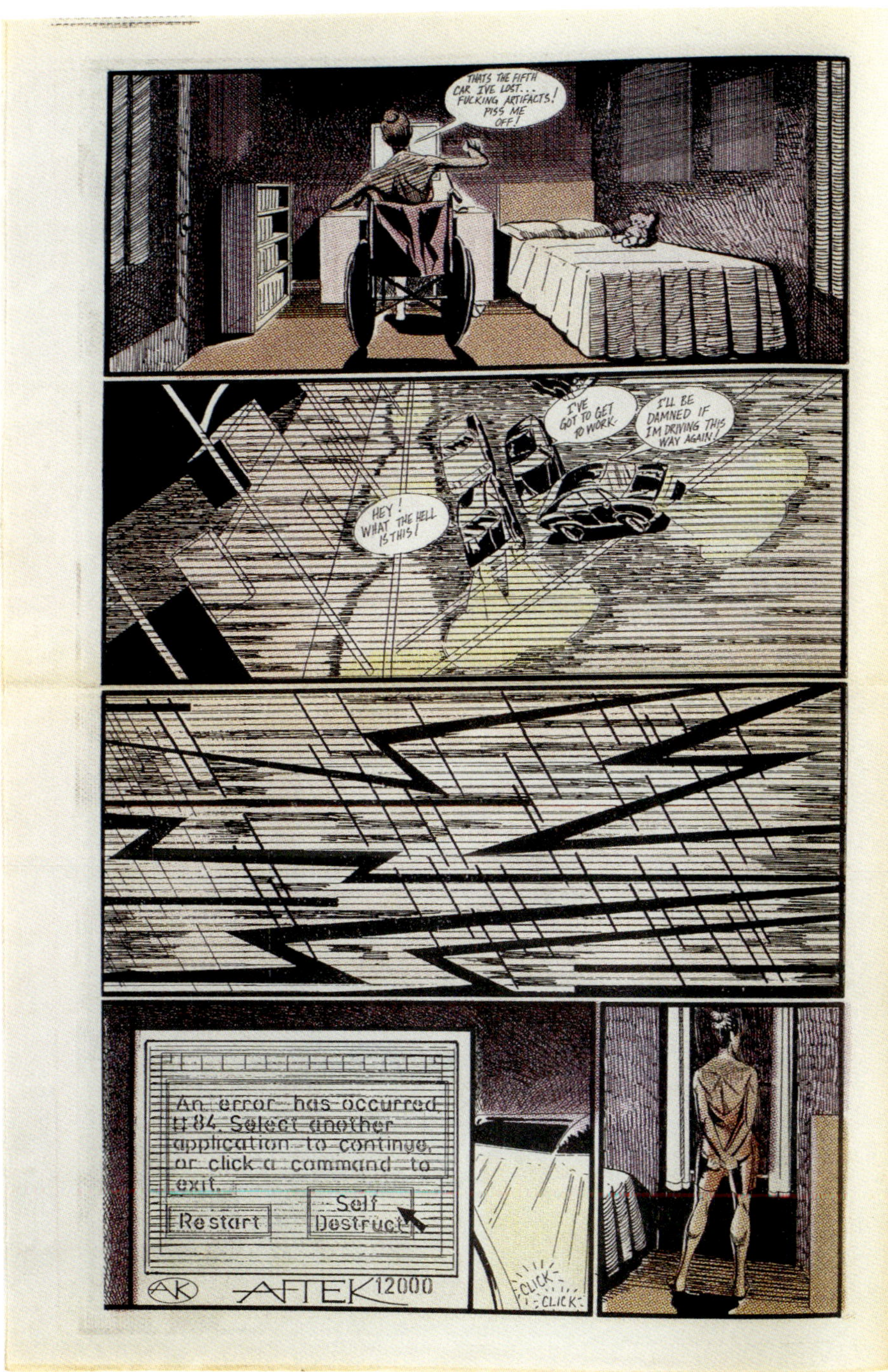
THATS THE FIFTH CAR IVE LOST... FUCKING ARTIFACTS! PISS ME OFF!
I'VE GOT TO GET TO WORK.
I'LL BE DAMNED IF IM DRIVING THIS WAY AGAIN!
HEY! WHAT THE HELL IS THIS!
An error has occurred #84. Select another application to continue, or click a command to exit.
Restart
Self Destruct
AK
AFTEK 12000
CLICK CLICK

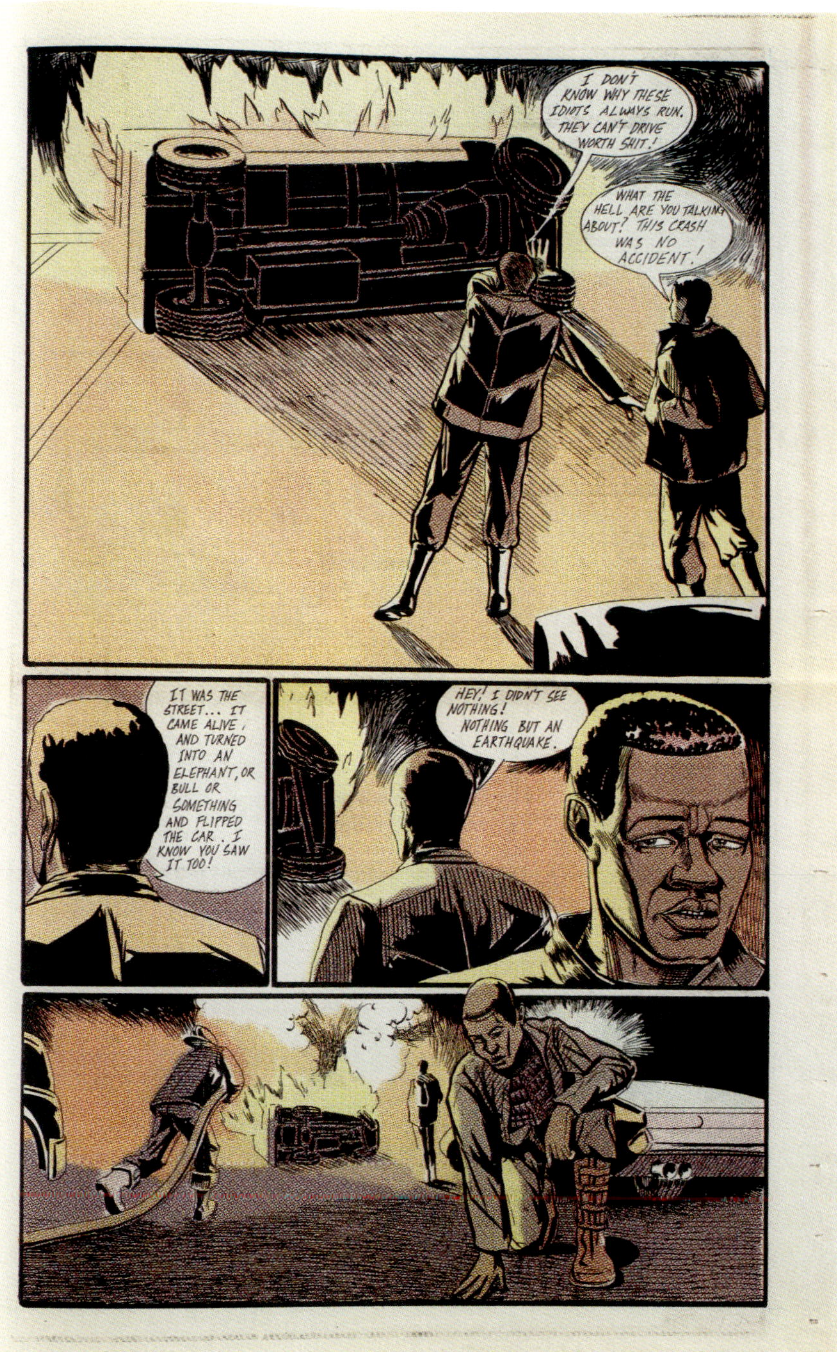
I DON'T KNOW WHY THESE IDIOTS ALWAYS RUN. THEY CAN'T DRIVE WORTH SHIT.!
WHAT THE HELL ARE YOU TALKING ABOUT? THIS CRASH WAS NO ACCIDENT.!
IT WAS THE STREET... IT CAME ALIVE, AND TURNED INTO AN ELEPHANT, OR BULL OR SOMETHING AND FLIPPED THE CAR. I KNOW YOU SAW IT TOO!
HEY! I DIDN'T SEE NOTHING! NOTHING BUT AN EARTHQUAKE.

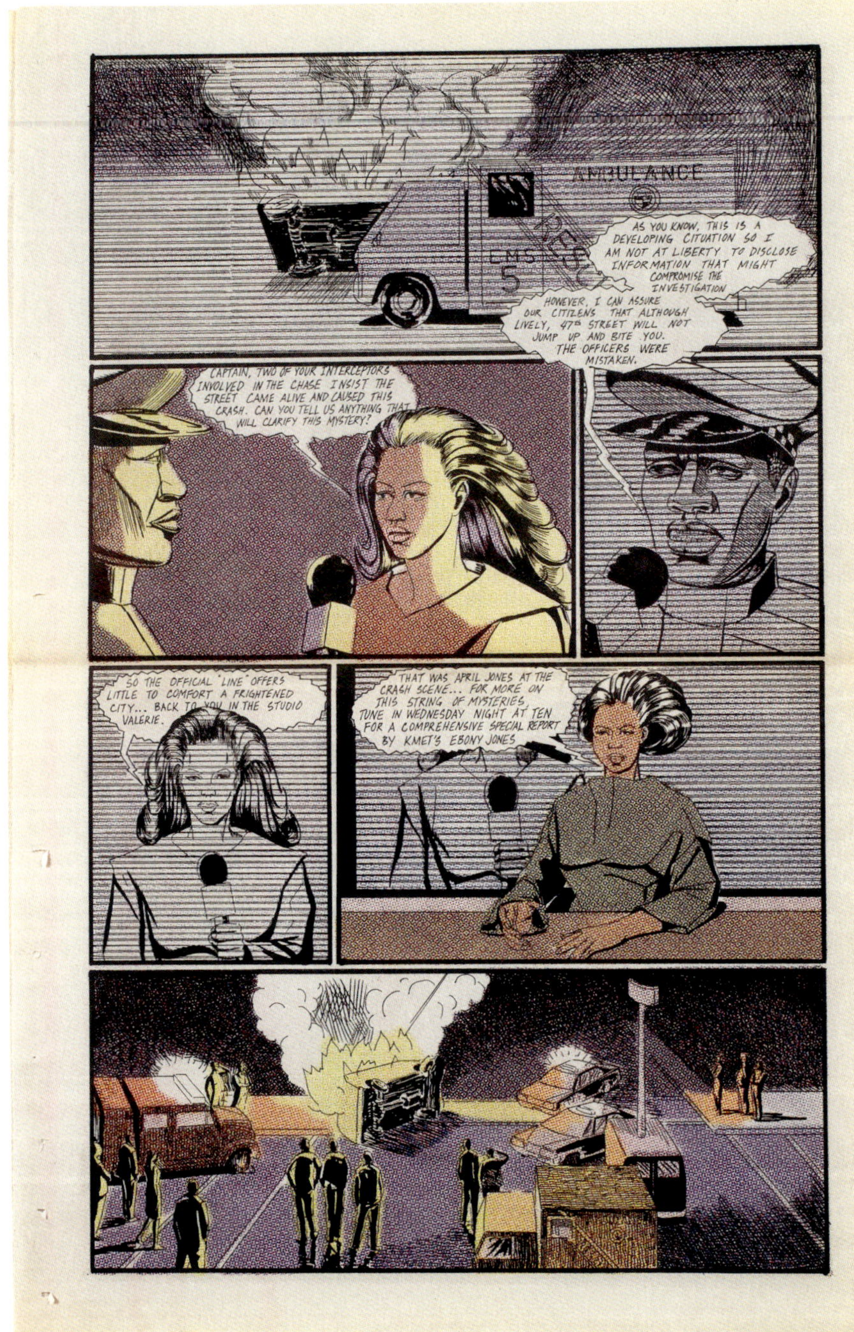
AMBULANCE
EMS 5
AS YOU KNOW, THIS IS A DEVELOPING CITUATION SO I AM NOT AT LIBERTY TO DISCLOSE INFORMATION THAT MIGHT COMPROMISE THE INVESTIGATION
HOWEVER, I CAN ASSURE OUR CITIZENS THAT ALTHOUGH LIVELY, 47th STREET WILL NOT JUMP UP AND BITE YOU. THE OFFICERS WERE MISTAKEN.
CAPTAIN, TWO OF YOUR INTERCEPTORS INVOLVED IN THE CHASE INSIST THE STREET CAME ALIVE AND CAUSED THIS CRASH. CAN YOU TELL US ANYTHING THAT WILL CLARIFY THIS MYSTERY?
SO THE OFFICIAL "LINE" OFFERS LITTLE TO COMFORT A FRIGHTENED CITY... BACK TO YOU IN THE STUDIO VALERIE.
THAT WAS APRIL JONES AT THE CRASH SCENE... FOR MORE ON THIS STRING OF MYSTERIES, TUNE IN WEDNESDAY NIGHT AT TEN FOR A COMPREHENSIVE SPECIAL REPORT BY KMET'S EBONY JONES

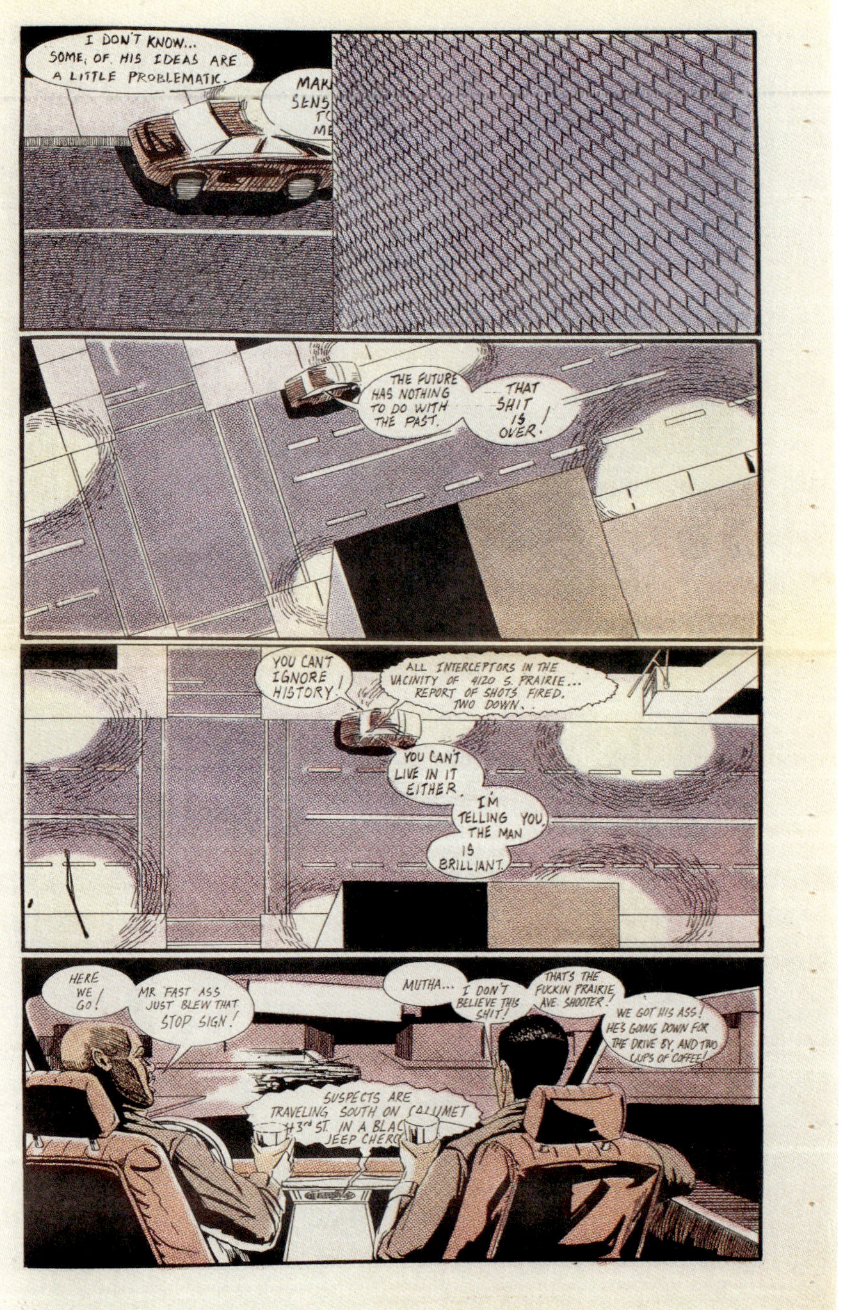
I DON'T KNOW... SOME OF HIS IDEAS ARE A LITTLE PROBLEMATIC.
THE FUTURE HAS NOTHING TO DO WITH THE PAST.
THAT SHIT IS OVER!
YOU CAN'T IGNORE HISTORY!
ALL INTERCEPTORS IN THE VACINITY OF 4120 S. PRAIRIE... REPORT OF SHOTS FIRED. TWO DOWN.
YOU CAN'T LIVE IN IT EITHER.
I'M TELLING YOU. THE MAN IS BRILLIANT.
HERE WE GO!
MR FAST ASS JUST BLEW THAT STOP SIGN!
MUTHA...
I DON'T BELIEVE THIS SHIT!
THAT'S THE FUCKIN PRAIRIE AVE. SHOOTER!
WE GOT HIS ASS! HE'S GOING DOWN FOR THE DRIVE BY, AND TWO CUPS OF COFFEE!
SUSPECTS ARE TRAVELING SOUTH ON CALUMET 43rd ST. IN A BLAC JEEP CHERO

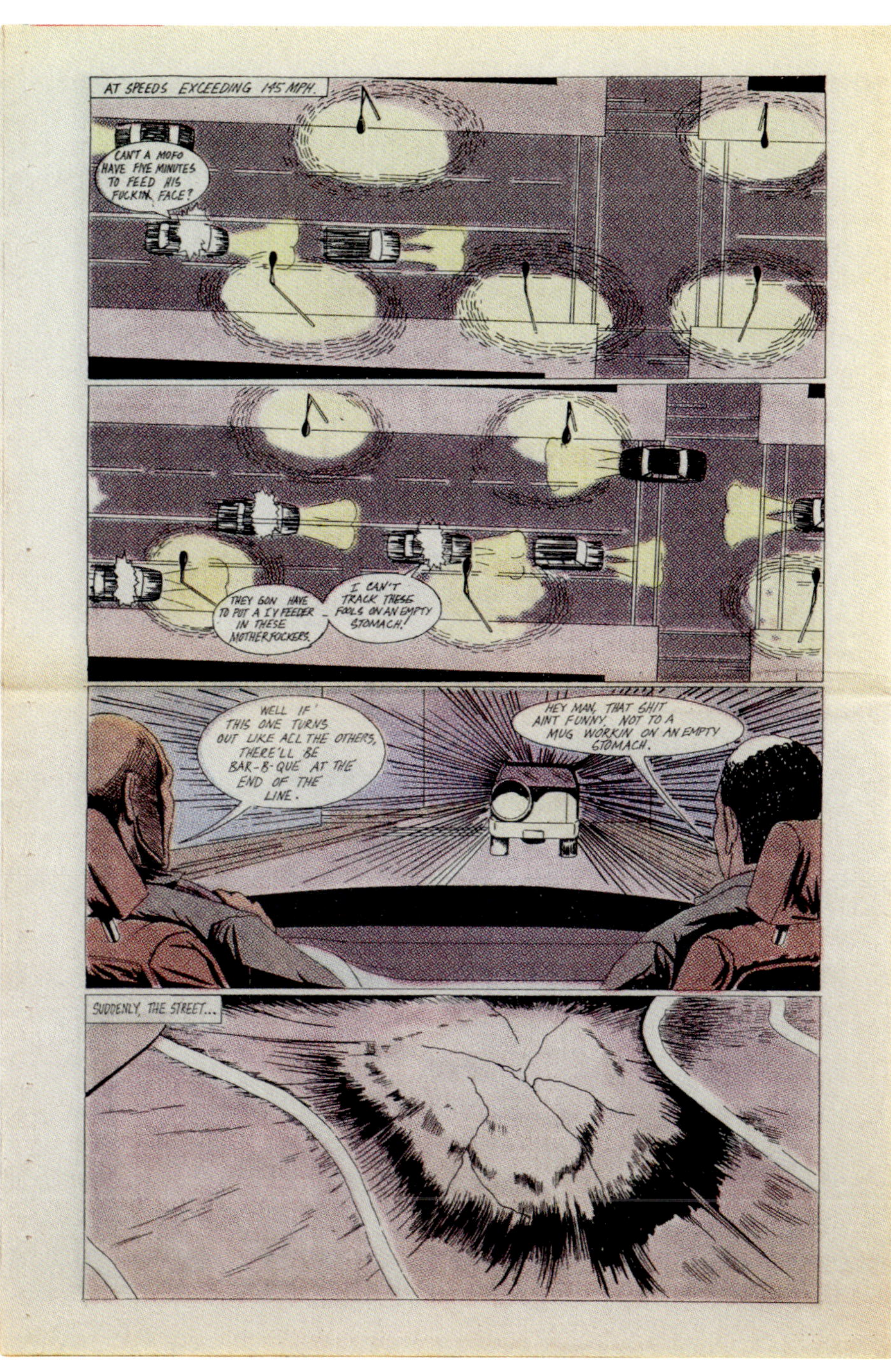

Rythm Mastr: Every Beat of My Heart **[1999–2000]**

1999–2000

RYTHM MASTR: TOWER OF POWER

The power of the five African sculpture-based superheroes fully manifests itself in the second episode of *Rythm Mastr*, when their joint efforts create a sonic field designed to protect a water tank from a mortar attack. Marshall drew attention to rooftop water tanks—a prominent and, at the time, vanishing feature of the Chicago cityscape—by using them as a base for his superheroes due to their resemblance to village huts. This is one of the very few episodes when Senufo, Ibeji, Nkisi, Oba, and Boli generate a cliff-hanger moment by verbalizing their thoughts. ("That was close. The sonic field held this time, but they'll most certainly increase the explosive field"; "Soon there will be few of these structures left. We must move quickly now. Our time grows shorter.") In the rest of the series, the characters' presence is impactful but mostly silent.

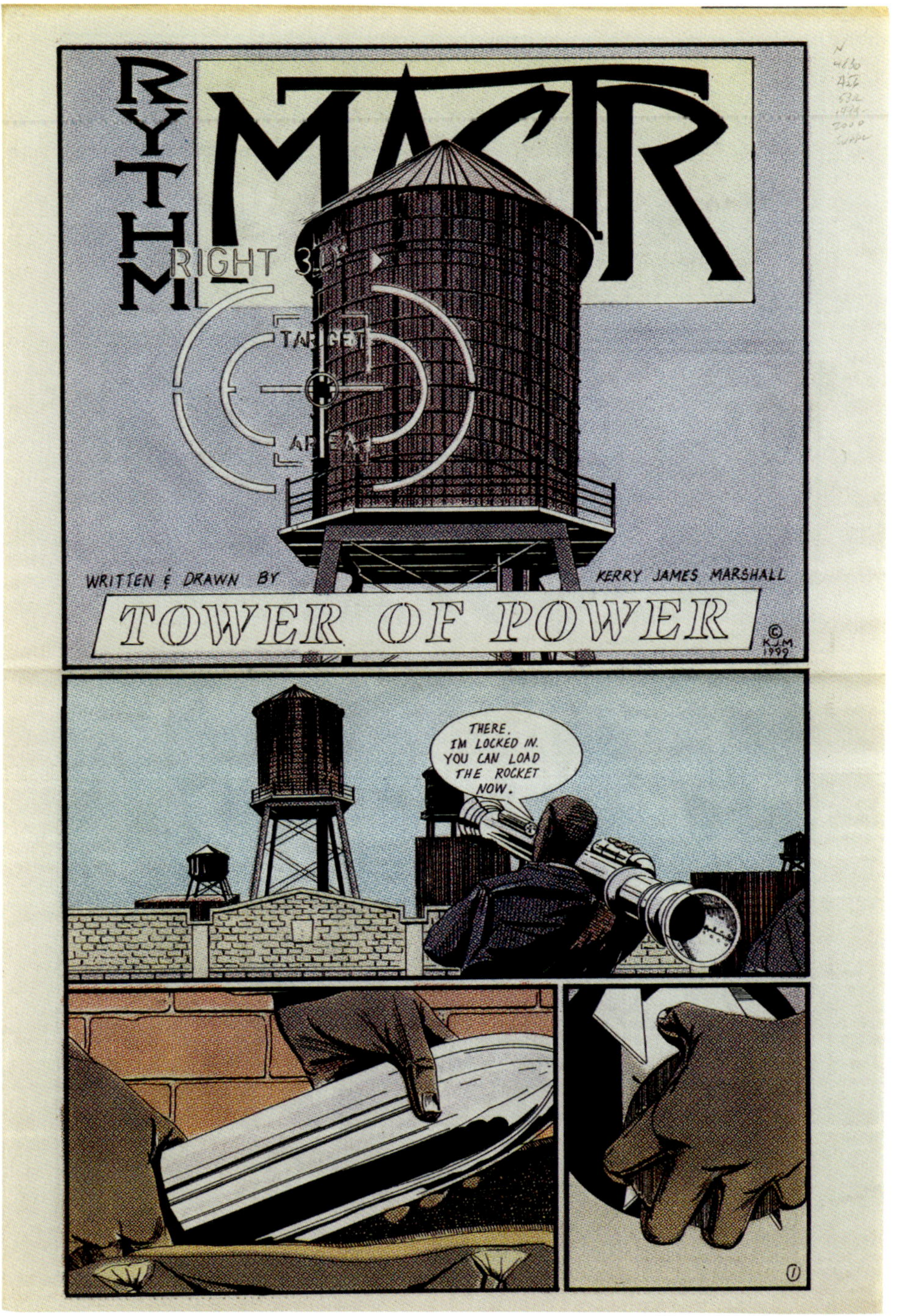

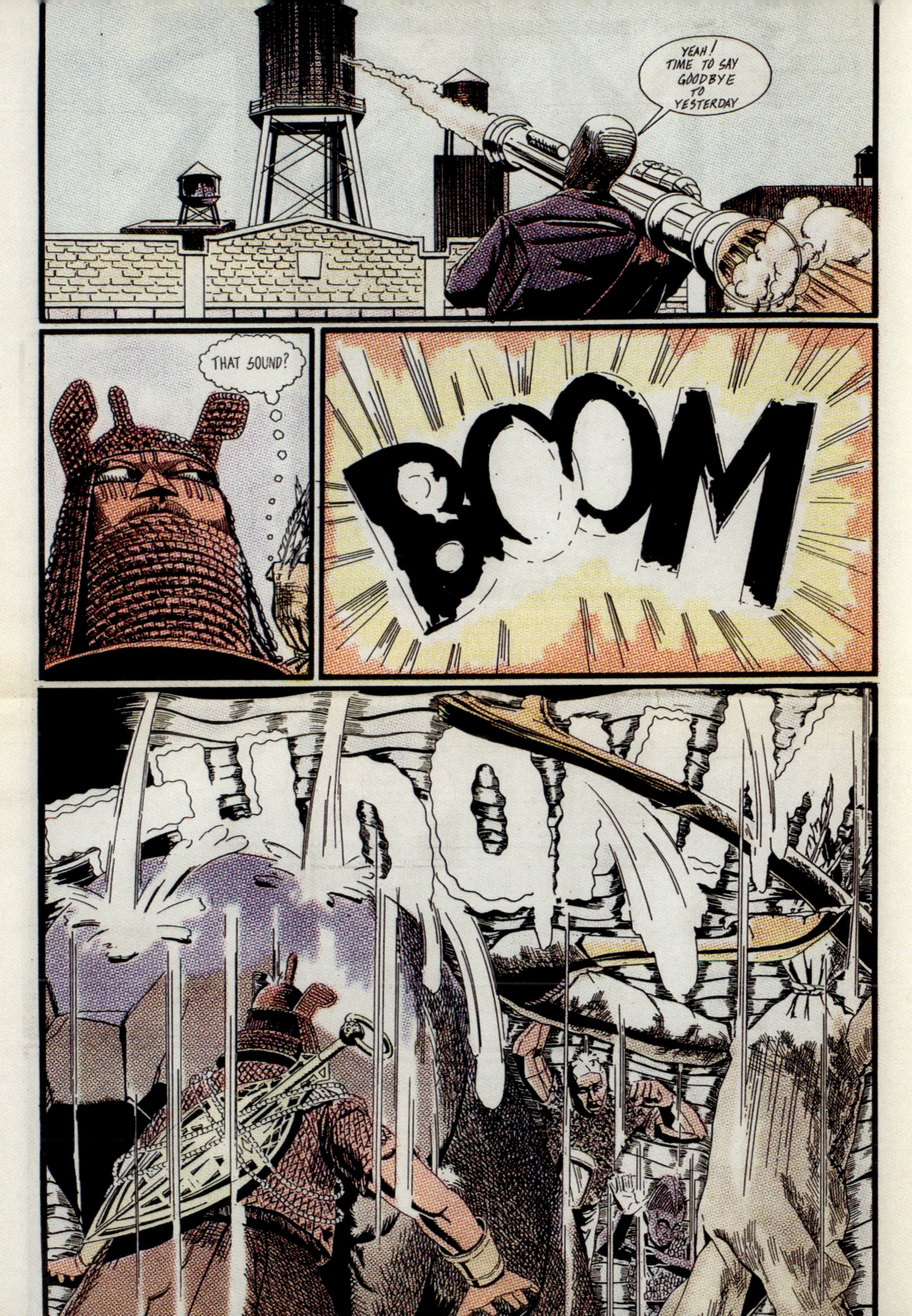
YEAH! TIME TO SAY GOODBYE TO YESTERDAY
THAT SOUND?
BOOM

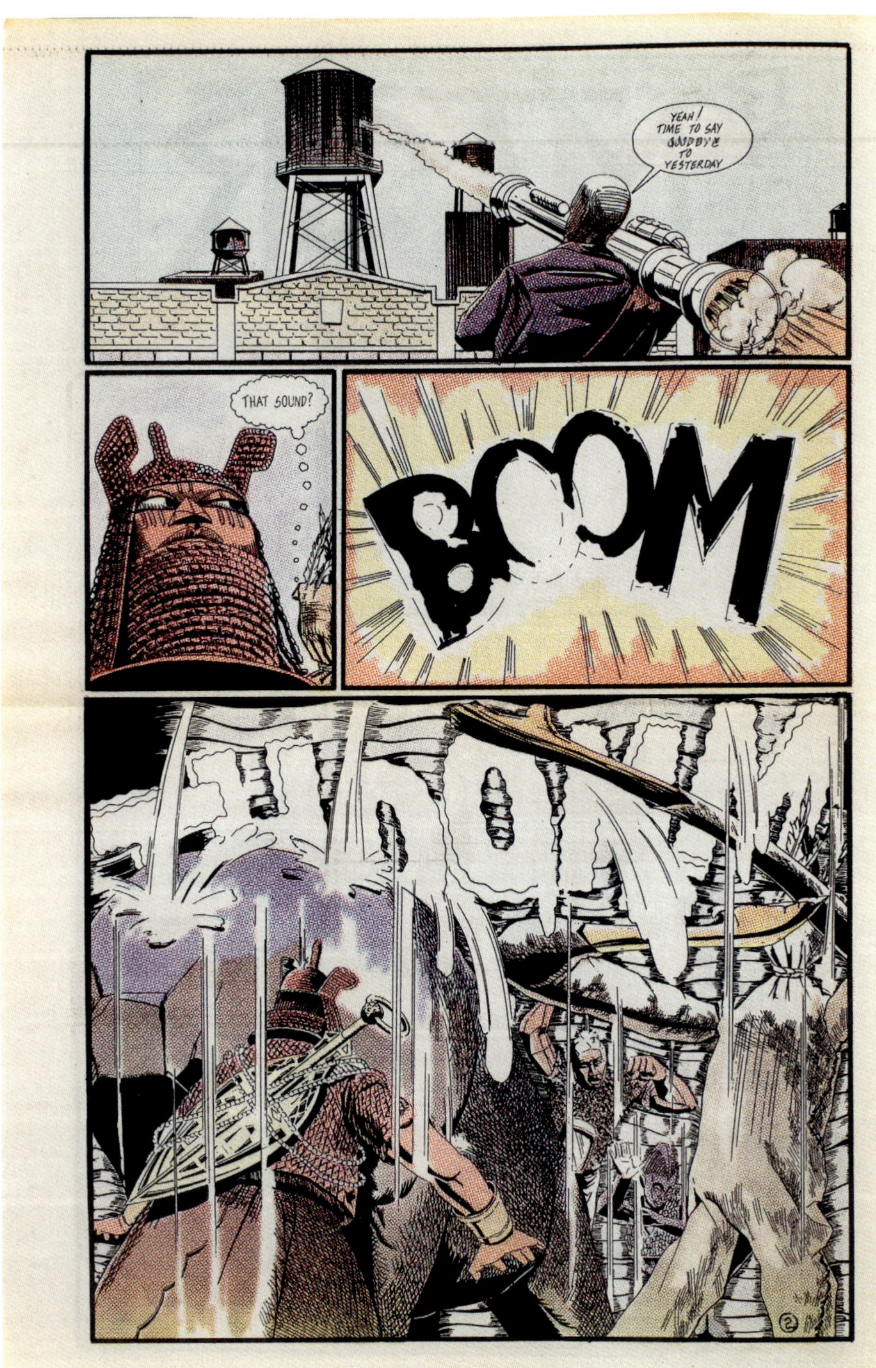
YEAH! TIME TO SAY
TO YESTERDAY
THAT SOUND?
BOOM

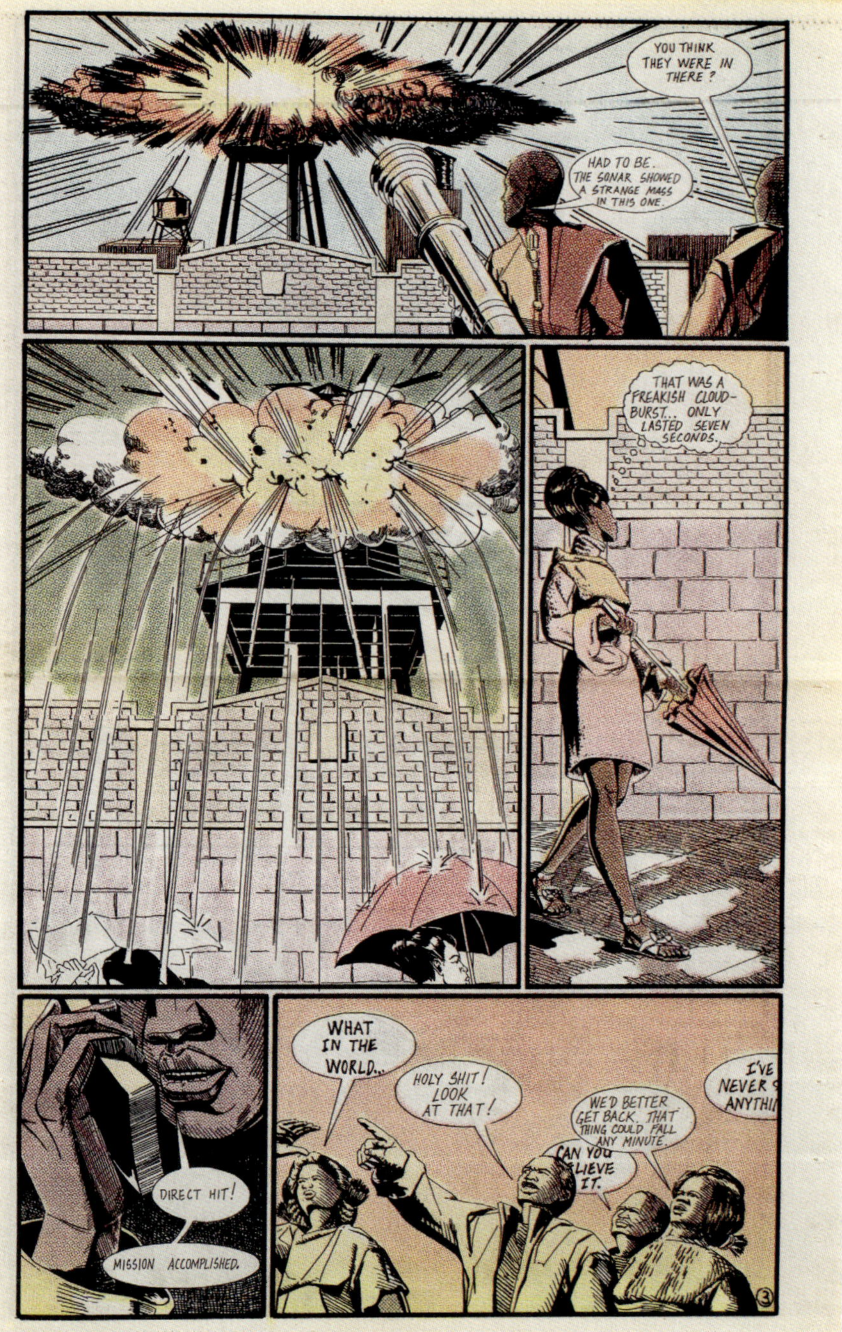
YOU THINK THEY WERE IN THERE?
HAD TO BE. THE SONAR SHOWED A STRANGE MASS IN THIS ONE.
THAT WAS A FREAKISH CLOUD-BURST... ONLY LASTED SEVEN SECONDS.
DIRECT HIT!
MISSION ACCOMPLISHED.
WHAT IN THE WORLD...
HOLY SHIT! LOOK AT THAT!
WE'D BETTER GET BACK. THAT THING COULD FALL ANY MINUTE.
I'VE NEVER

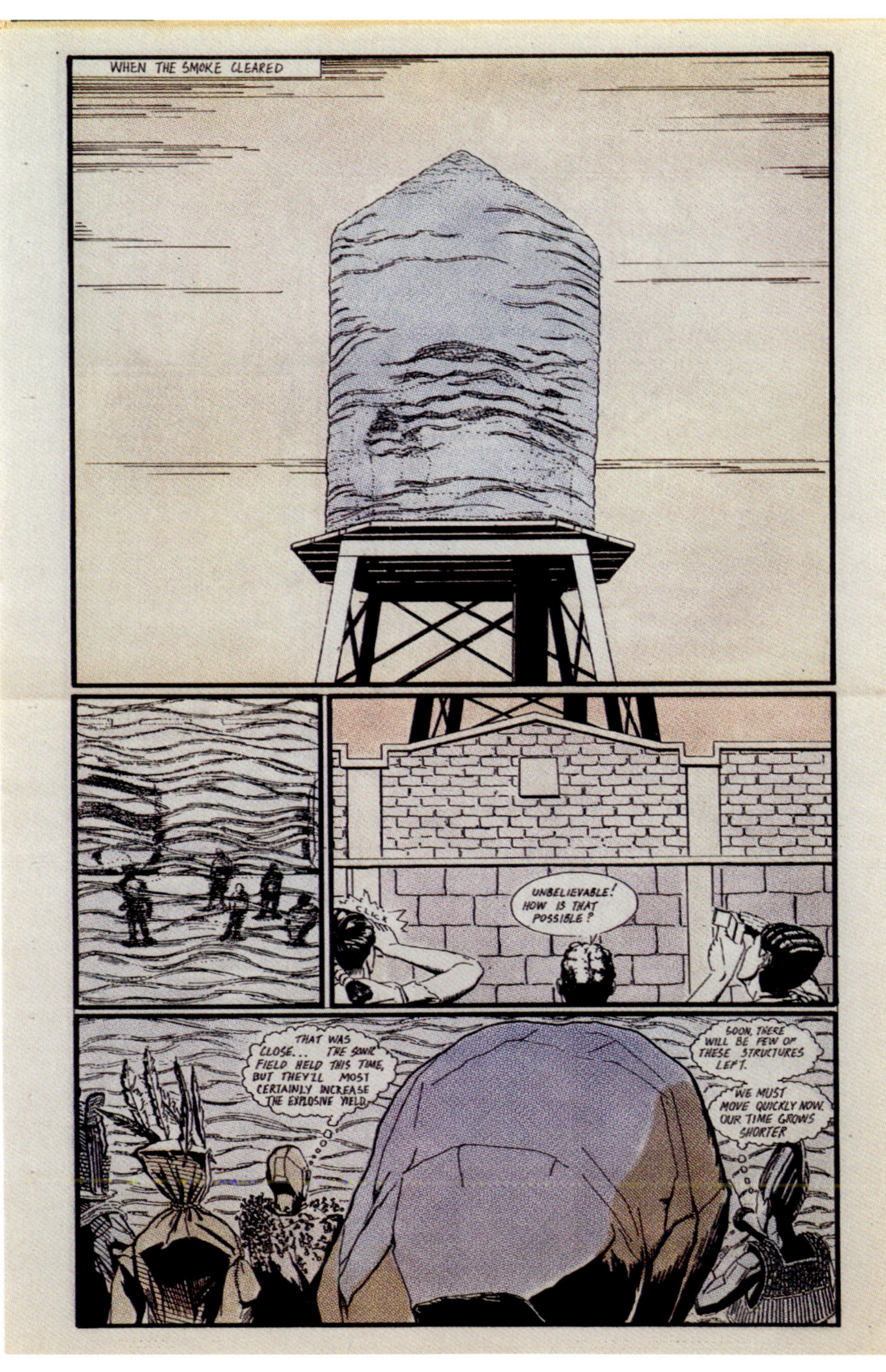

Rythm Mastr: Tower of Power **[1999–2000]**

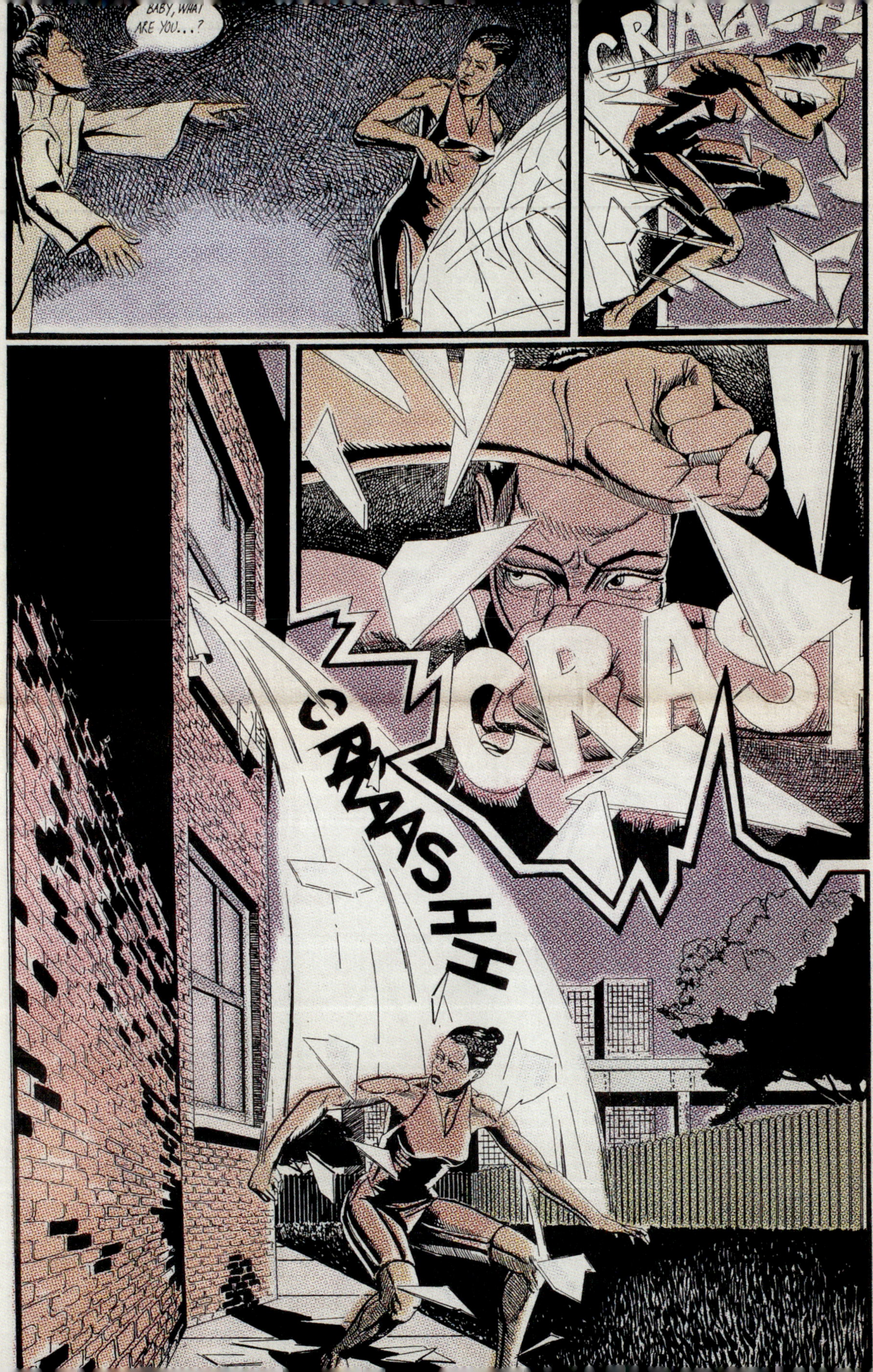

BABY, WHAT ARE YOU...?

CRAAASH

CRAS

CRAASHH

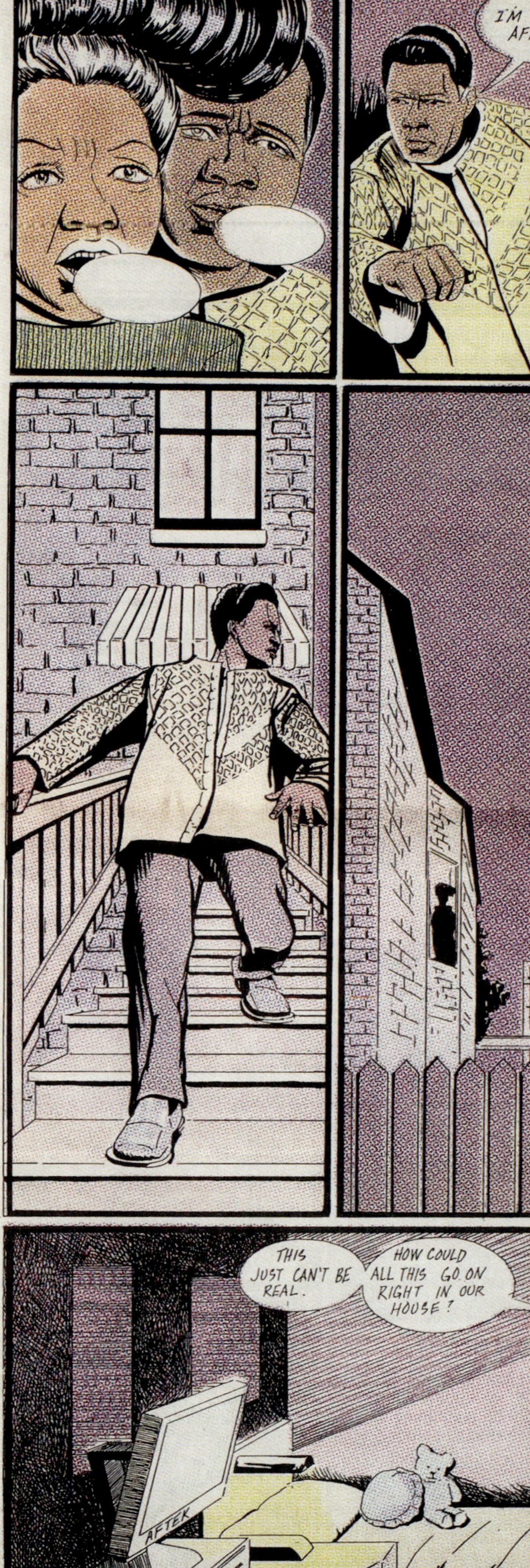

1999—2000

RYTHM MASTR: BULLETIN!

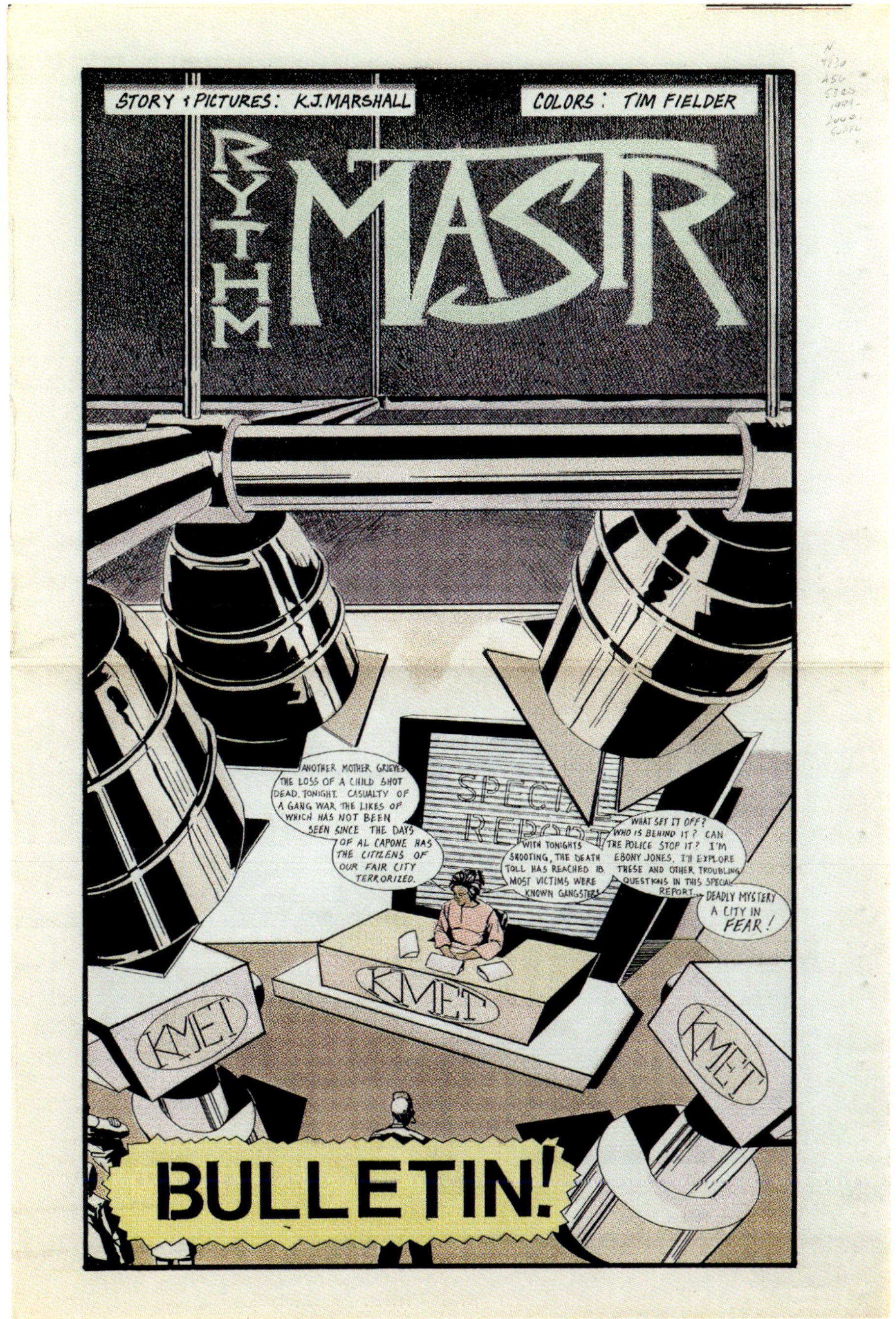

The third and final part of the first incarnation of *Rythm Mastr* focuses on Stasha—a master at robotics and Farrell's girlfriend. The difficulties superheroes traditionally encounter when called to reconcile their powers with their personal life is here illustrated by Stasha's concerned parents discovering their daughter's extraordinary abilities. "Bulletin!" is also important as it introduces the fictional TV station KMET. The media coverage of the events and the sensational way these are conveyed to the general public will become a recurrent theme.

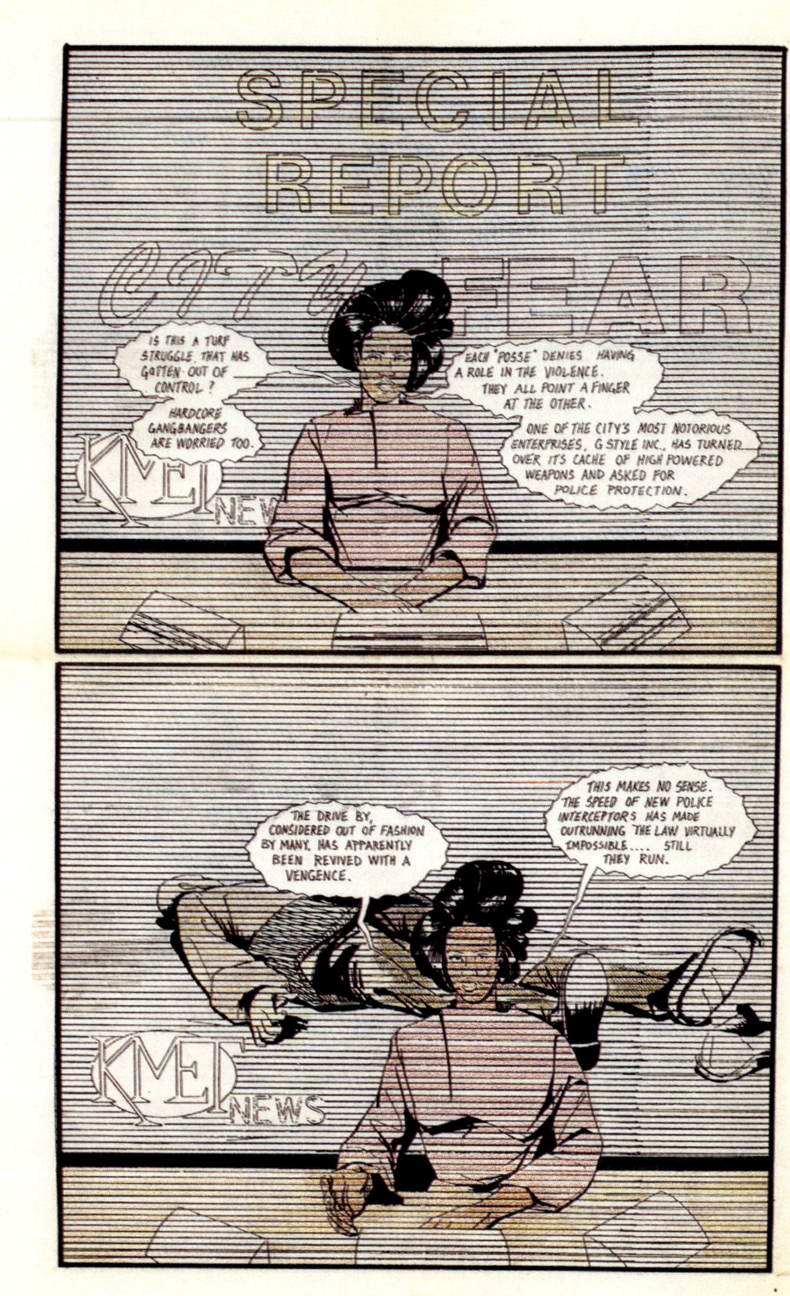
SPECIAL REPORT
CITY
FEAR
IS THIS A TURF STRUGGLE THAT HAS GOTTEN OUT OF CONTROL?
HARDCORE GANGBANGERS ARE WORRIED TOO.
EACH "POSSE" DENIES HAVING A ROLE IN THE VIOLENCE. THEY ALL POINT A FINGER AT THE OTHER.
ONE OF THE CITY'S MOST NOTORIOUS ENTERPRISES, G STYLE INC., HAS TURNED OVER ITS CACHE OF HIGH POWERED WEAPONS AND ASKED FOR POLICE PROTECTION.
KMET NEWS
THE DRIVE BY, CONSIDERED OUT OF FASHION BY MANY, HAS APPARENTLY BEEN REVIVED WITH A VENGENCE.
THIS MAKES NO SENSE. THE SPEED OF NEW POLICE INTERCEPTORS HAS MADE OUTRUNNING THE LAW VIRTUALLY IMPOSSIBLE.... STILL THEY RUN.
KMET NEWS

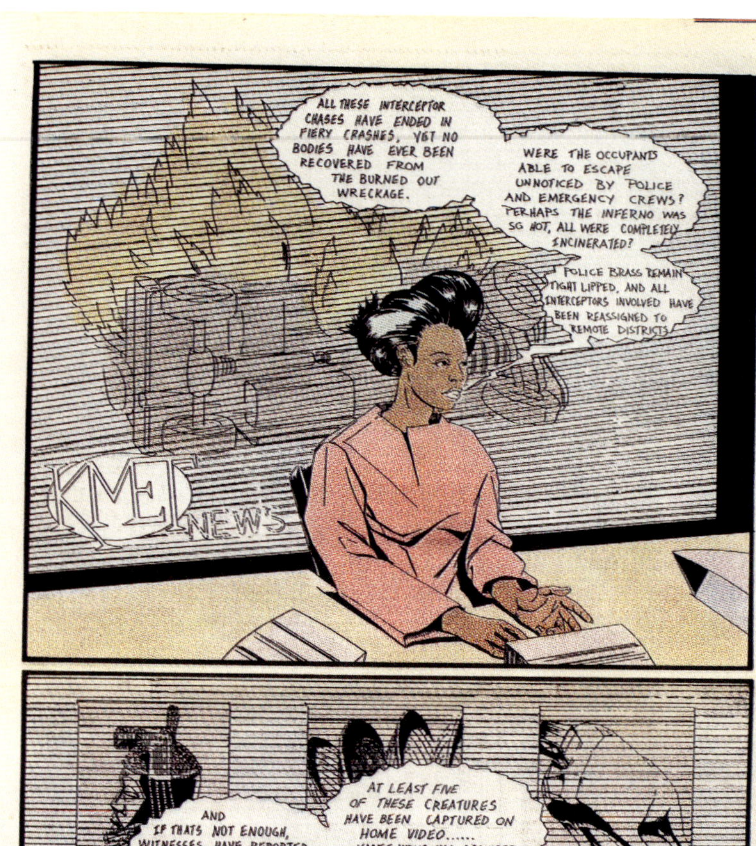
ALL THESE INTERCEPTOR CHASES HAVE ENDED IN FIERY CRASHES, YET NO BODIES HAVE EVER BEEN RECOVERED FROM THE BURNED OUT WRECKAGE.
WERE THE OCCUPANTS ABLE TO ESCAPE UNNOTICED BY POLICE AND EMERGENCY CREWS? PERHAPS THE INFERNO WAS SO HOT, ALL WERE COMPLETELY INCINERATED?
POLICE BRASS REMAIN TIGHT LIPPED, AND ALL INTERCEPTORS INVOLVED HAVE BEEN REASSIGNED TO REMOTE DISTRICTS.
KMET NEWS

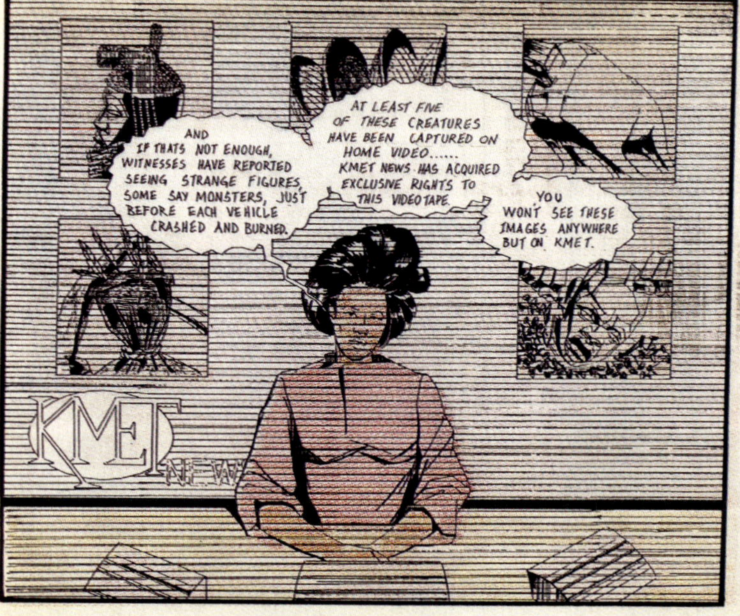
AND IF THATS NOT ENOUGH, WITNESSES HAVE REPORTED SEEING STRANGE FIGURES, SOME SAY MONSTERS, JUST BEFORE EACH VEHICLE CRASHED AND BURNED.
AT LEAST FIVE OF THESE CREATURES HAVE BEEN CAPTURED ON HOME VIDEO...... KMET NEWS HAS ACQUIRED EXCLUSIVE RIGHTS TO THIS VIDEOTAPE.
YOU WON'T SEE THESE IMAGES ANYWHERE BUT ON KMET.
KMET NEWS

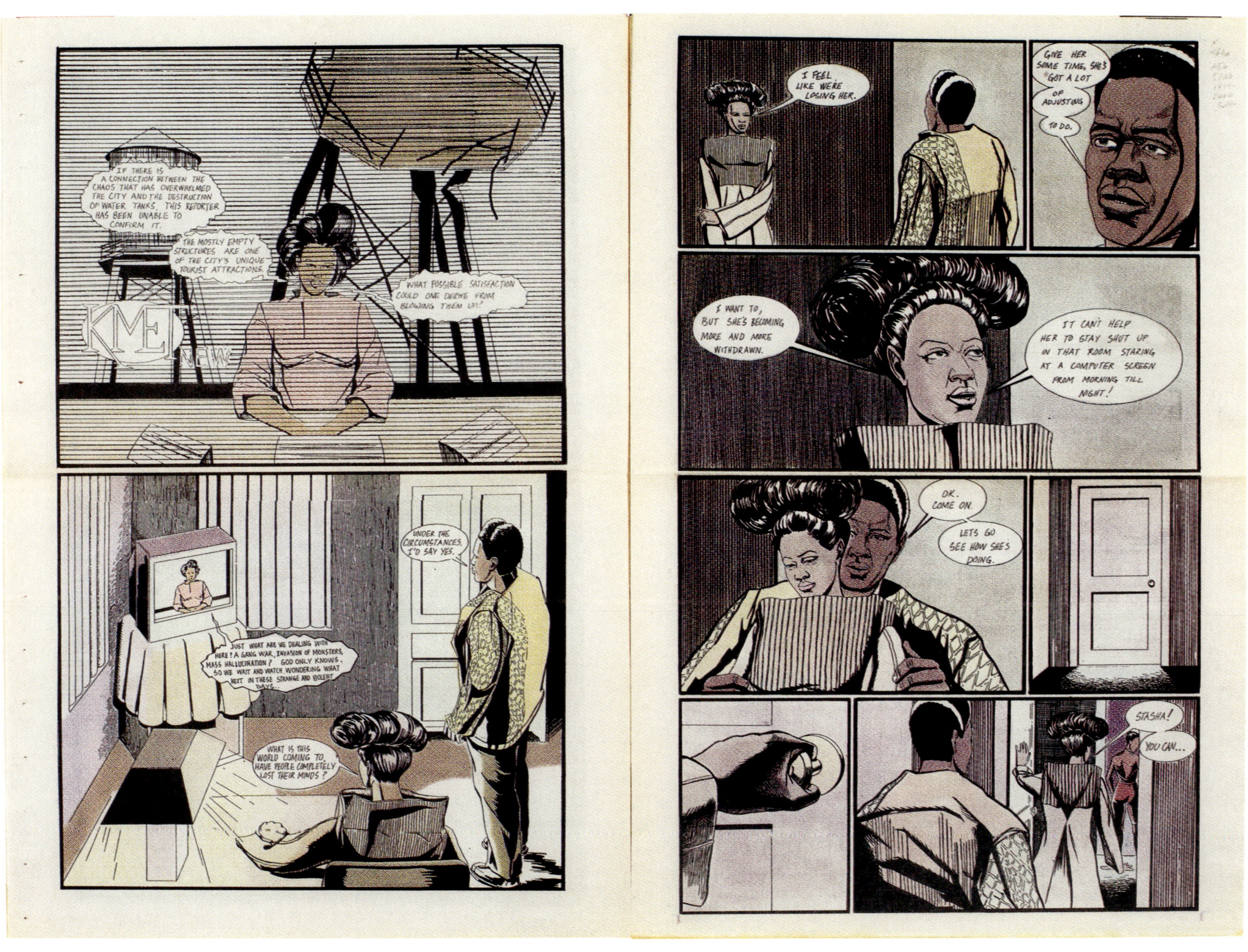
IF THERE IS A CONNECTION BETWEEN THE CHAOS THAT HAS OVERWHELMED THE CITY AND THE DESTRUCTION OF WATER TANKS, THIS REPORTER HAS BEEN UNABLE TO CONFIRM IT.
THE MOSTLY EMPTY STRUCTURES ARE ONE OF THE CITY'S UNIQUE TOURIST ATTRACTIONS.
WHAT POSSIBLE SATISFACTION COULD ONE DERIVE FROM BLOWING THEM UP?
KMEJ
UNDER THE CIRCUMSTANCES, I'D SAY YES.
JUST WHAT ARE WE DEALING WITH HERE? A GANG WAR, INVASION OF MONSTERS, MASS HALLUCINATION? GOD ONLY KNOWS. SO WE WAIT AND WATCH, WONDERING WHAT NEXT IN THESE STRANGE AND VIOLENT DAYS...
WHAT IS THIS WORLD COMING TO, HAVE PEOPLE COMPLETELY LOST THEIR MINDS?
I FEEL LIKE WE'RE LOSING HER.
GIVE HER SOME TIME, SHE'S GOT A LOT OF ADJUSTING TO DO.
I WANT TO, BUT SHE'S BECOMING MORE AND MORE WITHDRAWN.
IT CAN'T HELP HER TO STAY SHUT UP IN THAT ROOM STARING AT A COMPUTER SCREEN FROM MORNING TILL NIGHT!
OK. COME ON.
LETS GO SEE HOW SHE'S DOING.
STASHA!
YOU CAN...

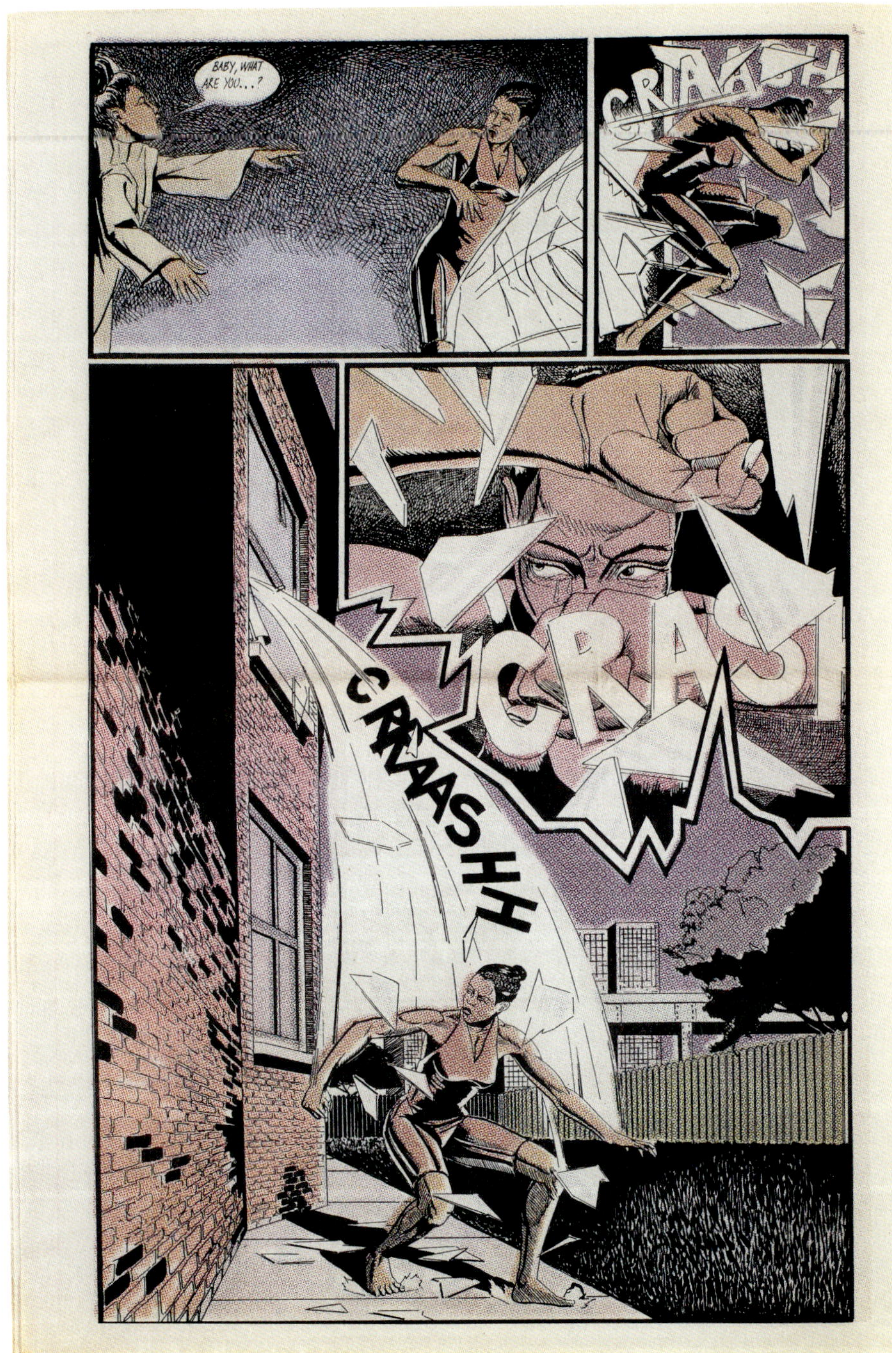
BABY, WHAT ARE YOU...?
CRAS
CRAASHH

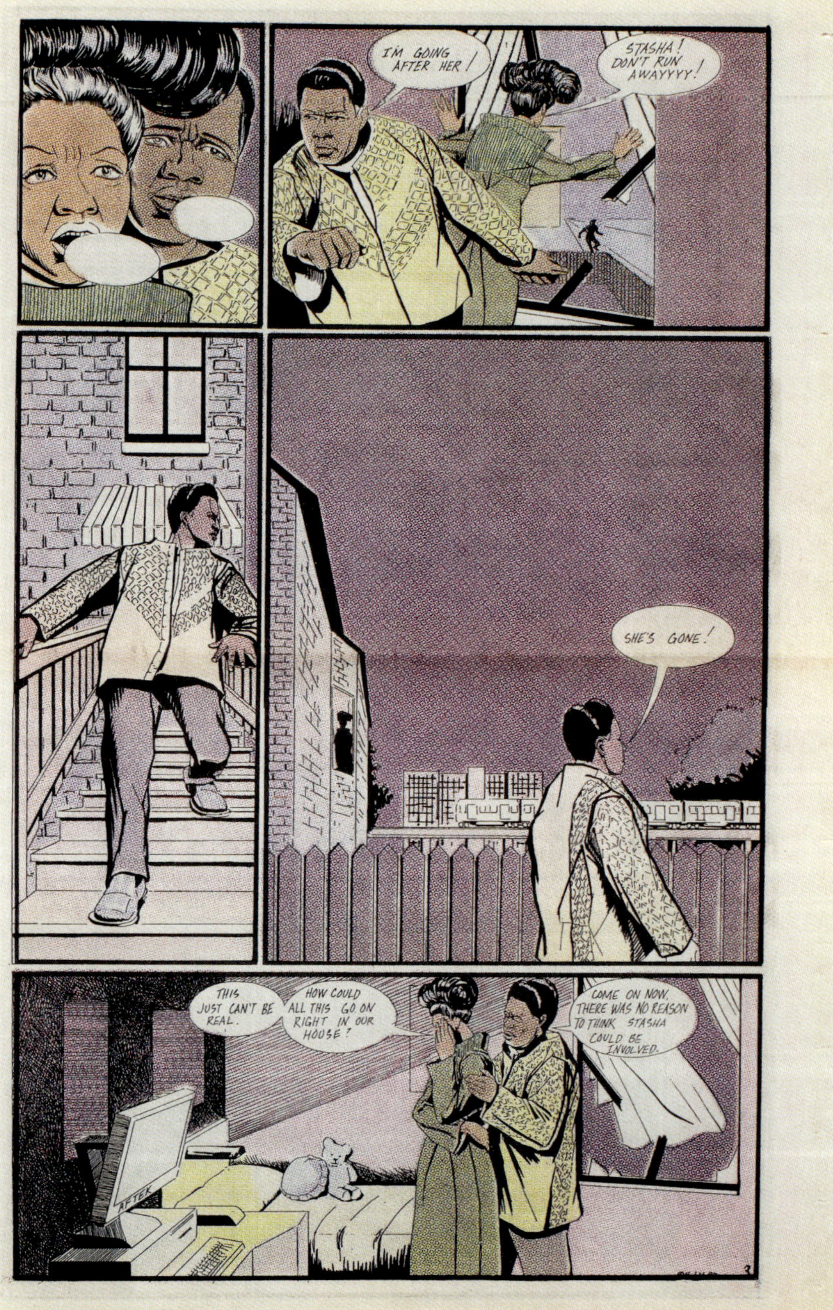
I'M GOING AFTER HER!
STASHA! DON'T RUN AWAYYYY!
SHE'S GONE!
THIS JUST CAN'T BE REAL.
HOW COULD ALL THIS GO ON RIGHT IN OUR HOUSE?
COME ON NOW, THERE WAS NO REASON TO THINK STASHA COULD BE INVOLVED.

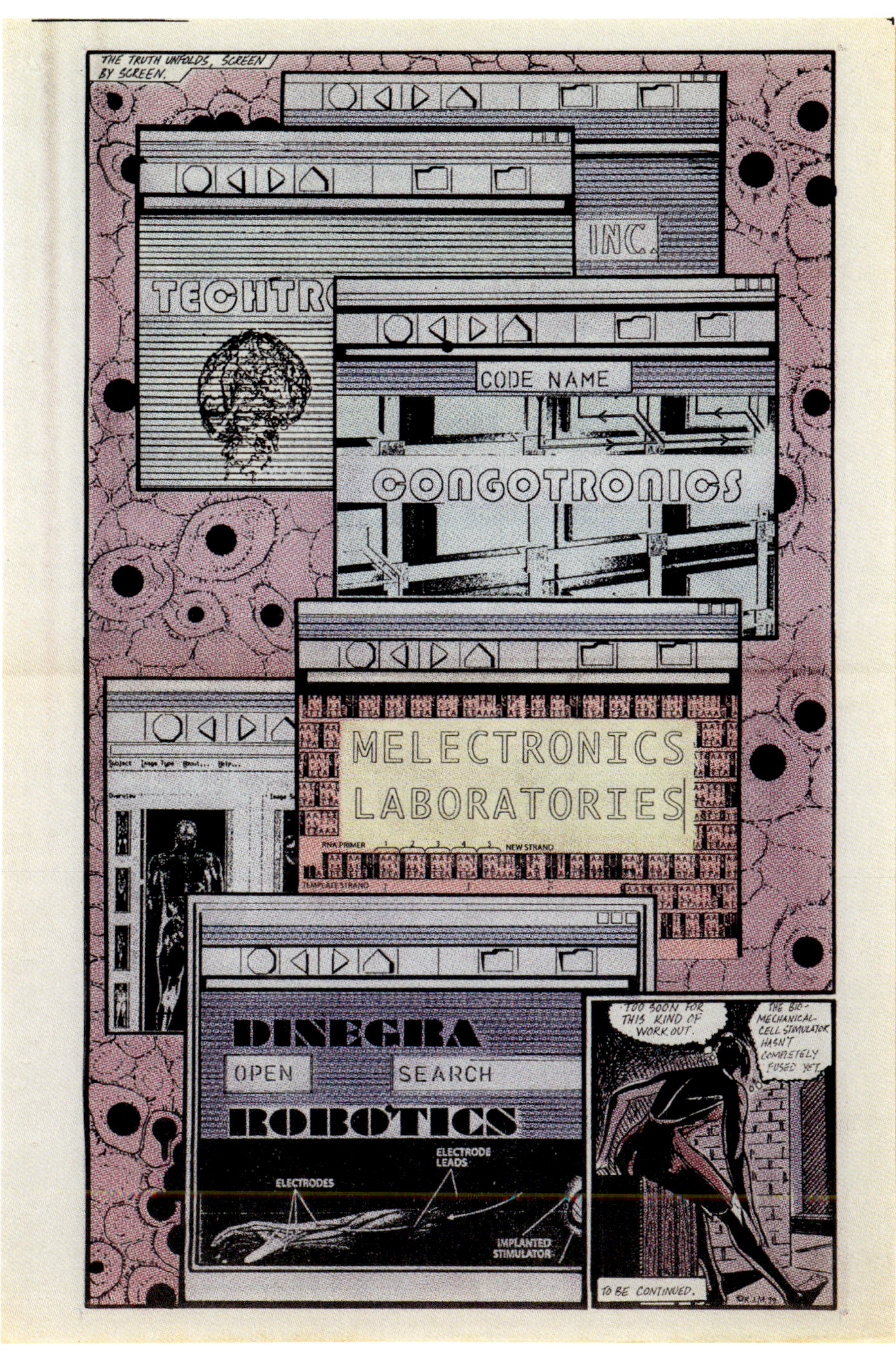
THE TRUTH UNFOLDS, SCREEN BY SCREEN.
INC.
TECHTR
CODE NAME
CONGOTRONICS
MELECTRONICS
LABORATORIES
RNA PRIMER
NEW STRAND
TEMPLATE STRAND
DISEGRA
OPEN
SEARCH
ROBOTICS
ELECTRODE LEADS
ELECTRODES
IMPLANTED STIMULATOR
TOO SOON FOR THIS KIND OF WORK OUT.
THE BIO-MECHANICAL CELL STIMULATOR HASN'T COMPLETELY FUSED YET.
TO BE CONTINUED.

1999

RYTHM MASTR: PITTSBURGH POST-GAZETTE

Series of eight weekly strips published in the *Pittsburgh Post-Gazette* during the Carnegie International 1999/2000. All 1999: November 2 (p. 41); November 9 (p. 31); November 16 (p. 29); November 23 (p. 39); November 30 (p. 49); December 7 (p. 35); December 14 (p. 39); December 21 (p. 51)

For the duration of the 1999/2000 Carnegie International, Marshall published a weekly *Rythm Mastr* comic strip in the *Pittsburgh Post-Gazette*. Aptly focusing on media reports, the story arc develops over eight single-panel episodes featuring KMET's anchor Ebony Jones and correspondent Cheryl Jones. The latter's interview with the self-proclaimed "keeper of the culture" Kuntinkantin Robinson (his name possibly a variation of Kunta Kinte, the protagonist of Alex Haley's 1976 novel *Roots: The Saga of an American Family*) sheds light on the African artifacts that have gone missing from The Ancient Egyptian Museum. The sculptures have not been stolen but instead have left of their own volition because "it was time"—thereby kicking off a new phase in the "liberation struggle." The panel from November 16, 1999 openly refers to Chicago as the city where *Rythm Mastr* takes place. In the following years, Marshall would make this reference subtler, eventually changing the name to Black Metropolis—an allusion to St. Clair Drake and Horace R. Cayton, Jr.'s eponymous book-length study, first published in 1945, about the Afro-American urban experience.

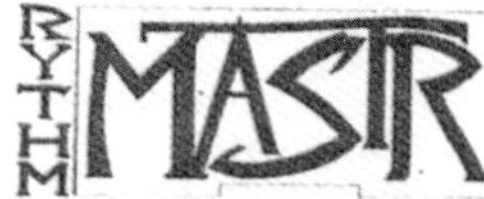

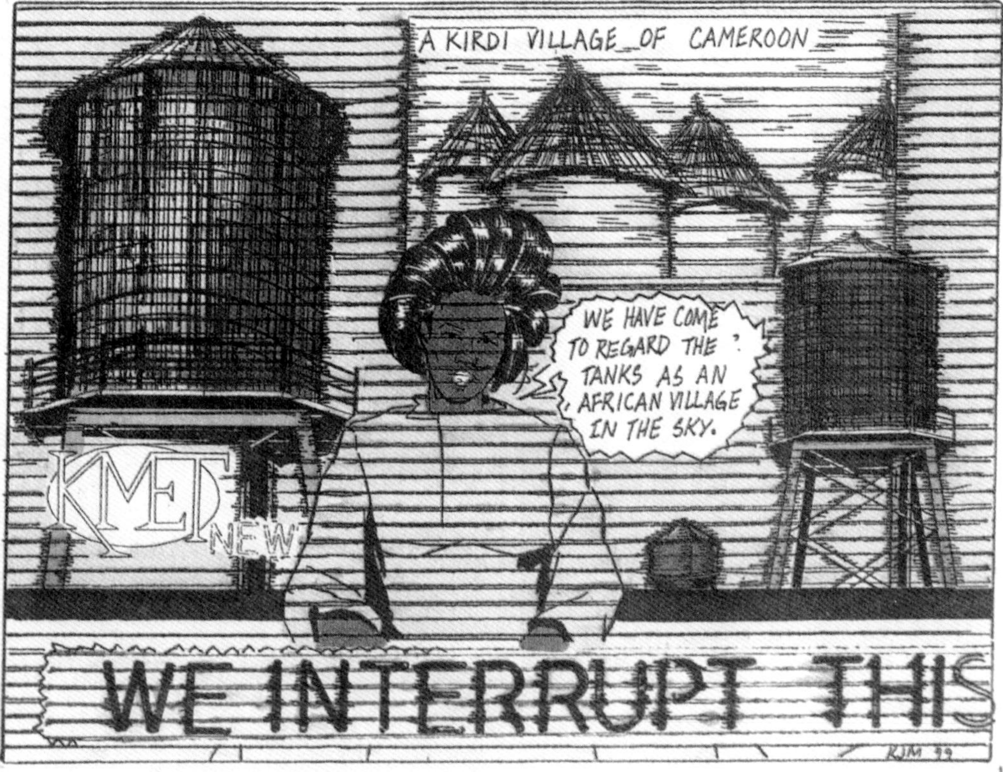

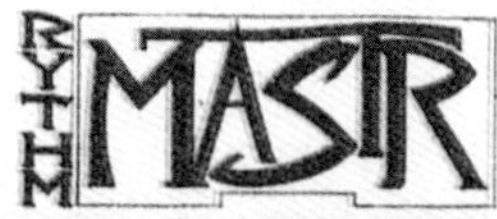

Second of eight panels. Last week: A TV newscast feature story was interrupted by breaking news.

This cartoon is a component of artist Kerry James Marshall's installation in the 1999 Carnegie International, which may be seen at the Carnegie Museum of Art through March 26, 2000.

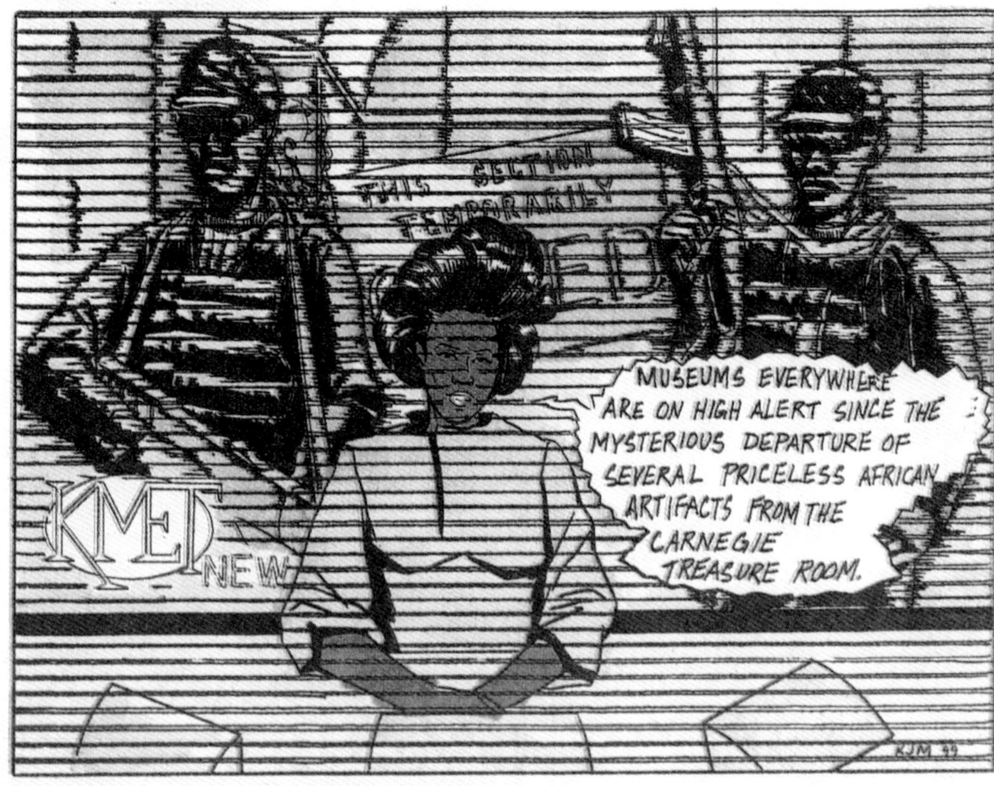

Pittsburgh Post-Gazette

Tuesday, November 9, 1999

INSIDE

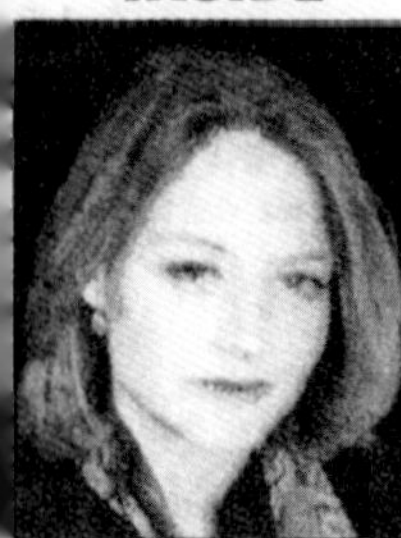

Jodie Foster

…ven though Jodie Foster …s she could make more …ney than she has ever …le, she won't do the "Si…ce of the Lambs" sequel …ause it is too grisly.
…OPLE, PAGE D-7.

…ivorced women often … themselves in financial …os. However, certified di…ce planners can help …n avoid the pitfalls.
…ESTYLE, PAGE D-2.

…he Open Stage Theater …duction of "Booth" at …nburg Studio presents an …resting look at the Booth …ily, regarded as among … world's leading Shake…areans.
…E, PAGE D-3.

…Gary & Mike" is the lat… animated show hitting …ne time in hopes of be…ing the next "Simpsons."
…LEVISION, PAGE D-6.

ALSO INSIDE

…all of all.

A telephone survey of Americans found that 76 percent were "not at all likely" or "not very likely" to take a vacation when the annual odometer turns over to 2000. They either want to spend the holiday at home or are turned off by possible Y2K computer glitches, claustrophobic crowds, lack of time or money.

That leaves a combined 24 percent who said they were very or somewhat likely to travel. And three out of five of them planned to use their own car, truck or RV — with only a third intending to fly, which is seen as dicey by nervous vacationers.

You can celebrate the millennium

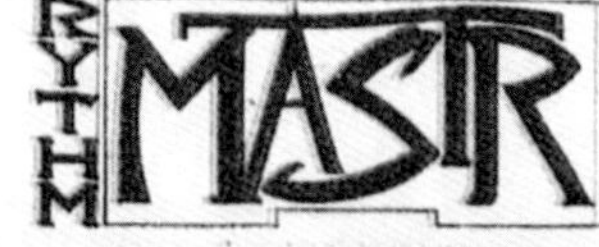

largest game of musical chairs. And, strangely enough, it has nothing to do with saving parking spaces during a snowstorm.

The outdoor game, at Liberty Avenue and Sixth Street, is one of scores of activities planned for New Year's Eve. You can party on the Roberto Clemente Bridge with homegrown musicians The Clarks, tour

SEE **PARTIES,** PAGE D-4

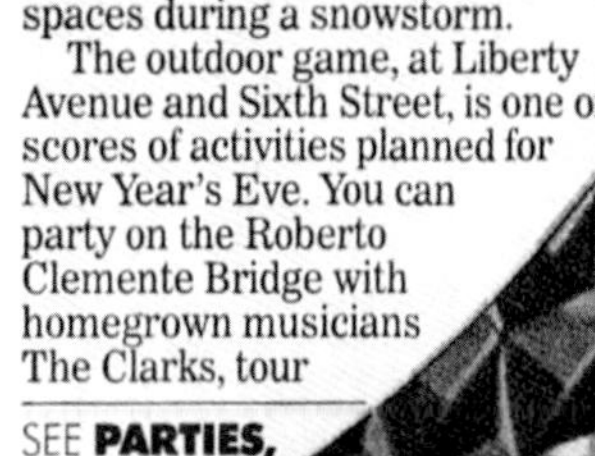

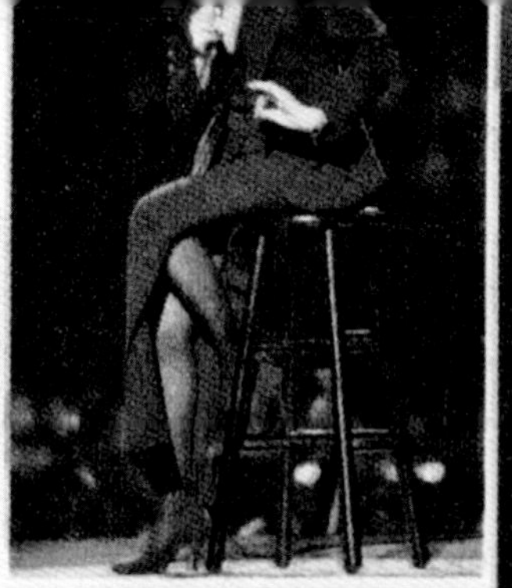

Las Vegas, with packages starting at $3,999. If your schedule won't permit you to catch her party, don't worry. Disney World's celebration runs for 15 months.

RYTHM MASTR

Second of eight panels. Last week: A TV newscast feature story was interrupted by breaking news.

This cartoon is a component of artist Kerry James Marshall's installation in the 1999 Carnegie International, which may be seen at the Carnegie Museum of Art through March 26, 2000.

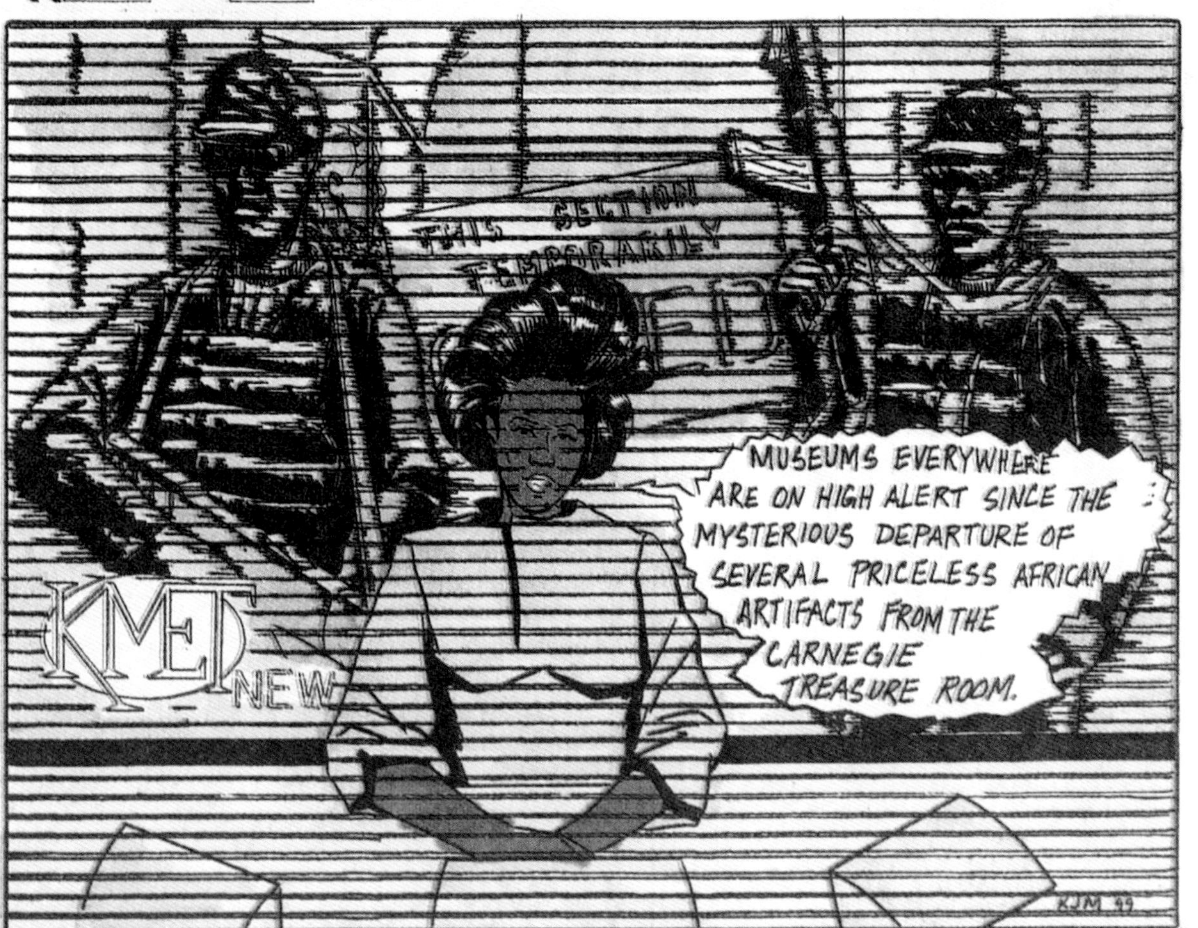

keep my answers simple and straightforward. If I had given goofy longer answers, I ran the risk of being interesting, and then some poor kid might have put aside his dream of going to medical school in favor of becoming a journalist. That would be a terrible thing to have on the conscience.

But I would like now to repeat the questions, my simple answers and then the longer clarifying answers that remained unsaid.

Why did you choose this occupation?

I like to write.

(Actually, my father was able to use his influence to get me a job. To my mind, family influence is not the worst crime, relatively speaking. The best advice for an eighth-grader seeking a job is to skip the career fairs and get to know Sheriff Pete DeFazio.)

To be utterly truthful, I don't like writing so much as I like to finish writing. The act of writing is too much like real work to be fun, and no sane person wants to do real work for a living.

What skills do you use in your job?

Writing skills, computer skills. (Also skills involving walking to the water fountain creatively and, of course, bladder-control skills — some of those editorial meetings can really drag on.

What kind of education or training is needed?

A bachelor's degree in journalism. (Or a degree of concussion from the University of Hard Knocks, which is what I have.)

What kinds of hours do you work in your job?

About 9.30 a.m. to 6.30 p.m. usually. (But it's nonstop, nose to the grindstone and no time for lunch. Also Sunday work on occasion. Payroll department, please note.)

Describe your work environment.

A regular office. (A regular office staffed by crazed and insecure egotists.)

What is the long range (next 10 years) outlook for workers in your occupation?

Good in the short term; the Internet has made long-range prediction difficult, but there'll always be journalists. (Sorry!)

This role model business is a cinch. Feel free to model yourself after me now that you have been fully informed.

Reg Henry's e-mail address is rhenry@post-gazette.com.

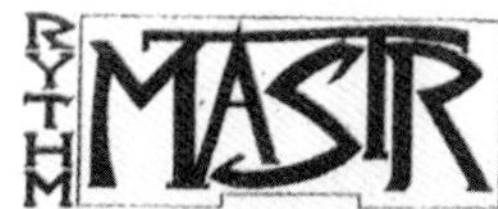

Third of eight panels. Last week: Live TV footage of armed guards posted at the museum after priceless African artifacts disappear from the Carnegie Treasure Room.

This cartoon is a component of artist Kerry James Marshall's installation in the 1999 Carnegie International, which may be seen at the Carnegie Museum of Art through March 26, 2000.

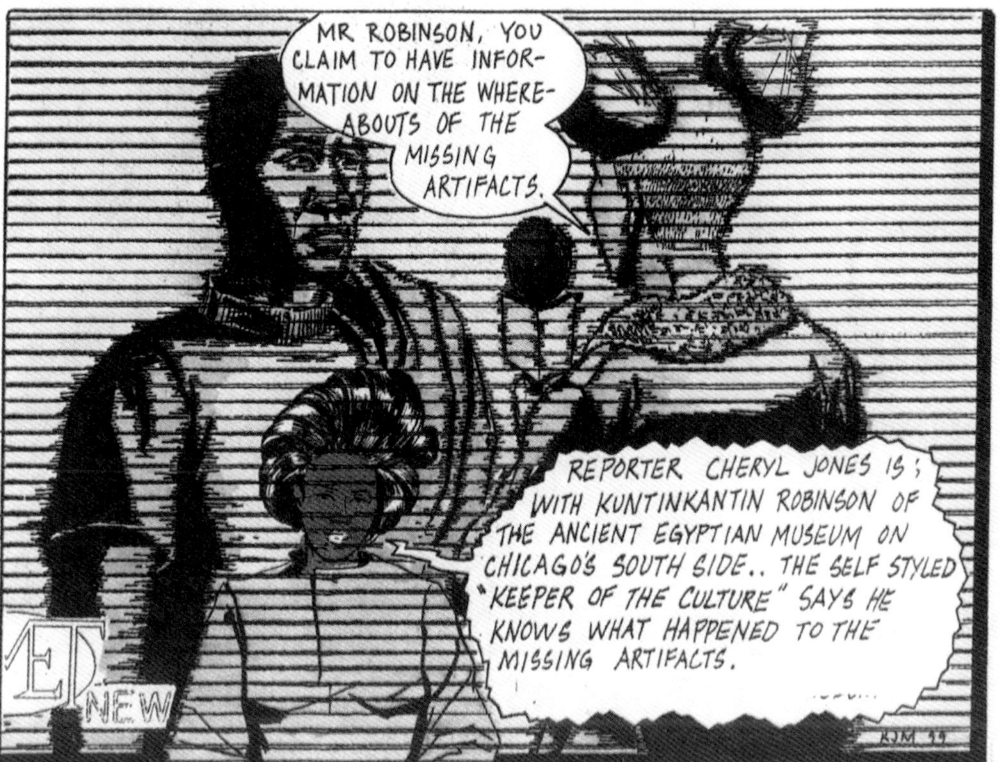

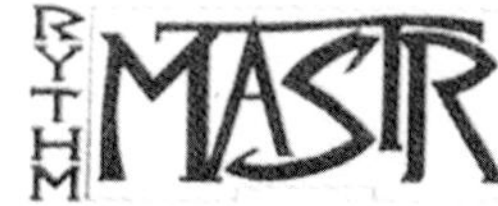

Fourth of eight panels. Last week: A TV reporter asks self-styled "keeper of the culture" Kuntinkantin Robinson for information about the African artifacts that were recently stolen from a local museum.

This cartoon is a component of artist Kerry James Marshall's installation in the 1999 Carnegie International, which may be seen at the Carnegie Museum of Art through March 26, 2000.

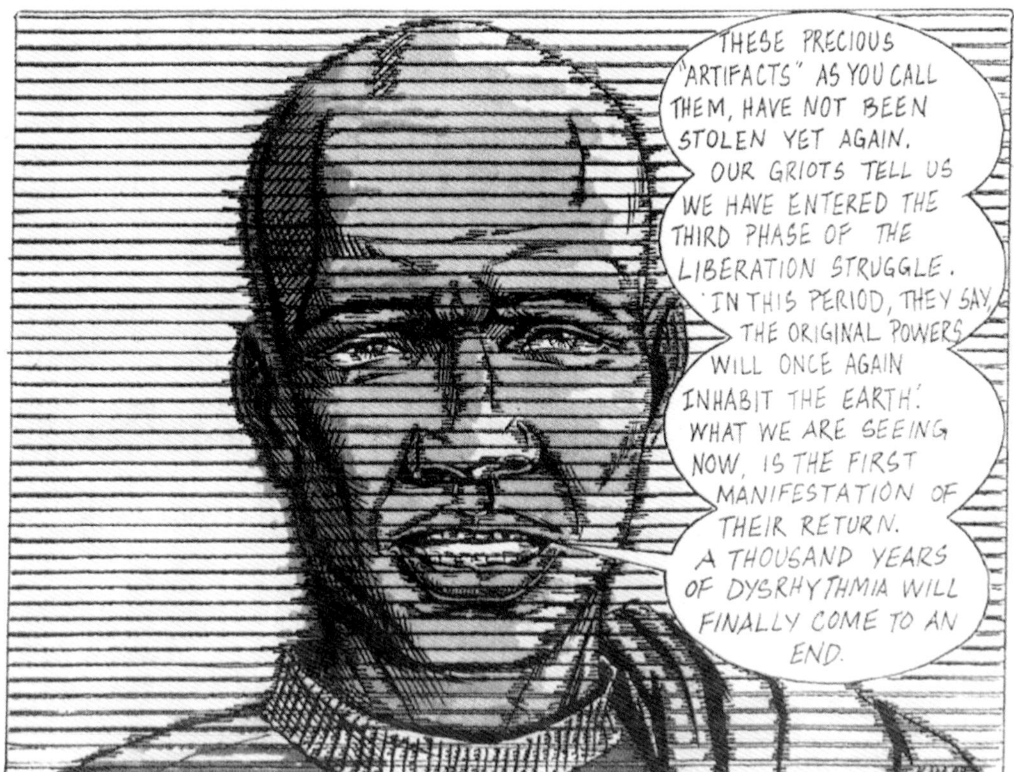

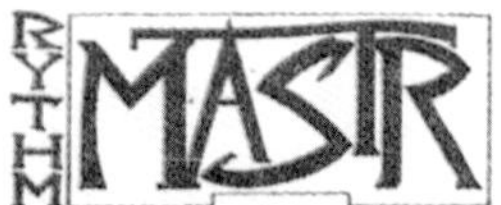

Fifth of eight panels. Last week: The self-styled "keeper of the culture" tells a TV reporter that the African artifacts that disappeared from a museum weren't stolen, but rather have become part of the liberation struggle to return the original powers of the Earth to control.

This cartoon is a component of artist Kerry James Marshall's installation in the 1999 Carnegie International, which may be seen at the Carnegie Museum of Art through March 26, 2000.

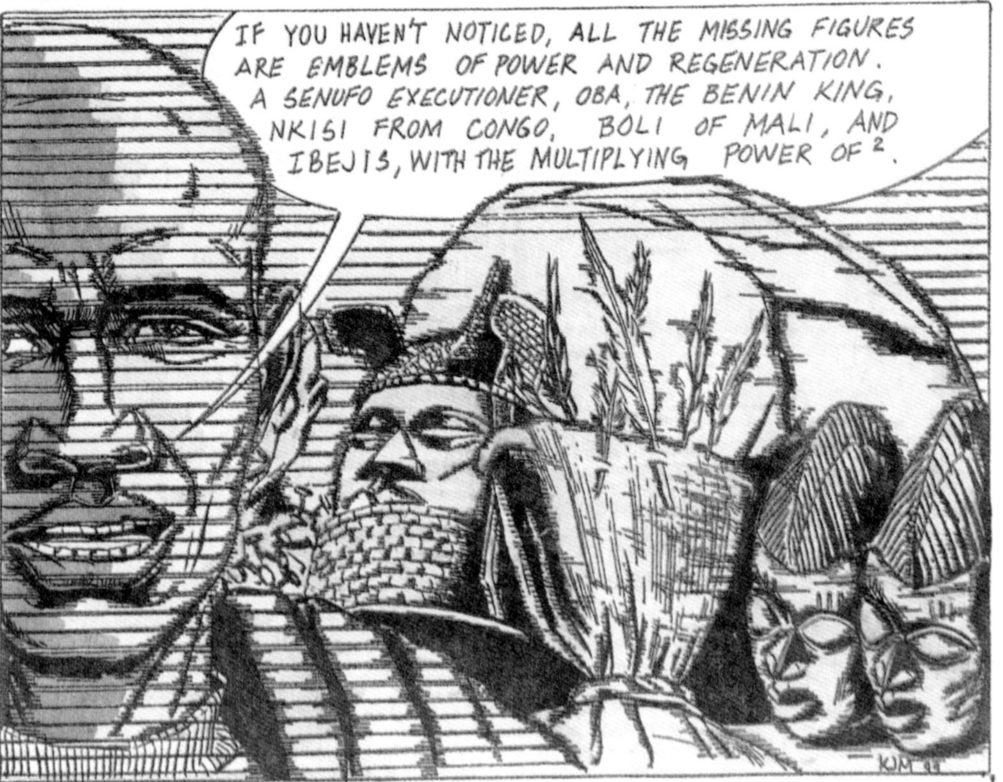

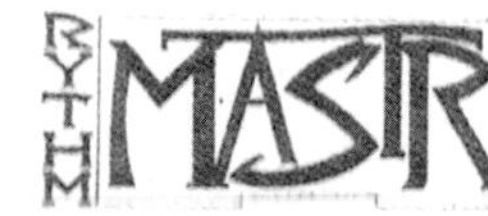

Sixth of eight panels. Last week: The self-styled "keeper of the culture" points out that missing African figures are all emblems of power and regeneration that have joined the street struggle to restore traditional cultural practices.

This cartoon is a component of artist Kerry James Marshall's installation in the 1999 Carnegie International, which may be seen at the Carnegie Museum of Art through March 26, 2000.

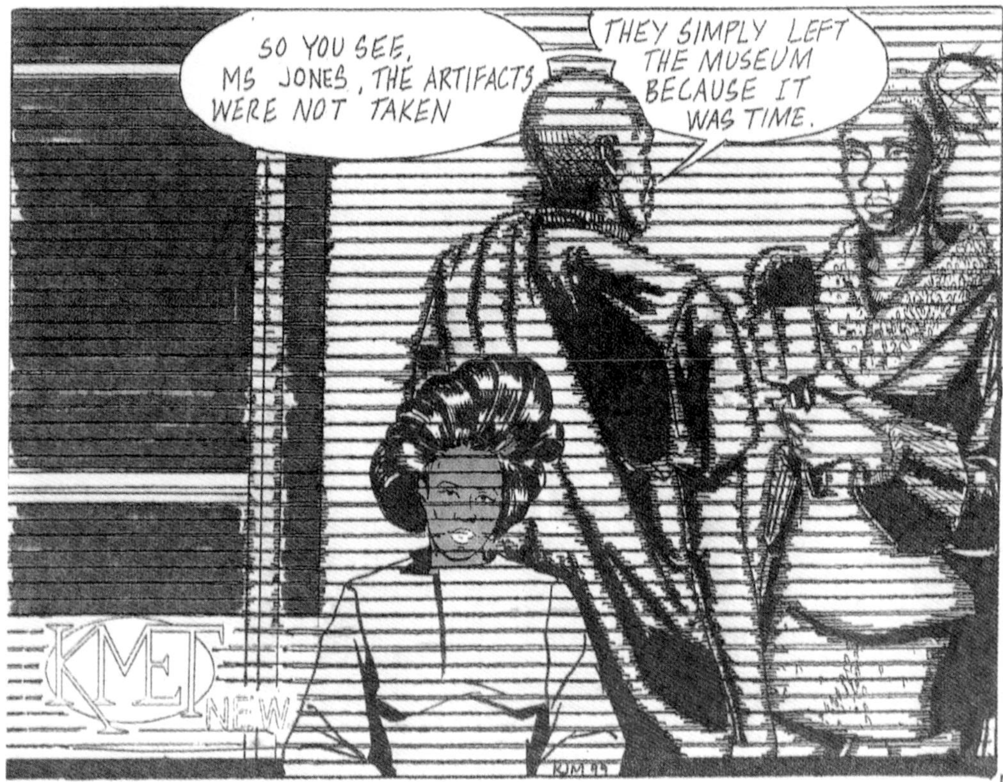

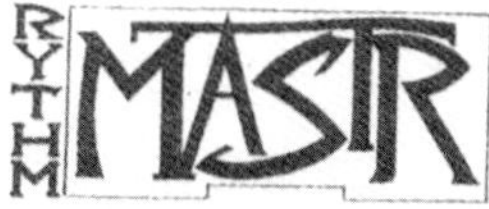

Seventh of eight panels. Last week: The self-styled "keeper of the culture" tells a TV reporter that African artifacts missing from a museum weren't taken, but rather left on their own to join the struggle to restore traditional cultural powers.

This cartoon is a component of artist Kerry James Marshall's installation in the 1999 Carnegie International, which may be seen at the Carnegie Museum of Art through March 26, 2000.

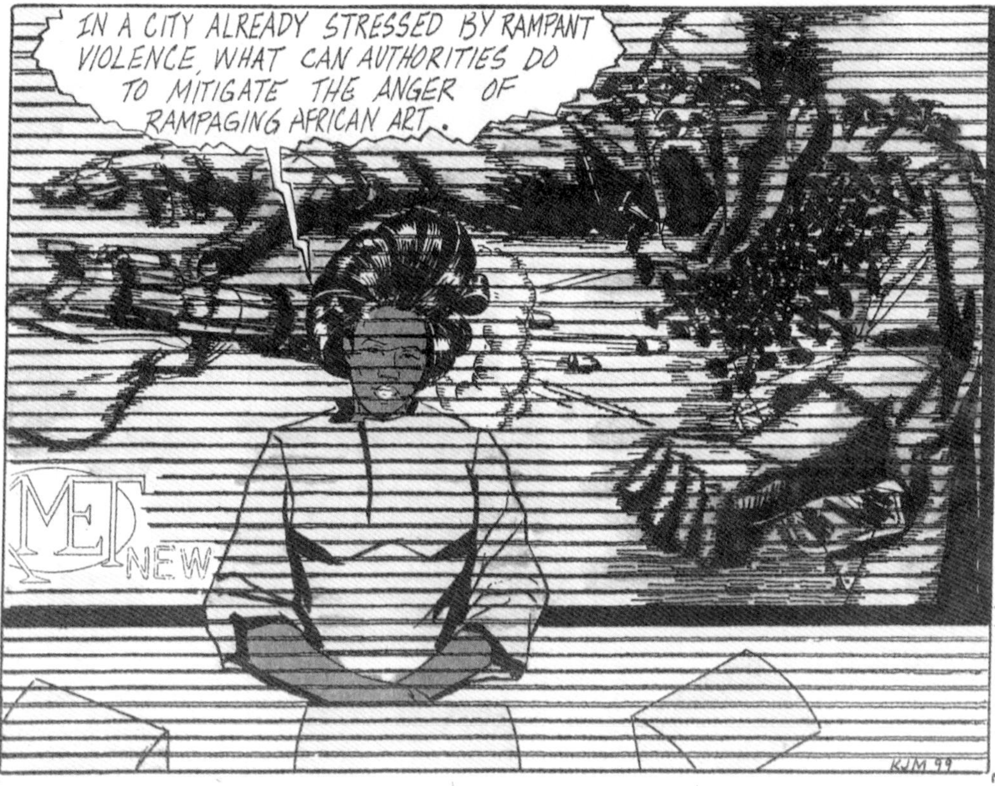

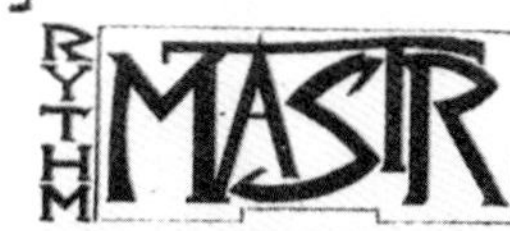

Eighth of eight panels. Last week: A TV newscaster asks how authorities can deal with rampaging African art in an already violent city, while in the background news footage shows a charging Congo *nkisi* (power figure) being gunned down.

This cartoon is a component of artist Kerry James Marshall's installation in the 1999 Carnegie International, which may be seen at the Carnegie Museum of Art through March 26, 2000.

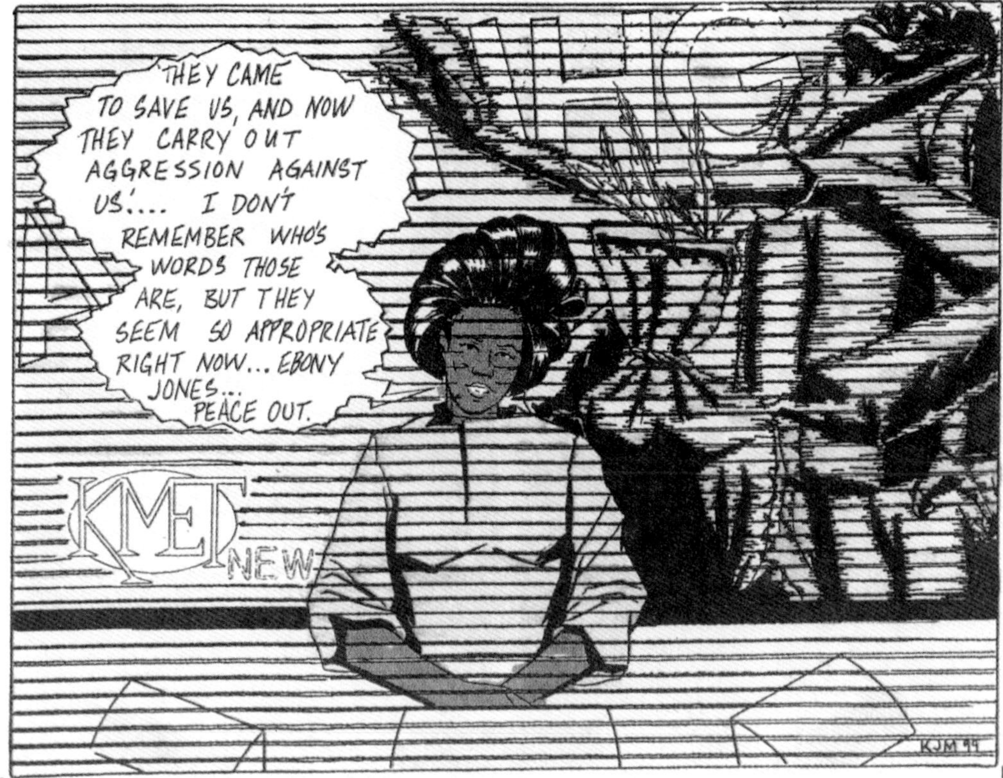

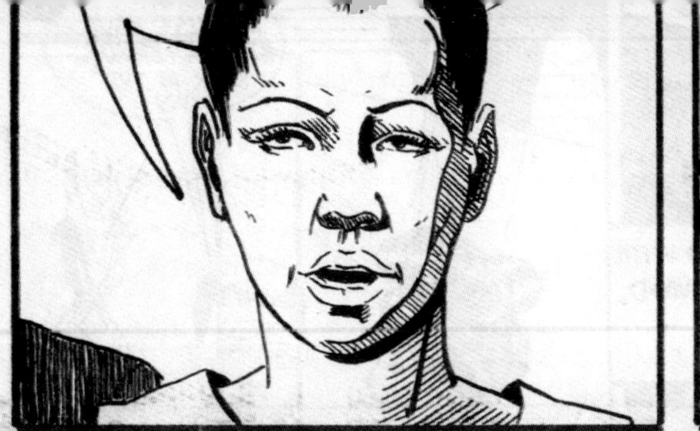

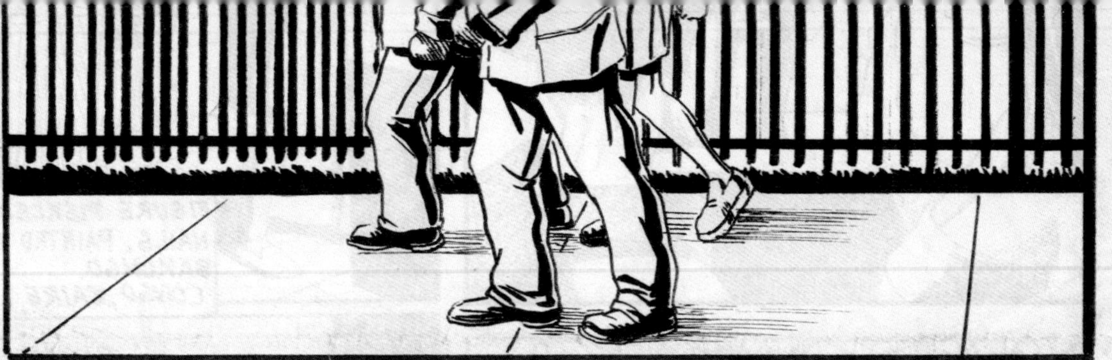

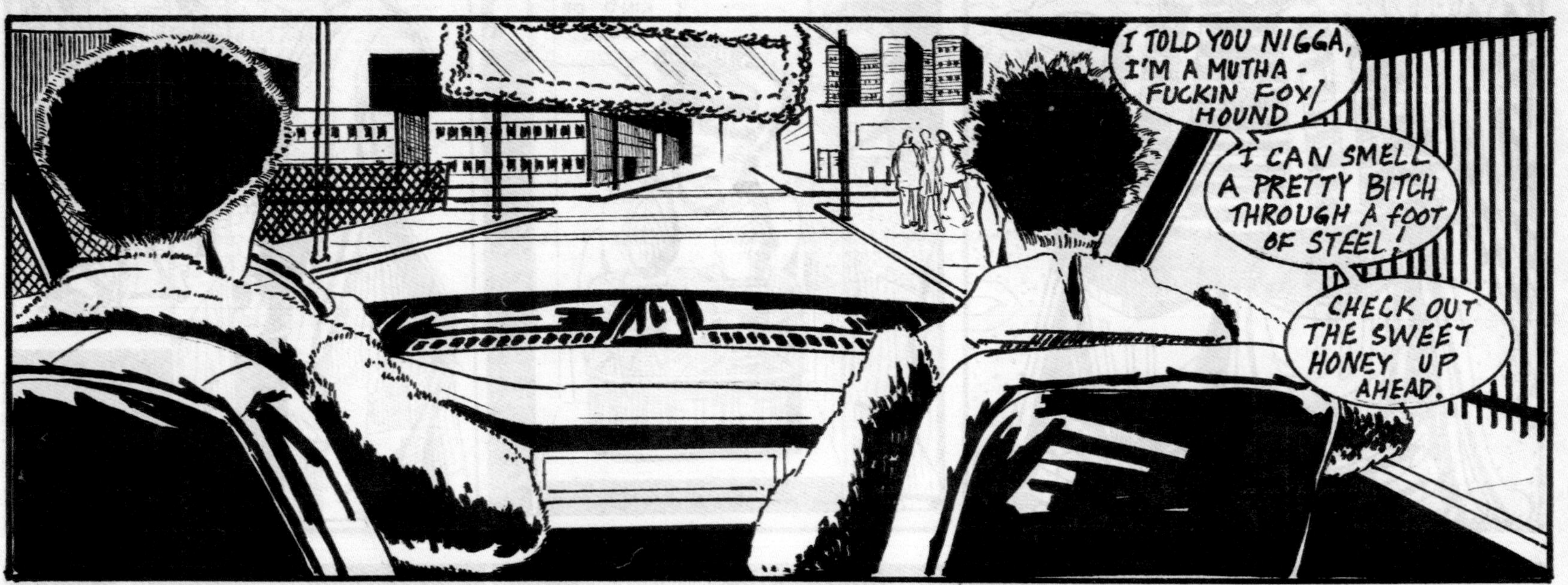
I TOLD YOU NIGGA, I'M A MUTHA-FUCKIN FOX/HOUND
I CAN SMELL A PRETTY BITCH THROUGH A FOOT OF STEEL!
CHECK OUT THE SWEET HONEY UP AHEAD.

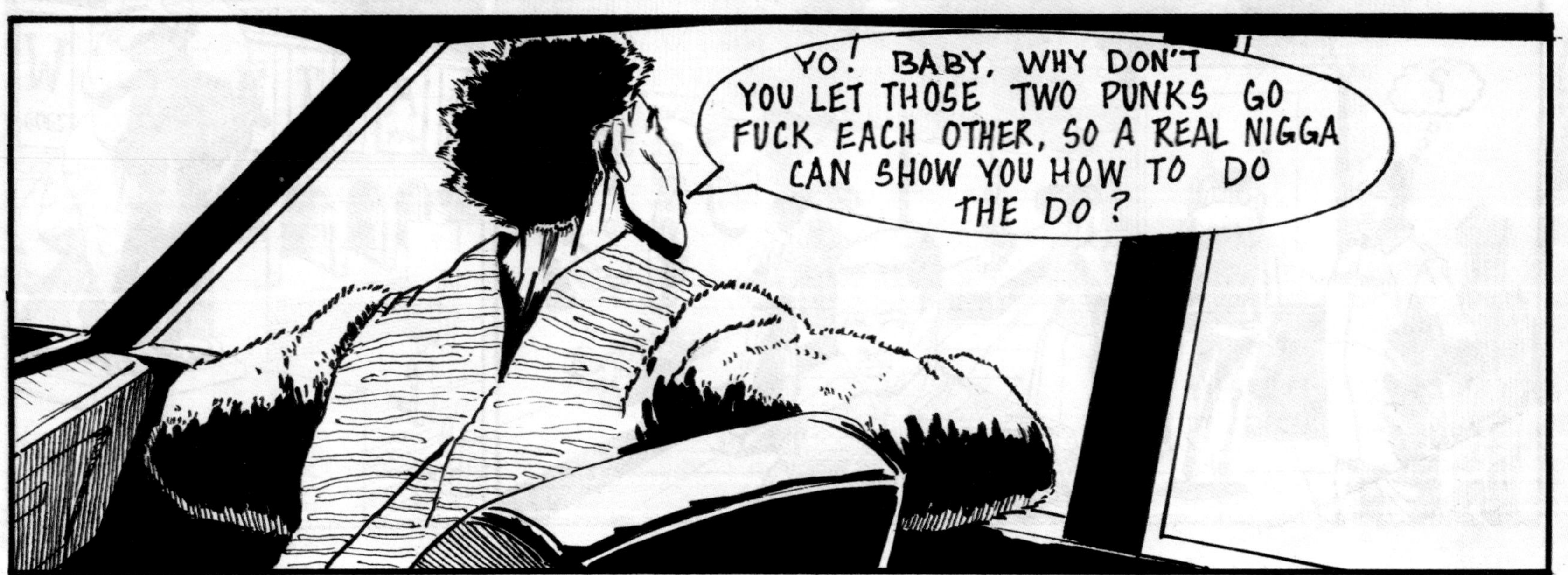
YO! BABY, WHY DON'T YOU LET THOSE TWO PUNKS GO FUCK EACH OTHER, SO A REAL NIGGA CAN SHOW YOU HOW TO DO THE DO?

2001

RYTHM MASTR (NICC, ANTWERP)

Two double-sided offset lithographs on folded newsprint

Sheets: 17×11 ¼ in. (43×28.5 cm) folded; 17×22 ½ in. (43×57 cm) unfolded

Edition: unknown

Printed by Newsweb Corporation, Chicago. Produced for *The Big Show*, NICC, Antwerp, 2001

When curator Wim Peeters invited Marshall to show *Rythm Mastr* at NICC in Antwerp in 2001, the artist took the exhibition as an opportunity to revisit *Rythm Mastr* and make changes that would end up having a lasting impact on the series. One of these revisions was to make the strip in black and white, a decision reached after examining *Marvel Essentials*, a collection of vintage stories from the 1980s later reprinted on coarse matte paper. The enhancing effect of the absence of color on Marshall's drawings sealed the visual presentation of *Rythm Mastr*, which from then on would be almost exclusively inked in black and white. The eight-page story arc expands on the events that would forever alter Stasha and Farrell's lives. A heavily restyled Nkisi is the only one from the original five Yoruba superheroes to be featured in this segment. This is the last known part of the series laid out as a comic book page, in a mix of pure grids, vertical and horizontal staggering, and blockage. Stasha's flight, to Farrell's concern, is presented here for the first time, laying the groundwork for an extensive series of prints and panels on the subject.

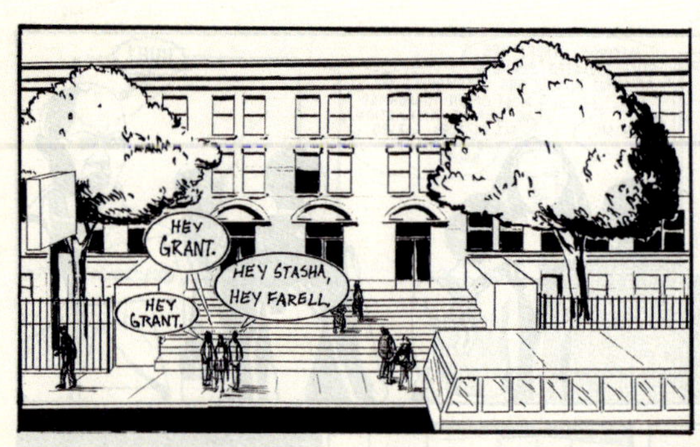
HEY GRANT.
HEY STASHA, HEY FARELL.
HEY GRANT.

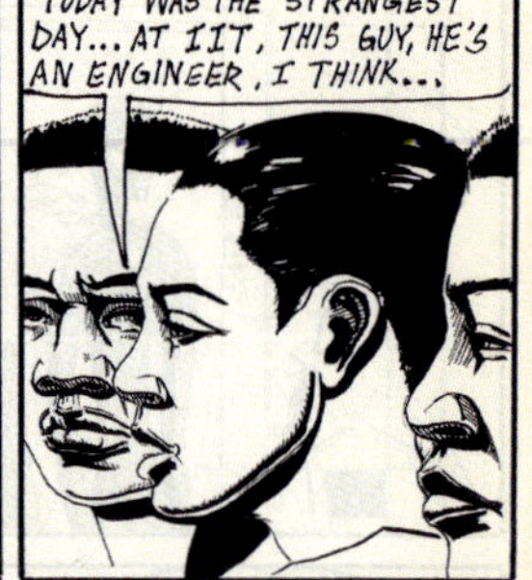
TODAY WAS THE STRANGEST DAY... AT IIT, THIS GUY, HE'S AN ENGINEER, I THINK...

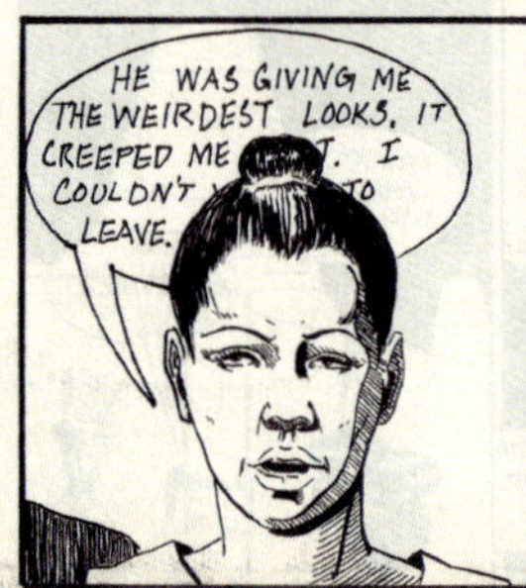
HE WAS GIVING ME THE WEIRDEST LOOKS, IT CREEPED ME T. I COULDN'T TO LEAVE.

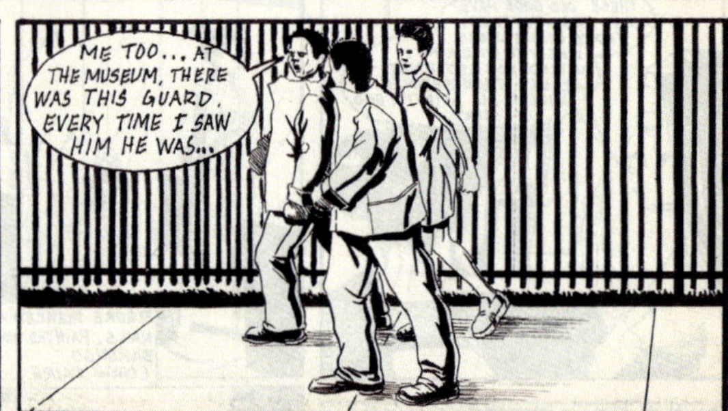
ME TOO... AT THE MUSEUM, THERE WAS THIS GUARD. EVERY TIME I SAW HIM HE WAS...

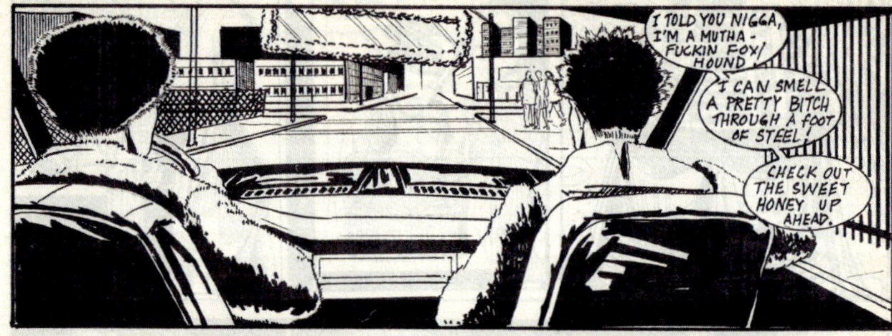
I TOLD YOU NIGGA, I'M A MUTHA-FUCKIN FOX HOUND!
I CAN SMELL A PRETTY BITCH THROUGH A FOOT OF STEEL!
CHECK OUT THE SWEET HONEY UP AHEAD.

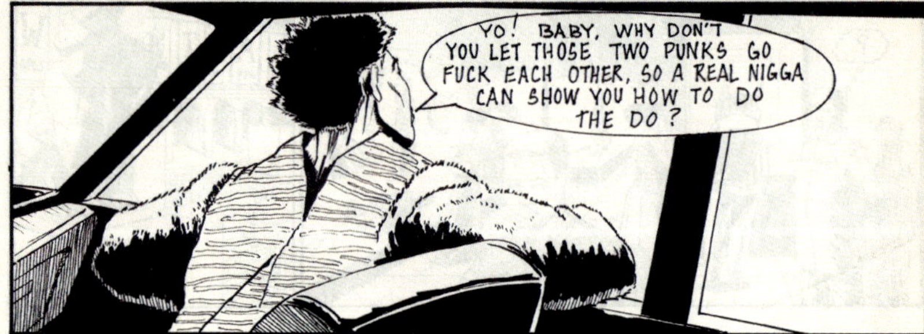
YO! BABY, WHY DON'T YOU LET THOSE TWO PUNKS GO FUCK EACH OTHER, SO A REAL NIGGA CAN SHOW YOU HOW TO DO THE DO?

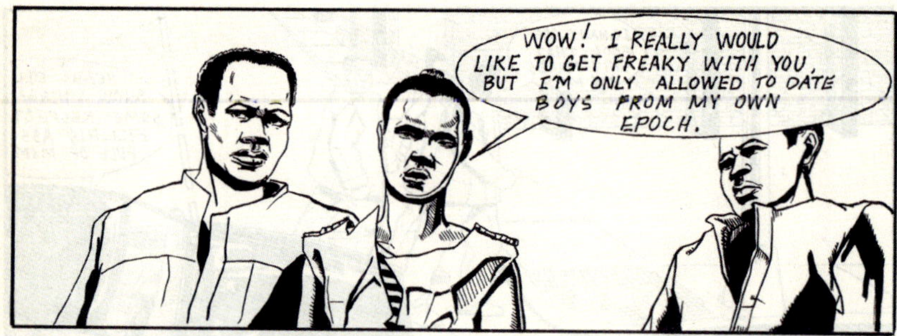
WOW! I REALLY WOULD LIKE TO GET FREAKY WITH YOU, BUT I'M ONLY ALLOWED TO DATE BOYS FROM MY OWN EPOCH.

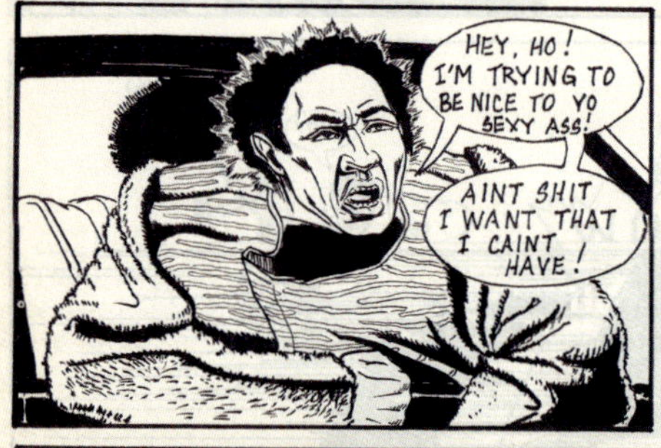
HEY, HO! I'M TRYING TO BE NICE TO YO SEXY ASS!
AINT SHIT I WANT THAT I CAINT HAVE!

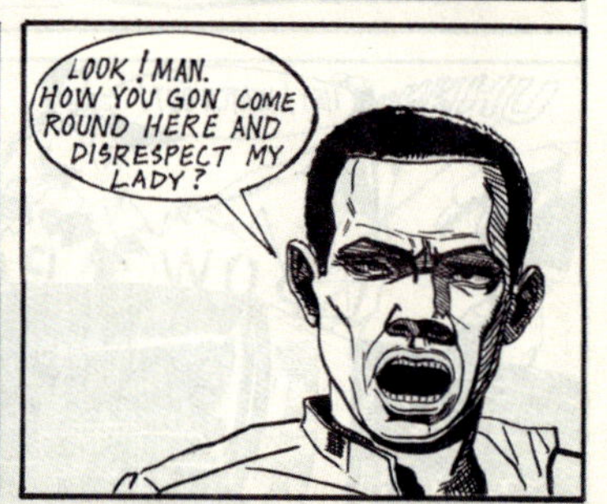
LOOK! MAN. HOW YOU GON COME ROUND HERE AND DISRESPECT MY LADY?

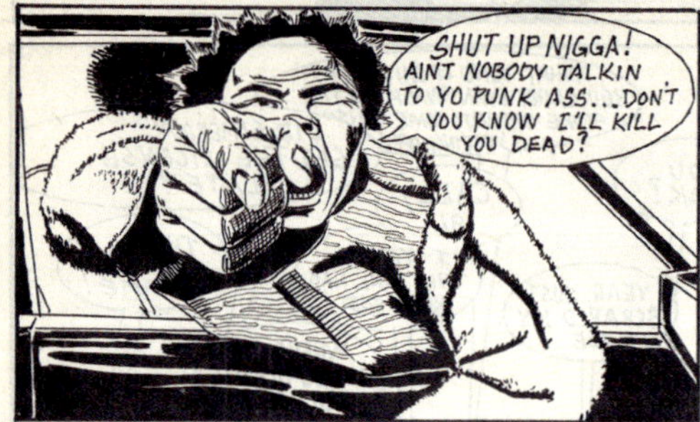
SHUT UP NIGGA! AIN'T NOBODY TALKIN TO YO PUNK ASS... DON'T YOU KNOW I'LL KILL YOU DEAD?

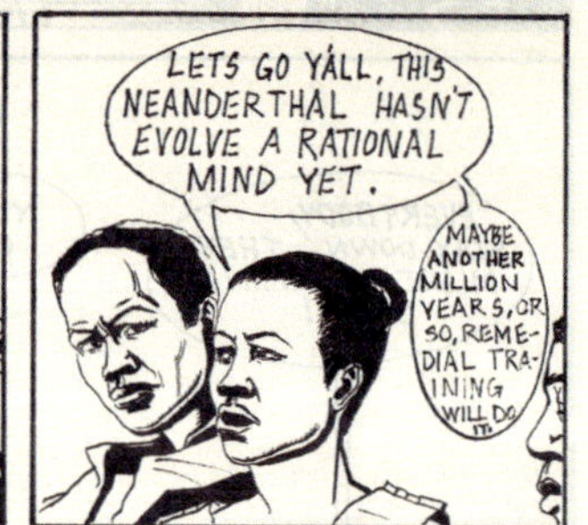
LETS GO YALL, THIS NEANDERTHAL HASN'T EVOLVE A RATIONAL MIND YET.
MAYBE ANOTHER MILLION YEARS, OR SO, REME-DIAL TRA-INING WILL DO IT.

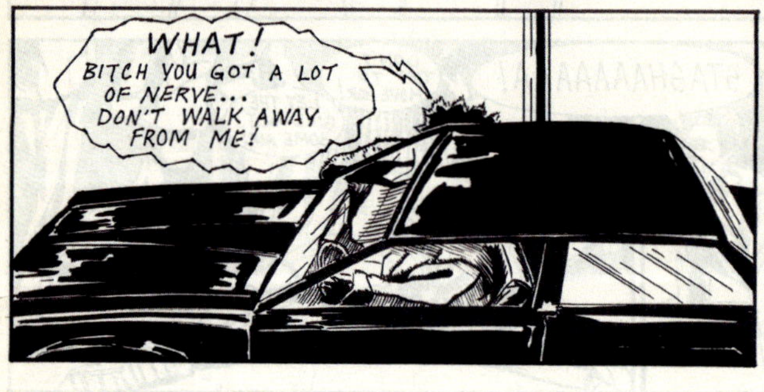
WHAT! BITCH YOU GOT A LOT OF NERVE... DON'T WALK AWAY FROM ME!

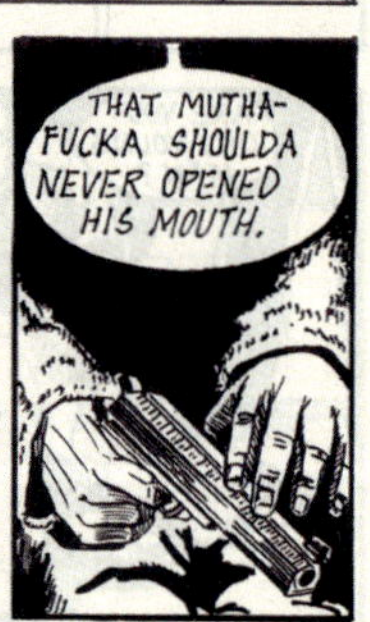
THAT MUTHA-FUCKA SHOULDA NEVER OPENED HIS MOUTH.

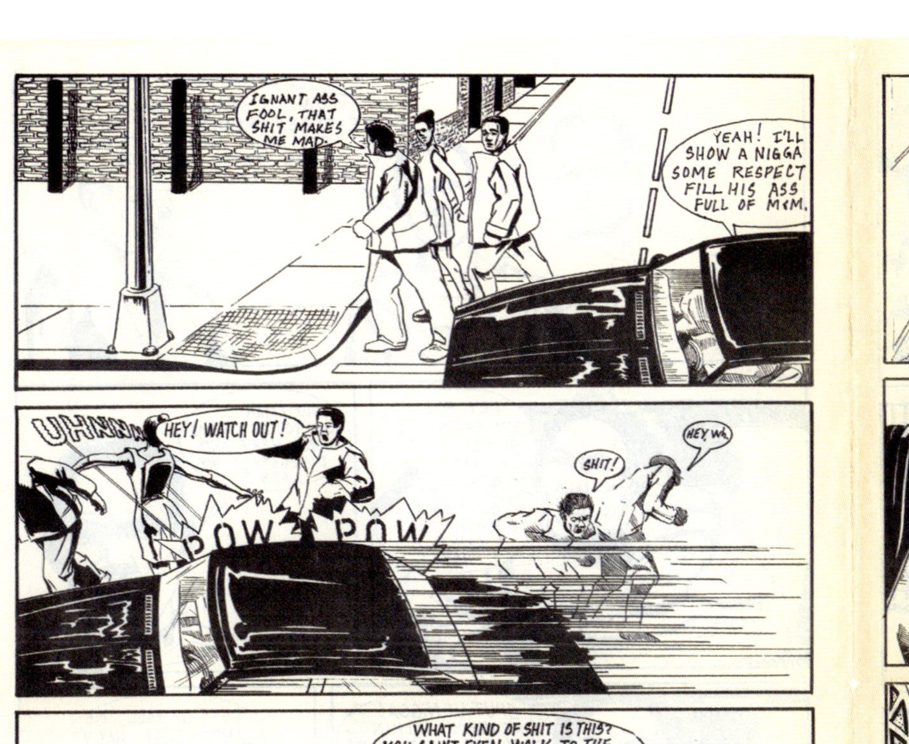
IGNANT ASS FOOL, THAT SHIT MAKES ME MAD.
YEAH! I'LL SHOW A NIGGA SOME RESPECT FILL HIS ASS FULL OF M&M.
UHNNN
HEY! WATCH OUT!
SHIT!
HEY, W...
POW POW

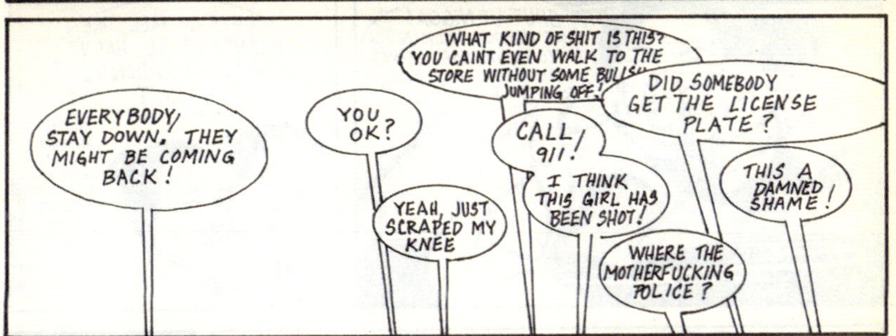
EVERYBODY STAY DOWN. THEY MIGHT BE COMING BACK!
YOU OK?
YEAH, JUST SCRAPED MY KNEE
WHAT KIND OF SHIT IS THIS? YOU CAINT EVEN WALK TO THE STORE WITHOUT SOME BULLS... JUMPING OFF!
CALL 911!
I THINK THIS GIRL HAS BEEN SHOT!
DID SOMEBODY GET THE LICENSE PLATE?
THIS A DAMNED SHAME!
WHERE THE MOTHERFUCKING POLICE?

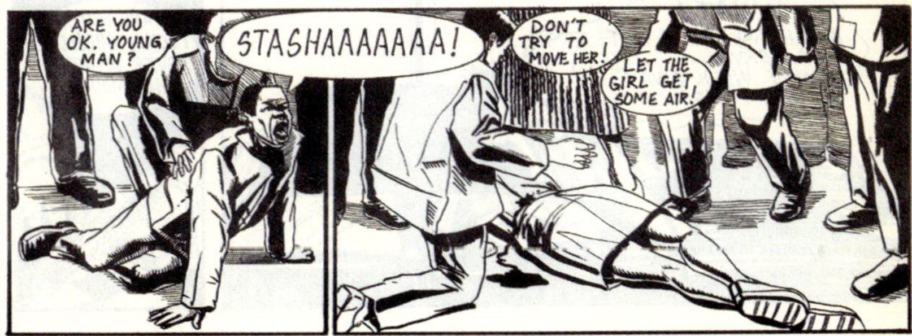
ARE YOU OK, YOUNG MAN?
STASHAAAAAAA!
DON'T TRY TO MOVE HER!
LET THE GIRL GET SOME AIR!

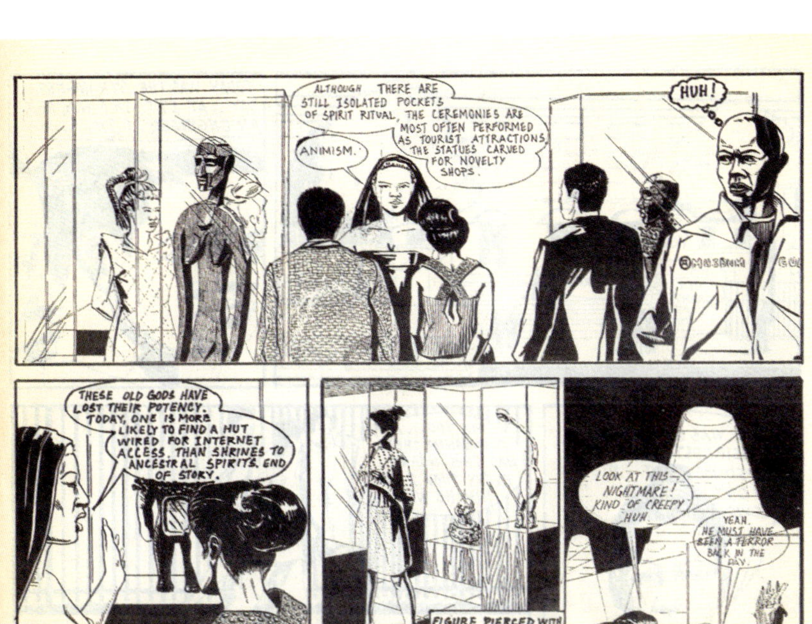
ALTHOUGH THERE ARE STILL ISOLATED POCKETS OF SPIRIT RITUAL, THE CEREMONIES ARE MOST OFTEN PERFORMED AS TOURIST ATTRACTIONS, THE STATUES CARVED FOR NOVELTY SHOPS.
ANIMISM.
HUH!
THESE OLD GODS HAVE LOST THEIR POTENCY. TODAY, ONE IS MORE LIKELY TO FIND A HUT WIRED FOR INTERNET ACCESS THAN SHRINES TO ANCESTRAL SPIRITS. END OF STORY.

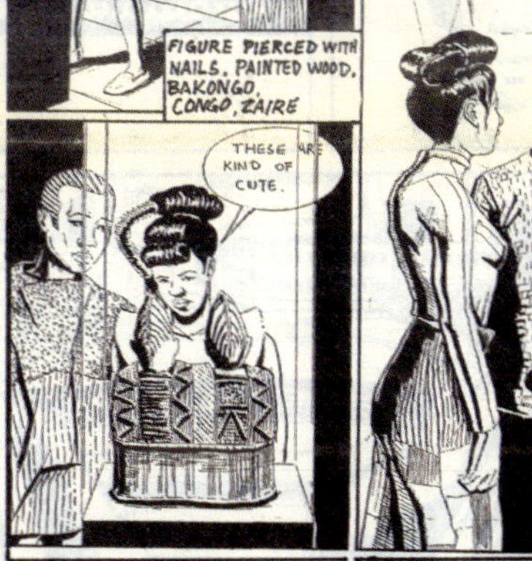
FIGURE PIERCED WITH NAILS, PAINTED WOOD, BAKONGO, CONGO, ZAIRE
LOOK AT THIS NIGHTMARE! KIND OF CREEPY HUH.
YEAH, HE MUST HAVE BEEN A TERROR BACK IN THE DAY.

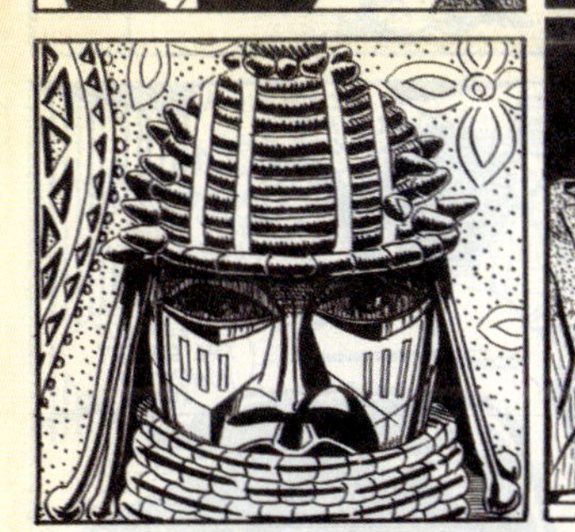
THESE ARE KIND OF CUTE.

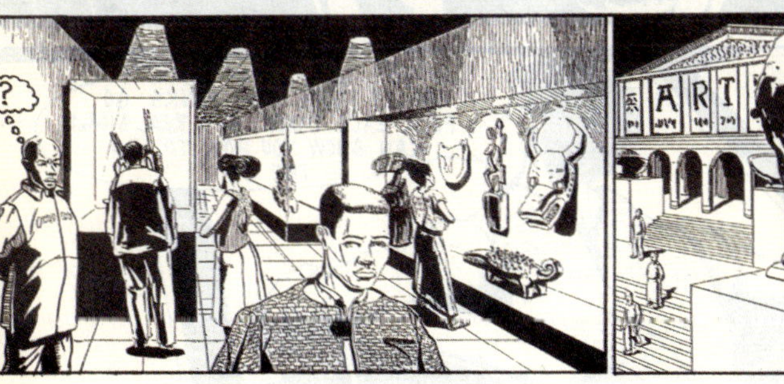
?
ART

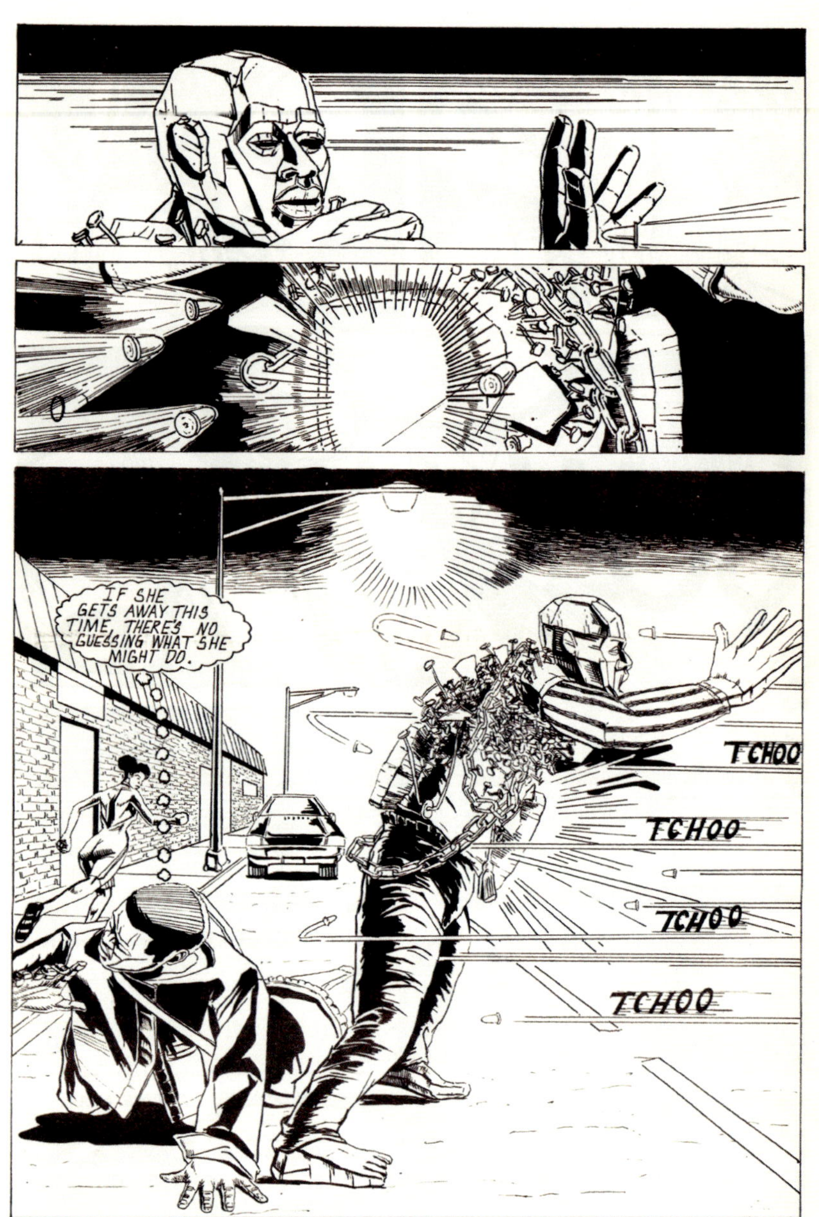
IF SHE GETS AWAY THIS TIME, THERE'S NO GUESSING WHAT SHE MIGHT DO.
TCHOO
TCHOO
TCHOO
TCHOO

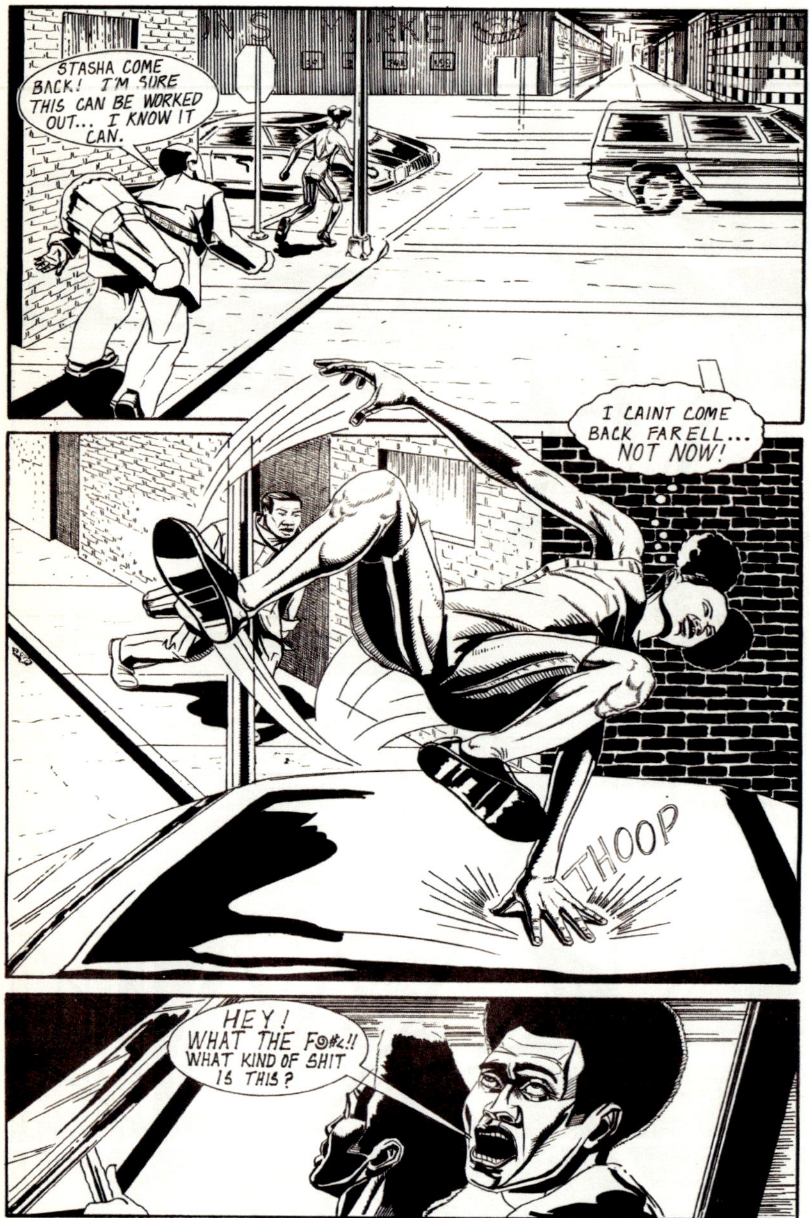
STASHA COME BACK! I'M SURE THIS CAN BE WORKED OUT... I KNOW IT CAN.
I CAINT COME BACK FARELL... NOT NOW!
THOOP
HEY! WHAT THE F@#¢!! WHAT KIND OF SHIT IS THIS?

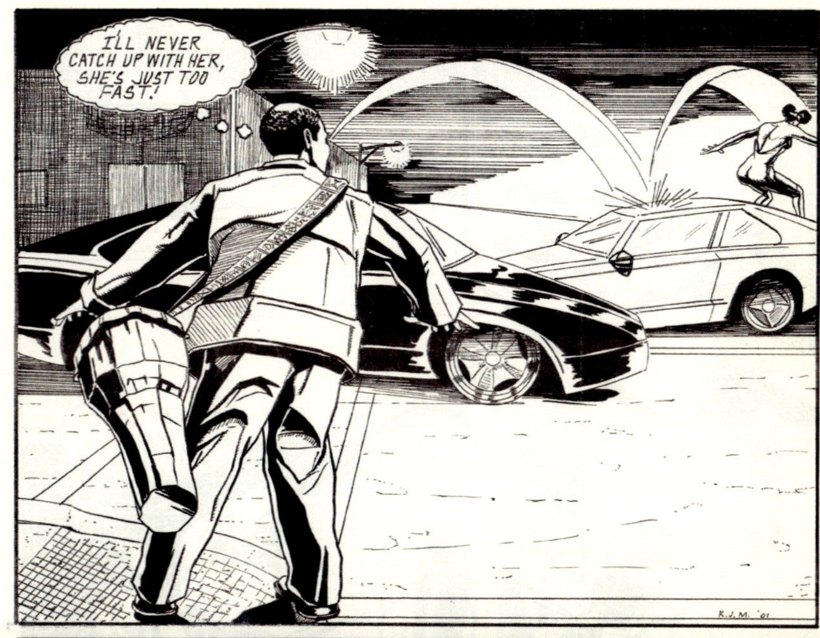
I'LL NEVER CATCH UP WITH HER, SHE'S JUST TOO FAST!
K.J.M. '01

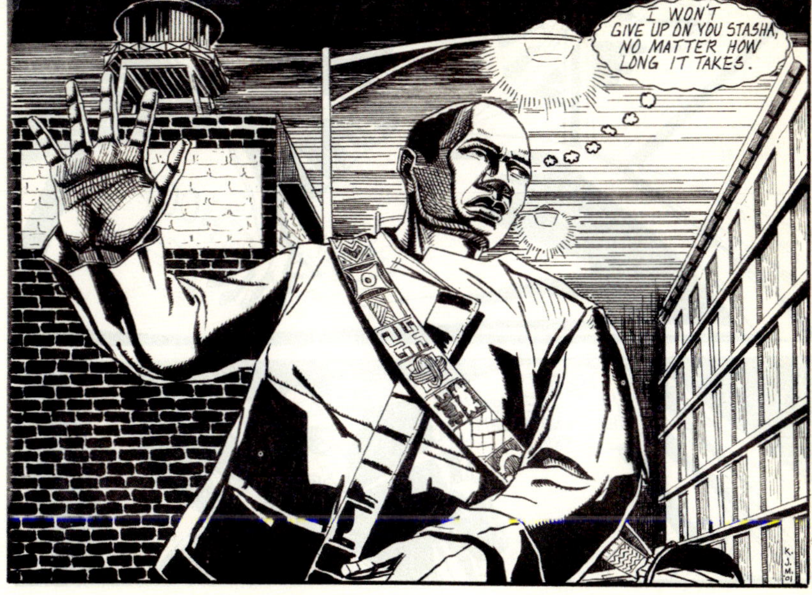
I WON'T GIVE UP ON YOU STASHA, NO MATTER HOW LONG IT TAKES.

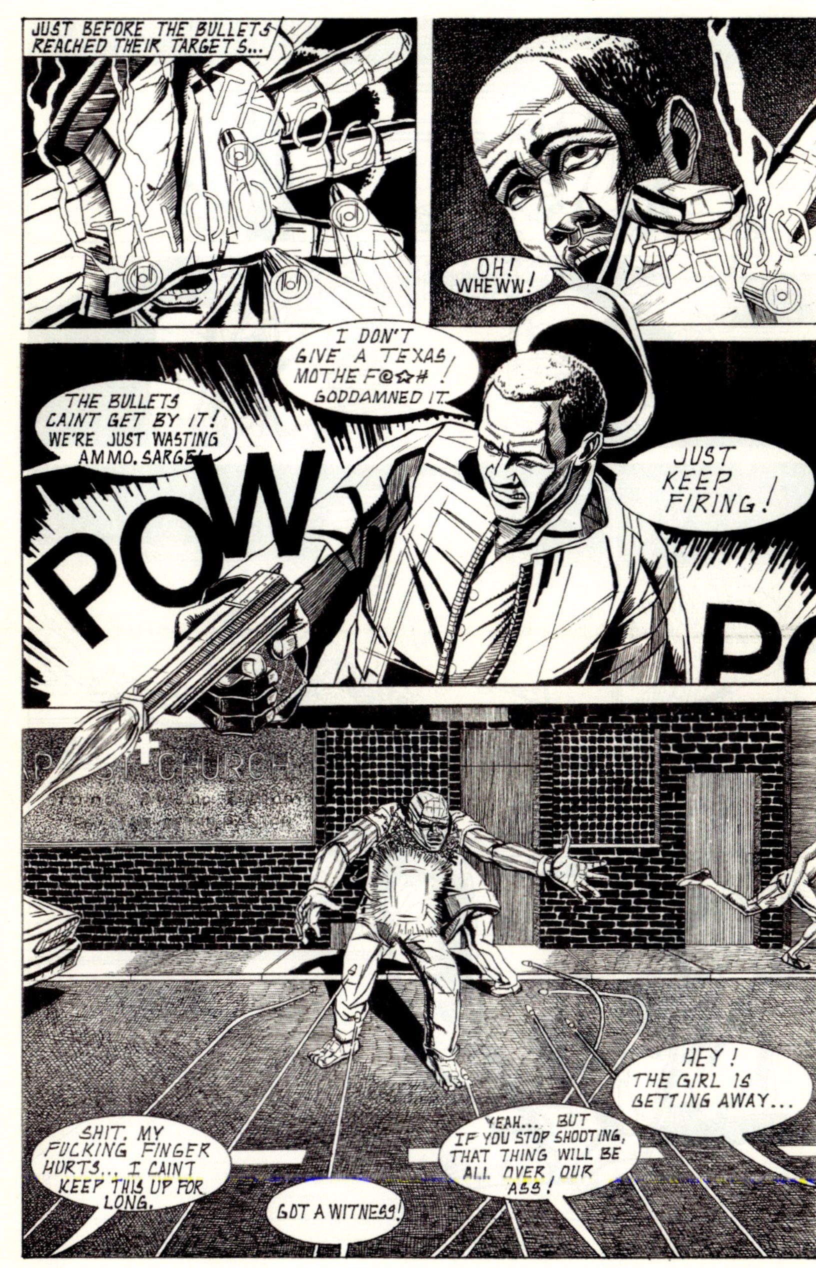
JUST BEFORE THE BULLETS REACHED THEIR TARGETS...
THOO
THOO
OH! WHEWW!
THOO
I DON'T GIVE A TEXAS MOTHE F@✿# ! GODDAMNED IT.
THE BULLETS CAINT GET BY IT! WE'RE JUST WASTING AMMO, SARGE!
JUST KEEP FIRING!
POW
SHIT, MY FUCKING FINGER HURTS... I CAINT KEEP THIS UP FOR LONG.
GOT A WITNESS!
YEAH... BUT IF YOU STOP SHOOTING, THAT THING WILL BE ALL OVER OUR ASS!
HEY! THE GIRL IS GETTING AWAY...

2003

ADRIFT

Inkjet on Plexiglas mounted on lightboxes

Each 48×36 in. (121.9×91.4 cm)

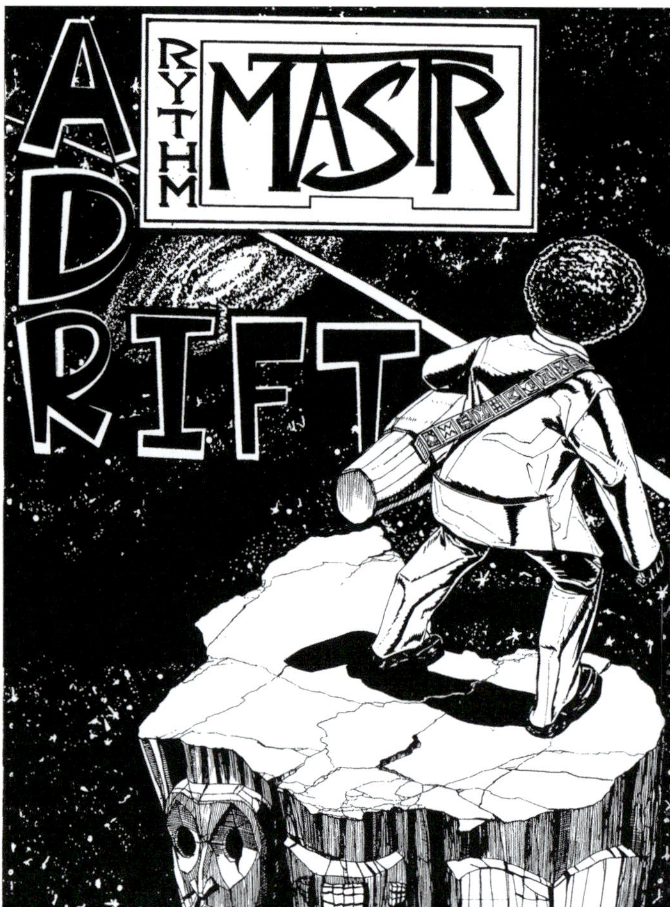

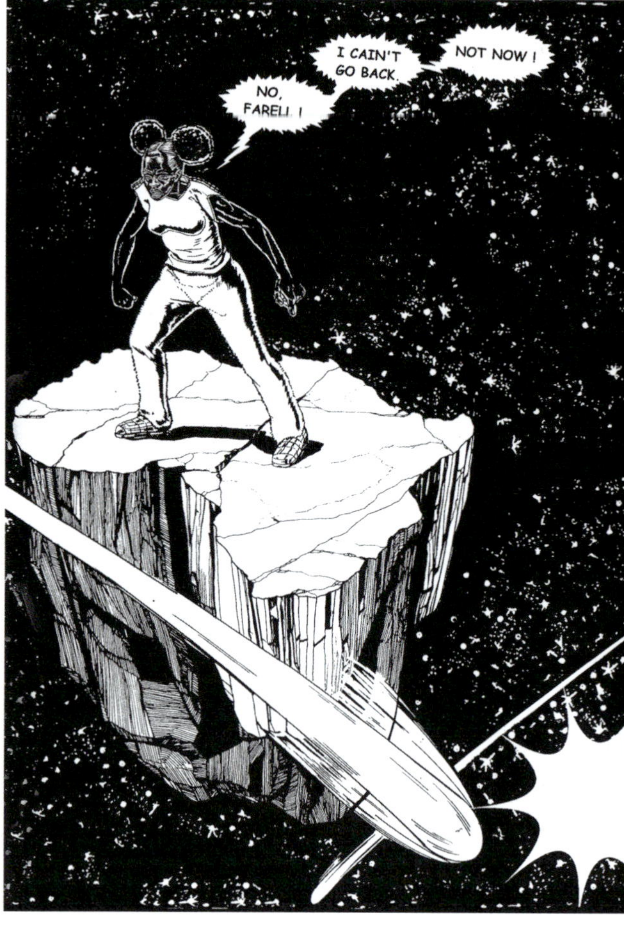

The philosophical battle between the two main protagonists of *Rythm Mastr*—Stasha's pragmatism versus Farrell's spiritualism—is the subject of the five-panel lightbox *Adrift* (2003). Set in outer space, with talking drums and satellites floating around a starry sky, the drawing is one of the most detailed of the series so far. Farrell's look is here subject to some developments: an afro is now firmly in place instead of the army haircut he sported in his previous outings. The cosmic debris supporting Farrell and Stasha is shaped like the African continent with the significant difference that Farrell's is carved with African masks. Marshall reinforced the cosmic vibe of the scenario by transferring the drawing onto a lightbox—a formal solution he would later discard.

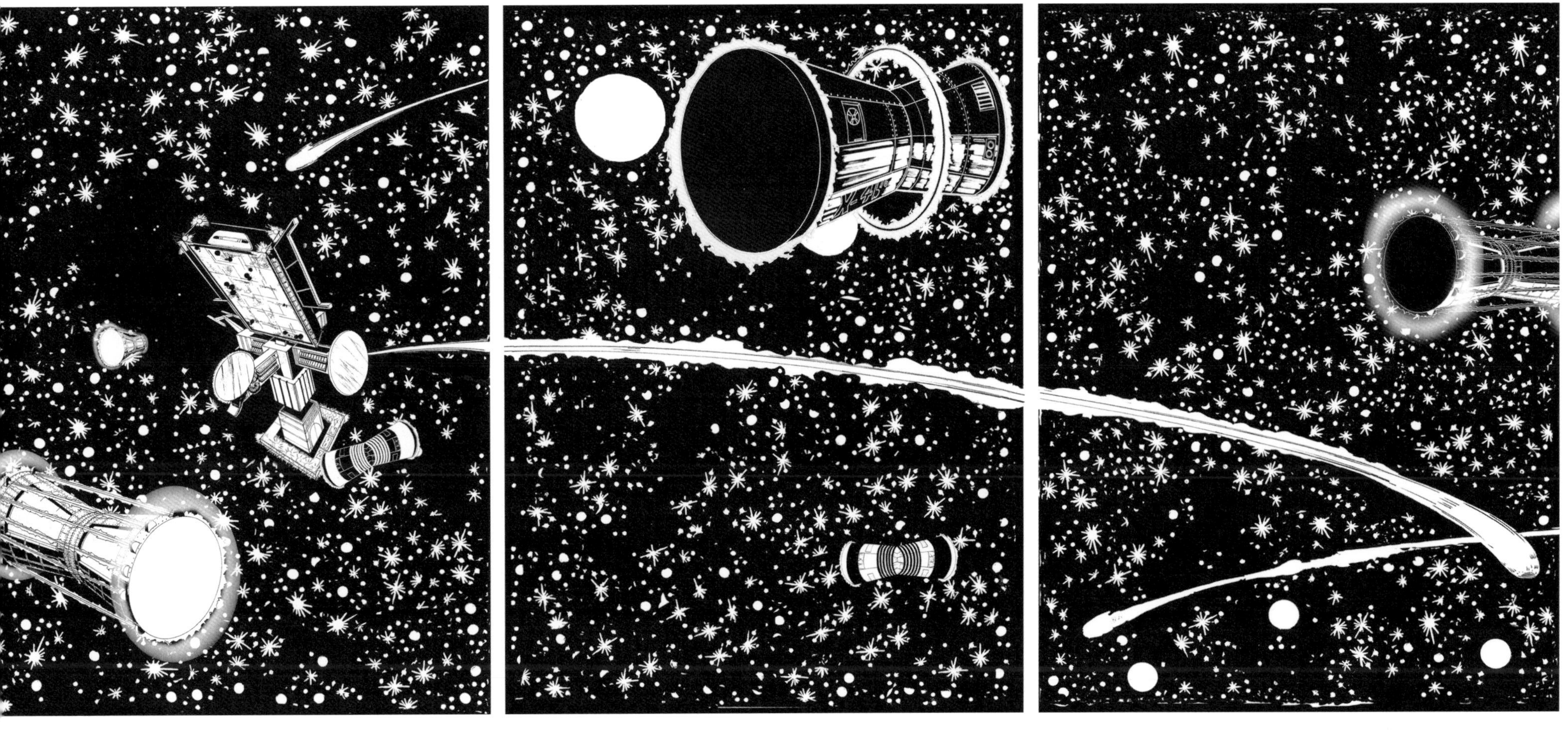

2003–2008

RYTHM MASTR DAILIES

Inkjet on newsprint

23×32 in. (58.5×81.5 cm)

44 unique compositions

Printed by the artist at Kinko's, Chicago

Marshall's introduction of the "Dailies" in 2003 contributed to considerably expanding the range and scope of *Rythm Mastr*. Inspired by the flexibility and breadth of possibility offered by the daily newspaper comics format, over the years Marshall has used the "Dailies" to present a rich variety of characters and situations, at times reprising elements and repositioning them in different contexts. If from a narrative standpoint the "Dailies" add little to the main story arc, their backup stories and vignettes further delve into the setting in which *Rythm Mastr* takes place, giving the author the opportunity to provide freewheeling commentary on a number of topics. Sociopolitical and art historical subjects are often debated, occasionally in vernacular Black English or in a foreign language, depending on where the piece is exhibited. Among the most notable additions are the Ho's Stroll (later renamed On the Stroll) and P-Van segments, who will introduce a set of future recurring characters. Although there seems to be a general convention around how they need to be presented (P-Van, for example, invariably has three frames in a row), the "Dailies" are generally conspicuous for their apparent lack of visual structure. Panels are either crowded or empty, making it difficult to discern why and where characters show up. Architectural features also claim a bigger role, with Marshall faithfully reproducing garden fences, brick walls, street views, and buildings from his neighborhood, including his own studio in Bronzeville.

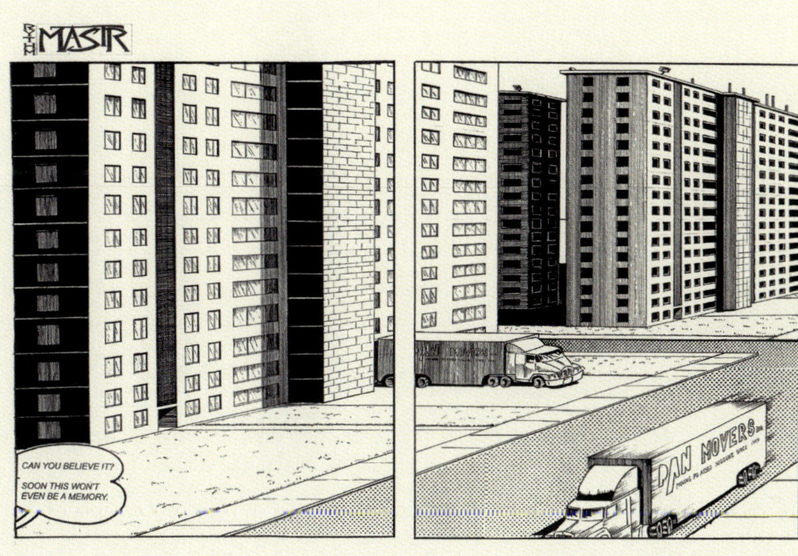
RYTHM MASTR
CAN YOU BELIEVE IT?
SOON THIS WON'T EVEN BE A MEMORY.
PAN MOVERS

RYTHM MASTR

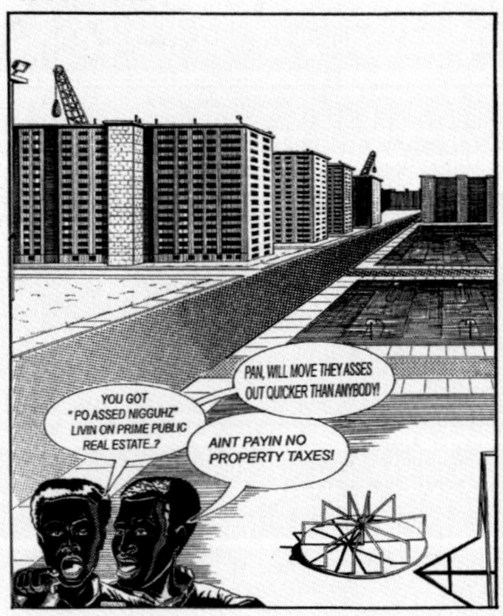
YOU GOT " PO ASSED NIGGUHZ" LIVIN ON PRIME PUBLIC REAL ESTATE..?
AINT PAYIN NO PROPERTY TAXES!
PAN, WILL MOVE THEY ASSES OUT QUICKER THAN ANYBODY!

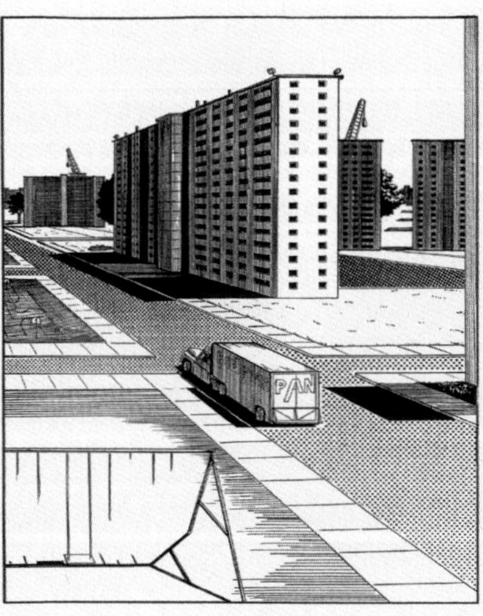
PAN

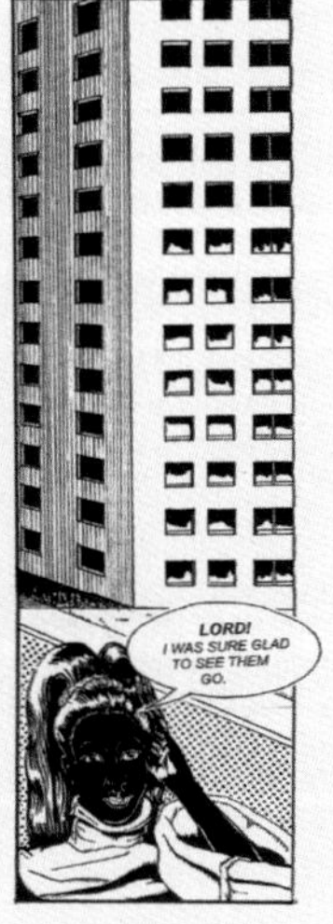
LORD! I WAS SURE GLAD TO SEE THEM GO.

RYTHM MASTR

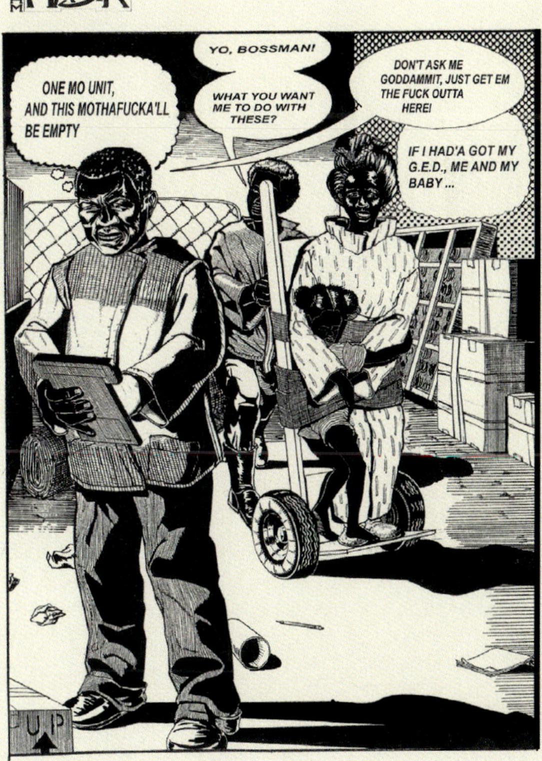

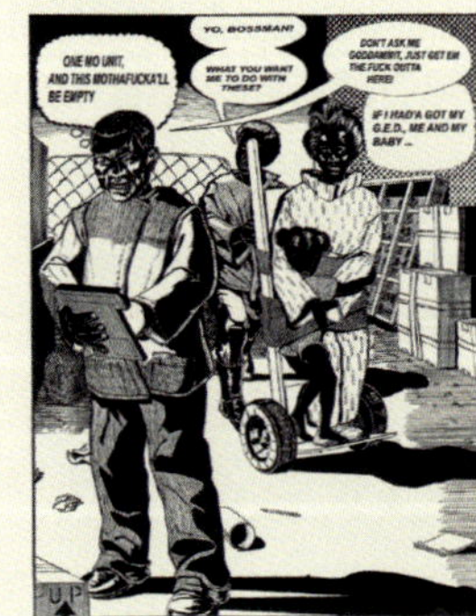
MASTR
ONE MO UNIT, AND THIS MOTHAFUCKA'LL BE EMPTY
YO, BOSSMAN!
WHAT YOU WANT ME TO DO WITH THESE?
DON'T ASK ME GODDAMMIT, JUST GET EM THE FUCK OUTTA HERE!
IF I HAD'A GOT MY G.E.D., ME AND MY BABY ...

RYTHM MASTR

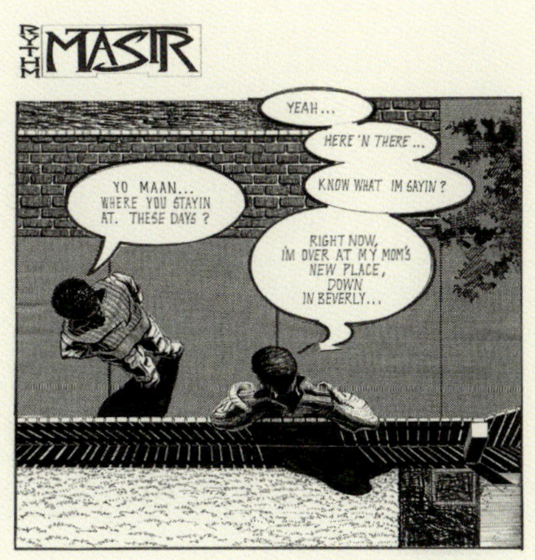
YO MAAN...
WHERE YOU STAYIN
AT. THESE DAYS ?
YEAH...
HERE 'N THERE...
KNOW WHAT IM SAYIN ?
RIGHT NOW,
IM OVER AT MY MOM'S
NEW PLACE,
DOWN
IN BEVERLY...

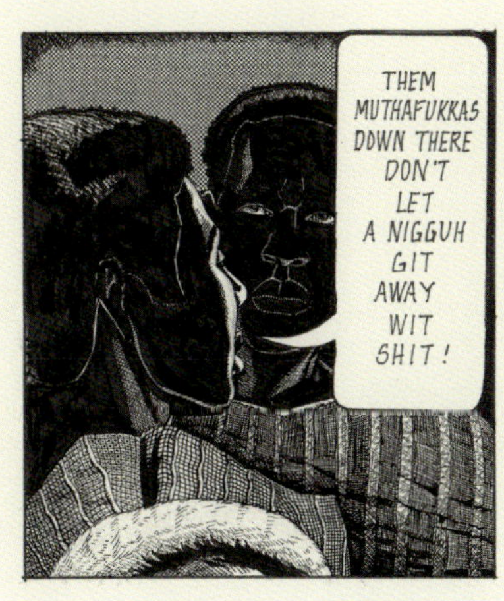
THEM
MUTHAFUKKAS
DOWN THERE
DON'T
LET
A NIGGUH
GIT
AWAY
WIT
SHIT !

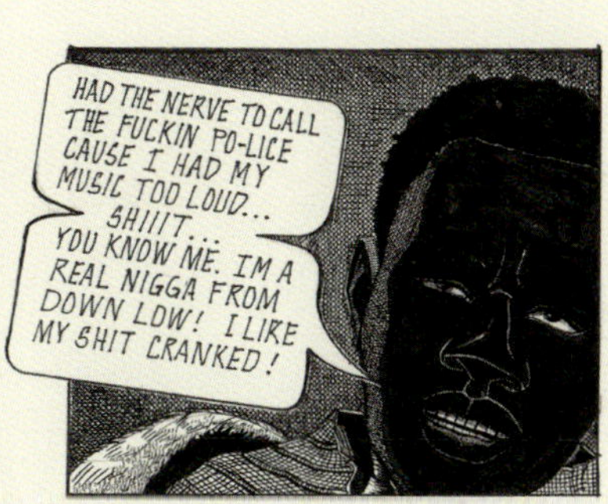
HAD THE NERVE TO CALL
THE FUCKIN PO-LICE
CAUSE I HAD MY
MUSIC TOO LOUD...
SHIIIT...
YOU KNOW ME. IM A
REAL NIGGA FROM
DOWN LOW! I LIKE
MY SHIT CRANKED !

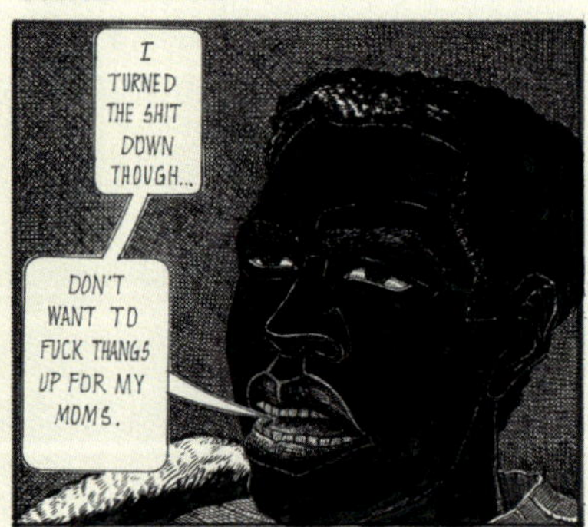
RYTHM
MASTR
I TURNED THE SHIT DOWN THOUGH...
DON'T WANT TO FUCK THANGS UP FOR MY MOMS.

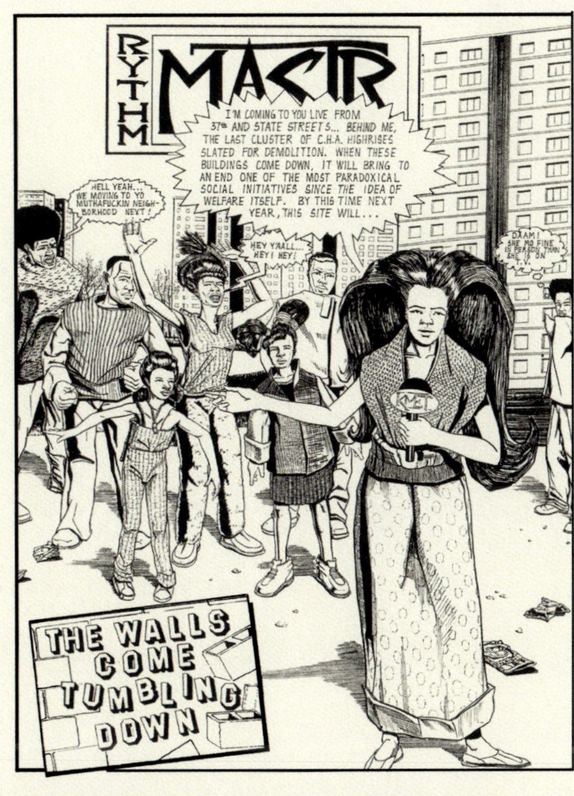
RYTHM
MASTR
I'M COMING TO YOU LIVE FROM 37th AND STATE STREETS... BEHIND ME, THE LAST CLUSTER OF C.H.A. HIGHRISES SLATED FOR DEMOLITION. WHEN THESE BUILDINGS COME DOWN, IT WILL BRING TO AN END ONE OF THE MOST PARADOXICAL SOCIAL INITIATIVES SINCE THE IDEA OF WELFARE ITSELF. BY THIS TIME NEXT YEAR, THIS SITE WILL...
HELL YEAH... WE MOVING TO YO MUTHAFUCKIN NEIGH-BORHOOD NEXT!
HEY Y'AALL... HEY! HEY!
DAAM! SHE MO FINE IN PERSON THAN SHE IS ON T.V.
THE WALLS COME TUMBLING DOWN

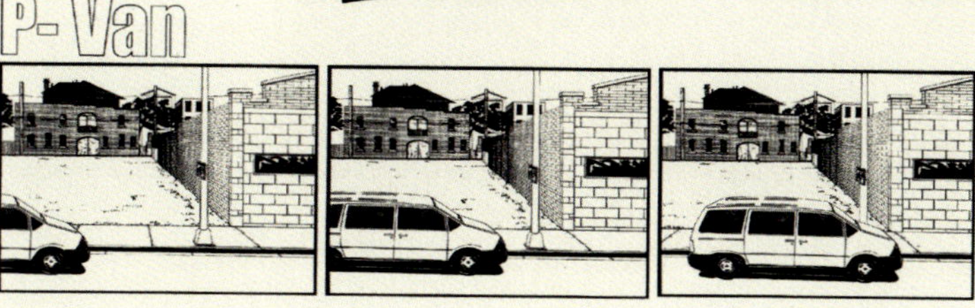
P- Van

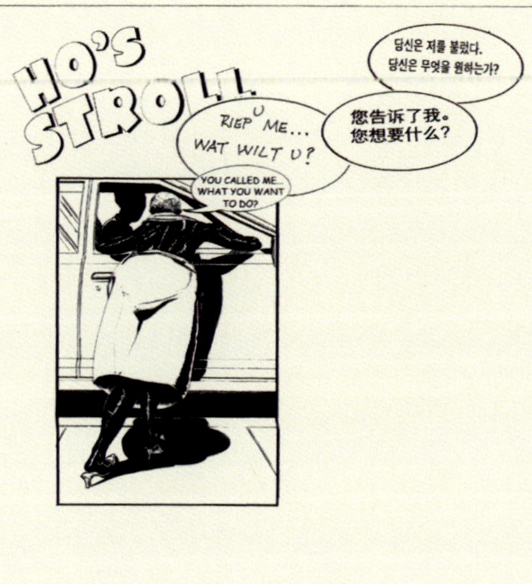
HO'S STROLL
당신은 저를 불렀다.
당신은 무엇을 원하는가?
您告诉了我。
您想要什么？
RIEP U ME...
WAT WILT U?
YOU CALLED ME...
WHAT YOU WANT
TO DO?

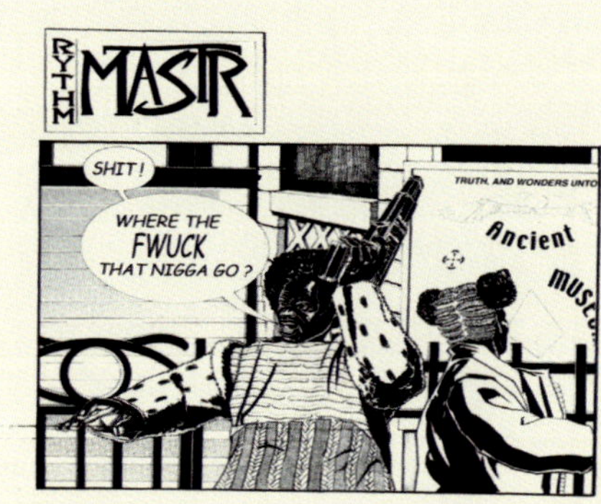
RYTHM MASTR
SHIT!
WHERE THE
FWUCK
THAT NIGGA GO?
TRUTH, AND WONDERS UNTO
Ancient

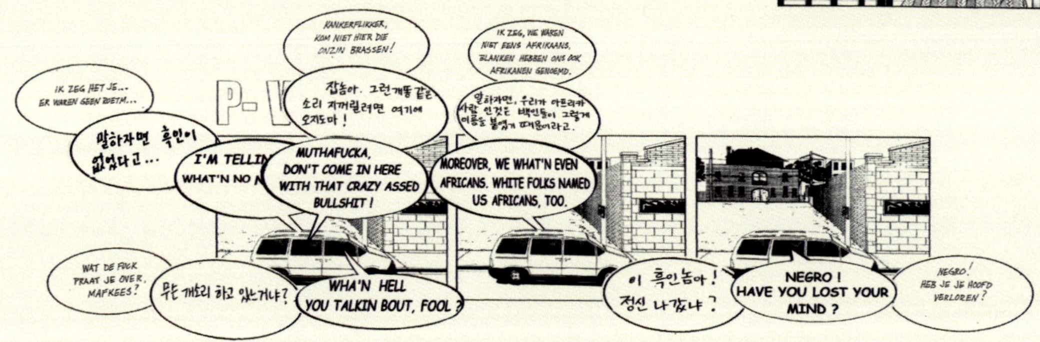
IK ZEG HET JE...
ER WAREN GEEN ROETM...
말하자면 흑인이
없었다고...
I'M TELLIN
WHAT'N NO
KANKERFLIKKER,
KOM NIET HIER DIE
ONZIN BRASSEN!
잡놈아. 그런 개똥 같은
소리 지꺼릴려면 여기에
오지도마!
MUTHAFUCKA,
DON'T COME IN HERE
WITH THAT CRAZY ASSED
BULLSHIT!
IK ZEG, WE WAREN
NIET EENS AFRIKAANS.
BLANKEN HEBBEN ONS OOK
AFRIKANEN GENOEMD.
말하자면, 우리가 아프리카
사람 인것은 백인들이 그렇게
이름을 붙였기 때문이라고.
MOREOVER, WE WHAT'N EVEN
AFRICANS. WHITE FOLKS NAMED
US AFRICANS, TOO.
WAT DE FUCK
PRAAT JE OVER,
MAFKEES?
무슨 개소리 하고 있는거냐?
WHA'N HELL
YOU TALKIN BOUT, FOOL?
이 흑인놈아!
정신 나갔냐?
NEGRO!
HAVE YOU LOST YOUR
MIND?
NEGRO!
HEB JE JE HOOFD
VERLOREN?

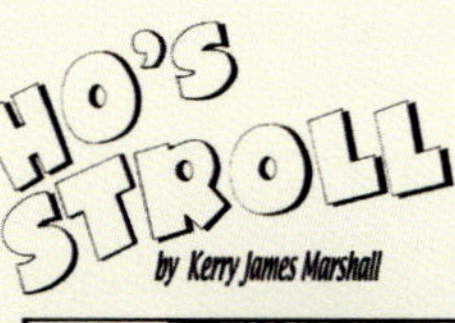
HO'S STROLL
by Kerry James Marshall

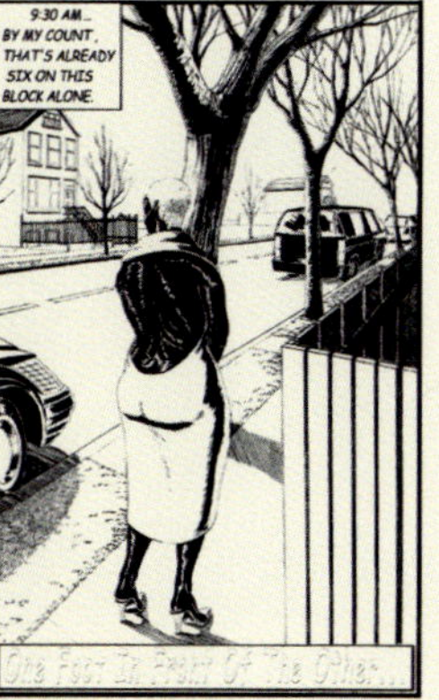
9:30 AM...
BY MY COUNT, THAT'S ALREADY SIX ON THIS BLOCK ALONE.
One Foot In Front Of The Other...

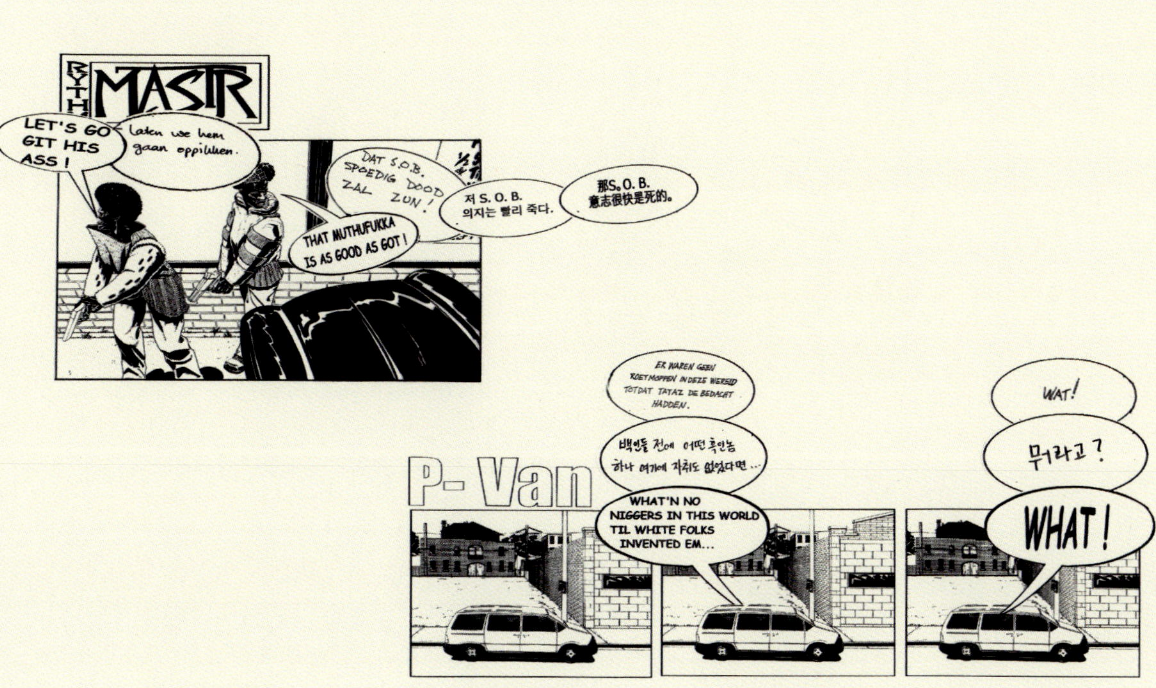
RYTHM MASTR
LET'S GO GIT HIS ASS!
laten we hem gaan oppikken.
THAT MUTHUFUKKA IS AS GOOD AS GOT!
DAT S.O.B. SPOEDIG DOOD ZAL ZIJN!
저 S. O. B. 의지는 빨리 죽다.
那S。O. B. 意志很快是死的。
P-Van
WHAT'N NO NIGGERS IN THIS WORLD TIL WHITE FOLKS INVENTED EM...
백인들 전에 어떤 흑인놈 하나 여기에 자취도 없었다면...
ER WAREN GEEN ROETMOPPEN IN DEZE WERELD TOTDAT TATA'Z DE BEDACHT HADDEN.
WHAT!
무라고?
WAT!

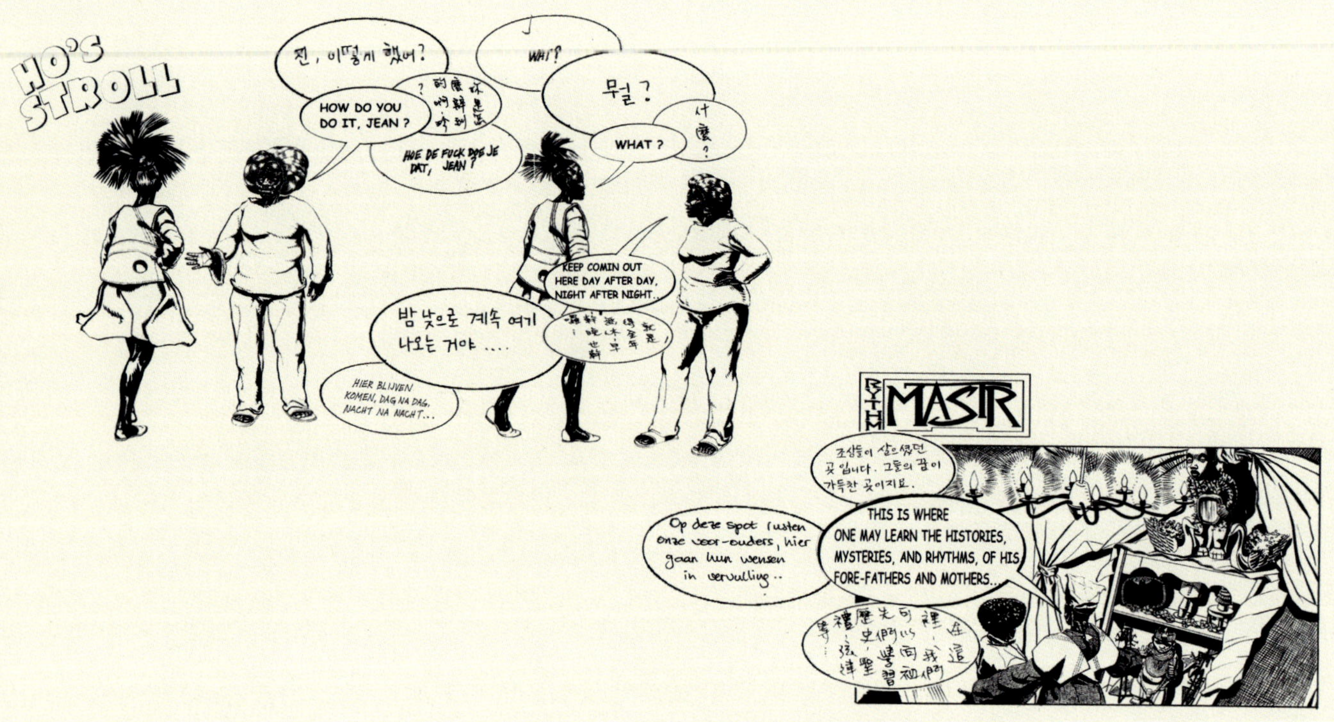
HO'S STROLL
진, 어떻게 했어?
HOW DO YOU DO IT, JEAN ?
HOE DE FUCK DOE JE DAT, JEAN ?
WHT?
뭘?
WHAT ?
什麼?
KEEP COMIN OUT HERE DAY AFTER DAY, NIGHT AFTER NIGHT...
밤 낮으로 계속 여기 나오는 거야 ....
HIER BLIJVEN KOMEN, DAG NA DAG, NACHT NA NACHT...
RYTHM MASTR
조상들이 살으셨던 곳 입니다. 그들의 꿈이 가득찬 곳이지요.
THIS IS WHERE ONE MAY LEARN THE HISTORIES, MYSTERIES, AND RHYTHMS, OF HIS FORE-FATHERS AND MOTHERS...
Op deze spot rusten onze voor-ouders, hier gaan hun wensen in vervulling..

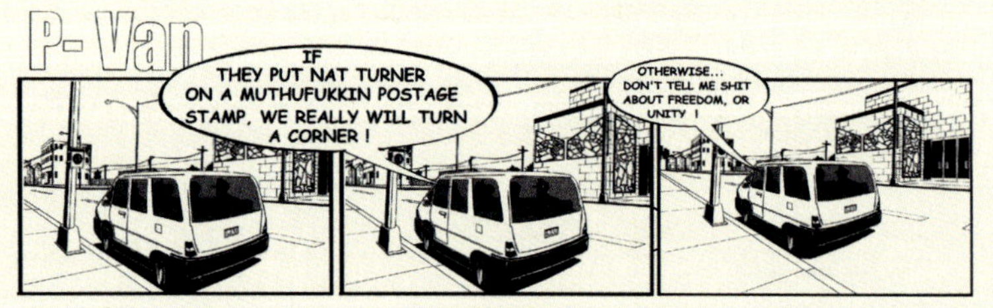
P- Van
IF THEY PUT NAT TURNER ON A MUTHUFUKKIN POSTAGE STAMP, WE REALLY WILL TURN A CORNER !
OTHERWISE... DON'T TELL ME SHIT ABOUT FREEDOM, OR UNITY !

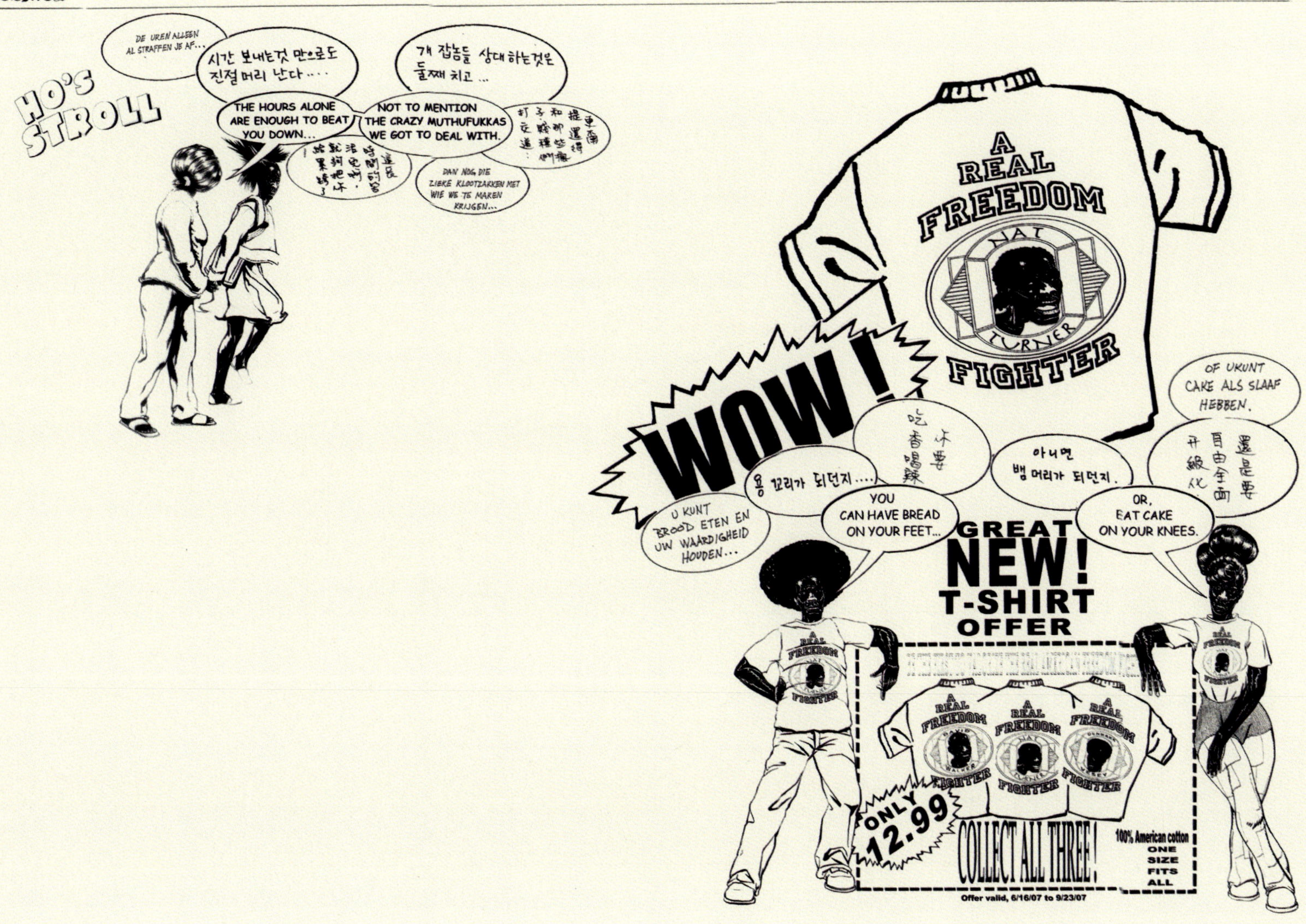
TIMES
HO'S STROLL
DE UREN ALLEEN AL STRAFFEN JE AF...
시간 보내는것 만으로도 진절머리 난다....
THE HOURS ALONE ARE ENOUGH TO BEAT YOU DOWN...
개 잡놈들 상대하는것은 둘째 치고 ...
NOT TO MENTION THE CRAZY MUTHUFUKKAS WE GOT TO DEAL WITH.
DAN NOG DIE ZIEKE KLOOTZAKKEN MET WIE WE TE MAKEN KRIJGEN...
A REAL FREEDOM
NAT TURNER
FIGHTER
WOW!
U KUNT BROOD ETEN EN UW WAARDIGHEID HOUDEN...
용 꼬리가 되던지....
不要吃香喝辣
YOU CAN HAVE BREAD ON YOUR FEET...
아니면 뱀 머리가 되던지.
OF UKUNT CAKE ALS SLAAF HEBBEN.
OR, EAT CAKE ON YOUR KNEES.
GREAT NEW! T-SHIRT OFFER
ONLY 12.99
COLLECT ALL THREE!
100% American cotton
ONE SIZE FITS ALL
Offer valid, 6/16/07 to 9/23/07

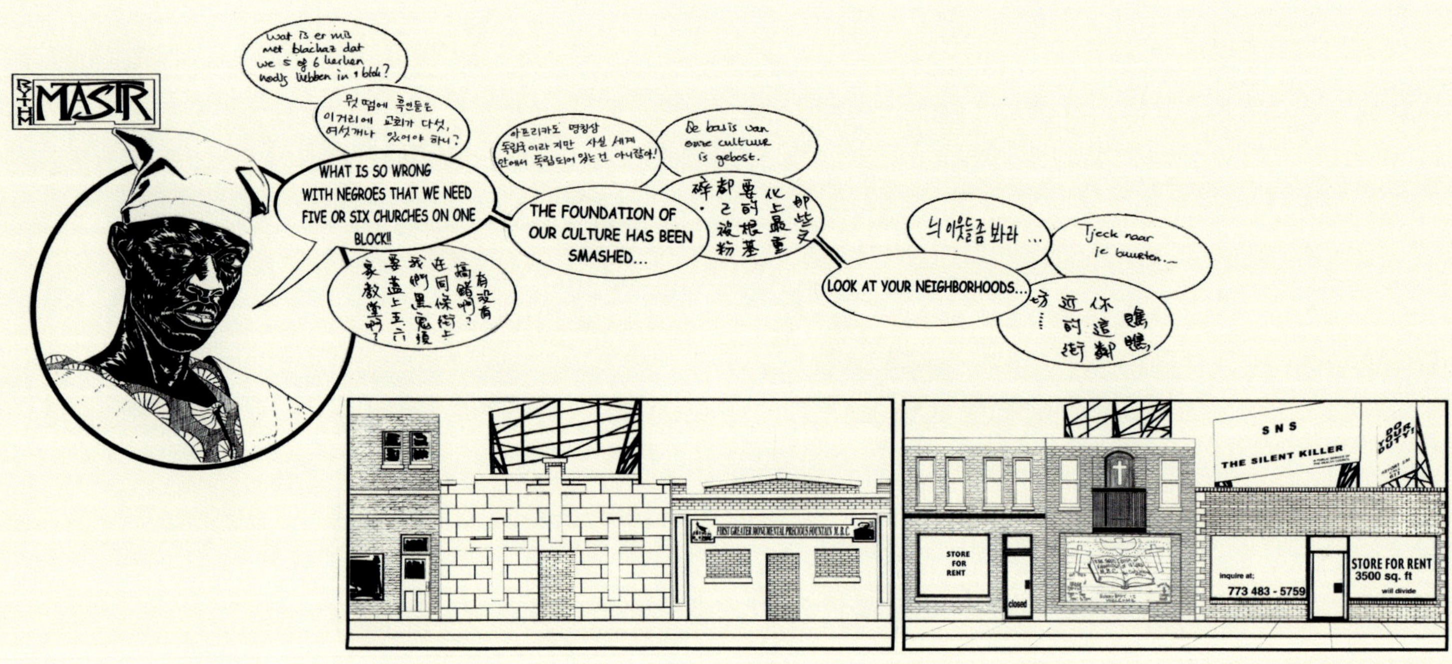
MASTR
WHAT IS SO WRONG WITH NEGROES THAT WE NEED FIVE OR SIX CHURCHES ON ONE BLOCK!!
Wat is er mis met blackaz dat we 5 of 6 kerken nodig hebben in 1 blok?
뭣 땜에 흑인들은 이거리에 교회가 다섯, 여섯개나 있어야 하니?
有没有搞錯啊？在同條街上我們黑鬼須要蓋上五、六家教堂啊？
THE FOUNDATION OF OUR CULTURE HAS BEEN SMASHED...
아프리카도 명칭상 독립국이라 지만 사실 세계 안에서 독립되어 있는 건 아니잖아!
De basis van onze cultuur is gebost.
那些文化上最重要的根基都已被粉碎·
LOOK AT YOUR NEIGHBORHOODS...
니 이웃들좀 봐라 ...
Tjeck naar je buurten...
瞧瞧你這鄰近的街坊……
STORE FOR RENT
closed
SNS
THE SILENT KILLER
inquire at:
773 483 - 5759
STORE FOR RENT
3500 sq. ft
will divide

P- Van

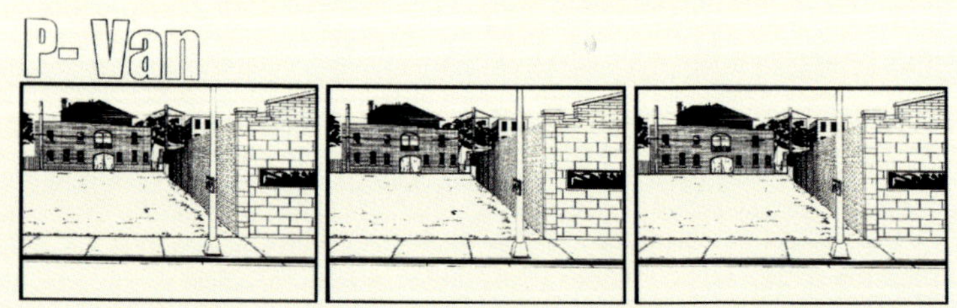

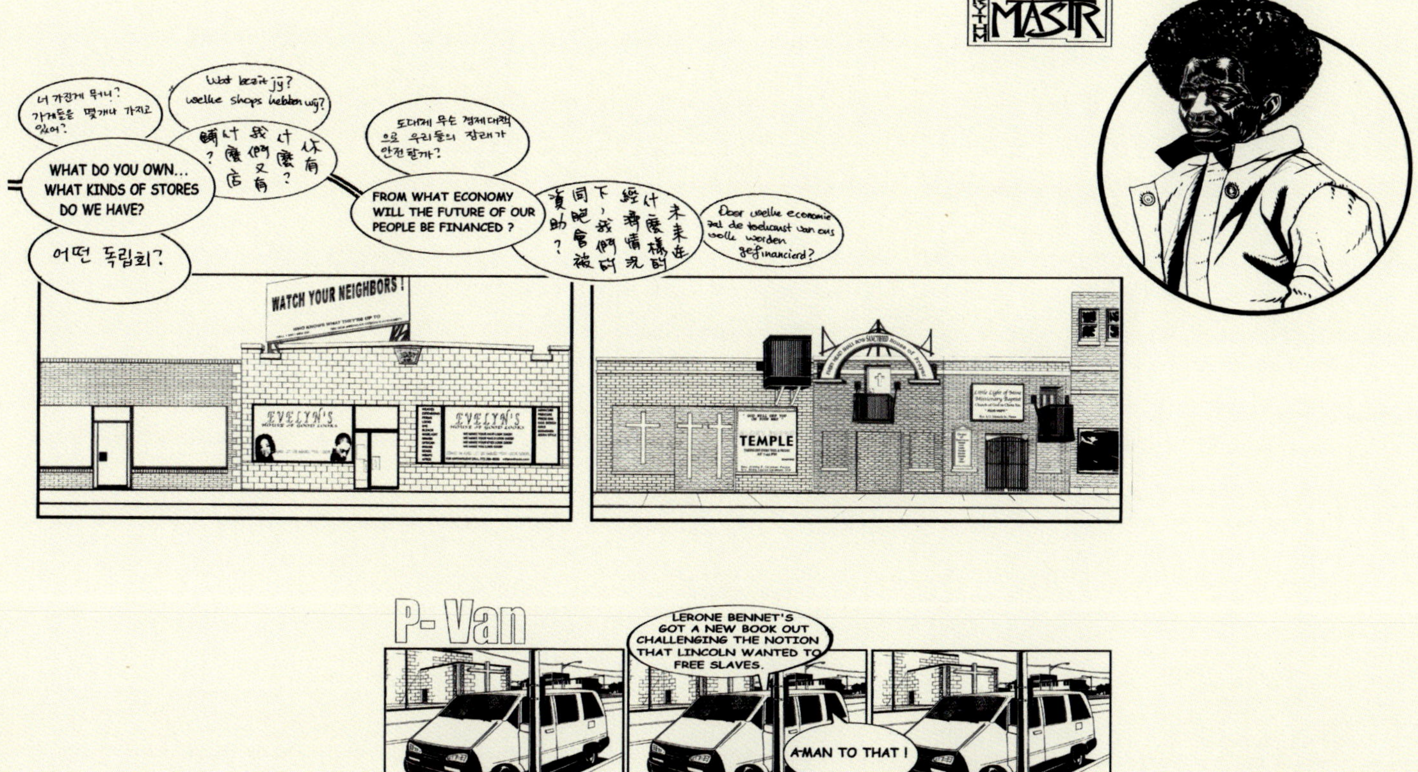
RYTHM MASTR
너 가진게 뭐니? 가게들을 몇개나 가지고 있어?
Wat bezit jij? welke shops hebben wij?
你有什麼？我們又有什麼店舖？
WHAT DO YOU OWN... WHAT KINDS OF STORES DO WE HAVE?
어떤 독립회?
도대체 무슨 경제대책으로 우리들의 장래가 안전할까?
FROM WHAT ECONOMY WILL THE FUTURE OF OUR PEOPLE BE FINANCED ?
未來在什麼樣的經濟情況下，我們的同胞會被資助？
Door welke economie zal de toekomst van ons volk worden gefinancierd?
WATCH YOUR NEIGHBORS !
EVELYN'S
TEMPLE
P- Van
LERONE BENNET'S GOT A NEW BOOK OUT CHALLENGING THE NOTION THAT LINCOLN WANTED TO FREE SLAVES.
A-MAN TO THAT !

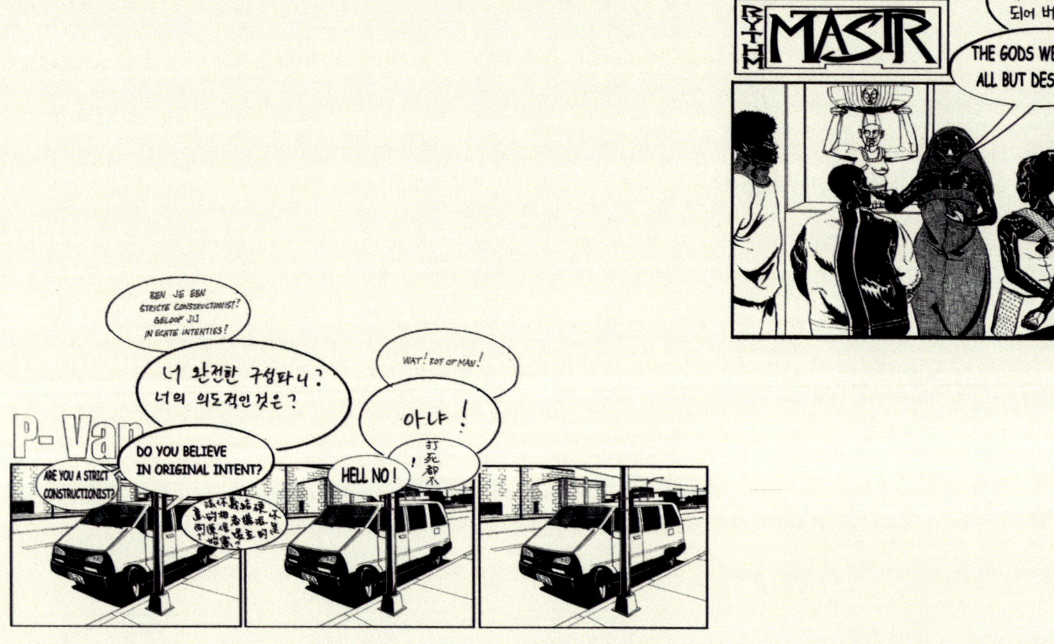
RYTHM MASTR
우리 신들은 다 파괴 되어 버리고....
De goden die wij hadden zijn bijna allemaal kapot gemaakt.
THE GODS WE HAD ARE ALL BUT DESTROYED...
P-Van
BEN JE EEN STRICTE CONSTRUCTIONIST? GELOOF JIJ IN ECHTE INTENTIES!
너 완전한 구성파니? 너의 의도적인 것은?
ARE YOU A STRICT CONSTRUCTIONIST?
DO YOU BELIEVE IN ORIGINAL INTENT?
WAT! ROT OP MAN!
아냐!
HELL NO!

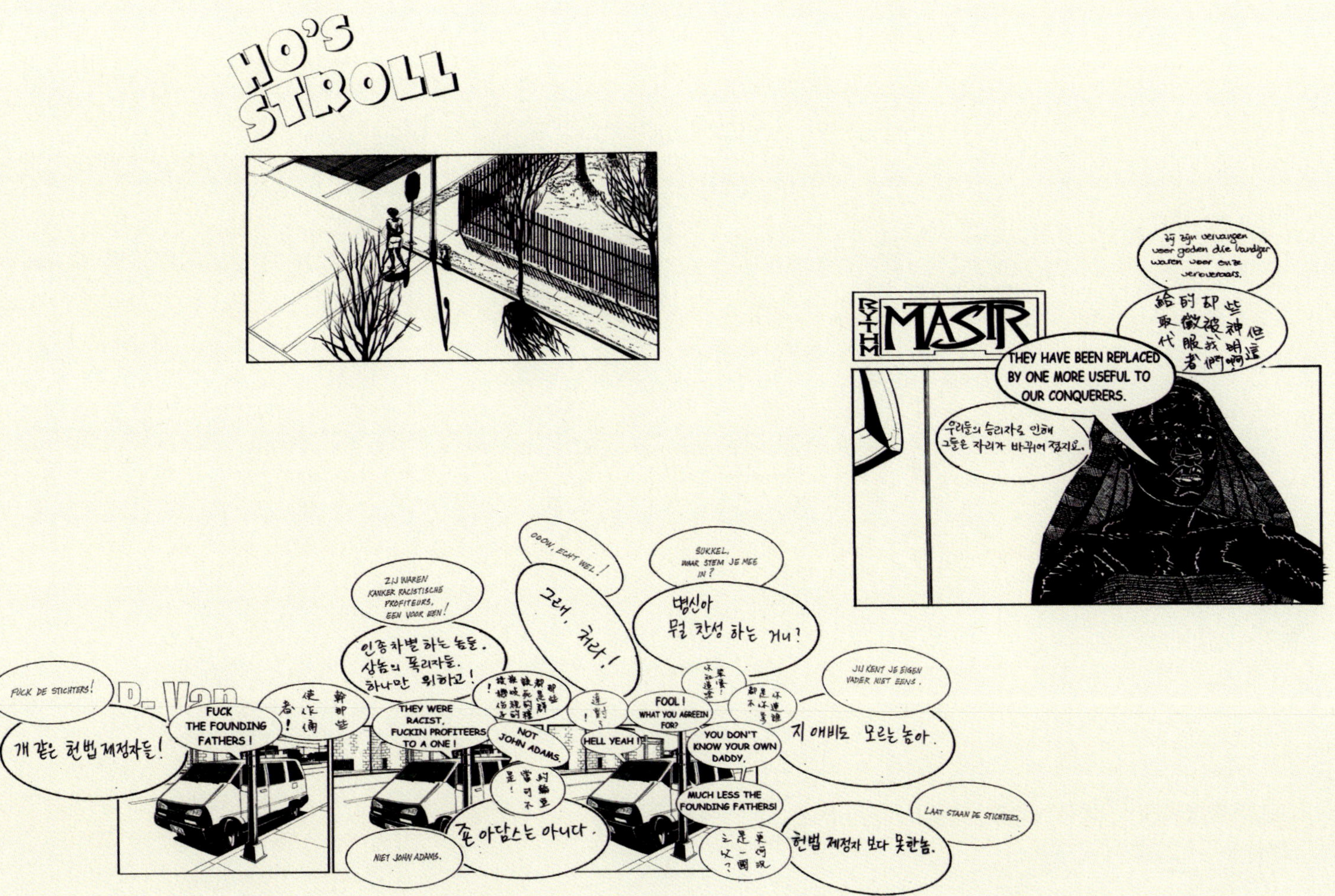
HO'S STROLL
RYTHM MASTR
THEY HAVE BEEN REPLACED BY ONE MORE USEFUL TO OUR CONQUERERS.
우리들의 승리자로 인해 그들은 자리가 바뀌어 졌지요.
zij zijn vervangen voor goden die handiger waren voor onze veroveraars.
D. Van
FUCK DE STICHTERS!
개 같은 헌법 제정자들!
FUCK THE FOUNDING FATHERS!
ZIJ WAREN KANKER RACISTISCHE PROFITEURS, EEN VOOR EEN!
인종차별 하는 놈들. 상놈의 폭리자들. 하나만 위하고!
THEY WERE RACIST, FUCKIN PROFITEERS TO A ONE!
NOT JOHN ADAMS.
존 아담스는 아니다.
NIET JOHN ADAMS.
OOOW, ECHT WEL!
그래, 처라!
HELL YEAH!
SUKKEL, WAAR STEM JE MEE IN?
병신아 뭘 찬성 하는 거니?
FOOL! WHAT YOU AGREEIN FOR?
YOU DON'T KNOW YOUR OWN DADDY.
지 애비도 모르는 놈아.
JIJ KENT JE EIGEN VADER NIET EENS.
MUCH LESS THE FOUNDING FATHERS!
헌법 제정자 보다 못한놈.
LAAT STAAN DE STICHTERS.

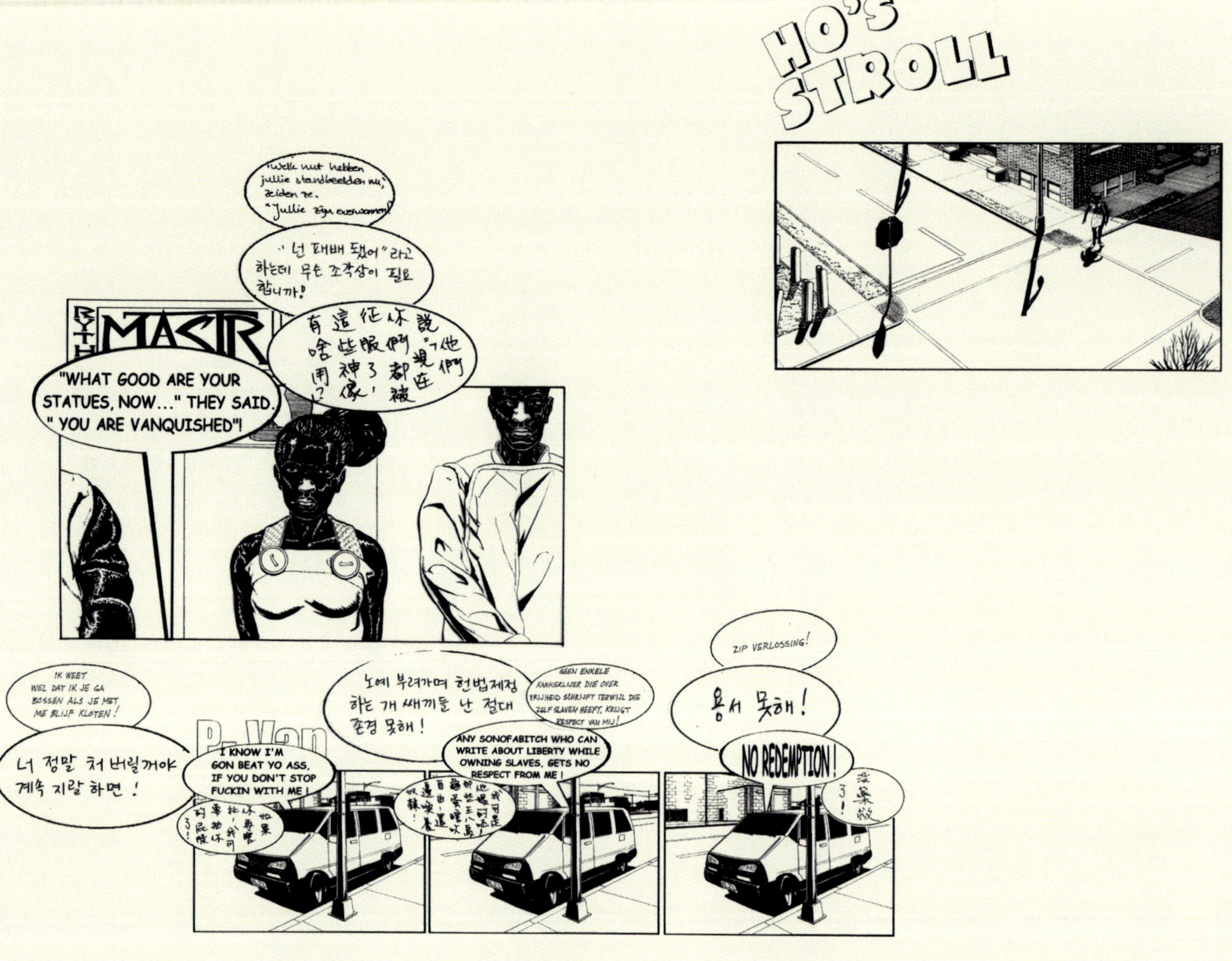
HO'S STROLL
"Welk nut hebben jullie standbeelden nu," zeiden ze. "Jullie zijn overwonnen!"
"넌 패배 됐어"라고 하는데 무슨 조각상이 필요 합니까!
"WHAT GOOD ARE YOUR STATUES, NOW..." THEY SAID. " YOU ARE VANQUISHED"!
IK WEET WEL DAT IK JE GA BOSSEN ALS JE MET ME BLIJF KLOTEN!
너 정말 처 버릴꺼야 계속 지랄 하면 !
I KNOW I'M GON BEAT YO ASS, IF YOU DON'T STOP FUCKIN WITH ME !
노예 부려가며 헌법제정 하는 개 새끼들 난 절대 존경 못해 !
GEEN ENKELE KANKERLIJER DIE OVER VRIJHEID SCHRIJFT TERWIJL DIE ZELF SLAVEN HEEFT, KRIJGT RESPECT VAN MIJ!
ANY SONOFABITCH WHO CAN WRITE ABOUT LIBERTY WHILE OWNING SLAVES, GETS NO RESPECT FROM ME !
ZIP VERLOSSING!
용서 못해 !
NO REDEMPTION !

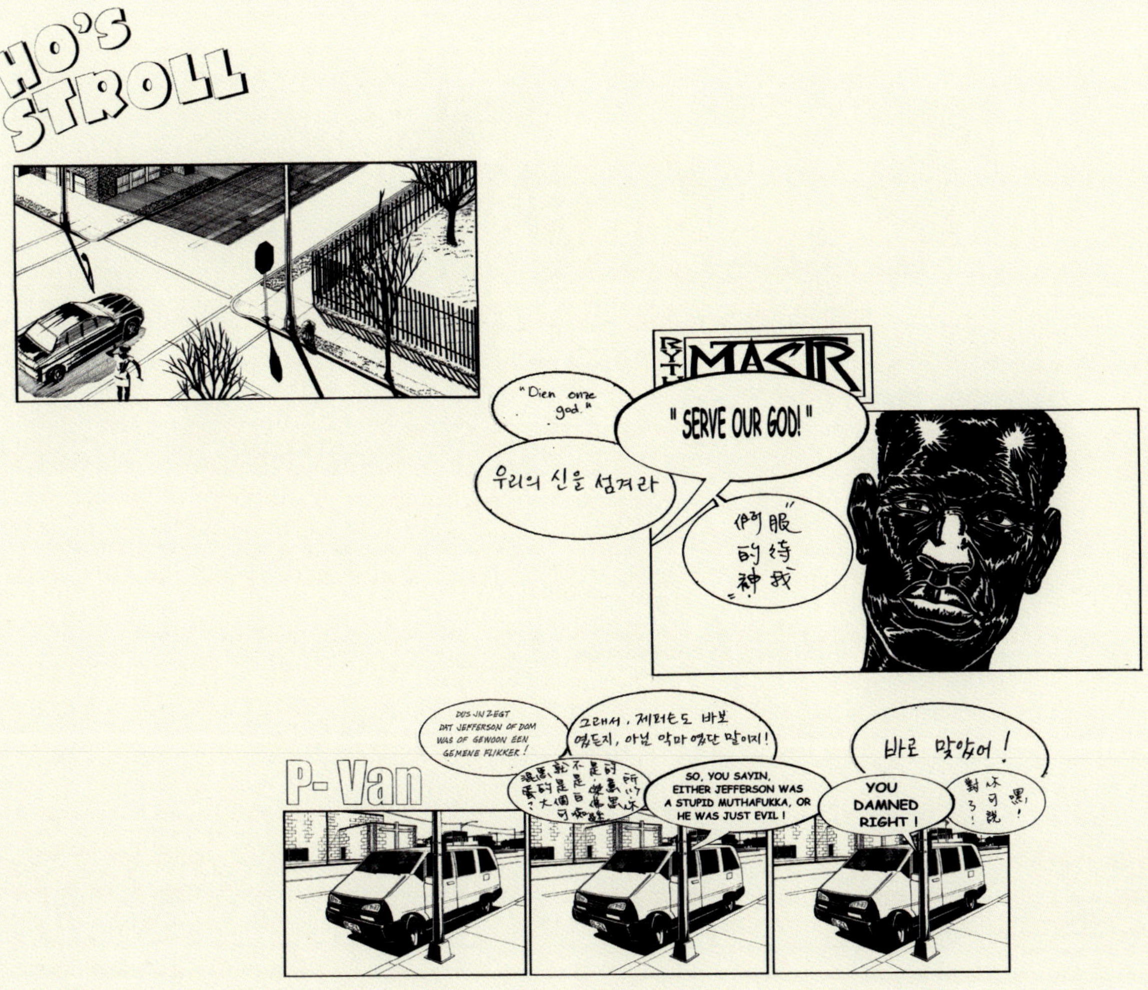
HO'S STROLL
MASTR
"Dien onze god."
우리의 신을 섬겨라
" SERVE OUR GOD! "
服侍我們的神
P- Van
DUS JIJ ZEGT DAT JEFFERSON OF DOM WAS OF GEWOON EEN GEMENE FLIKKER!
그래서, 제퍼슨도 바보 였든지, 아님 악마 였단 말이지!
SO, YOU SAYIN, EITHER JEFFERSON WAS A STUPID MUTHAFUKKA, OR HE WAS JUST EVIL!
바로 맞았어!
YOU DAMNED RIGHT!
嘿,你可說對了!

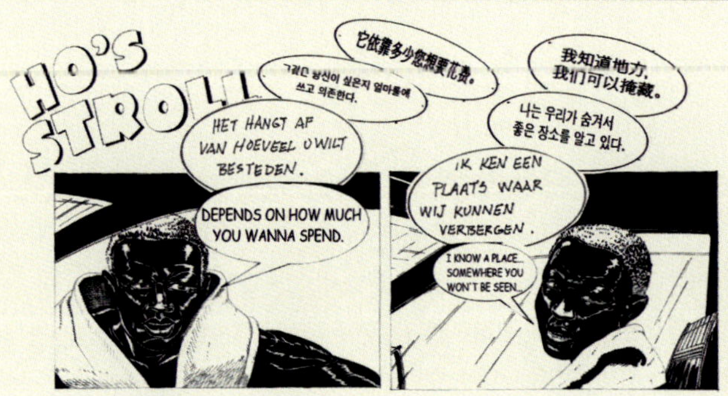
HO'S
它依靠多少您想要花费。
HET HANGT AF VAN HOEVEEL U WILT BESTEDEN.
DEPENDS ON HOW MUCH YOU WANNA SPEND.
我知道地方，我们可以掩藏。
나는 우리가 숨겨서 좋은 장소를 알고 있다.
IK KEN EEN PLAATS WAAR WIJ KUNNEN VERBERGEN.
I KNOW A PLACE... SOMEWHERE YOU WON'T BE SEEN...

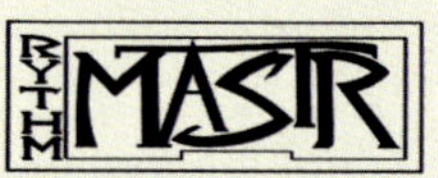
RYTHM MASTR

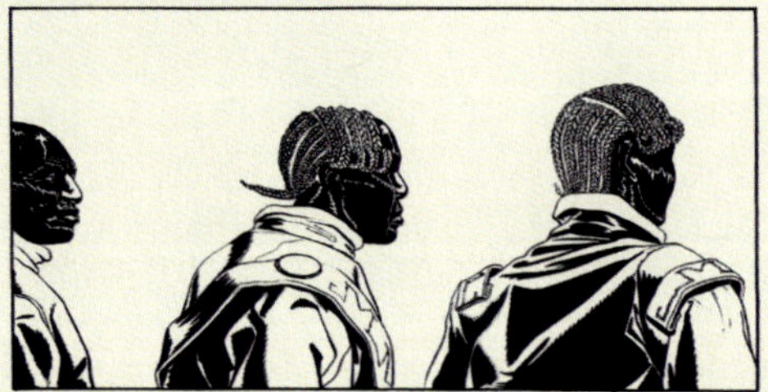

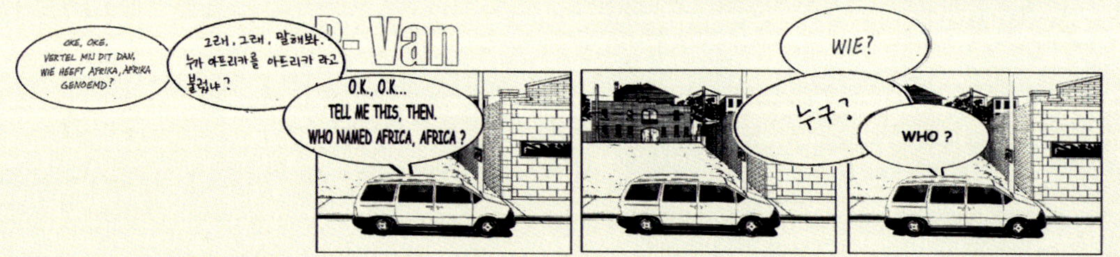
OKE, OKE. VERTEL MIJ DIT DAN, WIE HEEFT AFRIKA, AFRIKA GENOEMD?
그래, 그래, 말해봐. 누가 아프리카를 아프리카 라고 불렀나?
O.K., O.K... TELL ME THIS, THEN. WHO NAMED AFRICA, AFRICA ?
WIE?
누구?
WHO ?

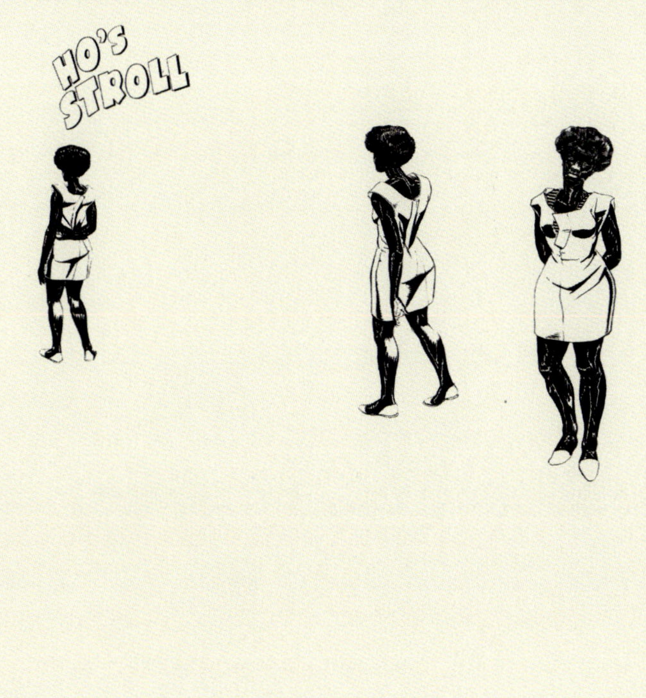
HO'S STROLL

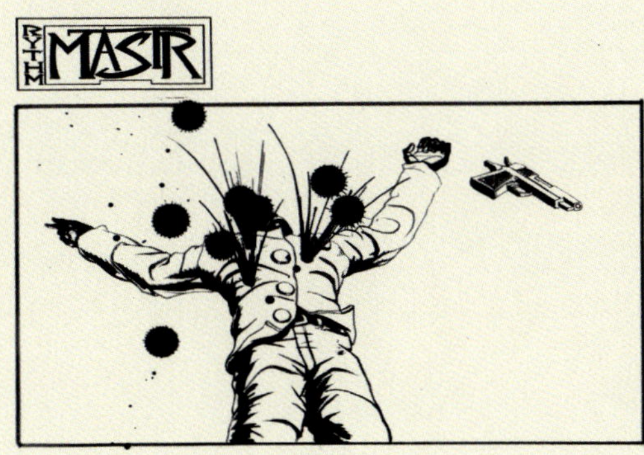
RYTHM MASTR

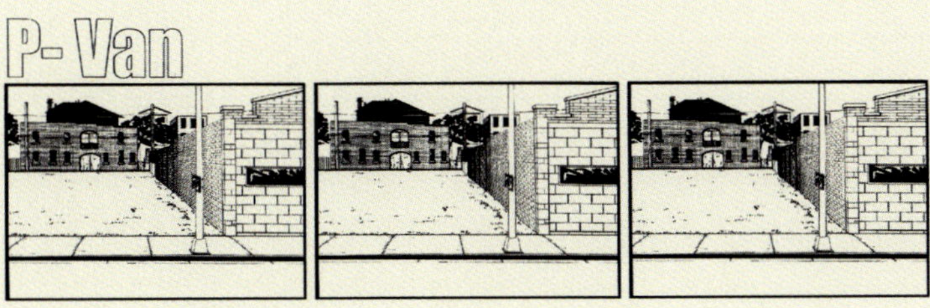
P-Van

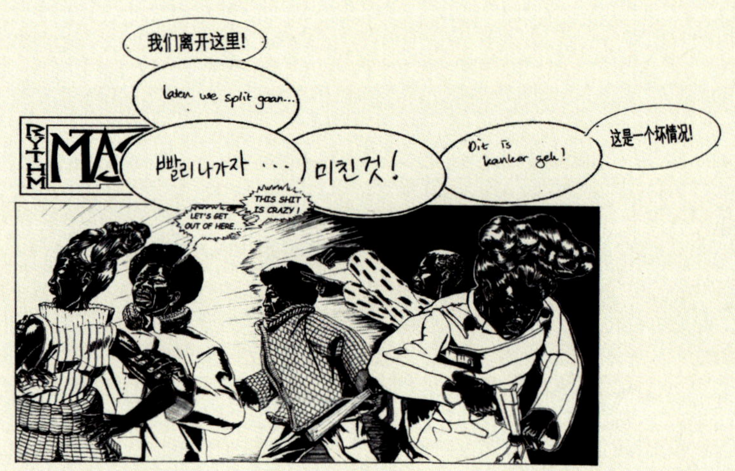

RYTHM
我们离开这里!
laten we split gaan...
빨리나가자 ...
미친것!
Dit is kanker geh!
这是一个坏情况!
LET'S GET OUT OF HERE...
THIS SHIT IS CRAZY!

P- Van

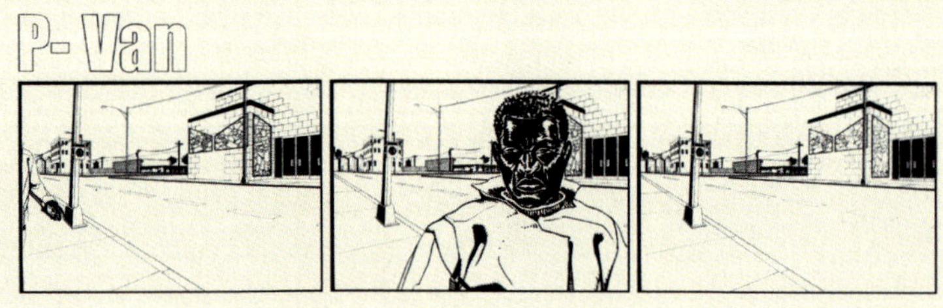

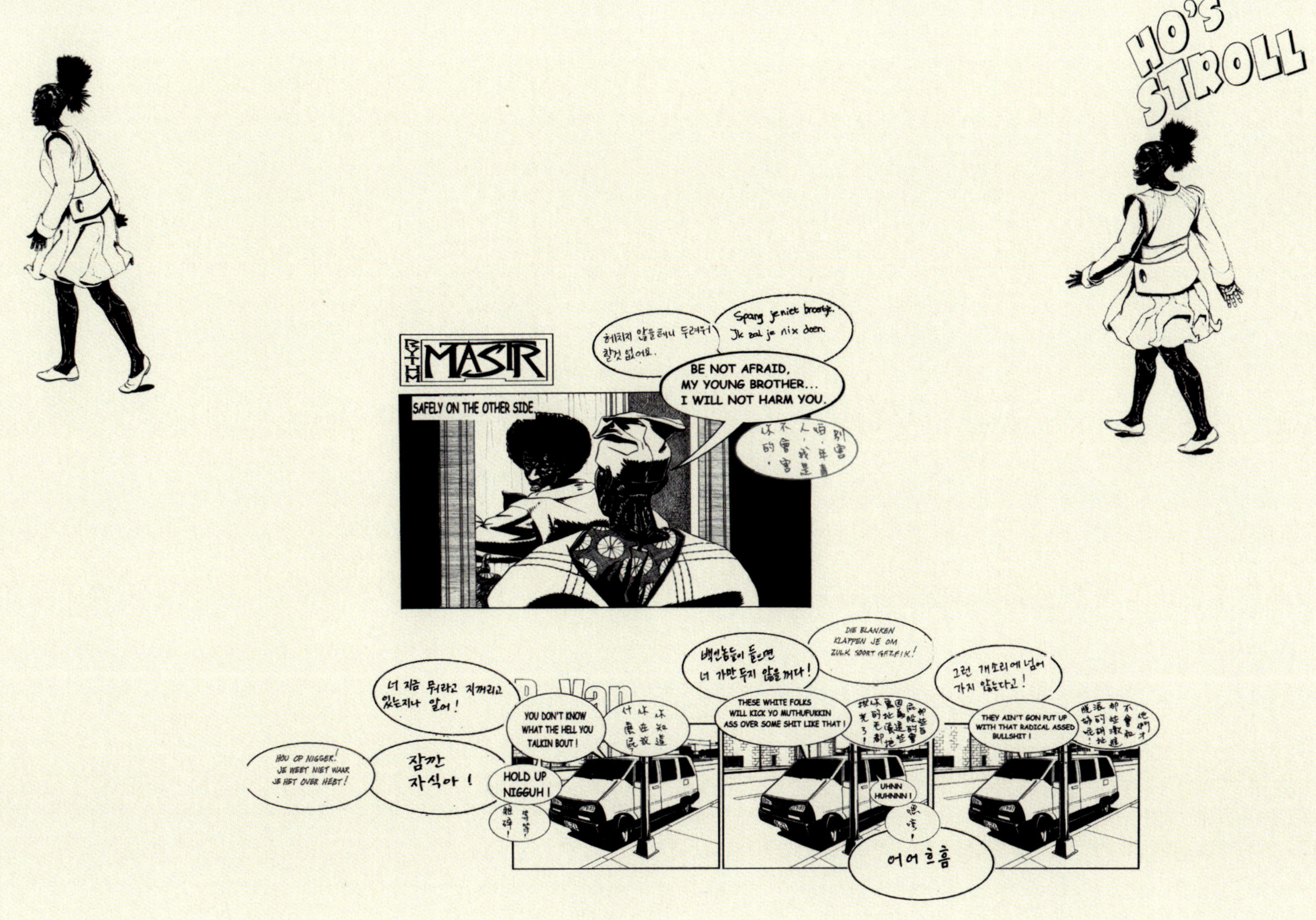
HO'S STROLL
RYTHM MASTR
SAFELY ON THE OTHER SIDE
헤치지 않을테니 두려워 할것 없어요.
Spang je niet broertje. Jk zal je nix doen.
BE NOT AFRAID, MY YOUNG BROTHER... I WILL NOT HARM YOU.
HOU OP NIGGER! JE WEET NIET WAAR JE HET OVER HEBT!
잠깐 자식아 !
HOLD UP NIGGUH !
너 지금 뭐라고 지껄리고 있는지나 알어 !
YOU DON'T KNOW WHAT THE HELL YOU TALKIN BOUT !
백인놈들이 들으면 너 가만 두지 않을꺼다 !
DIE BLANKEN KLAPPEN JE OM ZULK SOORT GEZEIK!
THESE WHITE FOLKS WILL KICK YO MUTHUFUKKIN ASS OVER SOME SHIT LIKE THAT !
UHNN HUHNNN !
어어 흐음
그런 개소리에 넘어 가지 않는다고 !
THEY AIN'T GON PUT UP WITH THAT RADICAL ASSED BULLSHIT !

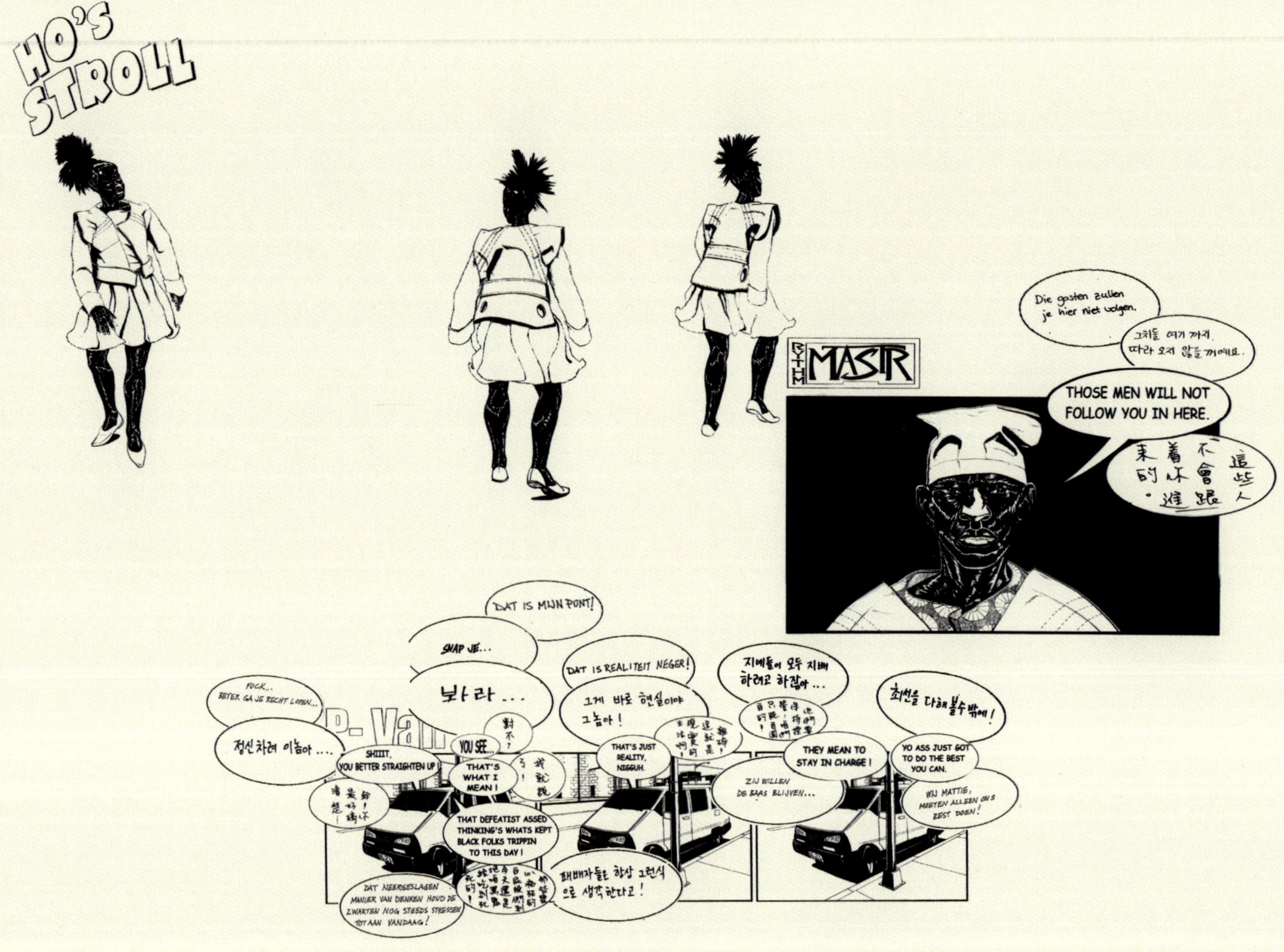
HO'S STROLL
RYTHM MASTR
Die gasten zullen je hier niet volgen.
그치들 여기 까지 따라 오지 않을 꺼에요.
THOSE MEN WILL NOT FOLLOW YOU IN HERE.
這些人不會跟着你進來的。
DAT IS MIJN PONT!
SNAP JE...
봐라 ...
FUCK... BETER GA JE RECHT LOPEN...
정신차려 이놈아 ....
SHIIIT, YOU BETTER STRAIGHTEN UP!
YOU SEE...
對不？
THAT'S WHAT I MEAN!
我就說了！
THAT DEFEATIST ASSED THINKING'S WHATS KEPT BLACK FOLKS TRIPPIN TO THIS DAY!
DAT NEERGESLAGEN MANIER VAN DENKEN HOUD DE ZWARTEN NOG STEEDS STRESSEN TOT AAN VANDAAG!
패배자들은 항상 그런식으로 생각한다고!
DAT IS REALITEIT NEGER!
그게 바로 현실이야 그놈아!
THAT'S JUST REALITY, NIGGUH.
지배들이 모두 지배 하려고 하잖아 ...
THEY MEAN TO STAY IN CHARGE!
ZIJ WILLEN DE BAAS BLIJVEN...
최선을 다해 볼수 밖에!
YO ASS JUST GOT TO DO THE BEST YOU CAN.
WIJ MATTIE, MOETEN ALLEEN ONS BEST DOEN!

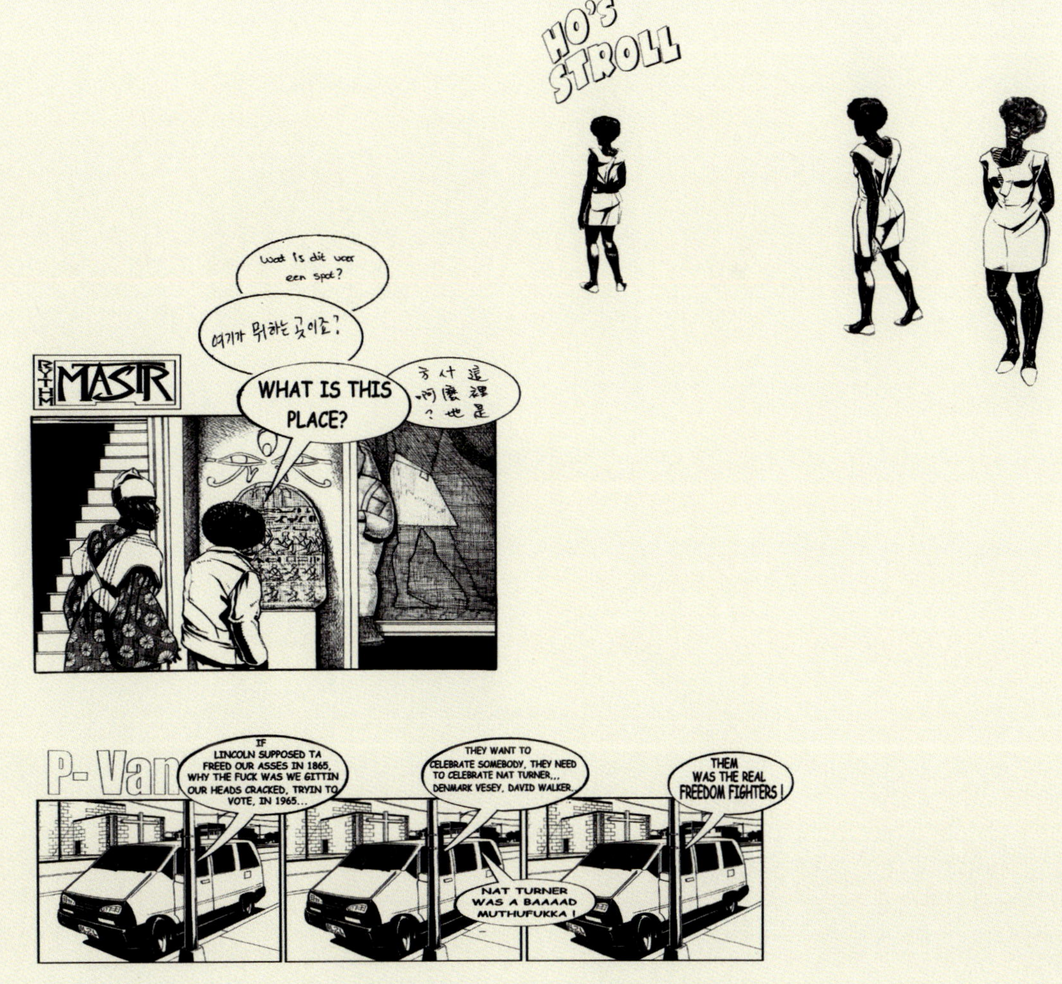
HO'S STROLL
RYTHM MASTR
Wat is dit voor een spot?
여기가 뭐하는 곳이죠?
WHAT IS THIS PLACE?
這裡是什麼地方啊?
P-Van
IF LINCOLN SUPPOSED TA FREED OUR ASSES IN 1865, WHY THE FUCK WAS WE GITTIN OUR HEADS CRACKED, TRYIN TO VOTE, IN 1965...
THEY WANT TO CELEBRATE SOMEBODY, THEY NEED TO CELEBRATE NAT TURNER,,, DENMARK VESEY, DAVID WALKER...
NAT TURNER WAS A BAAAAD MUTHUFUKKA !
THEM WAS THE REAL FREEDOM FIGHTERS !

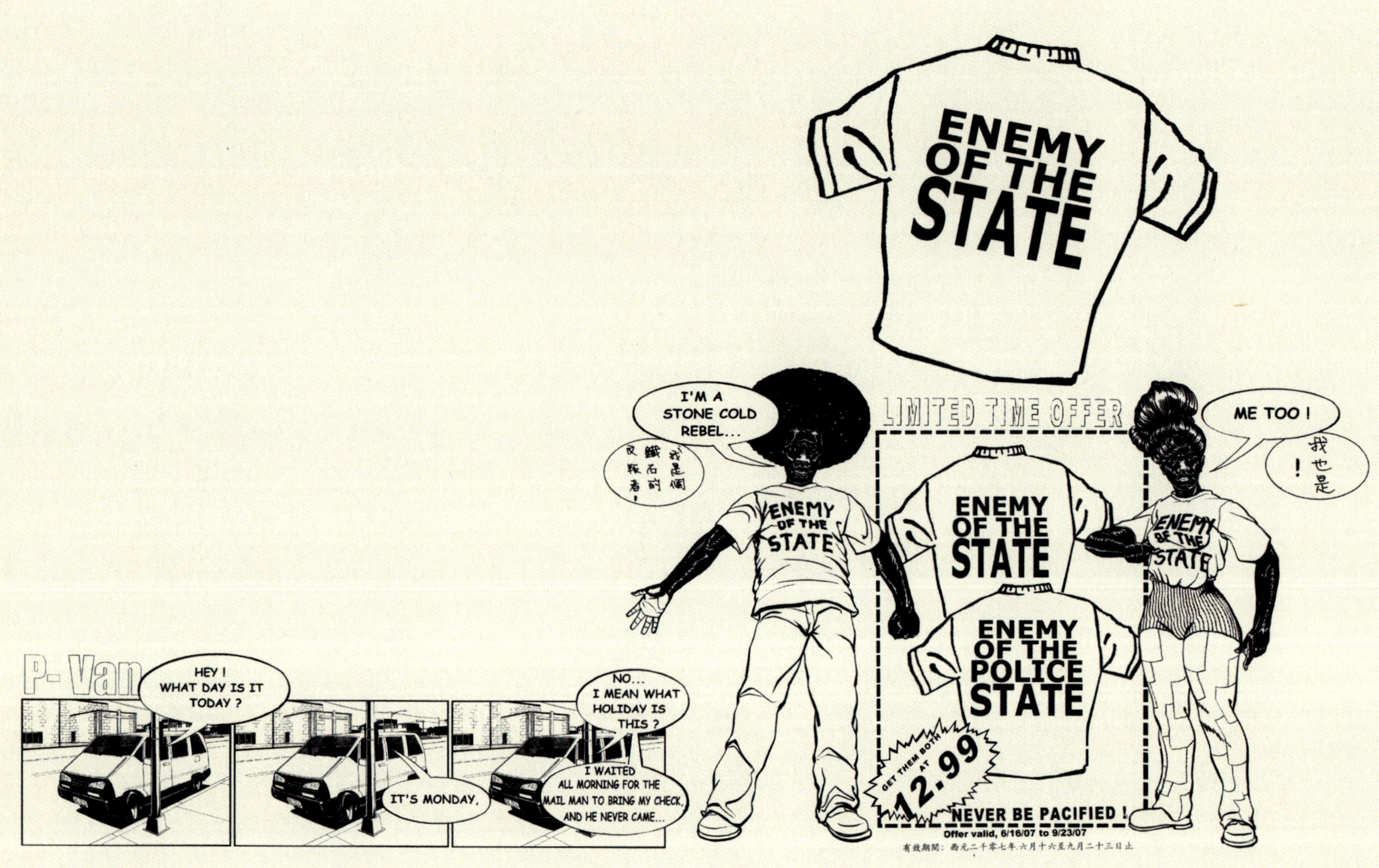
ENEMY OF THE STATE
I'M A STONE COLD REBEL...
我是個鐵石的反叛者！
LIMITED TIME OFFER
ENEMY OF THE STATE
ENEMY OF THE STATE
ENEMY OF THE POLICE STATE
GET THEM BOTH AT 12.99
NEVER BE PACIFIED !
Offer valid, 6/16/07 to 9/23/07
有效期間：西元二千零七年.六月十六至九月二十三日止
ME TOO !
我也是！
ENEMY OF THE STATE
P- Van
HEY ! WHAT DAY IS IT TODAY ?
IT'S MONDAY.
NO... I MEAN WHAT HOLIDAY IS THIS ?
I WAITED ALL MORNING FOR THE MAIL MAN TO BRING MY CHECK, AND HE NEVER CAME...

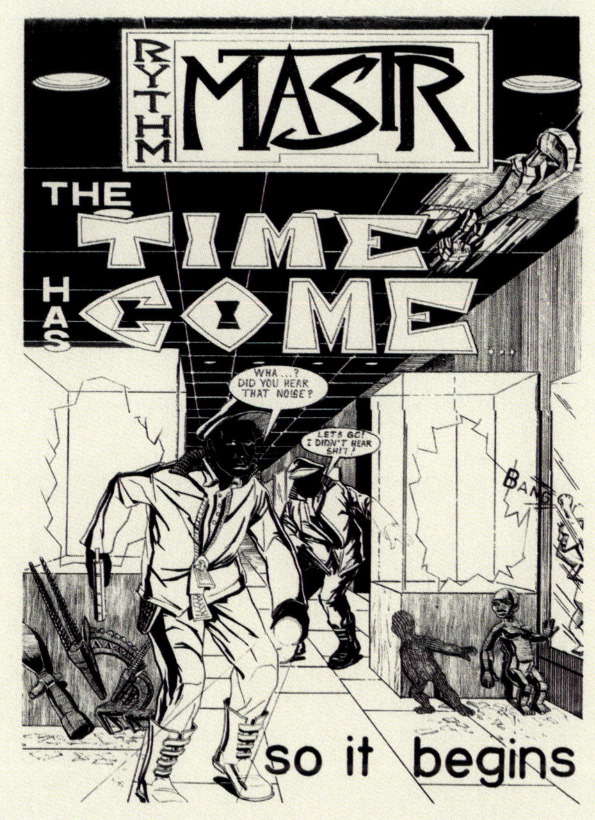
RYTHM MASTR
THE TIME HAS COME...
WHA...? DID YOU HEAR THAT NOISE?
LET'S GO! I DIDN'T HEAR SHIT!
BANG
so it begins

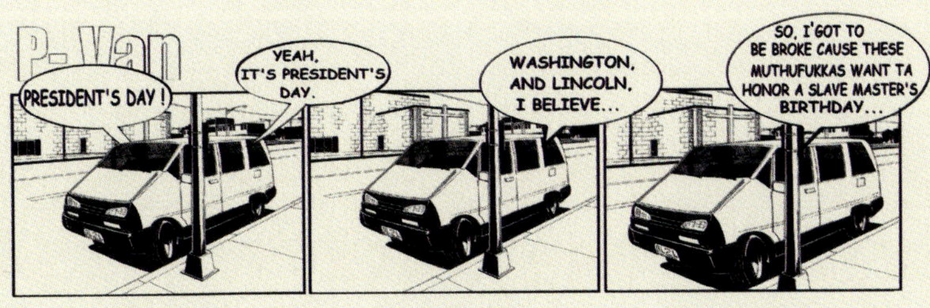
P-Van
PRESIDENT'S DAY!
YEAH, IT'S PRESIDENT'S DAY.
WASHINGTON, AND LINCOLN, I BELIEVE...
SO, I'GOT TO BE BROKE CAUSE THESE MUTHUFUKKAS WANT TA HONOR A SLAVE MASTER'S BIRTHDAY...

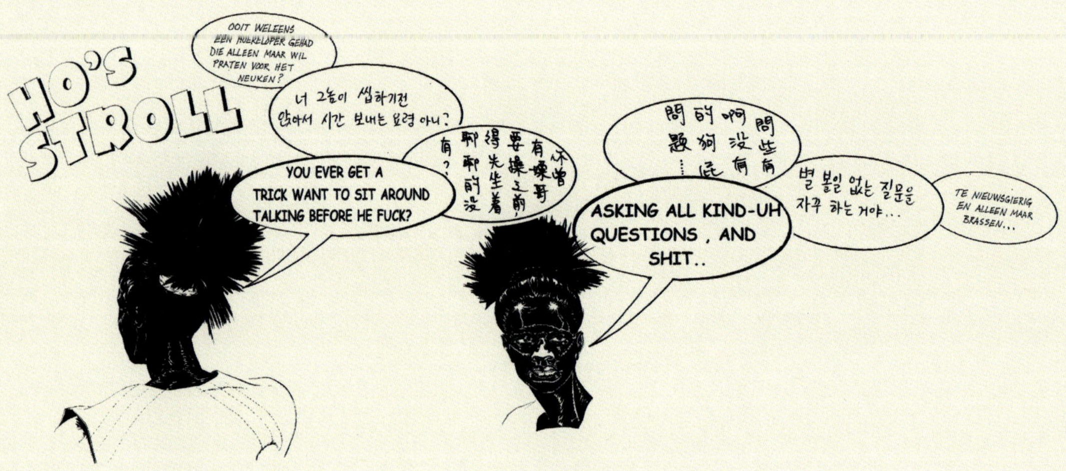
HO'S STROLL
OOIT WELEENS EEN HOERELOPER GEHAD DIE ALLEEN MAAR WIL PRATEN VOOR HET NEUKEN?
너 그놈이 씹하기전 앉아서 시간 보내는 요령 아니?
YOU EVER GET A TRICK WANT TO SIT AROUND TALKING BEFORE HE FUCK?
你曾有嫖哥要操之前，得先坐着聊聊的没有?
ASKING ALL KIND-UH QUESTIONS , AND SHIT..
問些有啊沒有的狗屁問題…
별 볼일 없는 질문을 자꾸 하는 거야...
TE NIEUWSGIERIG EN ALLEEN MAAR BRASSEN...

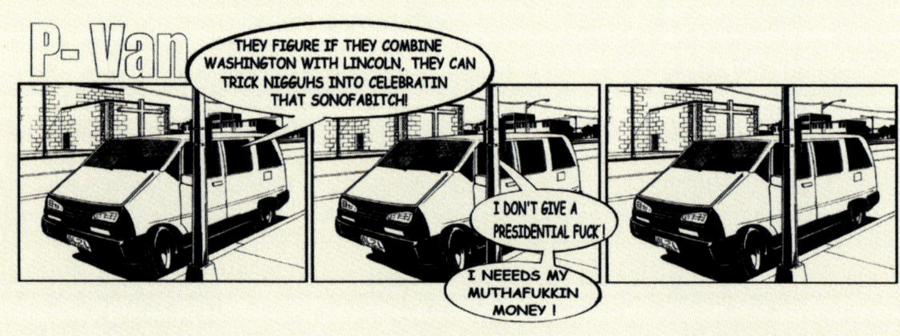
P- Van
THEY FIGURE IF THEY COMBINE WASHINGTON WITH LINCOLN, THEY CAN TRICK NIGGUHS INTO CELEBRATIN THAT SONOFABITCH!
I DON'T GIVE A PRESIDENTIAL FUCK!
I NEEEDS MY MUTHAFUKKIN MONEY !

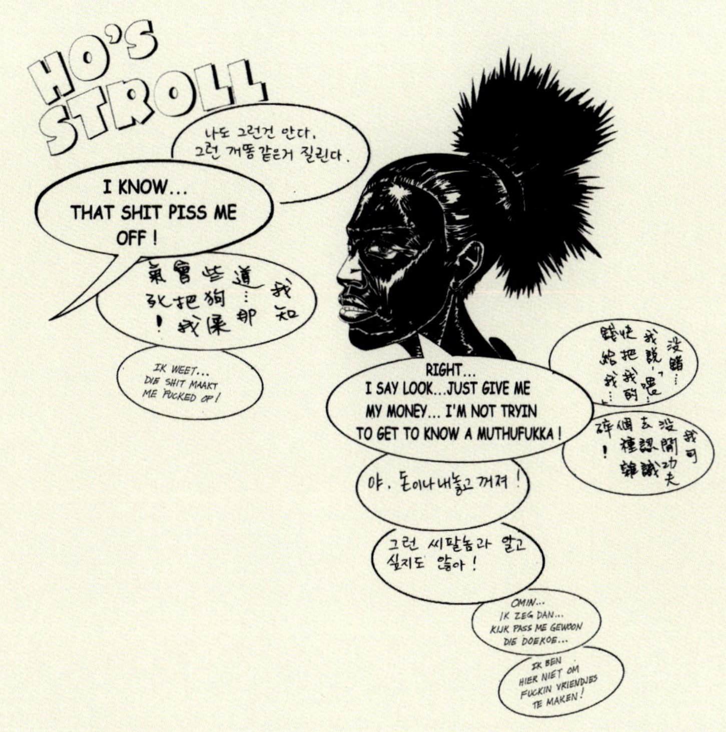
HO'S STROLL
나도 그런건 안다.
그런 개똥같은거 질린다.
I KNOW...
THAT SHIT PISS ME
OFF !
我知道…那些狗屎會把我氣死!
IK WEET...
DIE SHIT MAAKT
ME FUCKED OP!
RIGHT...
I SAY LOOK...JUST GIVE ME
MY MONEY... I'M NOT TRYIN
TO GET TO KNOW A MUTHUFUKKA !
야, 돈이나 내놓고 꺼져!
그런 씨팔놈과 알고
싶지도 않아!
沒錯…我說"喂"!快把我的錢給我…
我可沒閒功夫去認識個雜種!
OMIN...
IK ZEG DAN...
KIJK PASS ME GEWOON
DIE DOEKOE...
IK BEN
HIER NIET OM
FUCKIN VRIENDJES
TE MAKEN!

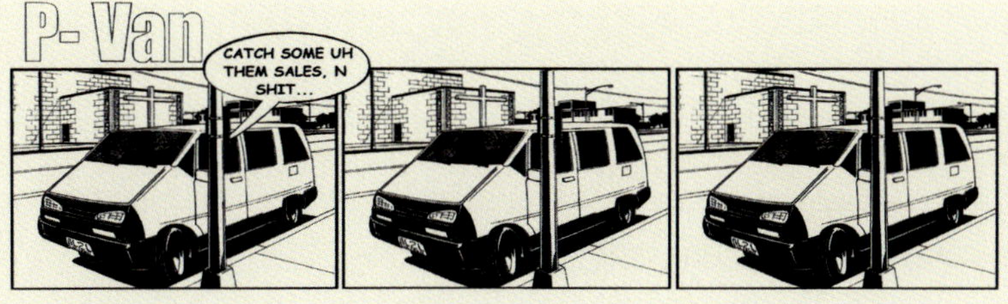
P- Van
CATCH SOME UH
THEM SALES, N
SHIT...

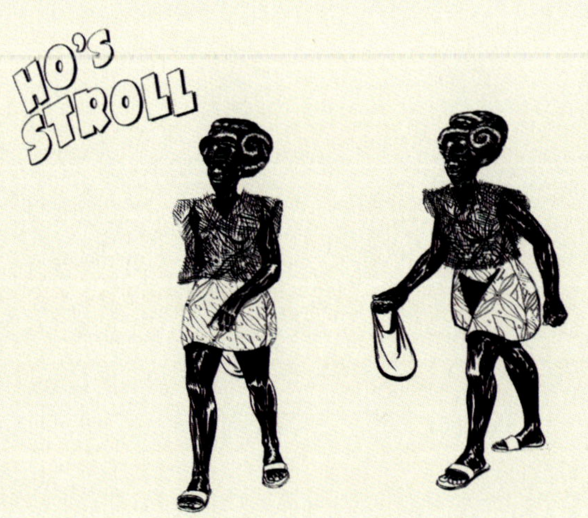
HO'S
STROLL

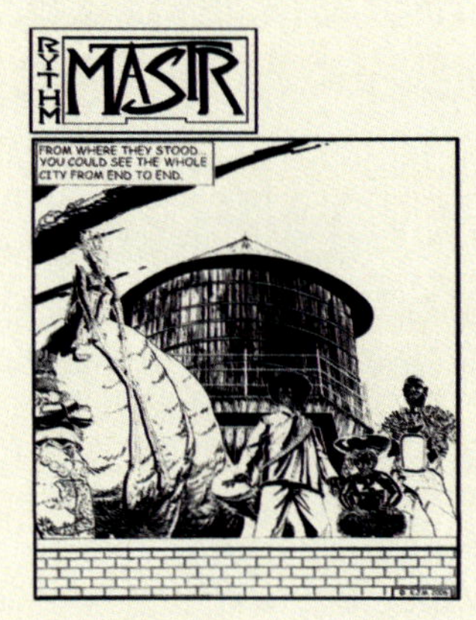
RYTHM
MASTR
FROM WHERE THEY STOOD...
YOU COULD SEE THE WHOLE
CITY FROM END TO END.

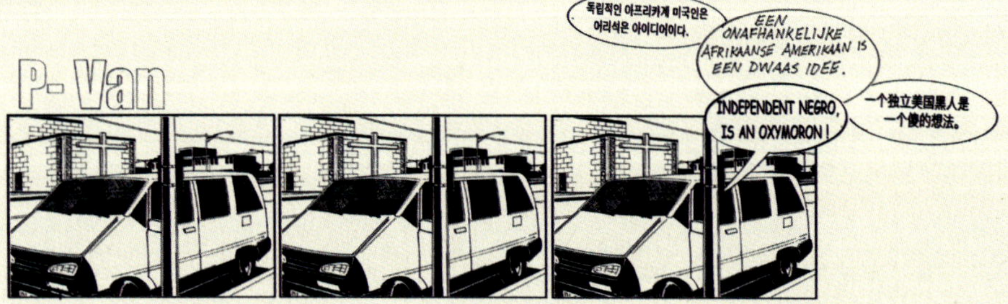
P-Van
INDEPENDENT NEGRO,
IS AN OXYMORON!
EEN ONAFHANKELIJKE AFRIKAANSE AMERIKAAN IS EEN DWAAS IDEE.
독립적인 아프리카계 미국인은 어리석은 아이디어이다.
一个独立美国黑人是一个傻的想法。

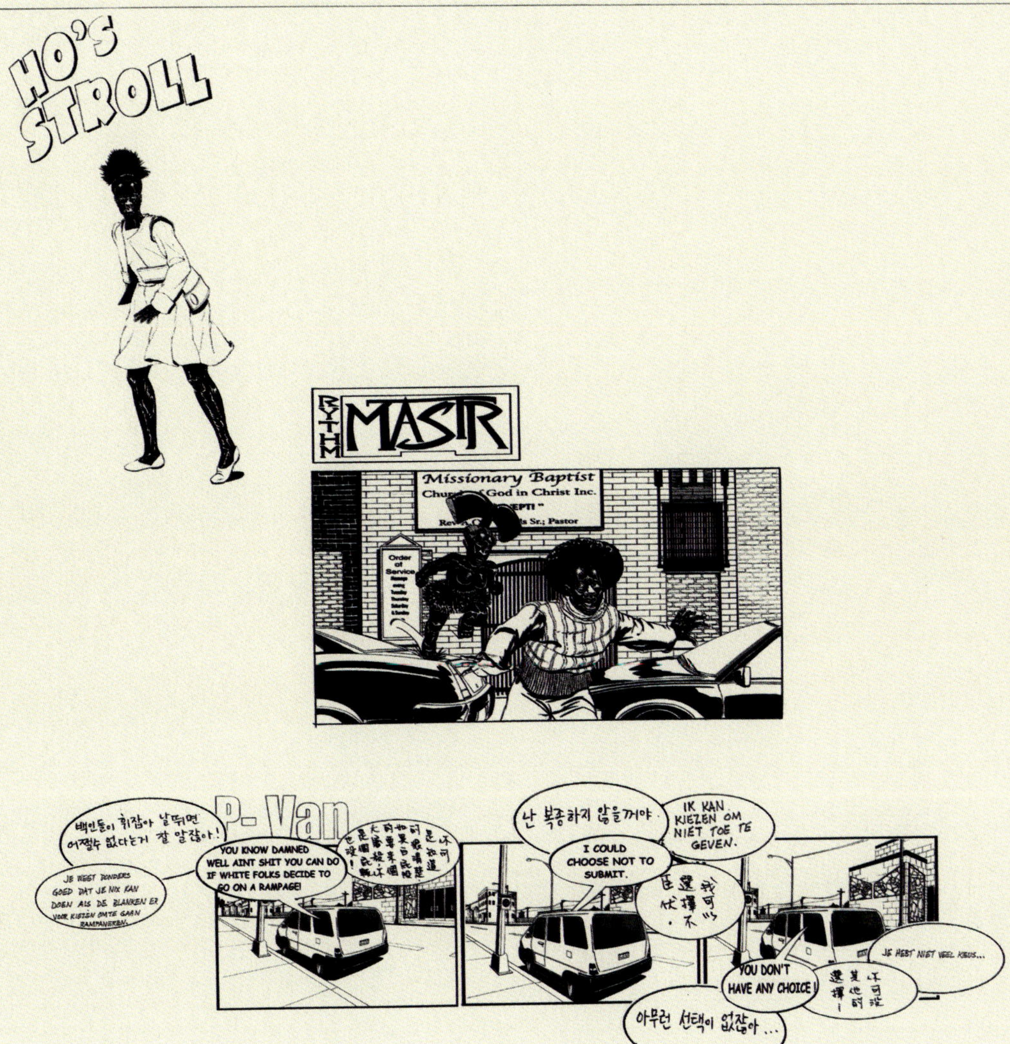
HO'S STROLL
RYTHM MASTR
Missionary Baptist
P- Van
백인들이 휘잡아 날뛰면 어쩔수 없다는거 잘 알잖아!
JE WEET DONDERS GOED DAT JE NIX KAN DOEN ALS DE BLANKEN ER VOOR KIEZEN OM TE GAAN RAMPANEREN.
YOU KNOW DAMNED WELL AINT SHIT YOU CAN DO IF WHITE FOLKS DECIDE TO GO ON A RAMPAGE!
난 복종하지 않을꺼야.
IK KAN KIEZEN OM NIET TOE TE GEVEN.
I COULD CHOOSE NOT TO SUBMIT.
YOU DON'T HAVE ANY CHOICE!
JE HEBT NIET VEEL KEUS...
아무런 선택이 없잖아...

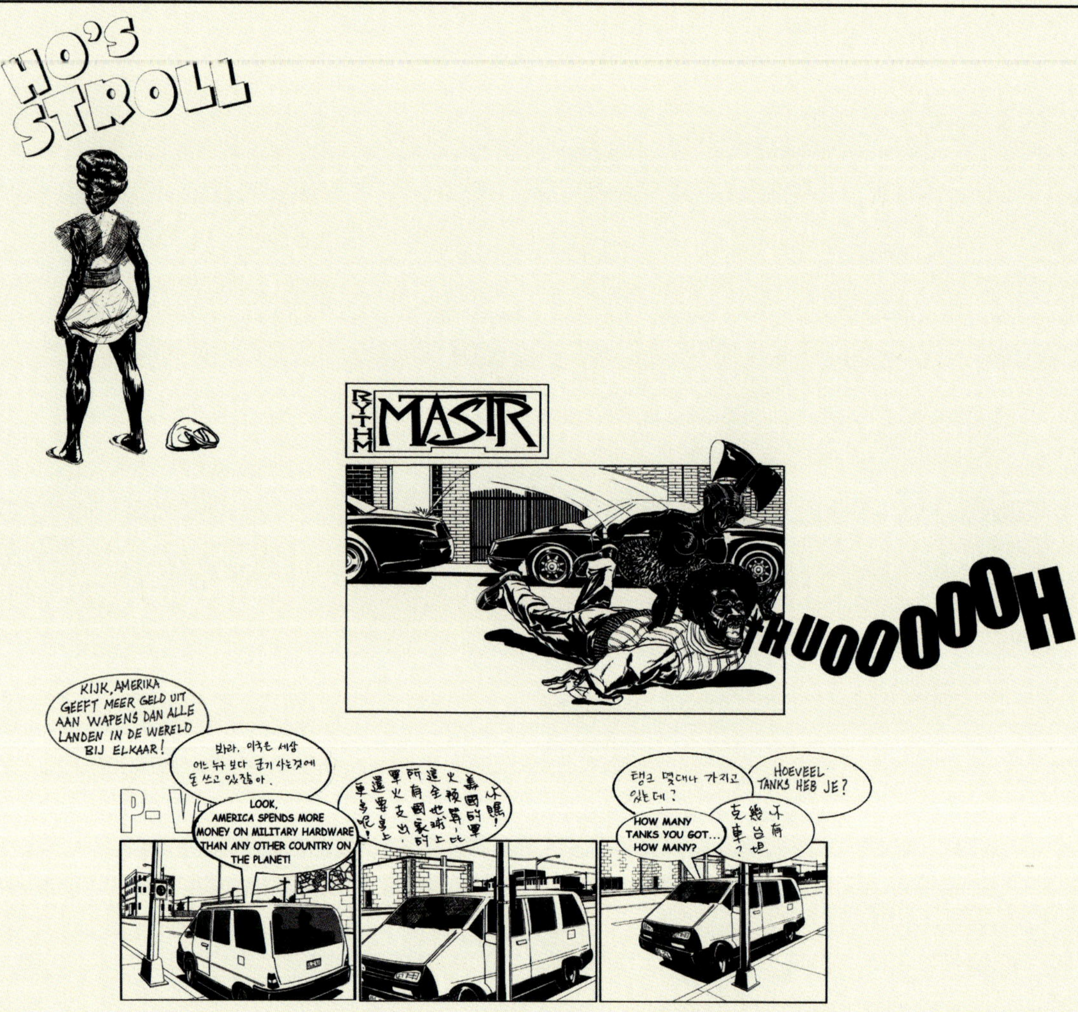
HO'S STROLL
RYTHM MASTR
THUOOOOOOH
KIJK, AMERIKA GEEFT MEER GELD UIT AAN WAPENS DAN ALLE LANDEN IN DE WERELD BIJ ELKAAR!
봐라. 미국은 세상 어느 누구 보다 군기 사는것에 돈 쓰고 있잖아.
LOOK, AMERICA SPENDS MORE MONEY ON MILITARY HARDWARE THAN ANY OTHER COUNTRY ON THE PLANET!
你瞧！美國的軍火預算，比全地球上所有國家的軍火支出，還要多上車多呢！
탱크 몇대나 가지고 있는데?
HOEVEEL TANKS HEB JE?
HOW MANY TANKS YOU GOT... HOW MANY?
你有幾台坦克車？

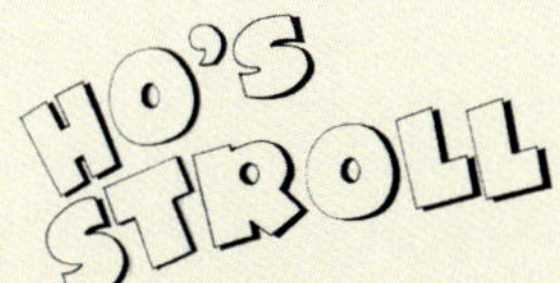
HO'S
STROLL

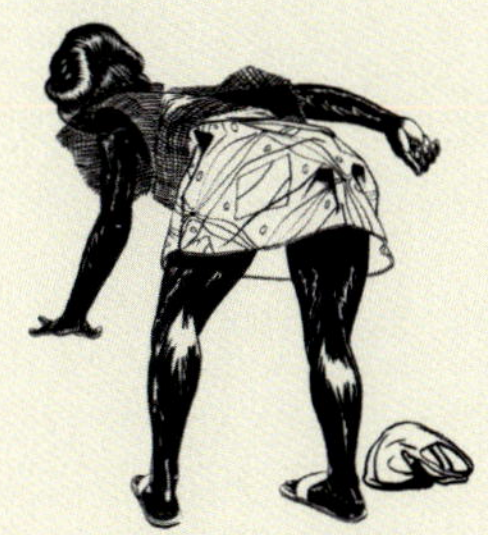

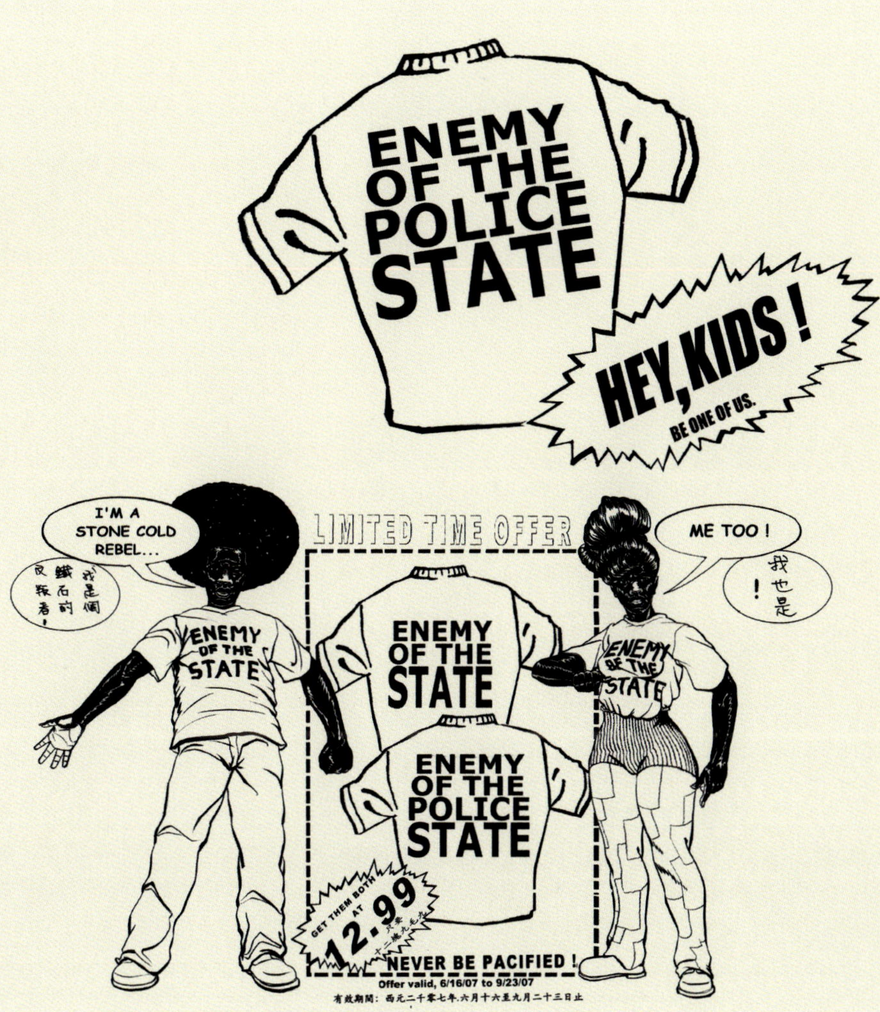
ENEMY
OF THE
POLICE
STATE
HEY, KIDS !
BE ONE OF US.
I'M A
STONE COLD
REBEL...
我是個鐵石的反叛者，
LIMITED TIME OFFER
ME TOO !
我也是！
ENEMY
OF THE
STATE
ENEMY
OF THE
STATE
ENEMY
OF THE
POLICE
STATE
ENEMY
OF THE
STATE
GET THEM BOTH
AT
12.99
只要十二塊九毛九
NEVER BE PACIFIED !
Offer valid, 6/16/07 to 9/23/07
有效期間：西元二千零七年.六月十六至九月二十三日止

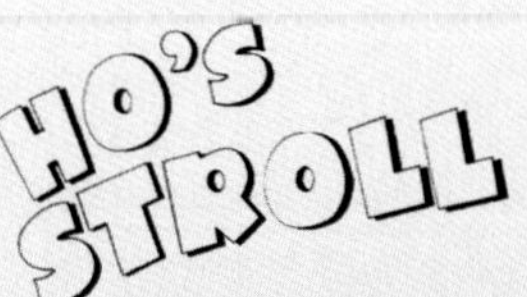
HO'S
STROLL

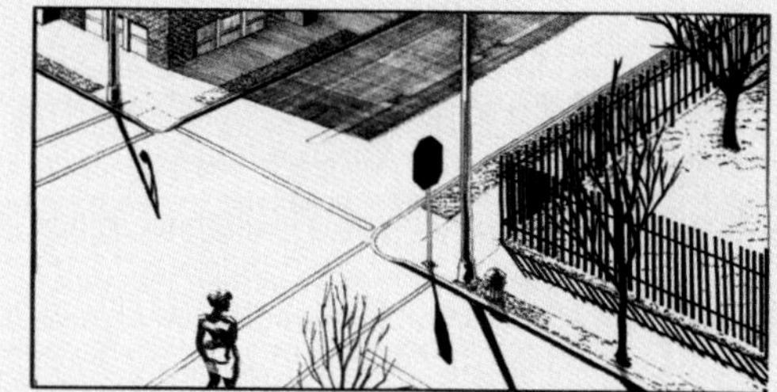

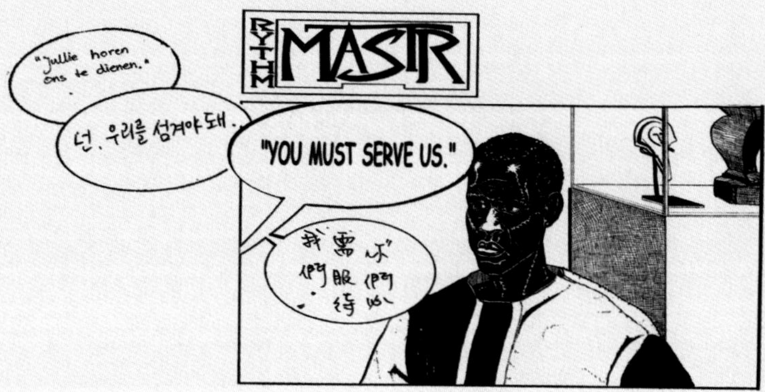
RYTHM MASTR
"Jullie horen ons te dienen."
넌, 우리를 섬겨야 돼..
"YOU MUST SERVE US."

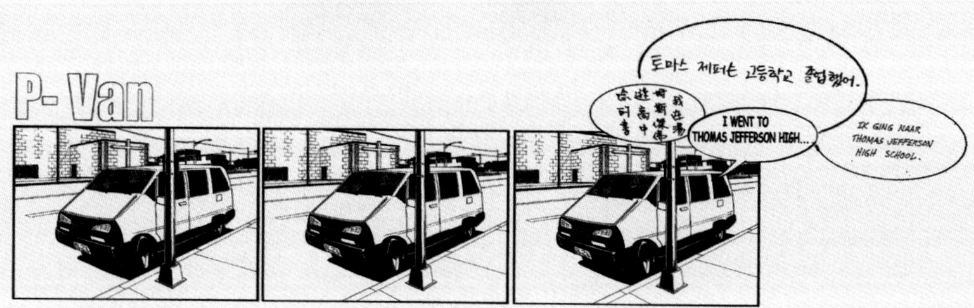
P- Van
토마스 제퍼슨 고등학교 졸업했어.
I WENT TO THOMAS JEFFERSON HIGH...
IK GING NAAR THOMAS JEFFERSON HIGH SCHOOL.

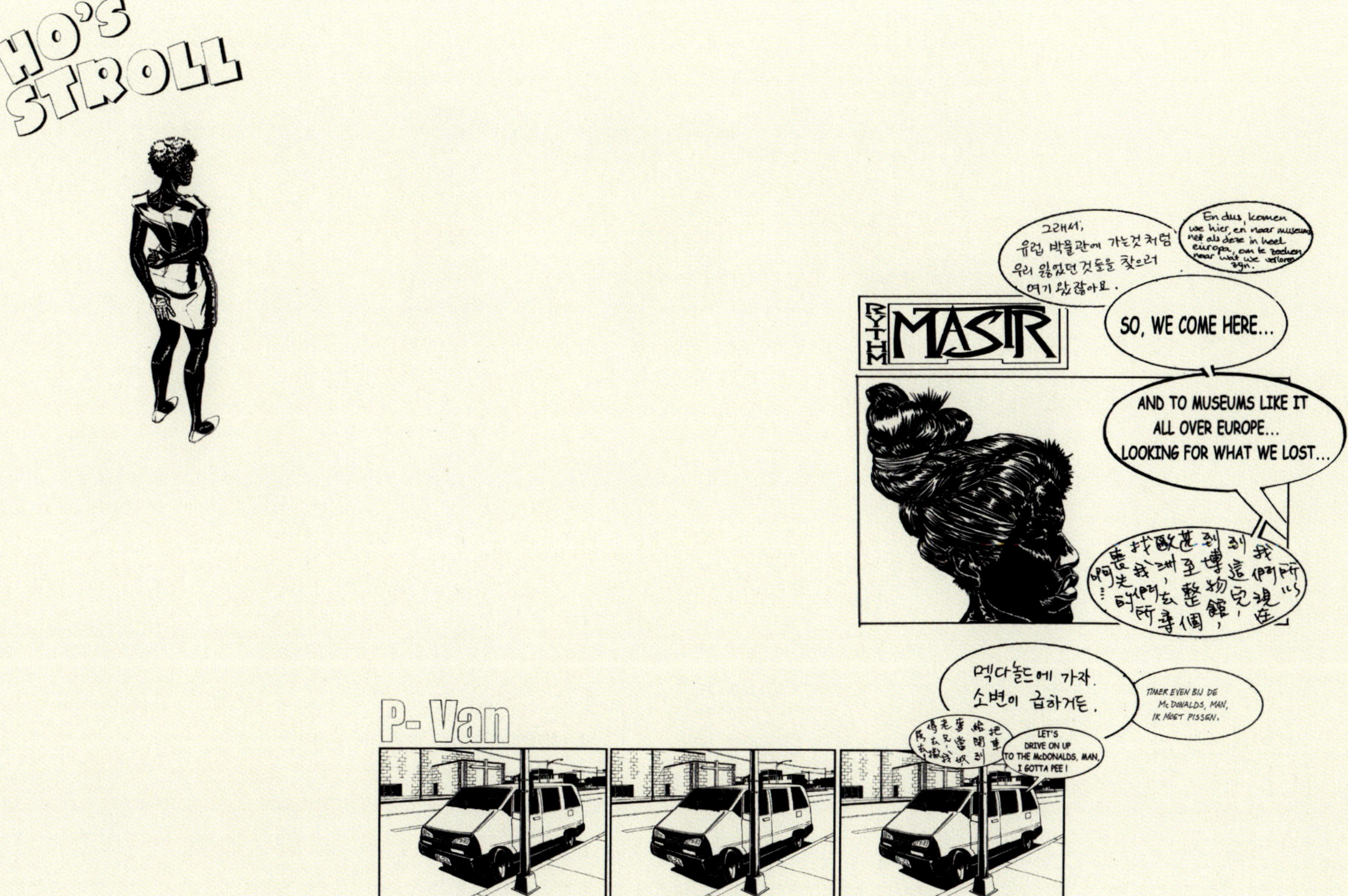
HO'S STROLL
RYTHM MASTR
그래서, 유럽 박물관에 가는것 처럼 우리 잃었던 것들을 찾으러 여기 왔잖아요.
En dus, komen we hier, en naar museums net als deze in heel europa, om te zoeken naar wat we verloren zijn.
SO, WE COME HERE...
AND TO MUSEUMS LIKE IT ALL OVER EUROPE... LOOKING FOR WHAT WE LOST...
P- Van
멕다놀드에 가자. 소변이 급하거든.
TIMER EVEN BIJ DE McDONALDS, MAN, IK MOET PISSEN.
LET'S DRIVE ON UP TO THE McDONALDS, MAN, I GOTTA PEE!

HO'S STROLL

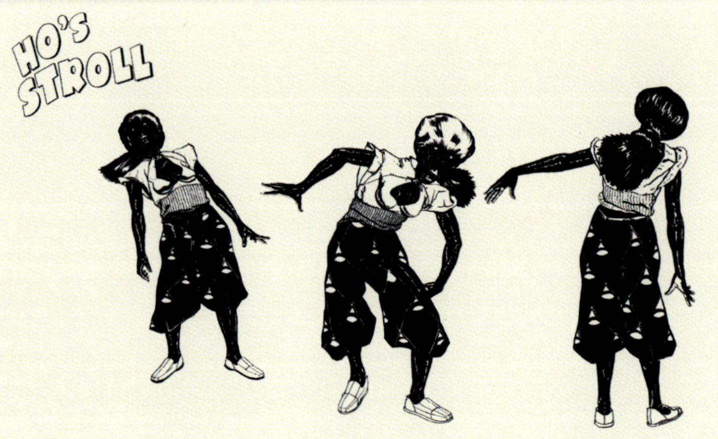

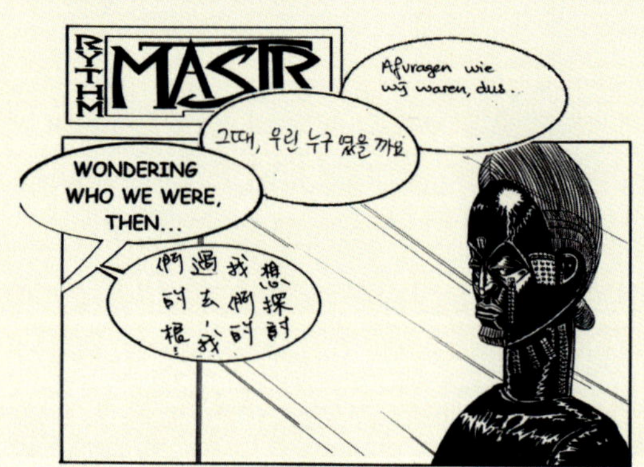

P- Van

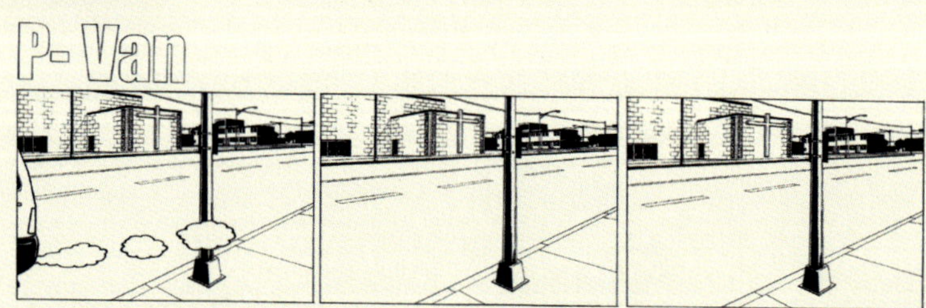

TIMES

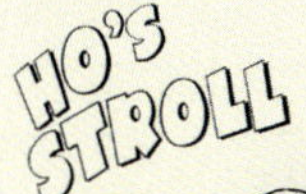

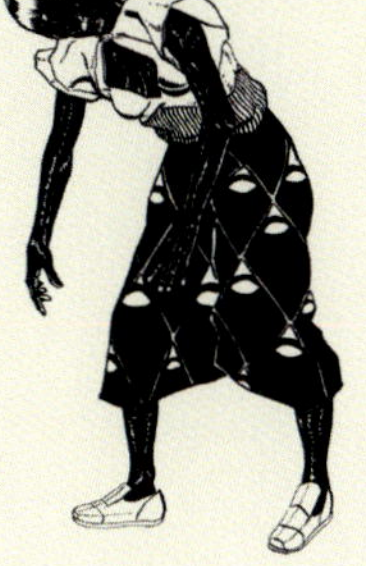

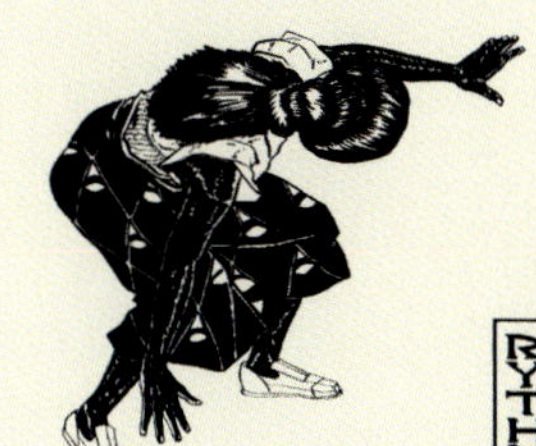

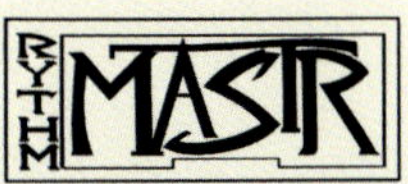

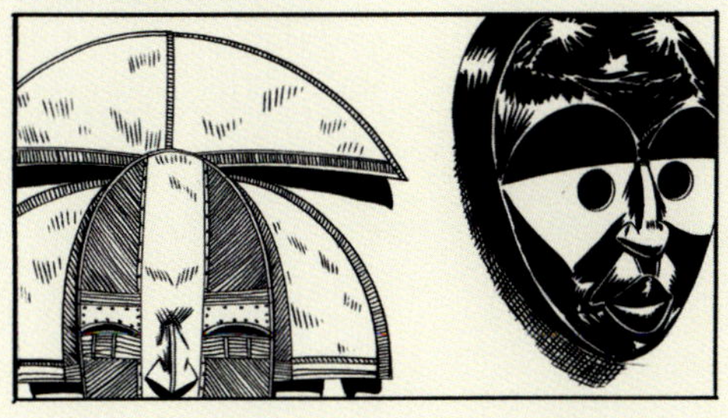

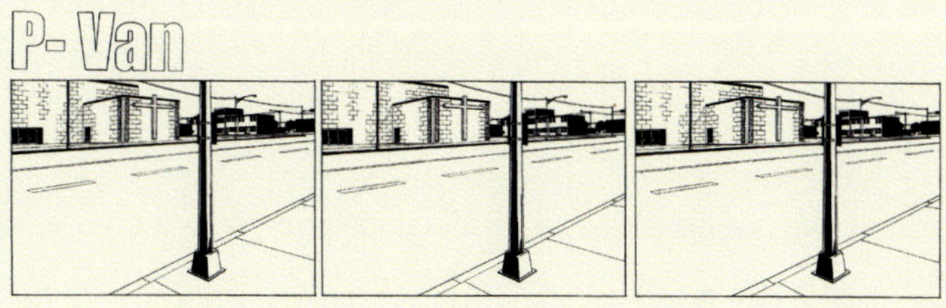

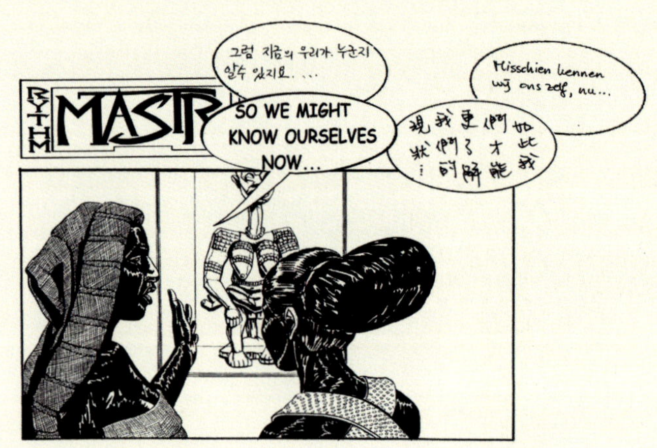
RYTHM MASTR
그럼 지금의 우리가. 누군지 알수 있지요. ...
SO WE MIGHT KNOW OURSELVES NOW...
如此我們才能更了解我們的現狀！
Misschien kennen wij ons zelf, nu...

P- Van

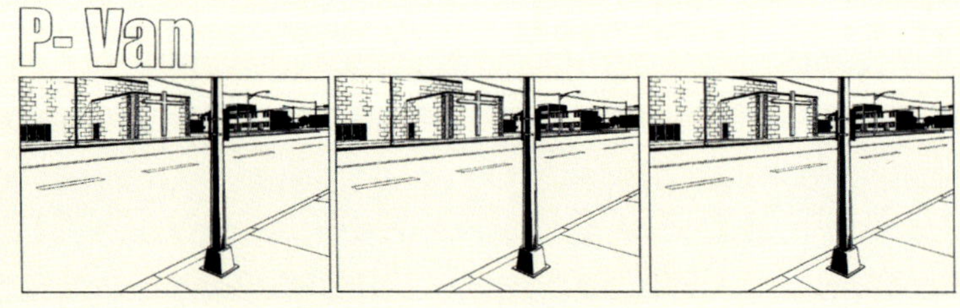

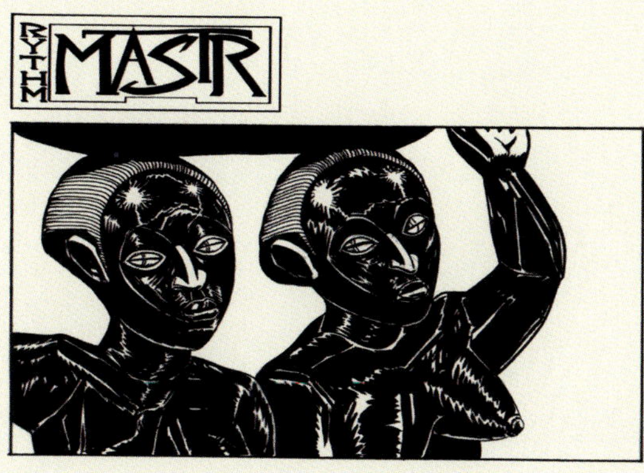
RYTHM MASTR

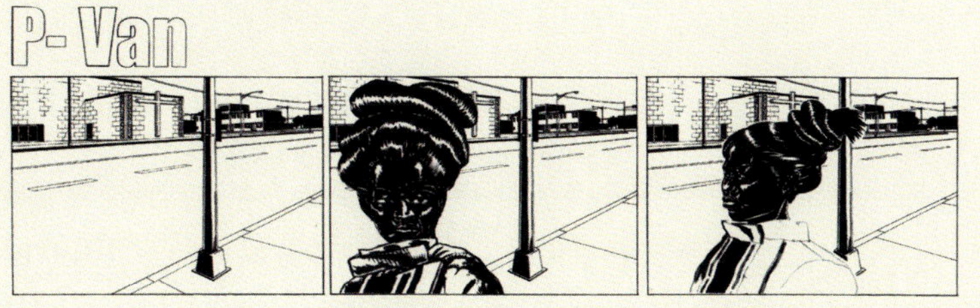
P- Van

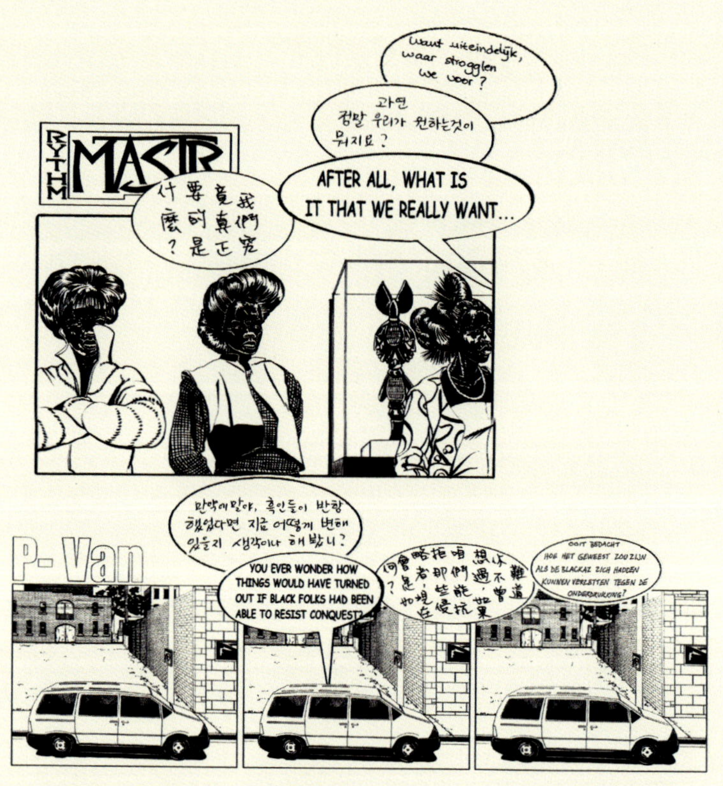
RYTHM MASTR
我們究竟真正要的是什麼？
AFTER ALL, WHAT IS IT THAT WE REALLY WANT...
과연 정말 우리가 원하는것이 뭐지요?
Want uiteindelijk, waar strogglen we voor?
P-Van
YOU EVER WONDER HOW THINGS WOULD HAVE TURNED OUT IF BLACK FOLKS HAD BEEN ABLE TO RESIST CONQUEST?
만약에 말야, 흑인들이 반항했었다면 지금 어떻게 변해 있을지 생각이나 해 봤니?
OOIT BEDACHT HOE HET GEWEEST ZOU ZIJN ALS DE BLACKAZ ZICH HADDEN KUNNEN VERLETTEN TEGEN DE ONDERDRUKKING?

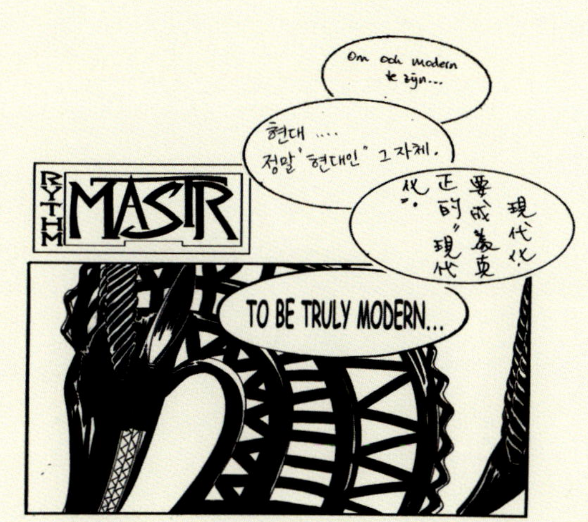
RYTHM MASTR
Om och modern te zijn...
현대 ....
정말 "현대인" 그 자체.
TO BE TRULY MODERN...

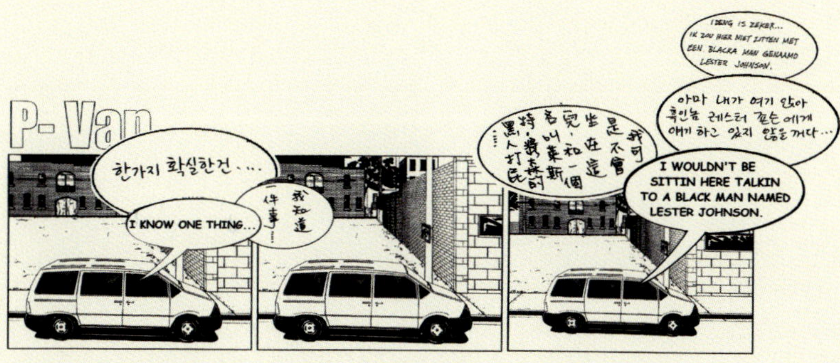
P-Van
한가지 확실한건....
I KNOW ONE THING...
我知道一件事!...
I DING IS ZEKER...
IK ZOU HIER NIET ZITTEN MET
EEN BLACKA MAN GENAAMD
LESTER JOHNSON.
아마 내가 여기 앉아
흑인놈 레스터 존슨에게
얘기 하고 있지 않을꺼다...
I WOULDN'T BE
SITTIN HERE TALKIN
TO A BLACK MAN NAMED
LESTER JOHNSON.

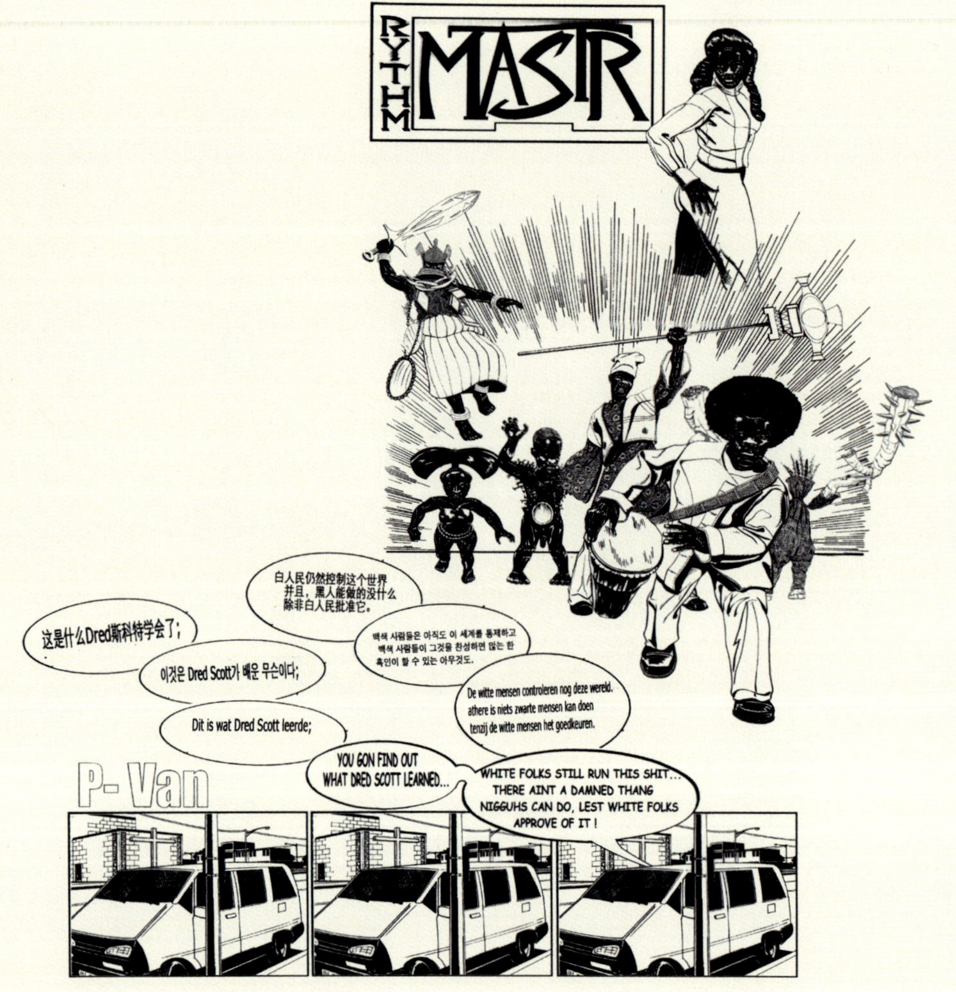
RYTHM MASTR
这是什么Dred斯科特学会了;
이것은 Dred Scott가 배운 무슨이다;
Dit is wat Dred Scott leerde;
白人民仍然控制这个世界 并且，黑人能做的没什么 除非白人民批准它。
백색 사람들은 아직도 이 세계를 통제하고 백색 사람들이 그것을 찬성하면 않는 한 흑인이 할 수 있는 아무것도.
De witte mensen controleren nog deze wereld. athere is niets zwarte mensen kan doen tenzij de witte mensen het goedkeuren.
P- Van
YOU GON FIND OUT WHAT DRED SCOTT LEARNED...
WHITE FOLKS STILL RUN THIS SHIT... THERE AINT A DAMNED THANG NIGGUHS CAN DO, LEST WHITE FOLKS APPROVE OF IT !

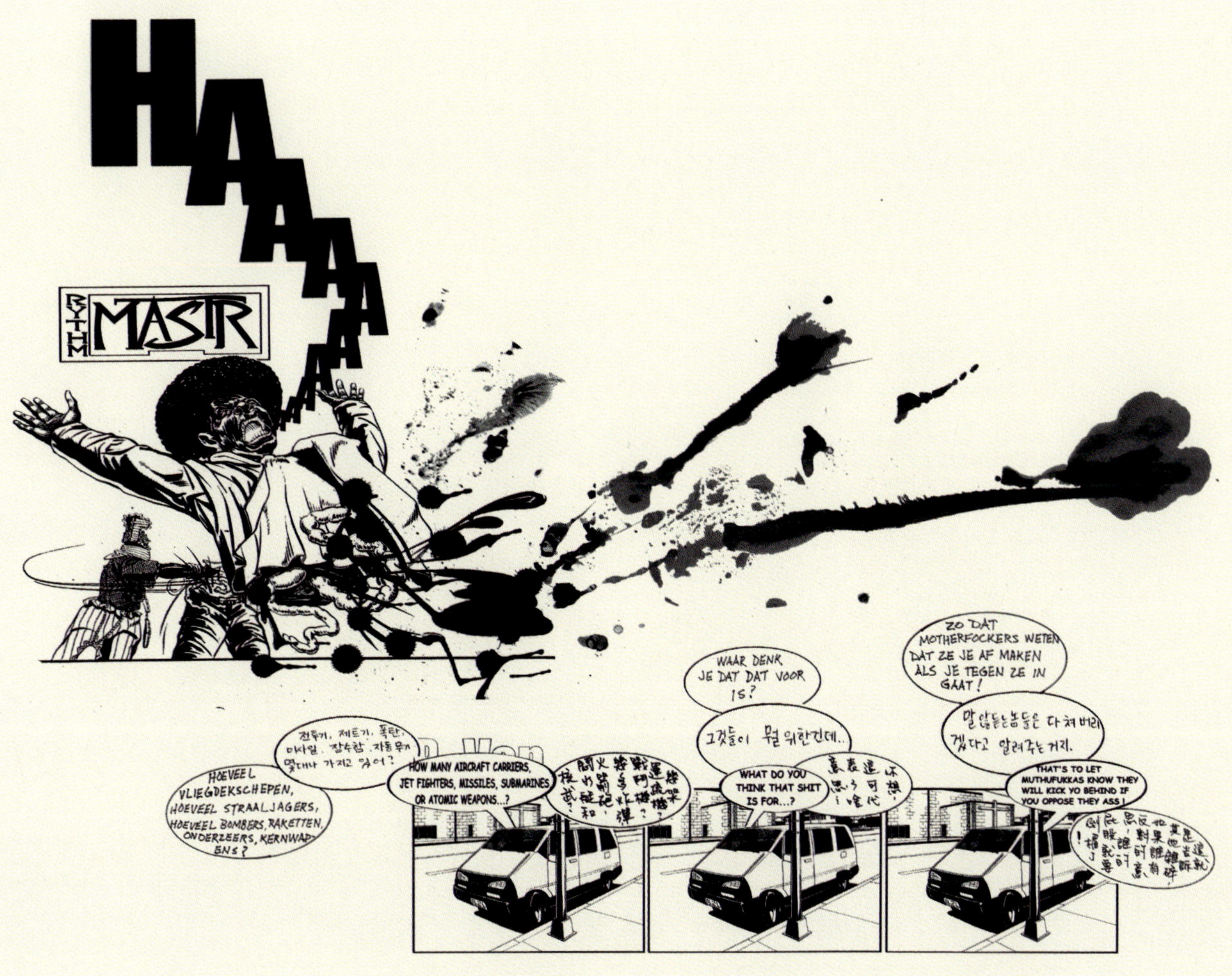
HAAAAAAAA
RYTHM MASTR
HOEVEEL VLIEGDEKSCHEPEN, HOEVEEL STRAALJAGERS, HOEVEEL BOMBERS, RAKETTEN, ONDERZEERS, KERNWAPENS?
HOW MANY AIRCRAFT CARRIERS, JET FIGHTERS, MISSILES, SUBMARINES OR ATOMIC WEAPONS...?
WAAR DENK JE DAT DAT VOOR IS?
그것들이 뭘 위한건데..
WHAT DO YOU THINK THAT SHIT IS FOR...?
ZO DAT MOTHERFOCKERS WETEN DAT ZE JE AF MAKEN ALS JE TEGEN ZE IN GAAT!
말안듣는놈들은 다 쳐 버리겠다고 알려주는 거지.
THAT'S TO LET MUTHUFUKKAS KNOW THEY WILL KICK YO BEHIND IF YOU OPPOSE THEY ASS!

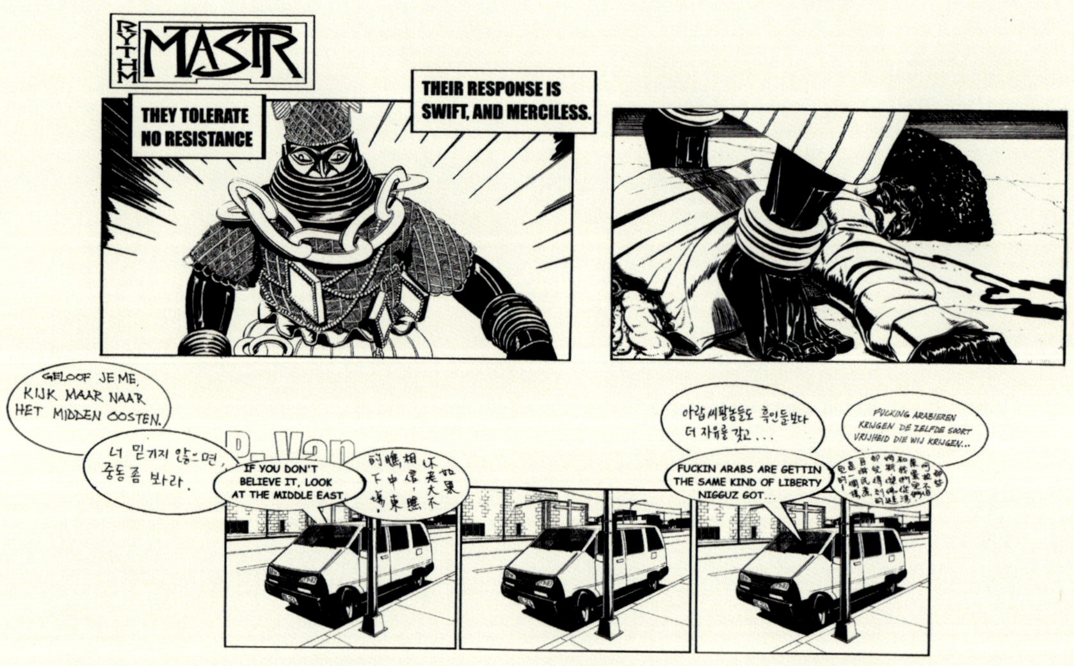
RYTHM MASTR
THEY TOLERATE NO RESISTANCE
THEIR RESPONSE IS SWIFT, AND MERCILESS.
GELOOF JE ME, KIJK MAAR NAAR HET MIDDEN OOSTEN.
너 믿기지 않으면, 중동좀 봐라.
IF YOU DON'T BELIEVE IT, LOOK AT THE MIDDLE EAST
아랍 씨팔놈들도 흑인들보다 더 자유를 갖고...
FUCKIN ARABS ARE GETTIN THE SAME KIND OF LIBERTY NIGGUZ GOT...
FUCKING ARABIEREN KRIJGEN DE ZELFDE SOORT VRIJHEID DIE WIJ KRIJGEN...

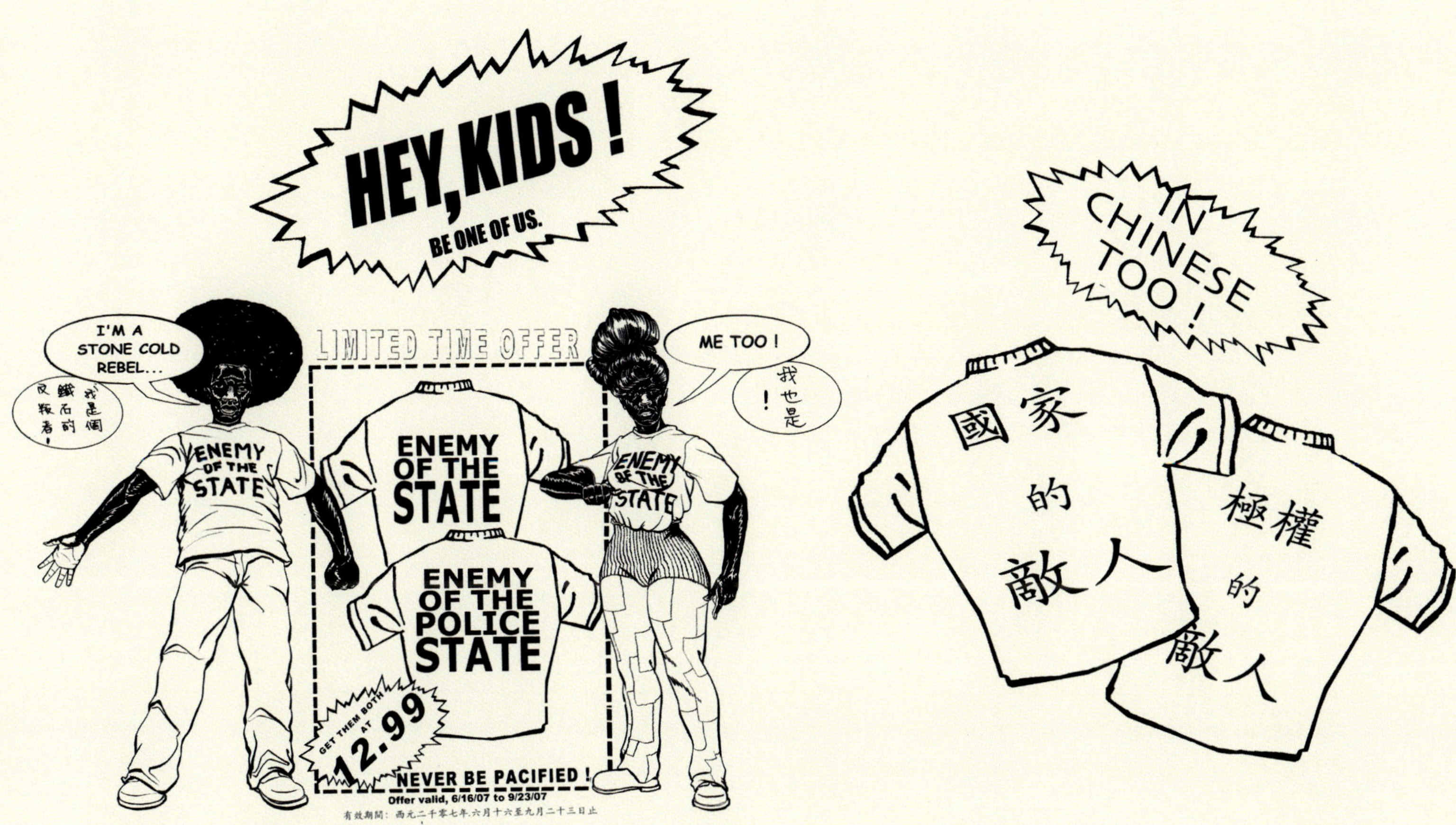
HEY, KIDS!
BE ONE OF US.
I'M A STONE COLD REBEL...
我是個鐵石的反叛者!
LIMITED TIME OFFER
ENEMY OF THE STATE
ENEMY OF THE STATE
ENEMY OF THE POLICE STATE
GET THEM BOTH AT 12.99
NEVER BE PACIFIED!
Offer valid, 6/16/07 to 9/23/07
有效期間: 西元二千零七年.六月十六至九月二十三日止
ENEMY OF THE STATE
ME TOO!
我也是!
IN CHINESE TOO!
國家的敵人
極權的敵人

2003–ONGOING

UNTITLED

Ink on paper

Seven of the superheroes from the series—Rythm Mastr, Farrell, Stasha, Senufo, Ibeji, Nkisi, and Oba—are the subject of one of the first collective portraits in the series. Originally included in the "Dailies," the drawing marks the philosophical division between Farrell and Stasha; Farrell leads the group while Stasha is represented on a different dimensional plane, overlooking the scene. On the occasion of the Los Angeles leg of Marshall's retrospective exhibition *Mastry* in 2017, a T-shirt featuring this image was produced as a gadget. It gained further prominence in 2025 when sported by the character Aziza in Branden Jacobs-Jenkins's Broadway play *Purpose.*

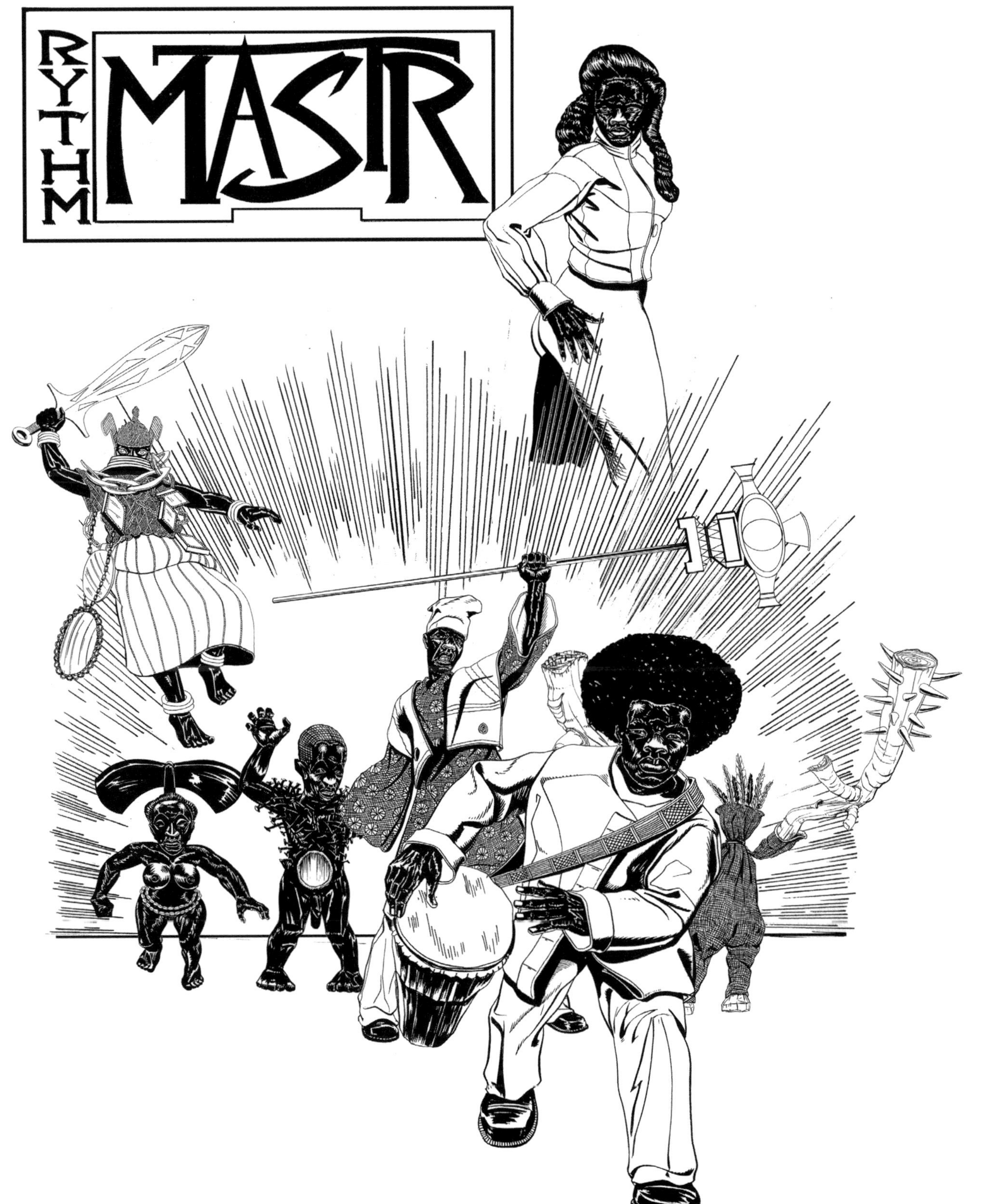
RYTHM
MASTR

2003–ONGOING

UNTITLED

Ink on paper

The drawing depicting Stasha and Farrell in *Rythm Mastr Dailies: Everything Will Be Alright, I Just Know It Will* and *Dailies: Everything Will Be Alright (Single)* is here proposed with a single balloon in English and the Rythm Mastr logo slightly positioned closer to the character.

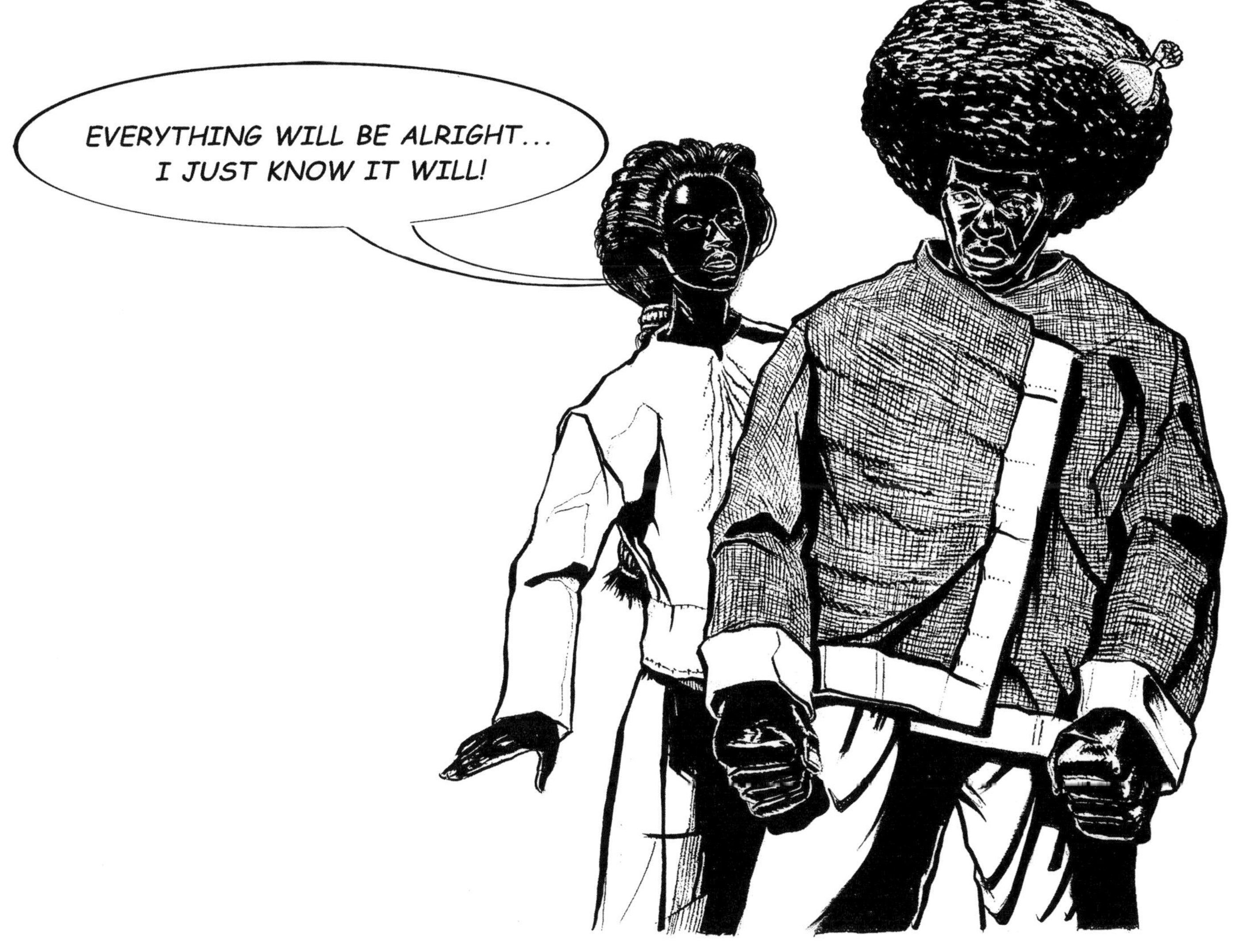
EVERYTHING WILL BE ALRIGHT... I JUST KNOW IT WILL!

2003–ONGOING

UNTITLED

Ink on paper

The vertical panel illustrates the façade of The Ancient Egyptian Museum. The broken glass suggest that the African artifacts have already left the building and that what we are seeing here is the aftermath of the episode that would lead to the events that will unfold in the series.

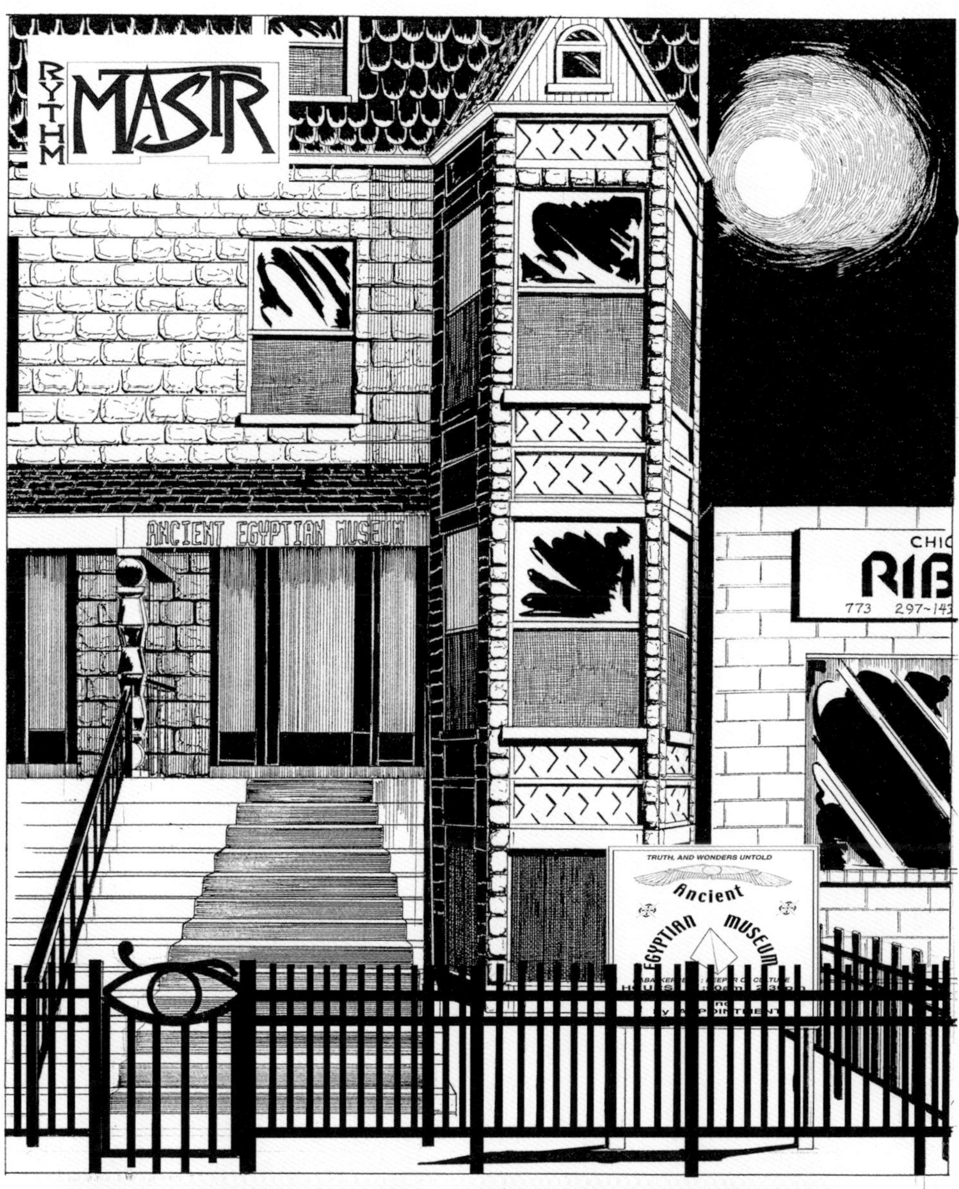

IN THIS HOUSE...

2003–2004

UNTITLED

Ink and graphite on paper, five parts

Each 30×41 ¾ in. (76.2×106 cm)

Museum of Modern Art, New York. Gift of the artist and Jack Shainman Gallery, and purchase

This set of drawings made with ink and graphite between 2003 and 2004 presents five different visual interpretations of a brief exchange between Farrell and Stasha. The comic book catchphrase "Everything will be alright, I just know it will" will end up earning mantra status, with the reassuring message becoming a regular fixture in future *Rythm Mastr*-related works. Marshall's fascination with this simple yet theatrical articulation was immediately put to use when he made inkjet versions of three of these drawings, now in the collection of the Museum of Modern Art in New York. The third incarnation of the series focuses on the only drawing where Stasha is not visible—the speech balloons belonging to someone outside the frame. Made as a helio-relief (a photo-mechanical woodcut in which light-sensitive emulsion is deployed to create a stencil through which a woodblock can be sandblasted), the piece was made following an invitation by Thomas Lucas, at the time director of printmaking at Lillstreet Art Center in Chicago. This is the first group of works where an afro comb is distinctly visible in Farrell's hair.

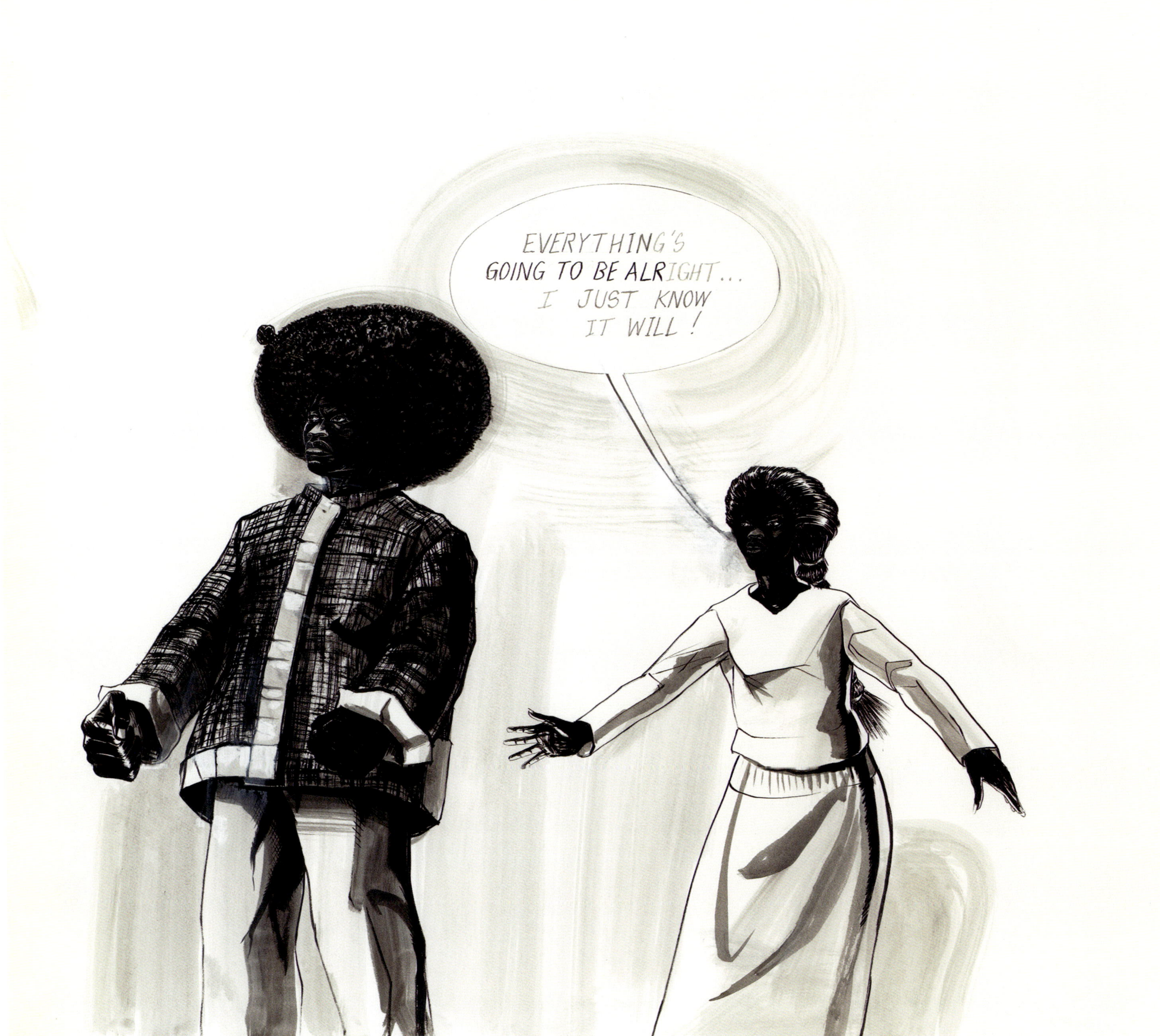
EVERYTHING'S GOING TO BE ALRIGHT... I JUST KNOW IT WILL!

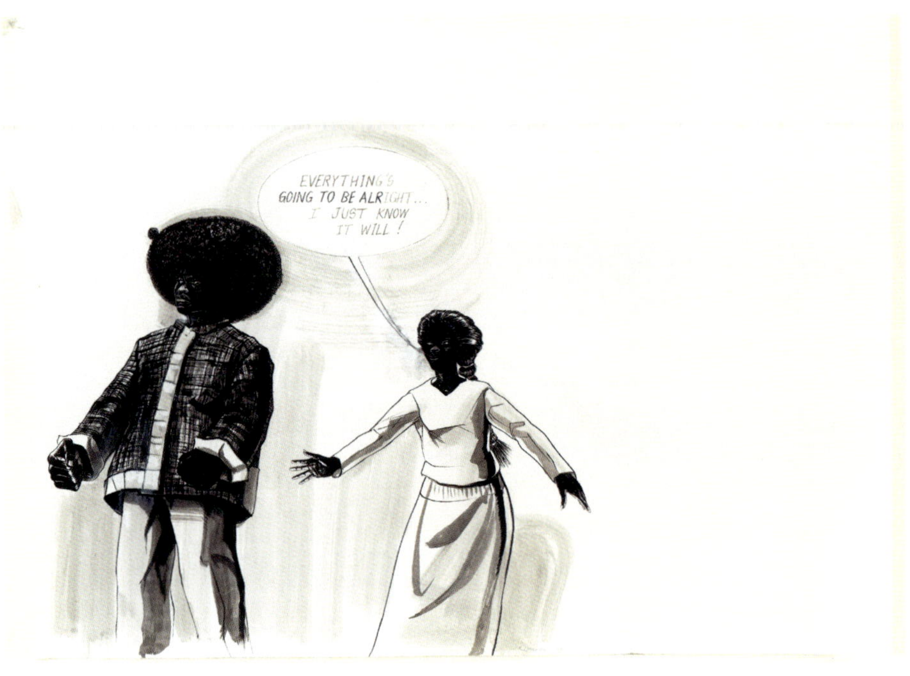
EVERYTHING'S GOING TO BE ALRIGHT... I JUST KNOW IT WILL!

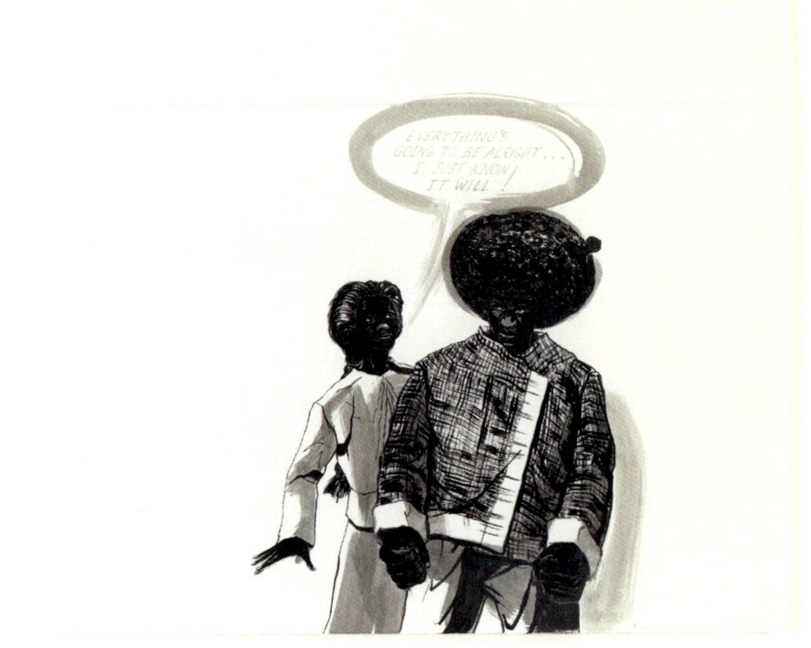
EVERYTHING'S GOING TO BE ALRIGHT... I JUST KNOW IT WILL!

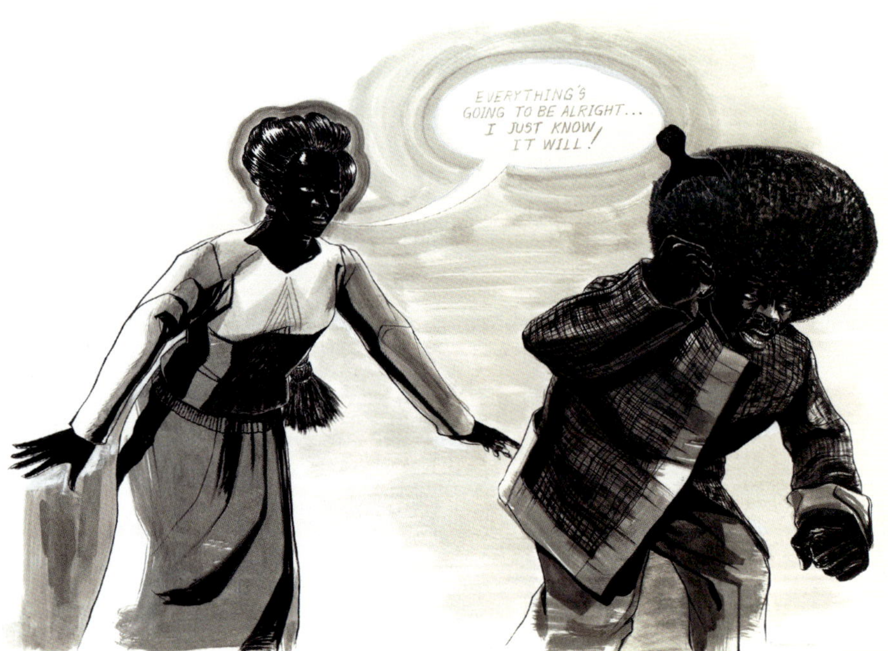
EVERYTHING'S GOING TO BE ALRIGHT... I JUST KNOW IT WILL!

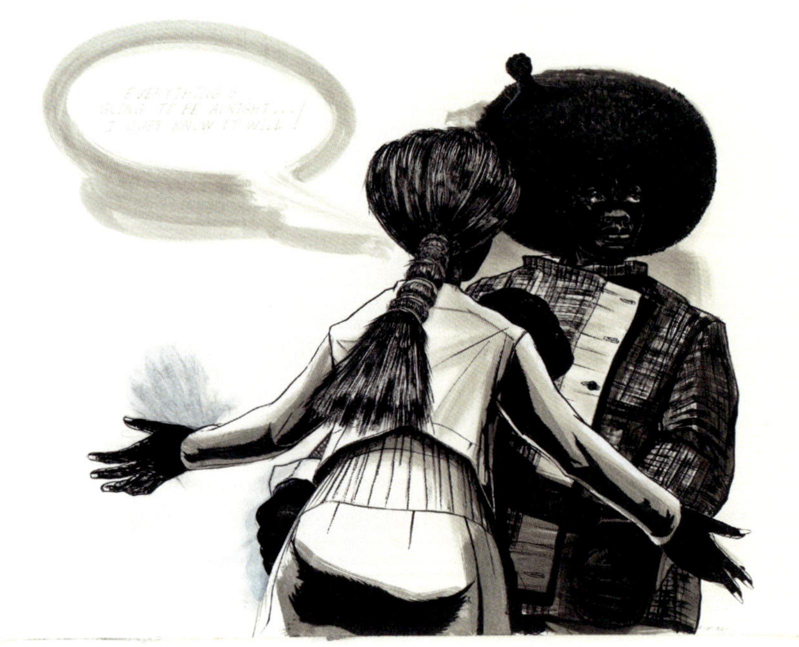

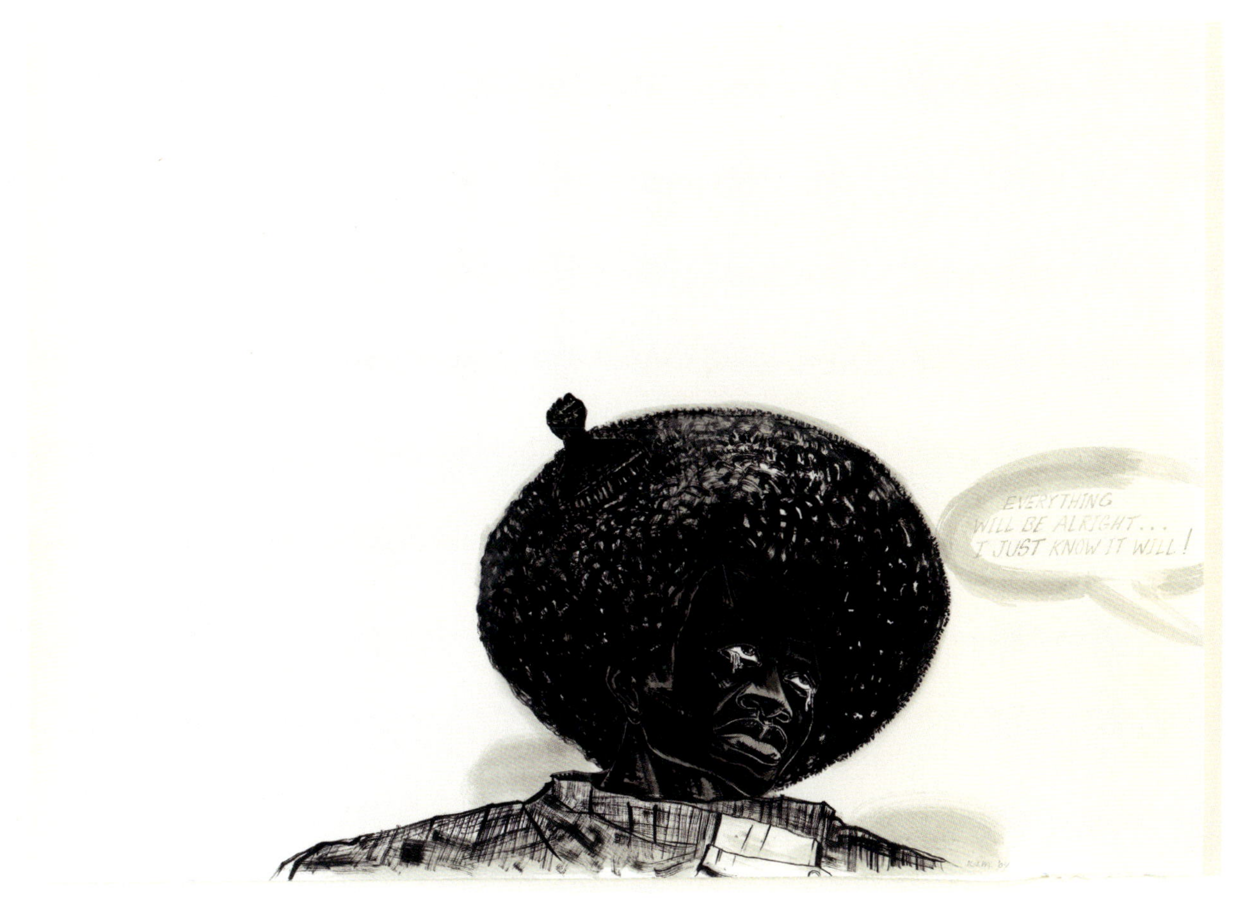

Untitled **[2004]**

2004

RYTHM MASTR DAILIES: EVERYTHING WILL BE ALRIGHT, I JUST KNOW IT WILL

Inkjet on newsprint

23×32 in. (58.5×81.5 cm)

Three unique compositions

Printed by the artist at Kinko's, Chicago

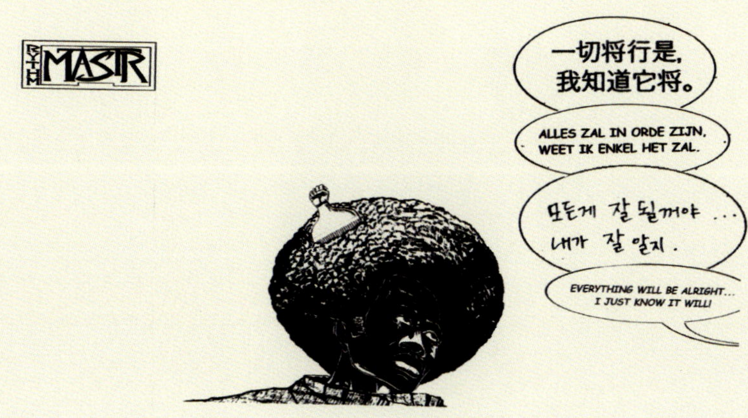
MASTR
一切将行是,
我知道它将。
ALLES ZAL IN ORDE ZIJN,
WEET IK ENKEL HET ZAL.
모든게 잘 될꺼야 ...
내가 잘 알지.
EVERYTHING WILL BE ALRIGHT...
I JUST KNOW IT WILL!

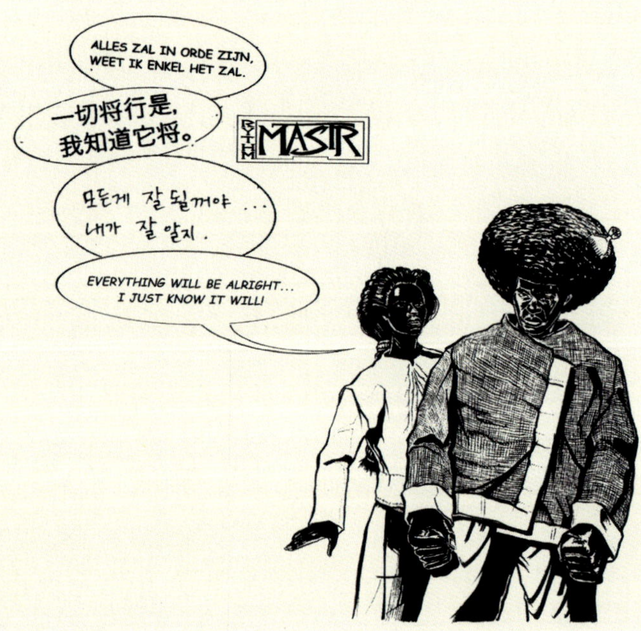
ALLES ZAL IN ORDE ZIJN, WEET IK ENKEL HET ZAL.
一切将行是，我知道它将。
RYTHM MASTR
모든게 잘 될꺼야 ... 내가 잘 알지.
EVERYTHING WILL BE ALRIGHT... I JUST KNOW IT WILL!

TIMES

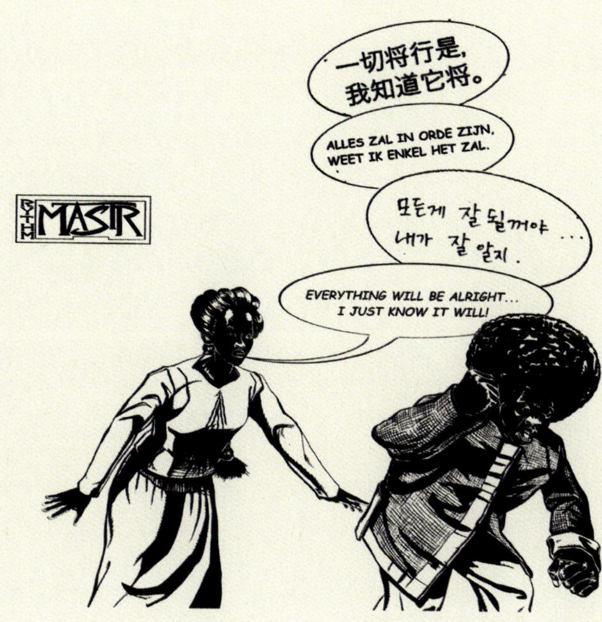

Rythm Mastr Dailies: Everything Will Be Alright, I Just Know It Will **[2004]**

2004

EVERYTHING WILL BE ALRIGHT

Sandblasted and hand-cut woodcut with screen print, printed in black and buff on Rives BFK gray with deckle edge

Image: 27 ½×41 ½ in. (70×105.5 cm), sheet: 30×44 in. (76×112 cm)

Edition: 25

Numbered, titled, signed, and dated in pencil

Printed by Thomas Lucas, Mary del Biasio, and Jessie Antonick at Hummingbird Press, Chicago. Published by Hummingbird Press, Chicago

2008–2009

RYTHM MASTR DAILIES: MONUMENTS FOR A NEW AMERICA

Inkjet on newsprint

23×32 in. (58.5×81.5 cm)

Printed by the artist at Kinko's, Chicago

As seen with the *Dailies*, Marshall has often used the narrative potential offered by *Rythm Mastr* to elaborate on sociopolitical themes he is interested in. *Monuments for a New America* focuses on Nat Turner, an enslaved carpenter who in 1831 led a four-day rebellion in Southampton County, Virginia. Between Turner's insurgence and the retaliatory action of the state troops, the fighting resulted in the death of over 150 people, including Turner himself, who was captured and sentenced to death after three months on the run. *Monuments for a New America* illustrates Marshall's position on the subject of historical cancellation: statues and sculptures erected to celebrate controversial figures or events should undergo modification rather than being left alone or toppled into oblivion. Noting that the nation's founding fathers were enslavers, Marshall proposes to install a winged Nat Turner breaking away from his chains on the obelisk in Washington, DC. P-Van, On the Stroll, and the Rythm Mastr corroborate the artist's view in a way that is consistent with their personalities. Initially presented in the "Dailies" as part of a subplot titled "At Last," *Monuments for a New America* would later be published, in a slightly different permutation, on the pages of the capital's newspaper, *The Washington Post*, on February 15, 2009. Art critic Blake Gopnik, who facilitated the project, observed around a decade later: "Washington's armed uprising against George III was not one-tenth as justified as Turner's against the men who dared to say they could own him." An additional panel for *Monuments for a New America* addresses the Liberty Bell in Philadelphia, which in Marshall's version is augmented by a gigantic hand holding it from above.

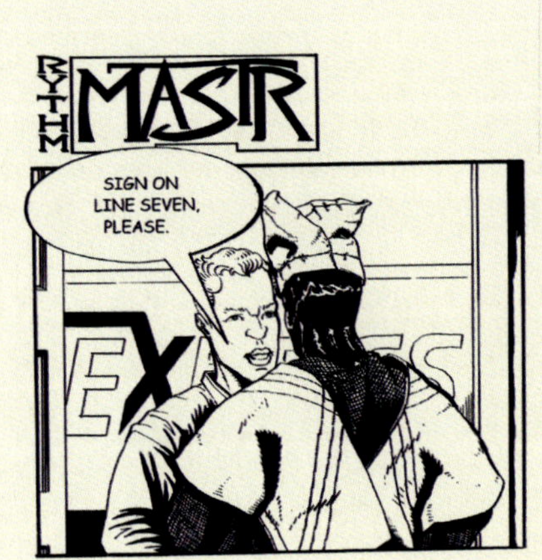
RYTHM
MASTR
SIGN ON LINE SEVEN, PLEASE.

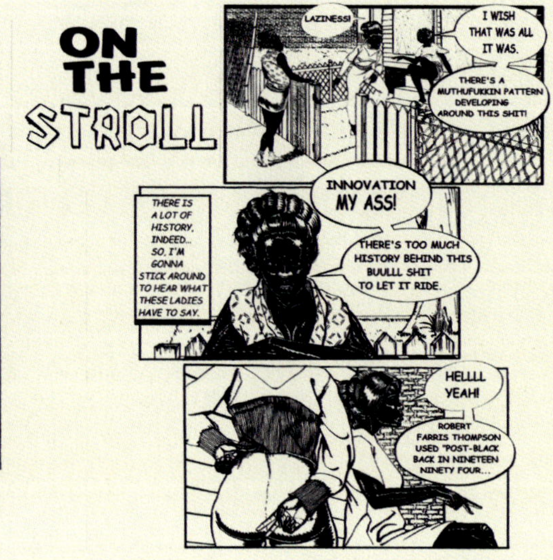
ON THE STROLL
LAZINESS!
I WISH THAT WAS ALL IT WAS.
THERE'S A MUTHUFUKKIN PATTERN DEVELOPING AROUND THIS SHIT!
THERE IS A LOT OF HISTORY, INDEED... SO, I'M GONNA STICK AROUND TO HEAR WHAT THESE LADIES HAVE TO SAY.
INNOVATION MY ASS!
THERE'S TOO MUCH HISTORY BEHIND THIS BUULLL SHIT TO LET IT RIDE.
HELLLL YEAH!
ROBERT FARRIS THOMPSON USED "POST-BLACK BACK IN NINETEEN NINETY FOUR...

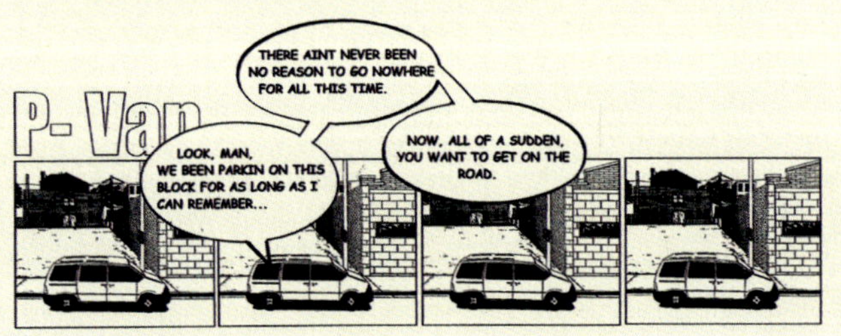
P-Van
LOOK, MAN, WE BEEN PARKIN ON THIS BLOCK FOR AS LONG AS I CAN REMEMBER...
THERE AINT NEVER BEEN NO REASON TO GO NOWHERE FOR ALL THIS TIME.
NOW, ALL OF A SUDDEN, YOU WANT TO GET ON THE ROAD.

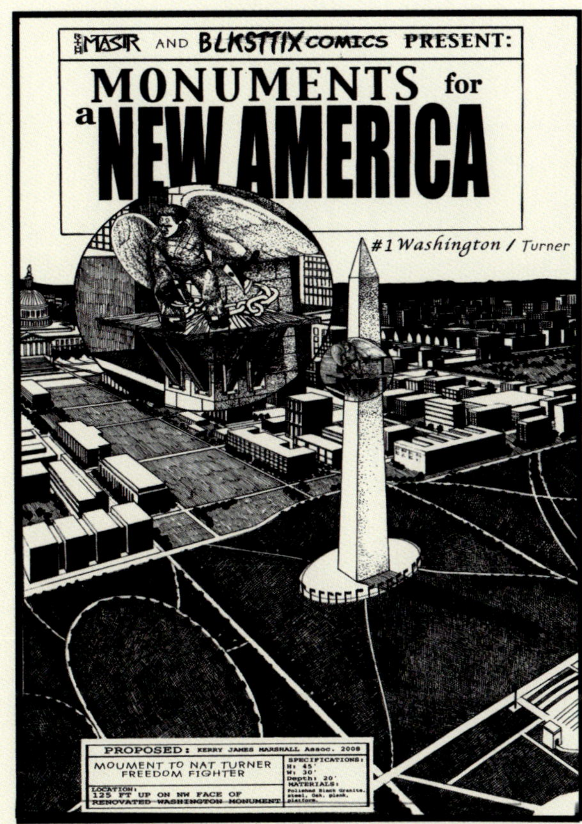

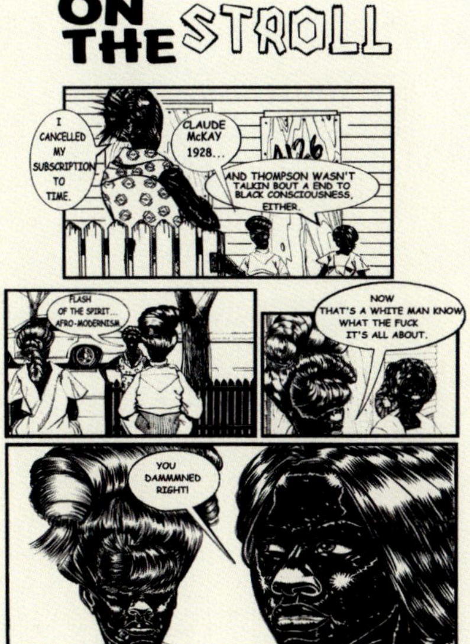

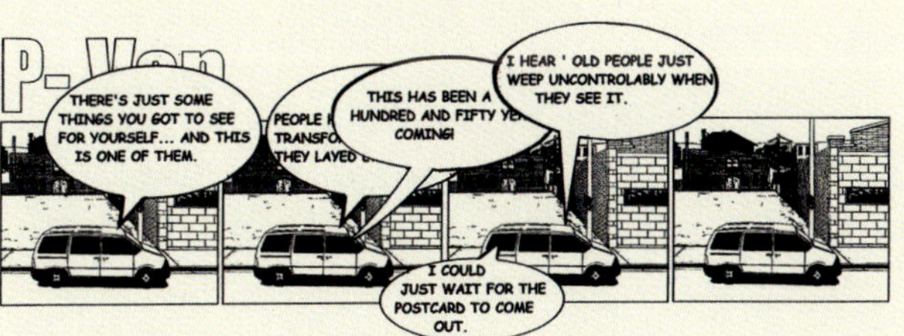

Rythm Mastr Dailies: Monuments for a New America [2008–2009]

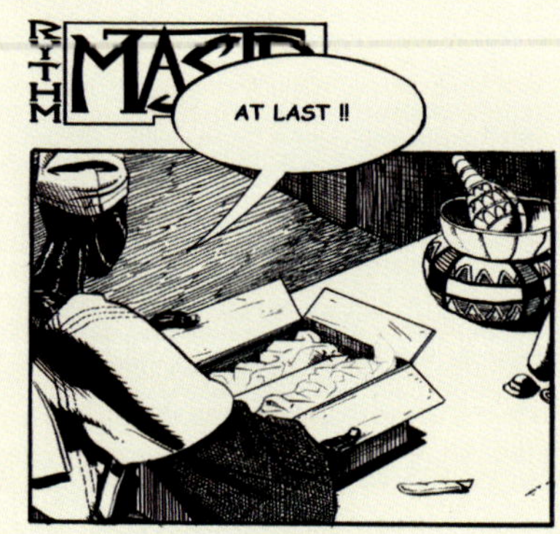
RITHM
AT LAST !!

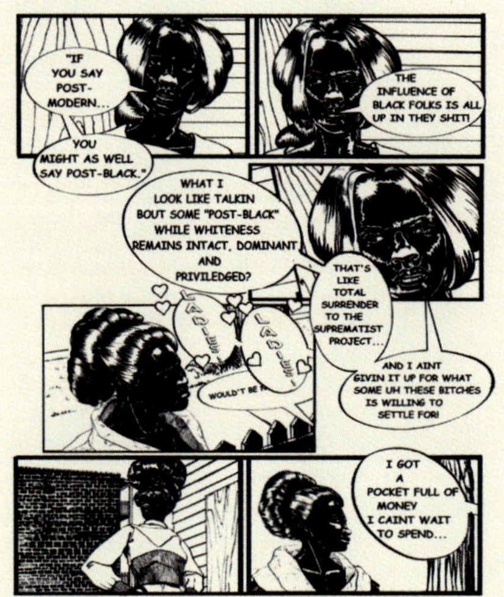
ON THE STROLL
"IF YOU SAY POST-MODERN...
YOU MIGHT AS WELL SAY POST-BLACK."
THE INFLUENCE OF BLACK FOLKS IS ALL UP IN THEY SHIT!
WHAT I LOOK LIKE TALKIN BOUT SOME "POST-BLACK" WHILE WHITENESS REMAINS INTACT, DOMINANT AND PRIVILEDGED?
THAT'S LIKE TOTAL SURRENDER TO THE SUPREMATIST PROJECT...
AND I AINT GIVIN IT UP FOR WHAT SOME UH THESE BITCHES IS WILLING TO SETTLE FOR!
WOULD'T BE
I GOT A POCKET FULL OF MONEY I CAINT WAIT TO SPEND...

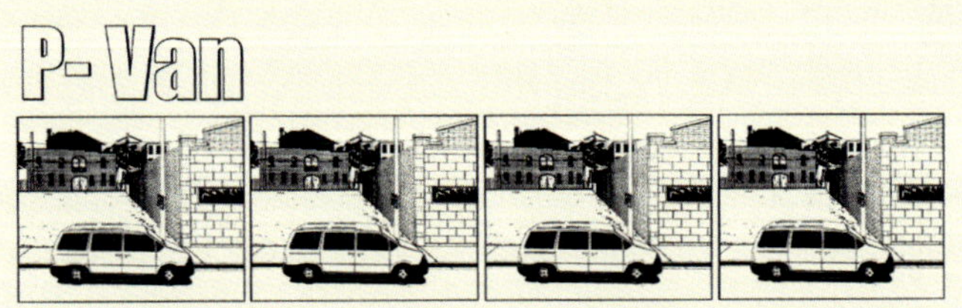
P- Van

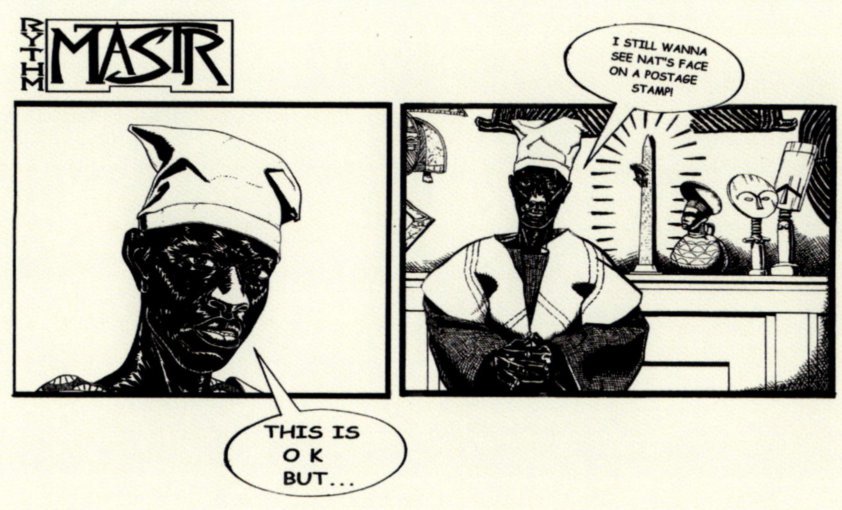
RYTHM MASTR
THIS IS O K BUT...
I STILL WANNA SEE NAT'S FACE ON A POSTAGE STAMP!

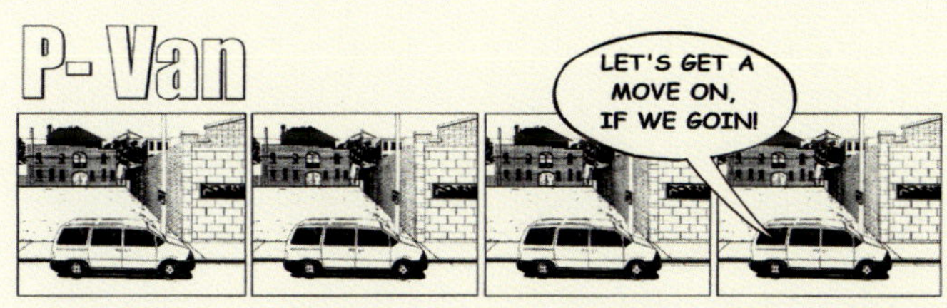
P-Van
LET'S GET A MOVE ON, IF WE GOIN!

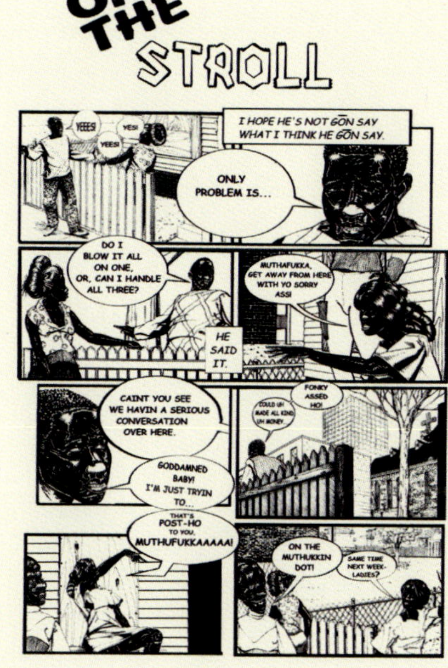
ON THE STROLL
YEEES!
YEES!
YES!
I HOPE HE'S NOT GŌN SAY WHAT I THINK HE GŌN SAY.
ONLY PROBLEM IS...
DO I BLOW IT ALL ON ONE, OR, CAN I HANDLE ALL THREE?
HE SAID IT.
MUTHAFUKKA, GET AWAY FROM HERE WITH YO SORRY ASS!
CAINT YOU SEE WE HAVIN A SERIOUS CONVERSATION OVER HERE.
GODDAMNED BABY! I'M JUST TRYIN TO...
COULD UH MADE ALL KIND UH MONEY...
FONKY ASSED HO!
THAT'S POST-HO TO YOU, MUTHUFUKKAAAAA!
ON THE MUTHUKKIN DOT!
SAME TIME NEXT WEEK LADIES?

2008–2009

MONUMENTS FOR A NEW AMERICA

Ink on paper

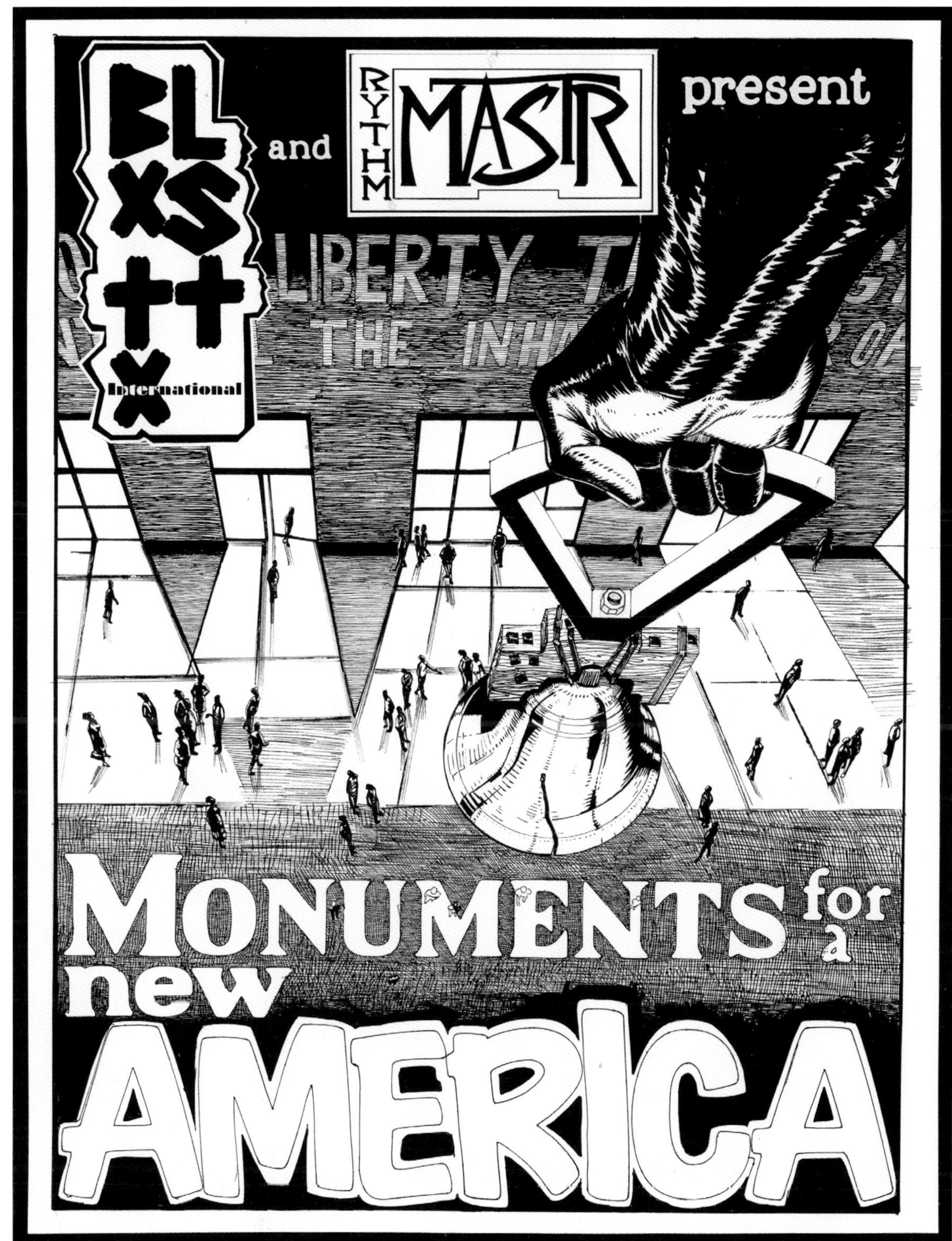
BL XS tt X
International
and
RYTHM MASTR
present
LIBERTY
THE
MONUMENTS for a new
AMERICA

2008–2009

MONUMENTS FOR A NEW AMERICA (WASHINGTON POST)

Double-page spread published in *The Washington Post*, M6–M7, Sunday, February 15, 2009

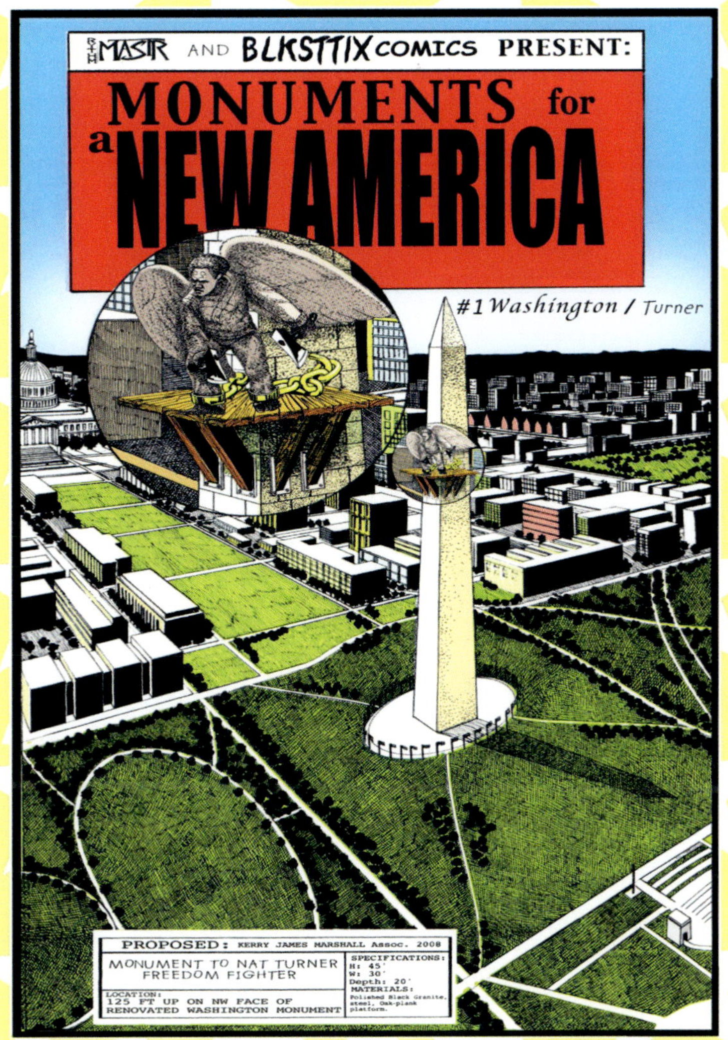
RYTHM MASTR AND BLKSTTIX COMICS PRESENT:
MONUMENTS for a NEW AMERICA
#1 Washington / Turner
PROPOSED: KERRY JAMES MARSHALL Assoc. 2008
MONUMENT TO NAT TURNER FREEDOM FIGHTER
LOCATION: 125 FT UP ON NW FACE OF RENOVATED WASHINGTON MONUMENT
SPECIFICATIONS: H: 45' W: 30' Depth: 20'
MATERIALS: Polished Black Granite, steel, Oak-plank platform.
next issue: JEFFERSON / Prosser

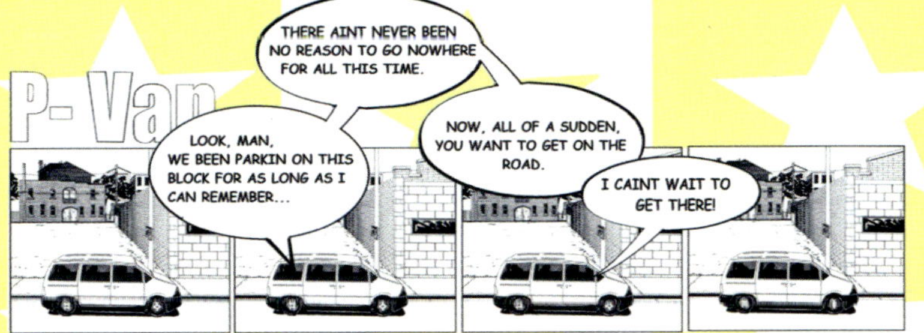
P-Van
LOOK, MAN, WE BEEN PARKIN ON THIS BLOCK FOR AS LONG AS I CAN REMEMBER...
THERE AINT NEVER BEEN NO REASON TO GO NOWHERE FOR ALL THIS TIME.
NOW, ALL OF A SUDDEN, YOU WANT TO GET ON THE ROAD.
I CAINT WAIT TO GET THERE!

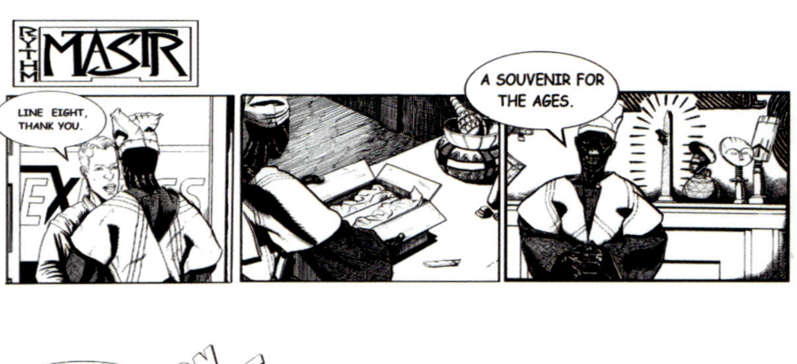
RYTHM MASTR
LINE EIGHT, THANK YOU.
A SOUVENIR FOR THE AGES.

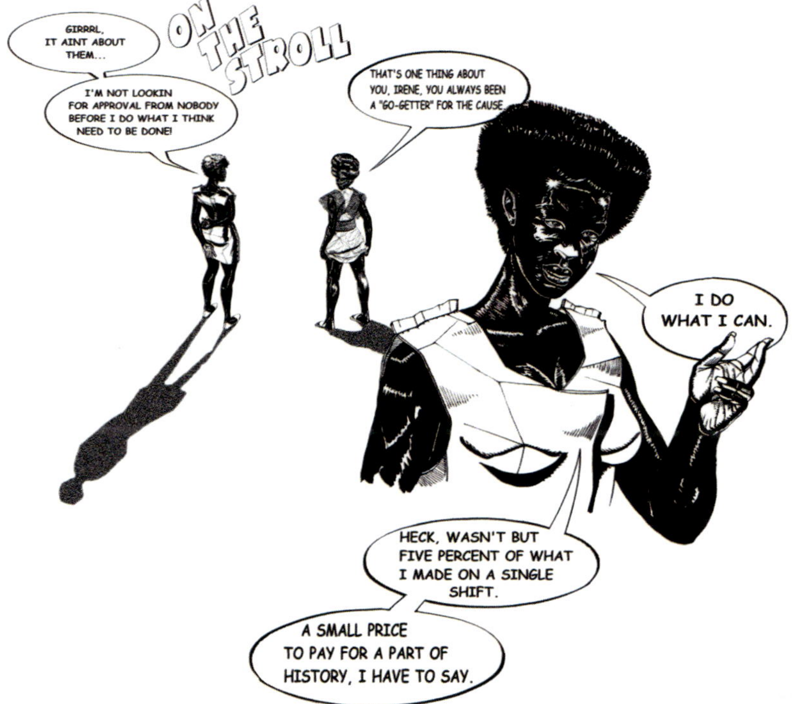
ON THE STROLL
GIRRRL, IT AINT ABOUT THEM...
I'M NOT LOOKIN FOR APPROVAL FROM NOBODY BEFORE I DO WHAT I THINK NEED TO BE DONE!
THAT'S ONE THING ABOUT YOU, IRENE, YOU ALWAYS BEEN A "GO-GETTER" FOR THE CAUSE.
I DO WHAT I CAN.
HECK, WASN'T BUT FIVE PERCENT OF WHAT I MADE ON A SINGLE SHIFT.
A SMALL PRICE TO PAY FOR A PART OF HISTORY, I HAVE TO SAY.

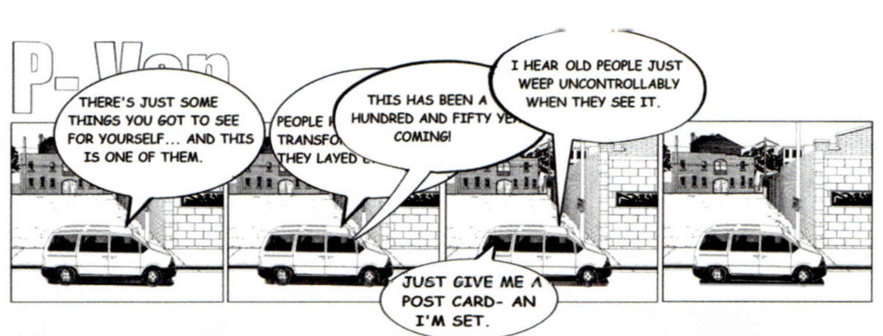
P-Van
THERE'S JUST SOME THINGS YOU GOT TO SEE FOR YOURSELF... AND THIS IS ONE OF THEM.
THIS HAS BEEN A HUNDRED AND FIFTY
COMING!
I HEAR OLD PEOPLE JUST WEEP UNCONTROLLABLY WHEN THEY SEE IT.
JUST GIVE ME A POST CARD- AN I'M SET.

2010

DAILIES

Nine screenprints printed in black and buff on Rives BFK paper

Image: each 21 ¼×29 in. (54×73.5 cm); sheet: each 22 ¼×30 in. (56.5×76 cm)

Edition: 5

Numbered, titled, signed, and dated in pencil

Printed by the artist and Thomas Lucas at Hummingbird Press, Chicago

Marshall's first attempt to silkscreen the *Dailies* produced nine prints of a newspaper-like tonality recapitulating or expanding on some of the themes explored over the previous six years. *This Is How it Begins* and *Origin* do not feature images—only words printed in small type. Respectively they read: "When ordinary men, women, and children will no longer tolerate limited access to the exalted places once denied to them. A hero emerges to lead the battle. That champion is the Rythm Mastr." And: "The new phoneme recalls the standard, rhythm, and the patois, riddim, or riddum. Its meaning is derived from the third definition of 'rhythm' found in the 1996 pocket *Oxford Dictionary*: '3: a pattern of successive strong and weak movements. This is combined with the noun, Mastr, or Master; 4: prevailing person; 11: a boy too young to be called Mr.' 'Rythm Mastr' is meant to avoid the implied dominance associated with the term Master, while retaining a link to history and culture." The third one, simply titled *Dailies*, illustrates the three principal characters—a running Farrell, an unusually quiet P-Van, and a woman from On the Stroll in her trademark pose, turning her back to the viewer. *The Time Has Come* shows the guards in The Ancient Egyptian Museum coming to the realization that some of the artifacts are gone, while just below them, Stasha and Farrell advertise T-shirts attractively priced at $12.99 celebrating Nat Turner as a freedom fighter. *Rythm Mastr* is a group portrait of the main characters in Farrell's corner: Senufo, Ibeji, Nkisi, Boli, Oba, the Rythm Mastr, and Farrell himself. The remaining four panels, all titled *Dailies* (*At Last*), offer a variation on the *Monuments for a New America* previously published in the *Washington Post*, with P-Van ready to leave the street where he is stationed 24/7 to go to DC, and one of the women from "On the Stroll" vindicating art historian Robert Farris Thompson for being the first one to coin the term "Post-Black" in the 1980s.

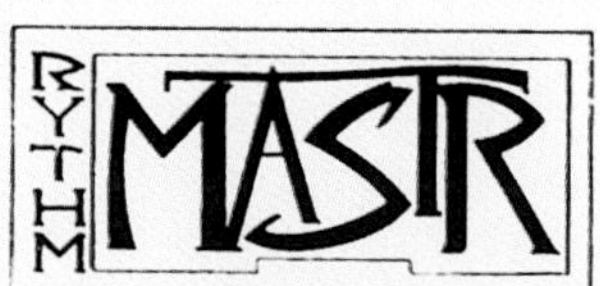

THIS IS HOW IT BEGINS

WHEN ORDINARY MEN WOMEN AND CHILDREN WILL NO LONGER TOLERATE LIMITED ACCESS TO THE EXALTED PLACES ONCE DENIED THEM.

A HERO EMERGES TO LEAD THE BATTLE THAT CHAMPION IS THE RYTHM MASTR

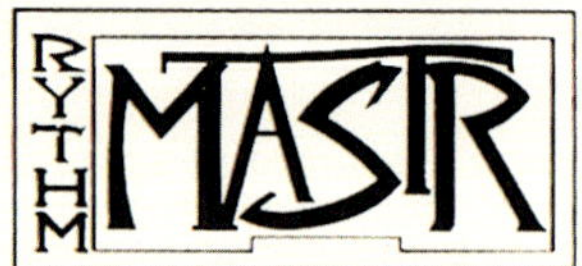

ORIGIN. THE NEW PHONEME RECALLS THE STANDARD, RHYTHM, AND THE PATOIS, RIDDIM, OR RIDDUM. ITS MEANING IS DERIVED FROM THE THIRD LEVEL DEFINITION OF RHYTHM FOUND IN THE 1996 POCKET OXFORD DICTIONARY. 3; A PATTERN OF SUCCESSIVE STRONG AND WEAK MOVEMENTS. THIS IS COMBINED WITH THE NOUN, MASTR, OR MASTER 4. PREVAILING PERSON. 11; A BOY TOO YOUNG TO BE CALLED MR. RYTHM MASTR IS MEANT TO AVOID THE IMPLIED DOMINANCE ASSOCIATED WITH THE TERM MASTER, WHILE RETAINING A LINK TO HISTORY AND CULTURE

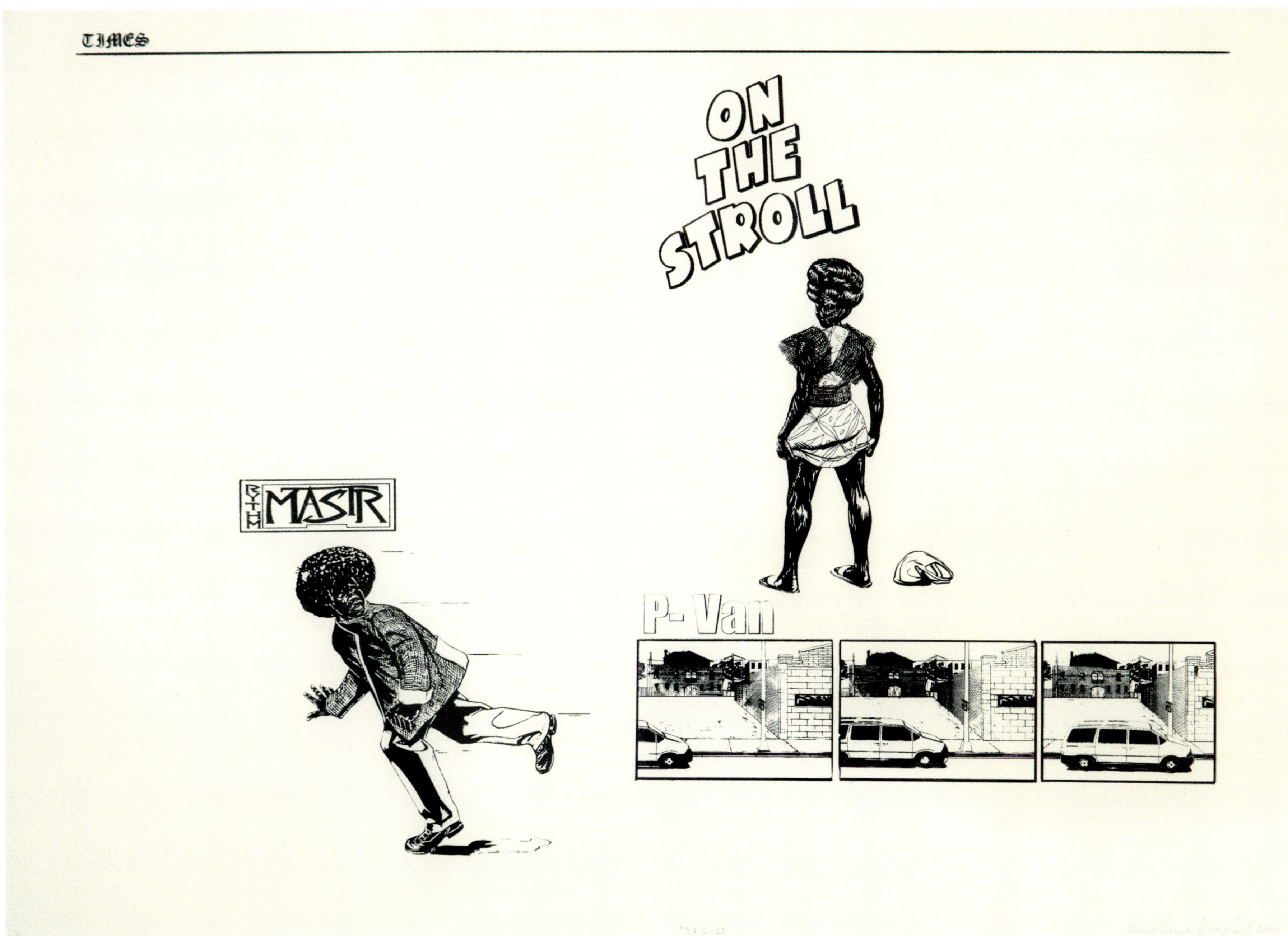
TIMES
ON THE STROLL
RYTHM MASTR
P- Van

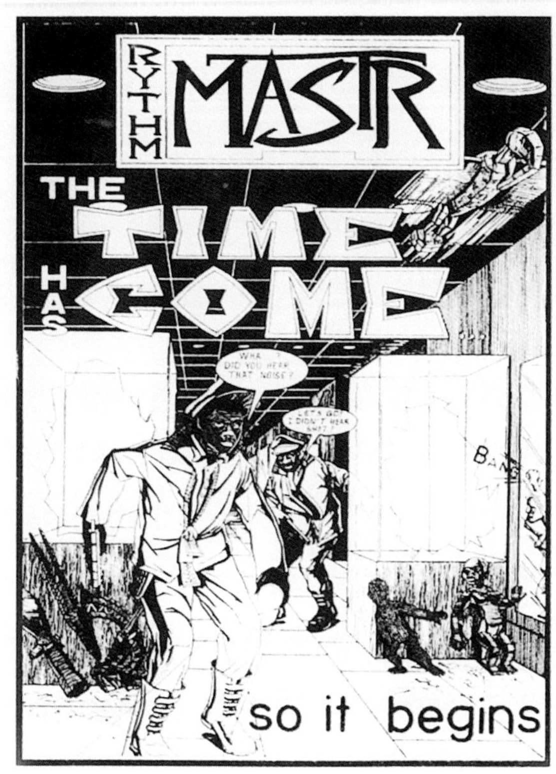
RYTHM
MASTR
THE TIME HAS COME
DID YOU HEAR THAT NOISE?
LET'S GO! I DIDN'T HEAR SHIT!
so it begins

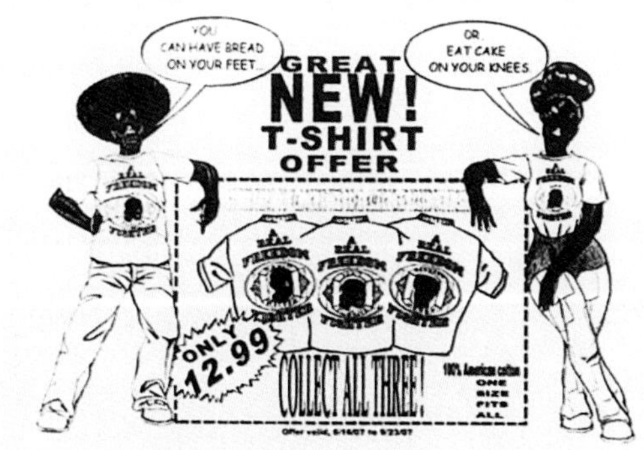
YOU CAN HAVE BREAD ON YOUR FEET...
OR EAT CAKE ON YOUR KNEES
GREAT NEW! T-SHIRT OFFER
ONLY 12.99
COLLECT ALL THREE!
ONE SIZE FITS ALL

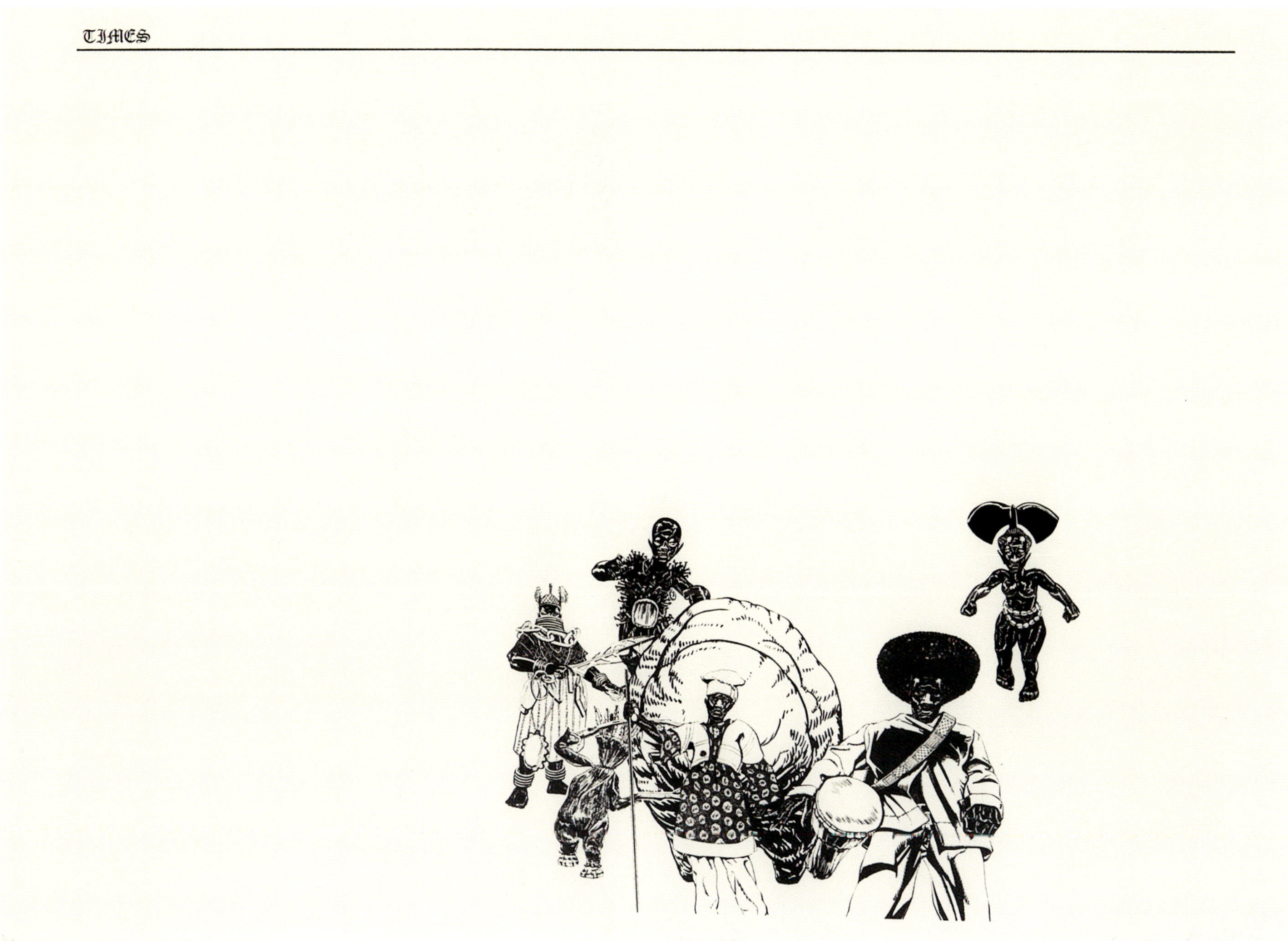
TIMES

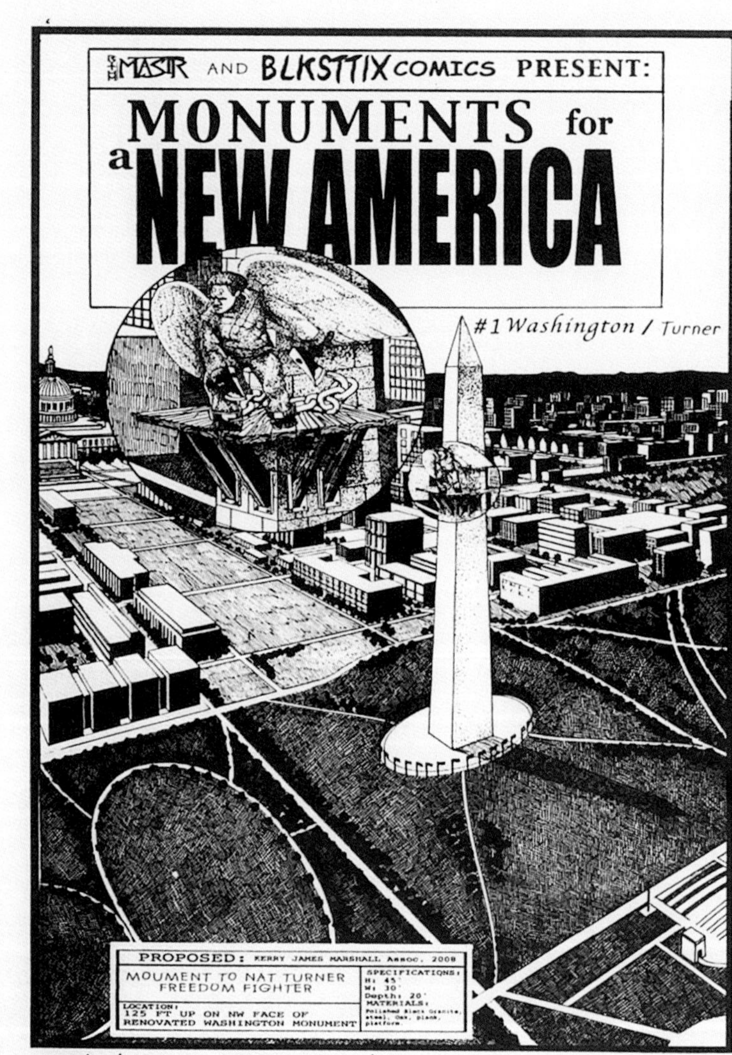
MASTR AND BLKSTTIX COMICS PRESENT:
MONUMENTS for a NEW AMERICA
#1 Washington / Turner
PROPOSED: KERRY JAMES MARSHALL Assoc. 2008
MOUMENT TO NAT TURNER FREEDOM FIGHTER
LOCATION: 125 FT UP ON NW FACE OF RENOVATED WASHINGTON MONUMENT
SPECIFICATIONS: H: 45' W: 30' Depth: 20'
MATERIALS:
next issue: JEFFERSON / Prosser

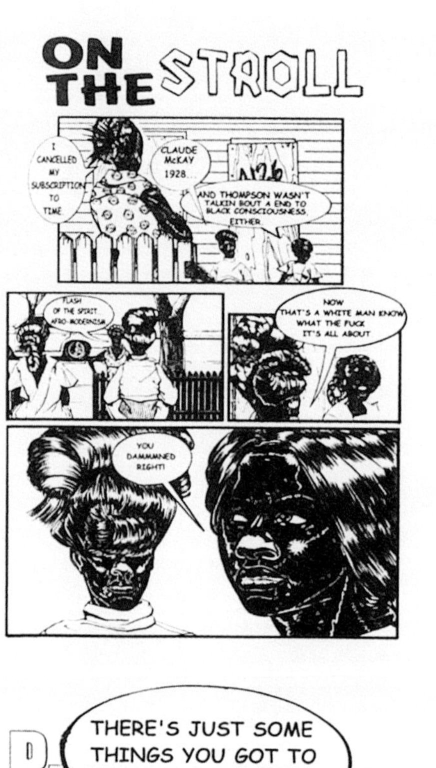
ON THE STROLL
I CANCELLED MY SUBSCRIPTION TO TIME.
CLAUDE McKAY 1928...
AND THOMPSON WASN'T TALKIN BOUT A END TO BLACK CONSCIOUSNESS, EITHER.
FLASH OF THE SPIRIT... AFRO-MODERNISM
NOW THAT'S A WHITE MAN KNOW WHAT THE FUCK IT'S ALL ABOUT
YOU DAMMNED RIGHT!

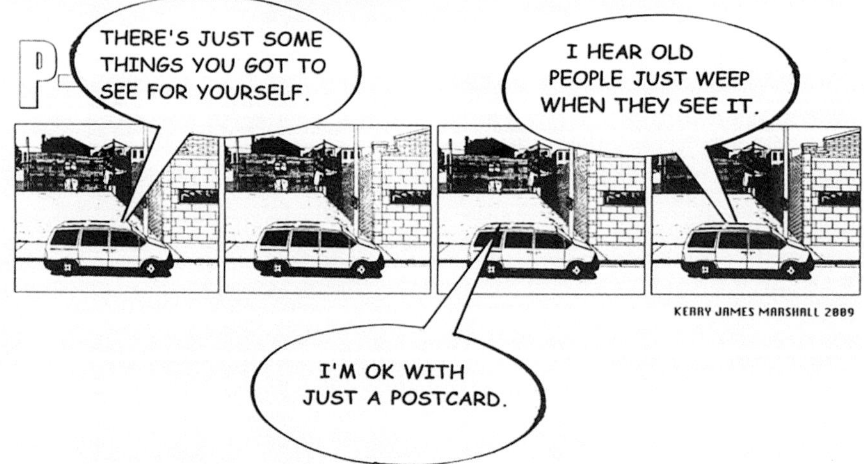
THERE'S JUST SOME THINGS YOU GOT TO SEE FOR YOURSELF.
I HEAR OLD PEOPLE JUST WEEP WHEN THEY SEE IT.
I'M OK WITH JUST A POSTCARD.
KERRY JAMES MARSHALL 2009

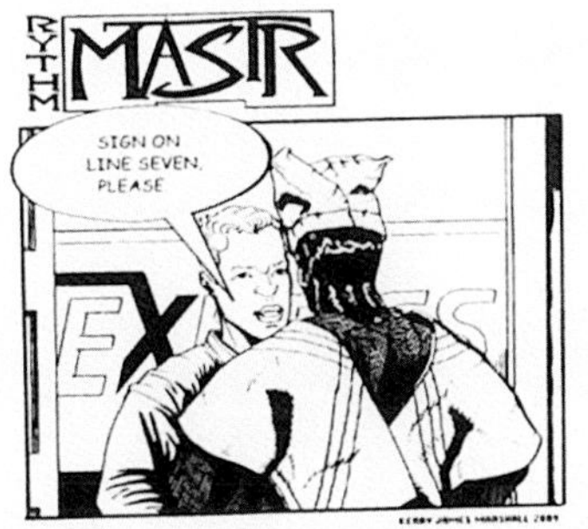
RYTHM MASTR
SIGN ON LINE SEVEN, PLEASE

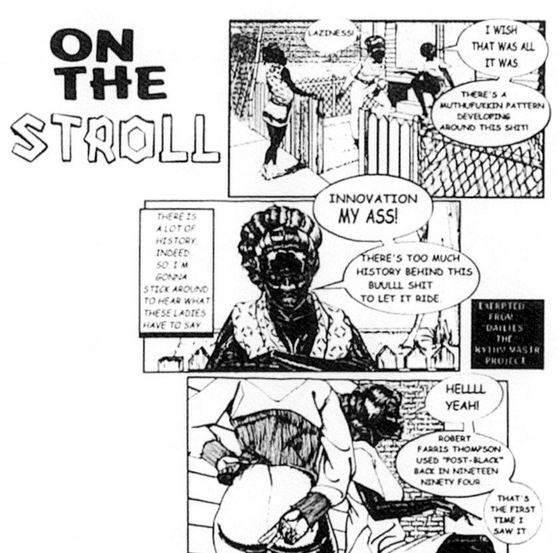
ON THE STROLL
LAZINESS!
I WISH THAT WAS ALL IT WAS
THERE'S A MUTHUFUKKIN PATTERN DEVELOPING AROUND THIS SHIT!
INNOVATION MY ASS!
THERE IS A LOT OF HISTORY, INDEED. SO, I'M GONNA STICK AROUND TO HEAR WHAT THESE LADIES HAVE TO SAY.
THERE'S TOO MUCH HISTORY BEHIND THIS BUULLL SHIT TO LET IT RIDE.
EXCERPTED FROM "DAILIES" THE RYTHM MASTR PROJECT
HELLLL YEAH!
ROBERT FARRIS THOMPSON USED "POST-BLACK" BACK IN NINETEEN NINETY FOUR
THAT'S THE FIRST TIME I SAW IT

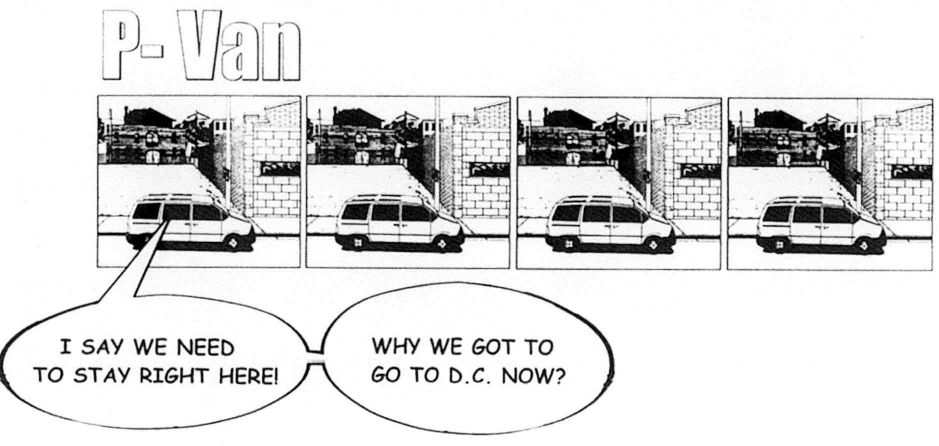
P-Van
I SAY WE NEED TO STAY RIGHT HERE!
WHY WE GOT TO GO TO D.C. NOW?

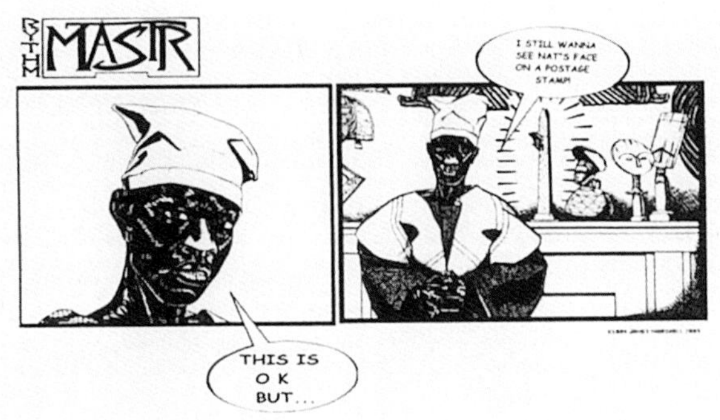
MASTR
THIS IS O K BUT...
I STILL WANNA SEE NAT'S FACE ON A POSTAGE STAMP!

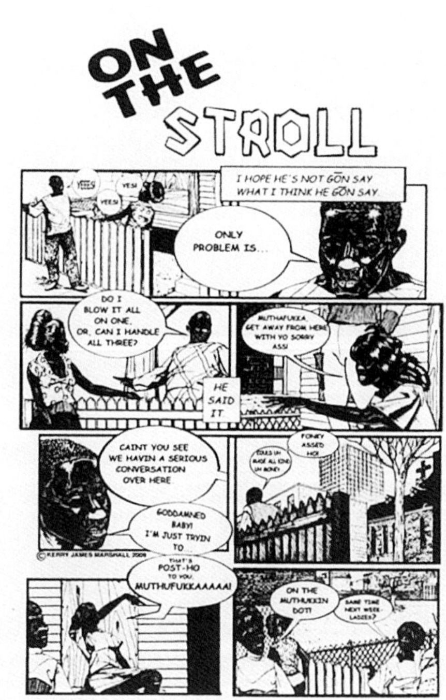
ON THE STROLL
I HOPE HE'S NOT GŌN SAY WHAT I THINK HE GŌN SAY
ONLY PROBLEM IS...
DO I BLOW IT ALL ON ONE, OR, CAN I HANDLE ALL THREE?
HE SAID IT
MUTHAFUKKA, GET AWAY FROM HERE WITH YO SORRY ASS!
CAINT YOU SEE WE HAVIN A SERIOUS CONVERSATION OVER HERE.
GODDAMNED BABY! I'M JUST TRYIN TO
FONEY ASSED HO!
©KERRY JAMES MARSHALL 2009
THAT'S POST-HO TO YOU, MUTHUFUKKAAAAA!
ON THE MUTHUKKIN DOT!
SAME TIME NEXT WEEK, LADIES?

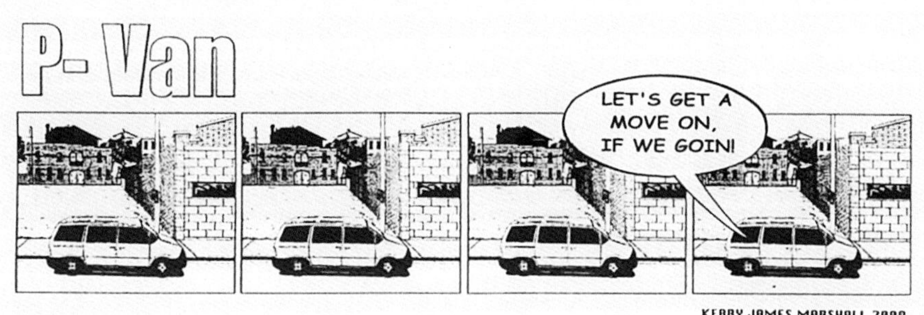
P- Van
LET'S GET A MOVE ON, IF WE GOIN!
KERRY JAMES MARSHALL 2009

TIMES

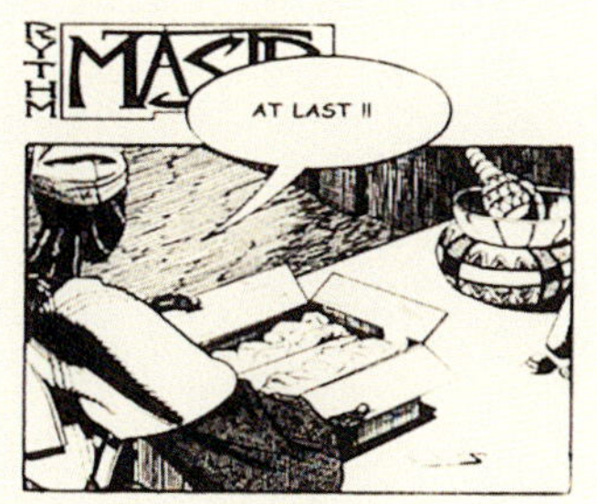

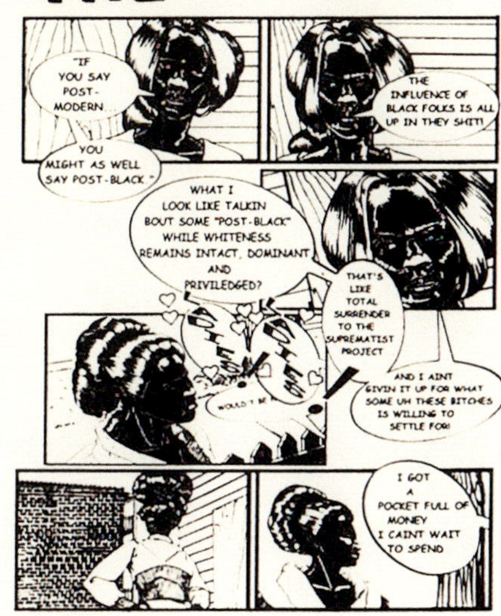

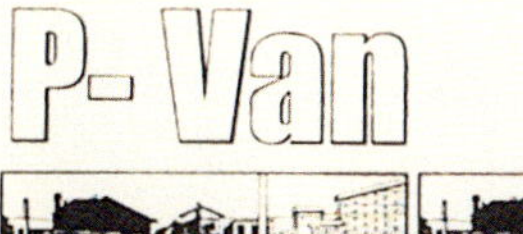

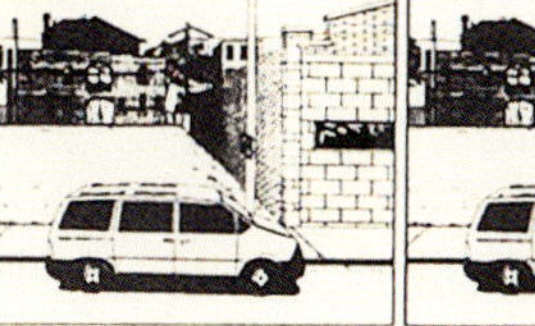
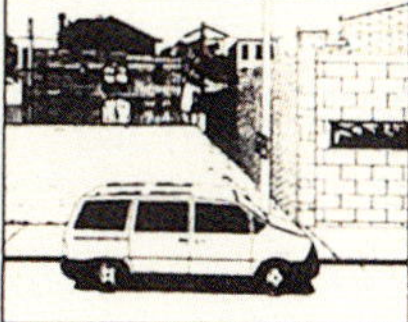
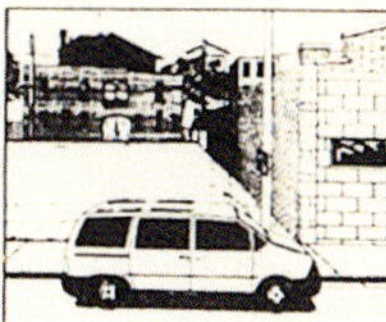
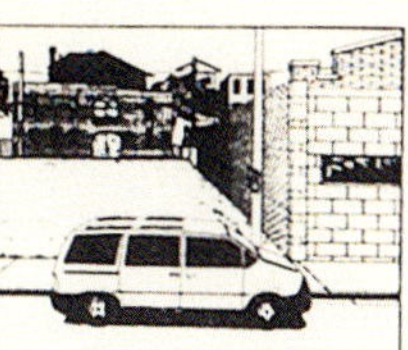

2010

IT'S SO HARD TO SAY GOODBYE (ESOPUS)

Artist project for *Esopus* 14 (spring 2010)

Ten pages in *Esopus*

Each 11×9 ½ in. (28×24 cm)

When the now defunct *Esopus* magazine—a New York-based annual publication featuring artists' projects—invited Marshall to contribute in 2010, it seemed only logical that he would revert to the *Rythm Mastr* universe to produce something that would resonate with the printed-matter format. The sixteen-page insert opens and closes with black-on-black road signs, with each exit number concealing a historical date:

Exit 1619 A / Black Metropolis / Next
(The arrival of the first slave ship from Africa)
Exit 1865 B / Black Metropolis / Return
(The date slavery was officially abolished)
Exit 1968 B / Black Metropolis / No Exit
(The year Martin Luther King, Jr. was assassinated)
Exit 2010 A / Black Metropolis / Return
(The year of the project's publication)

On the second double-page spread, Black Metropolis is represented by a busy street view combining well-known elements (a billboard announcing the "Monuments for a New America") with new ones that will soon earn a regular spot ("Jim Bey's Club"). The chapter concludes with the advertising-laced segment "Naps & Knots," in which the assumption that people speaking in "Ebonics" cannot have deep conversations is openly challenged. Two men engaged in a philosophical discussion pass the baton of the debate to two women after catcalling one of them and being elbowed out of the way.

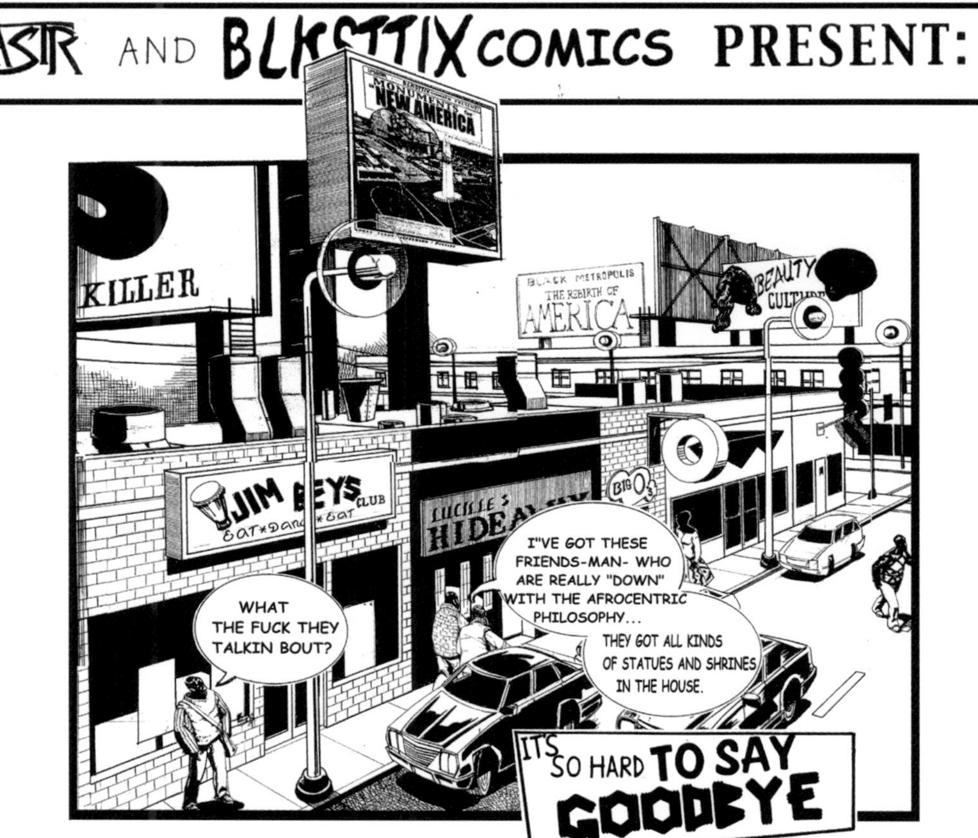

RYTHM MASTR AND BLKSTTIX COMICS PRESENT:
KILLER
NEW AMERICA
BLACK METROPOLIS THE REBIRTH OF AMERICA
BEAUTY CULTURE
JIM BEYS CLUB
LUCILLE'S HIDEA
BIG O'S
WHAT THE FUCK THEY TALKIN BOUT?
I"VE GOT THESE FRIENDS-MAN- WHO ARE REALLY "DOWN" WITH THE AFROCENTRIC PHILOSOPHY...
THEY GOT ALL KINDS OF STATUES AND SHRINES IN THE HOUSE.
ITS SO HARD TO SAY GOODBYE

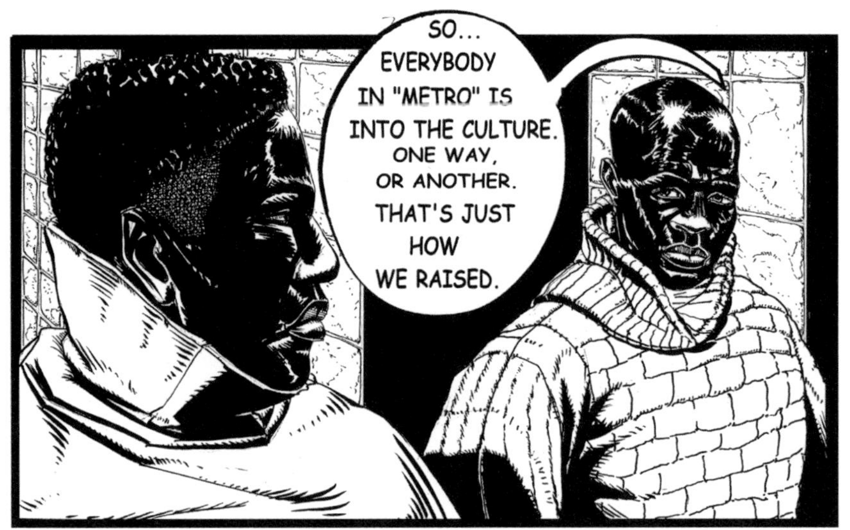
SO...
EVERYBODY
IN "METRO" IS
INTO THE CULTURE.
ONE WAY,
OR ANOTHER.
THAT'S JUST
HOW
WE RAISED.

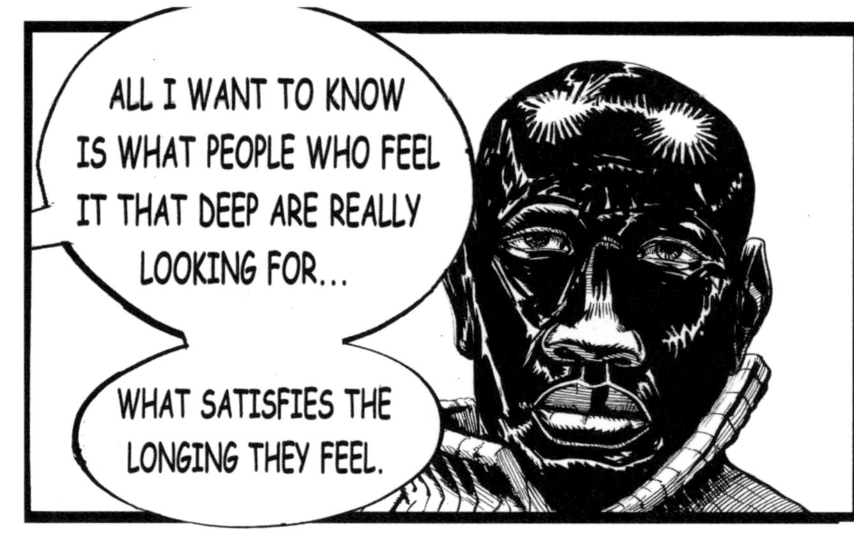
ALL I WANT TO KNOW
IS WHAT PEOPLE WHO FEEL
IT THAT DEEP ARE REALLY
LOOKING FOR...
WHAT SATISFIES THE
LONGING THEY FEEL.

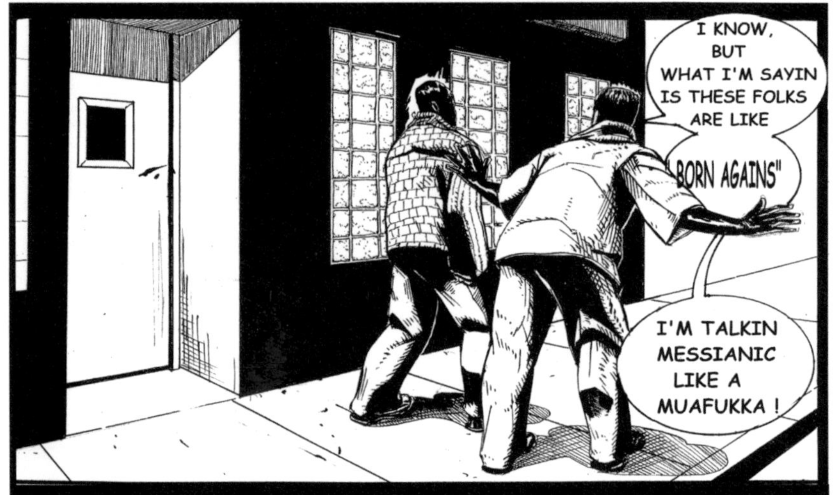
I KNOW,
BUT
WHAT I'M SAYIN
IS THESE FOLKS
ARE LIKE
"BORN AGAINS"
I'M TALKIN
MESSIANIC
LIKE A
MUAFUKKA !

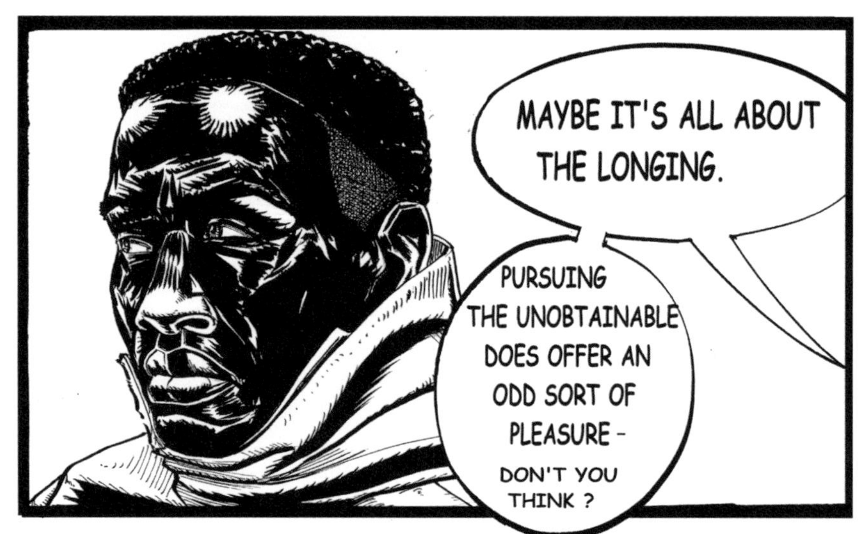
MAYBE IT'S ALL ABOUT
THE LONGING.
PURSUING
THE UNOBTAINABLE
DOES OFFER AN
ODD SORT OF
PLEASURE –
DON'T YOU
THINK ?

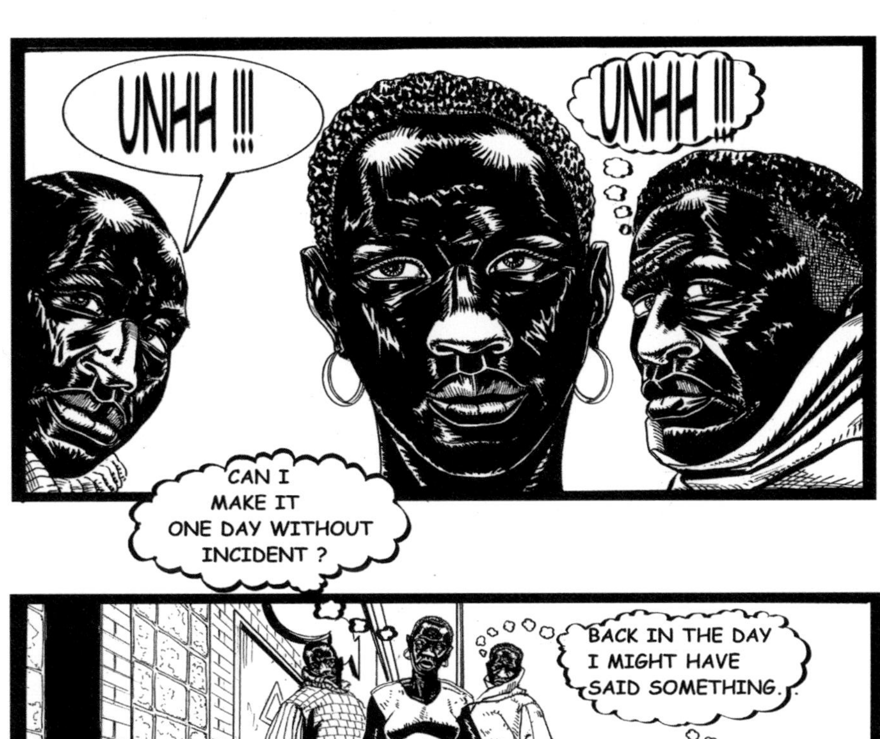
UNHH !!!
UNHH !!!
CAN I MAKE IT ONE DAY WITHOUT INCIDENT ?

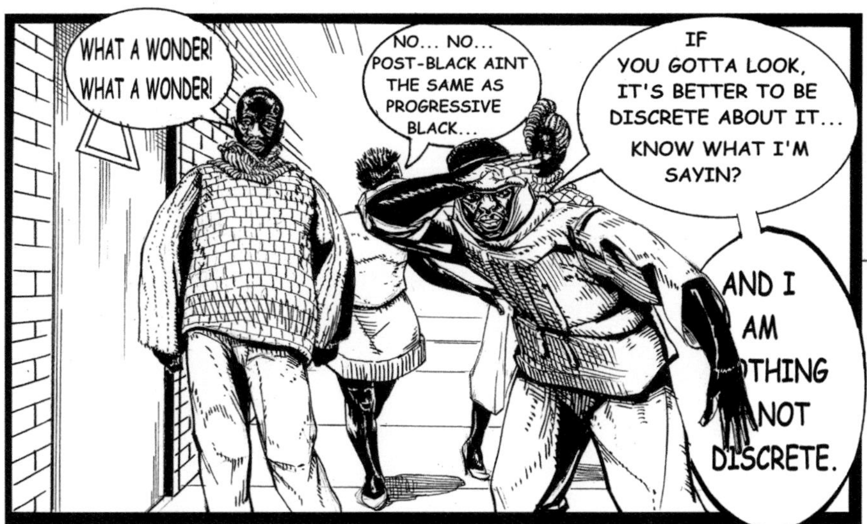
WHAT A WONDER! WHAT A WONDER!
NO... NO... POST-BLACK AINT THE SAME AS PROGRESSIVE BLACK...
IF YOU GOTTA LOOK, IT'S BETTER TO BE DISCRETE ABOUT IT... KNOW WHAT I'M SAYIN?
AND I AM THING NOT DISCRETE.

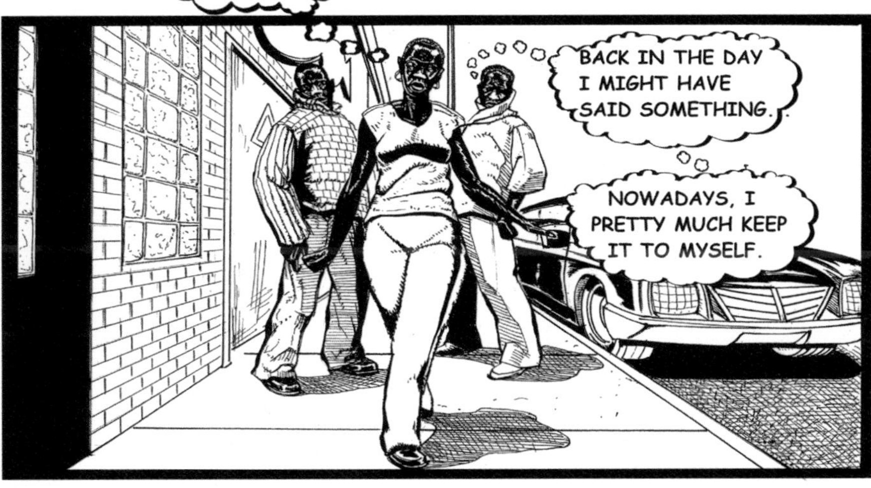
BACK IN THE DAY I MIGHT HAVE SAID SOMETHING.
NOWADAYS, I PRETTY MUCH KEEP IT TO MYSELF.

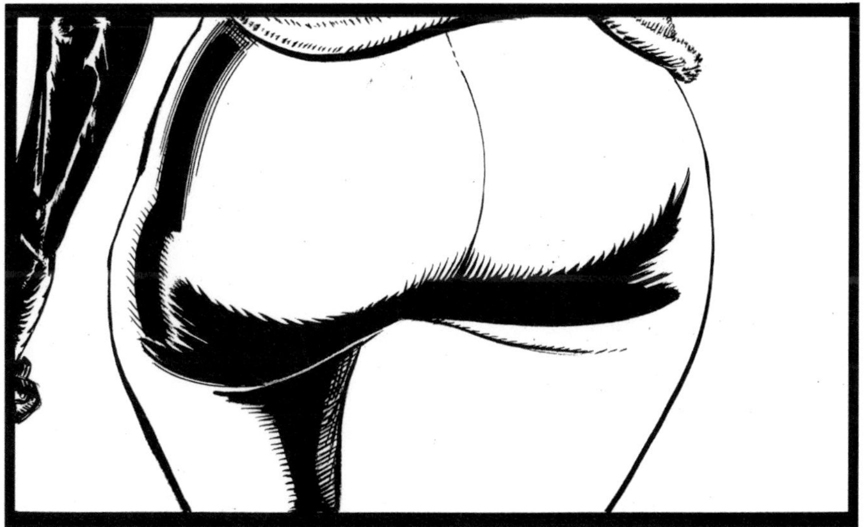

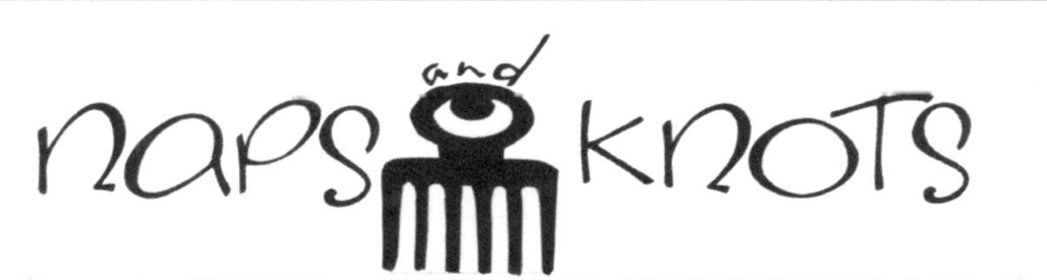
naps and knots

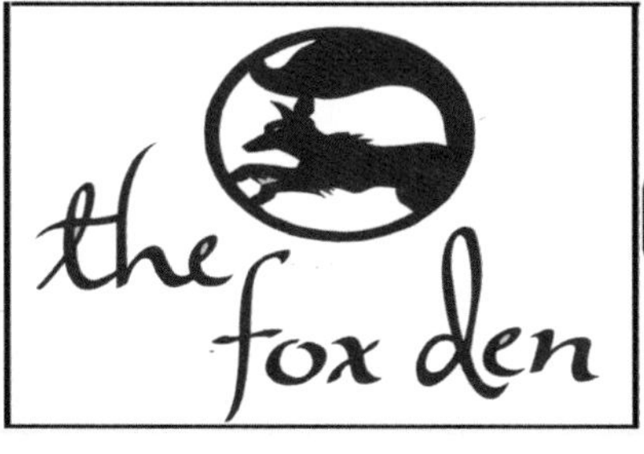
the fox den

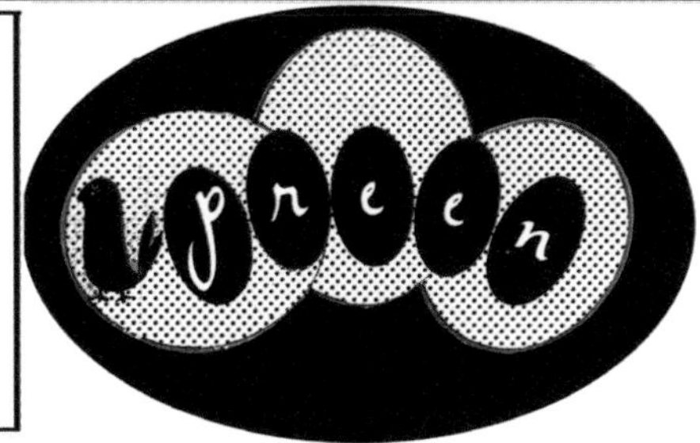

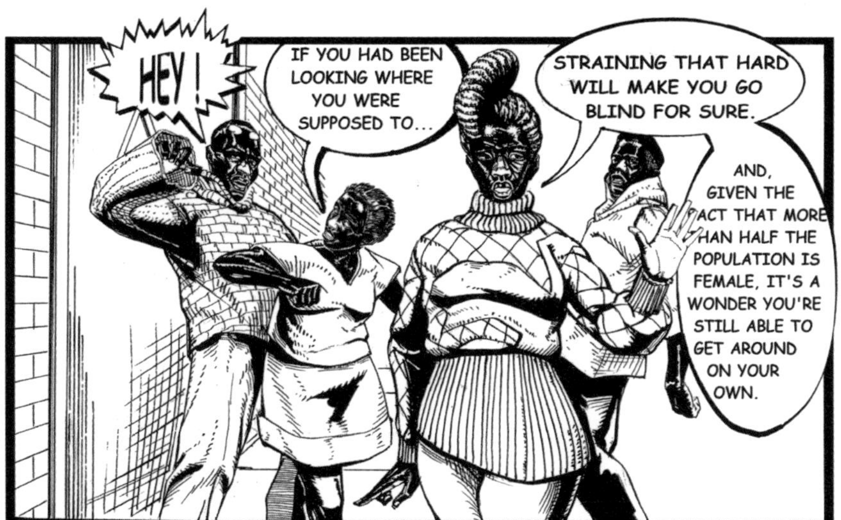
HEY!
IF YOU HAD BEEN LOOKING WHERE YOU WERE SUPPOSED TO...
STRAINING THAT HARD WILL MAKE YOU GO BLIND FOR SURE.
AND, GIVEN THE FACT THAT MORE THAN HALF THE POPULATION IS FEMALE, IT'S A WONDER YOU'RE STILL ABLE TO GET AROUND ON YOUR OWN.

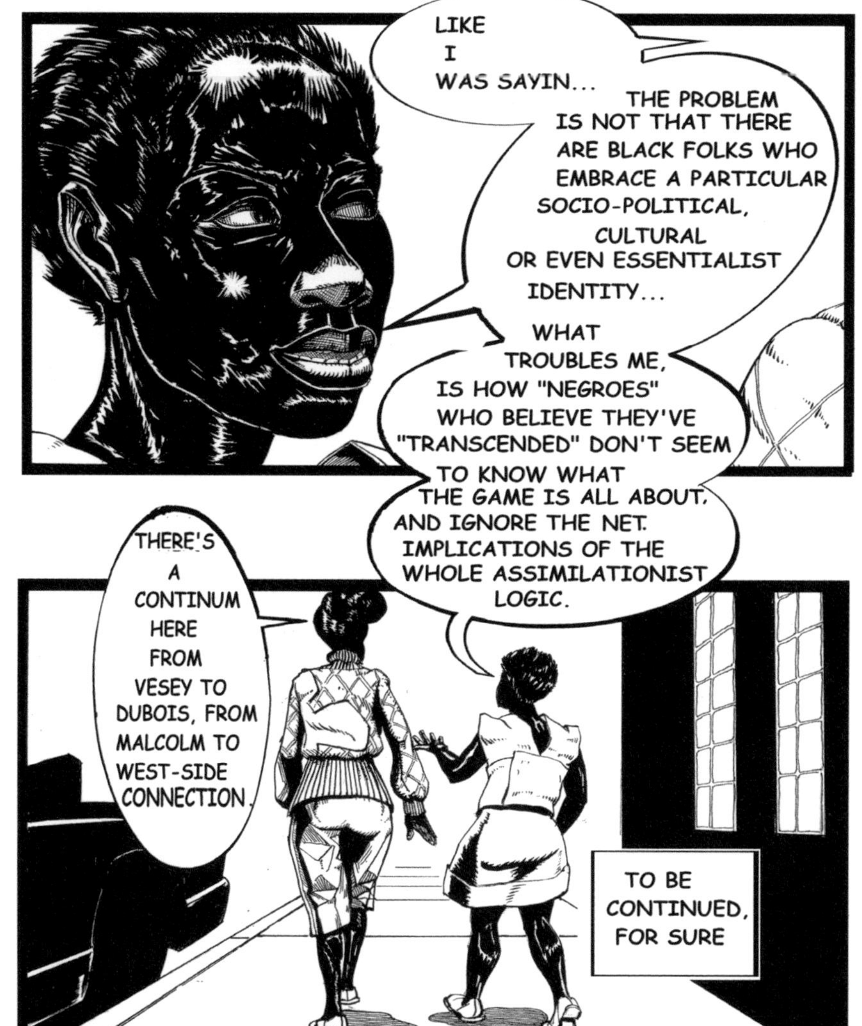
LIKE I WAS SAYIN... THE PROBLEM IS NOT THAT THERE ARE BLACK FOLKS WHO EMBRACE A PARTICULAR SOCIO-POLITICAL, CULTURAL OR EVEN ESSENTIALIST IDENTITY...
WHAT TROUBLES ME, IS HOW "NEGROES" WHO BELIEVE THEY'VE "TRANSCENDED" DON'T SEEM TO KNOW WHAT THE GAME IS ALL ABOUT, AND IGNORE THE NET. IMPLICATIONS OF THE WHOLE ASSIMILATIONIST LOGIC.
THERE'S A CONTINUM HERE FROM VESEY TO DUBOIS, FROM MALCOLM TO WEST-SIDE CONNECTION.
TO BE CONTINUED, FOR SURE

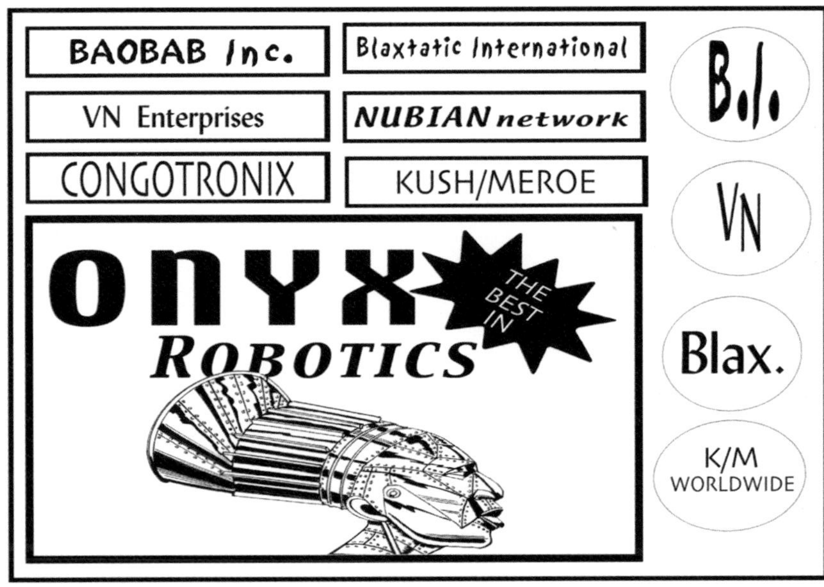
BAOBAB Inc.
Blaxtatic International
B.I.
VN Enterprises
NUBIAN network
CONGOTRONIX
KUSH/MEROE
VN
ONYX
THE BEST IN
ROBOTICS
Blax.
K/M
WORLDWIDE

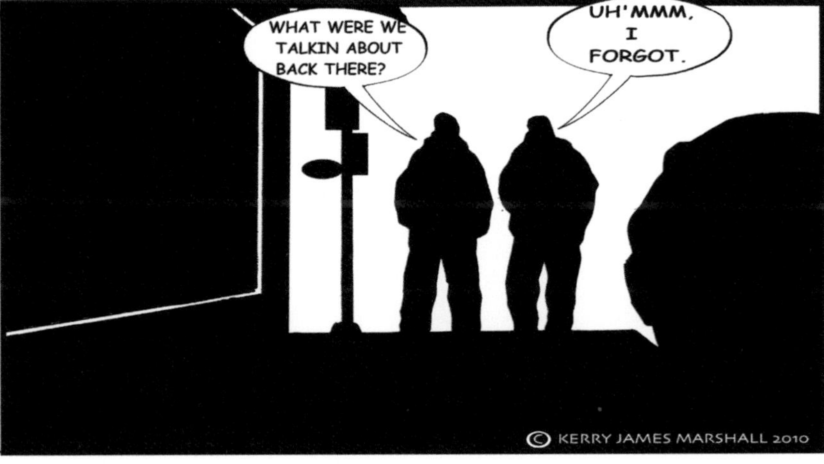
WHAT WERE WE TALKIN ABOUT BACK THERE?
UH'MMM, I FORGOT.
© KERRY JAMES MARSHALL 2010

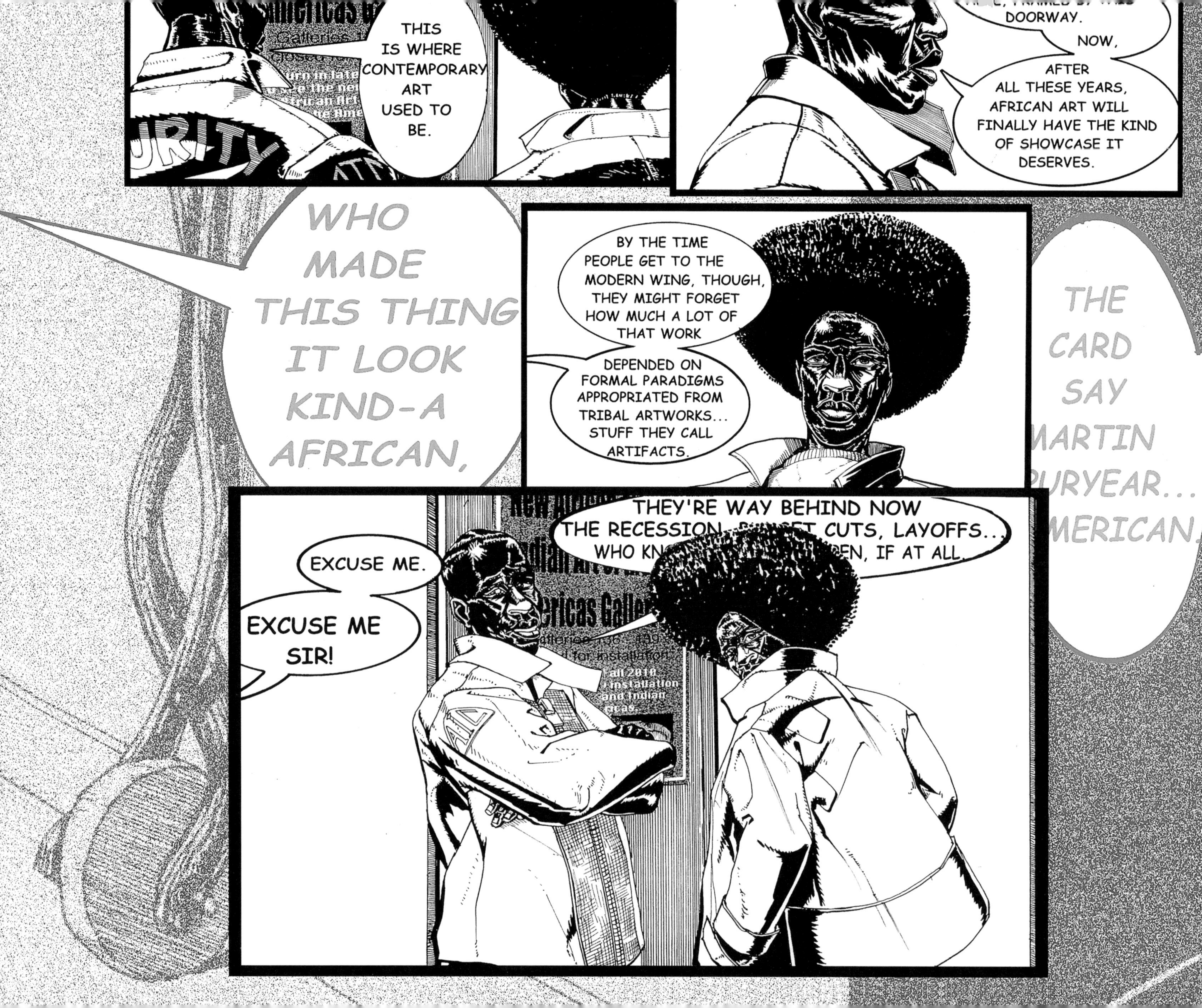
THIS IS WHERE CONTEMPORARY ART USED TO BE.
DOORWAY.
NOW,
AFTER ALL THESE YEARS, AFRICAN ART WILL FINALLY HAVE THE KIND OF SHOWCASE IT DESERVES.
WHO MADE THIS THING IT LOOK KIND-A AFRICAN,
BY THE TIME PEOPLE GET TO THE MODERN WING, THOUGH, THEY MIGHT FORGET HOW MUCH A LOT OF THAT WORK
DEPENDED ON FORMAL PARADIGMS APPROPRIATED FROM TRIBAL ARTWORKS... STUFF THEY CALL ARTIFACTS.
THE CARD SAY ARTIN URYEAR... MERICAN.
THEY'RE WAY BEHIND NOW THE RECESSION, CUTS, LAYOFFS... WHO KN EN, IF AT ALL.
EXCUSE ME.
EXCUSE ME SIR!

2016

ON THE STROLL

Ink on paper

Published in the catalogue accompanying Marshall's 2016 touring retrospective exhibition *Mastry* that originated at MCA Chicago, this four-page segment of *On the Stroll* is a collection of strips already featured in some of the "Dailies." The first spread opens with a rare personal interjection from Marshall on the story he is about to tell. ("There is a lot of history indeed...So, I'm gonna stick around to hear what these ladies have to say.") Standing metaphorically on opposite sides of the garden fence, two women from "On the Stroll" discuss a theme dear to Marshall—Robert Farris Thompson's use of the term "Post-Black" in 1994 and his intended meaning. ("And Thompson wasn't talking bout a end to Black consciousness either.") One of the women in the strip also mentions Claude McKay and the year 1928—probably a reference to the publication date of McKay's seminal novel *Home to Harlem*. On the second spread, two museum security guards comment on the delayed opening of a wing dedicated to African and Native American art. A woman visiting with her two children is vocal about her disappointment once she learns that the museum will not be visitable for another six months. The name of sculptor Martin Puryear (whose work inspired one of the artifacts in The Ancient Egyptian Museum) is visible in the background and is accompanied by the humorous exchange: "The Brancusis? That's a tribe in East Africa, aint it?"

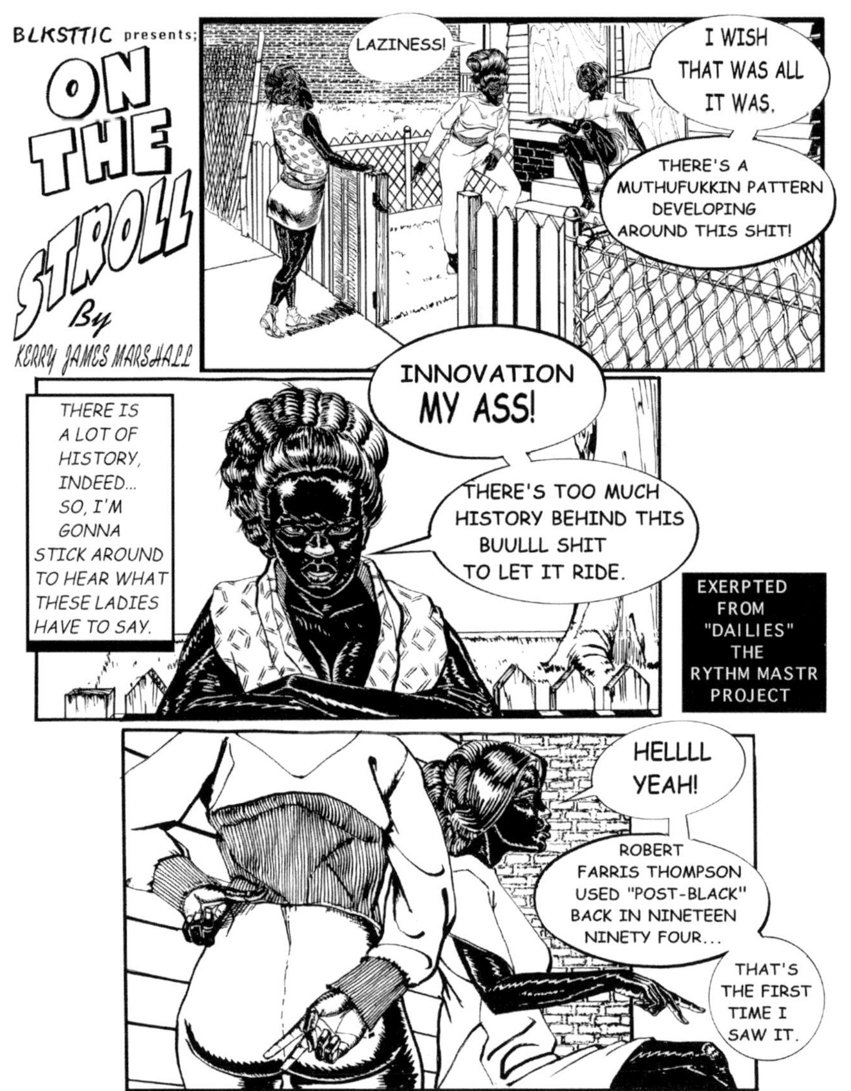

BLKSTTIC presents;
ON THE STROLL
By
KERRY JAMES MARSHALL
LAZINESS!
I WISH THAT WAS ALL IT WAS.
THERE'S A MUTHUFUKKIN PATTERN DEVELOPING AROUND THIS SHIT!
THERE IS A LOT OF HISTORY, INDEED... SO, I'M GONNA STICK AROUND TO HEAR WHAT THESE LADIES HAVE TO SAY.
INNOVATION MY ASS!
THERE'S TOO MUCH HISTORY BEHIND THIS BUULLL SHIT TO LET IT RIDE.
EXERPTED FROM "DAILIES" THE RYTHM MASTR PROJECT
HELLLL YEAH!
ROBERT FARRIS THOMPSON USED "POST-BLACK" BACK IN NINETEEN NINETY FOUR...
THAT'S THE FIRST TIME I SAW IT.

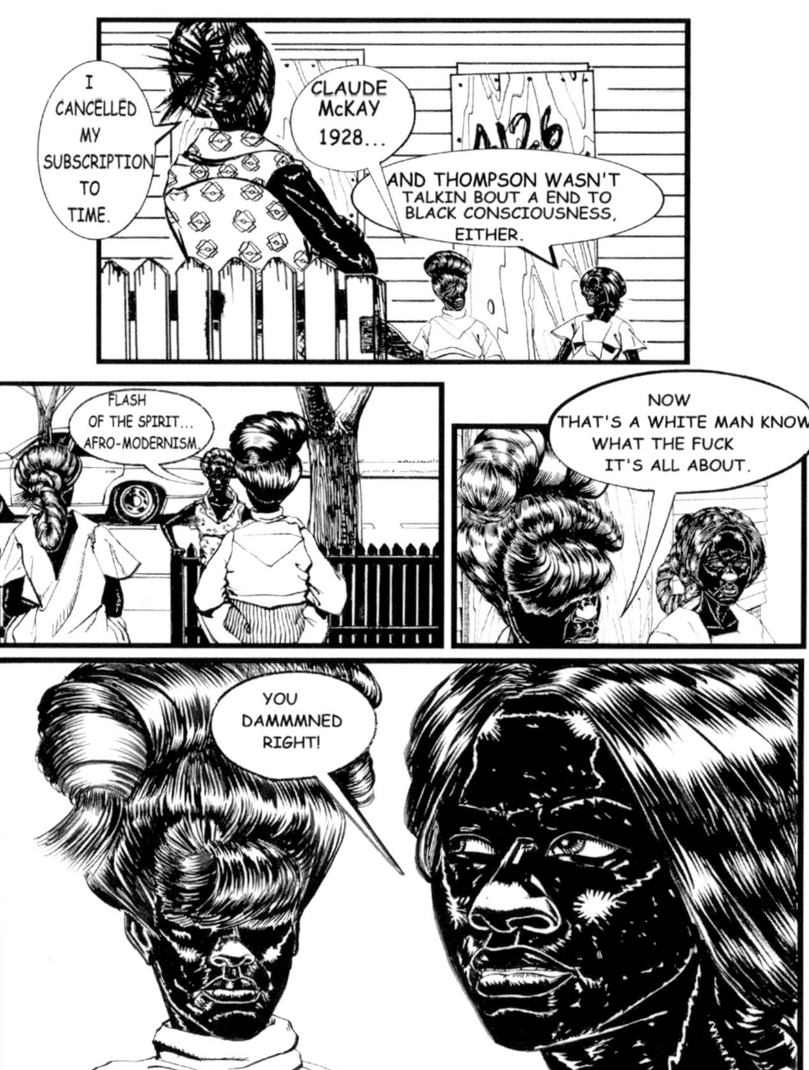

I CANCELLED MY SUBSCRIPTION TO TIME.
CLAUDE McKAY 1928...
AND THOMPSON WASN'T TALKIN BOUT A END TO BLACK CONSCIOUSNESS, EITHER.
FLASH OF THE SPIRIT... AFRO-MODERNISM
NOW THAT'S A WHITE MAN KNOW WHAT THE FUCK IT'S ALL ABOUT.
YOU DAMMMNED RIGHT!

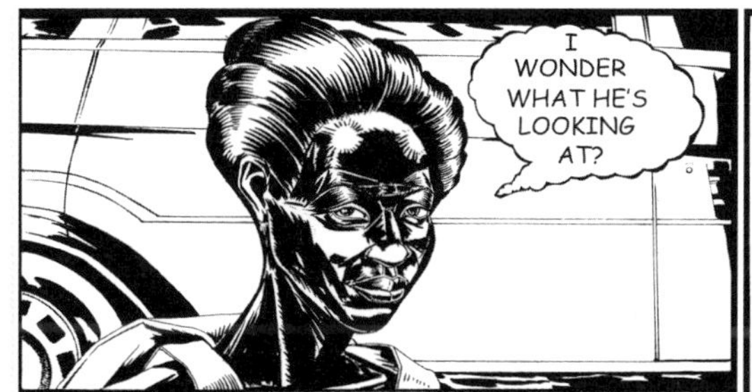
I WONDER WHAT HE'S LOOKING AT?

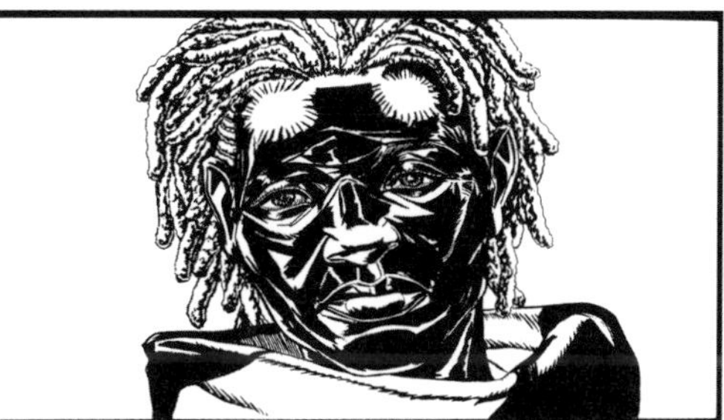

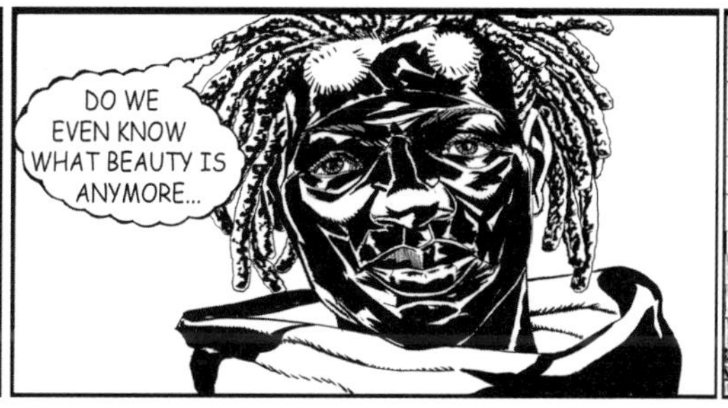
DO WE EVEN KNOW WHAT BEAUTY IS ANYMORE...

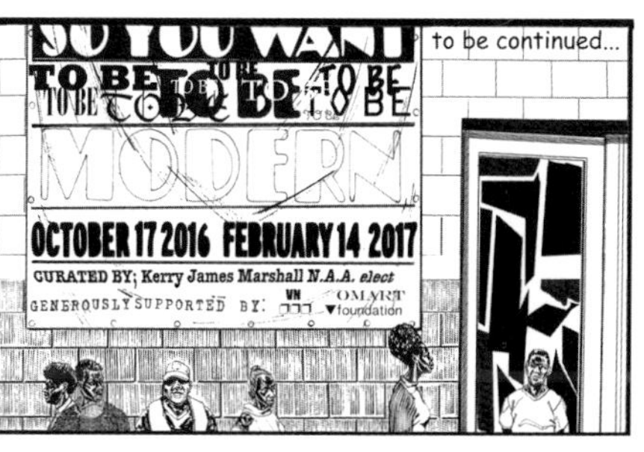
to be continued...
SO YOU WANT
TO BE
MODERN
OCTOBER 17 2016 FEBRUARY 14 2017
CURATED BY; Kerry James Marshall N.A.A. elect
GENEROUSLY SUPPORTED BY:
foundation

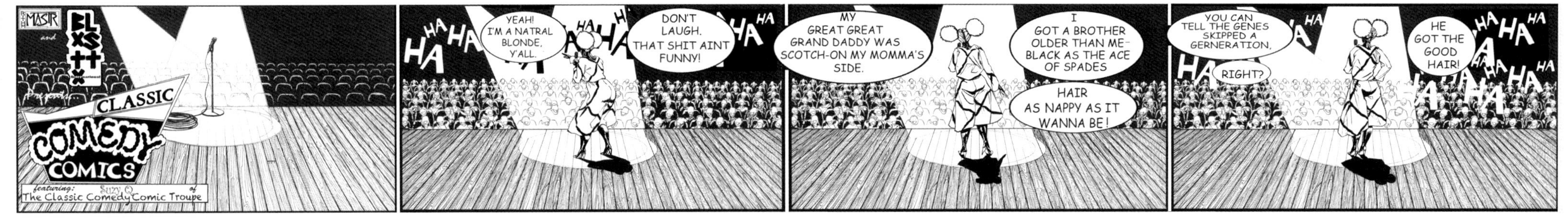

MASTR
and
Presents...
CLASSIC
COMEDY
COMICS
featuring: Suzy Q of
The Classic Comedy Comic Troupe
YEAH! I'M A NATRAL BLONDE, Y'ALL.
DON'T LAUGH. THAT SHIT AINT FUNNY!
MY GREAT GREAT GRAND DADDY WAS SCOTCH-ON MY MOMMA'S SIDE.
I GOT A BROTHER OLDER THAN ME-BLACK AS THE ACE OF SPADES
HAIR AS NAPPY AS IT WANNA BE!
YOU CAN TELL THE GENES SKIPPED A GERNERATION,
RIGHT?
HE GOT THE GOOD HAIR!

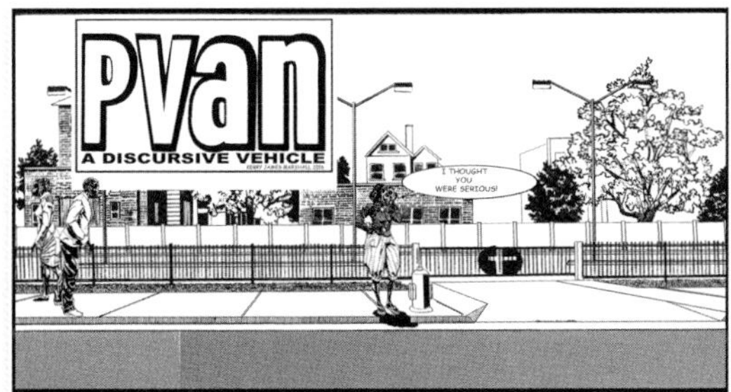
pvan
A DISCURSIVE VEHICLE
I THOUGHT YOU WERE SERIOUS!

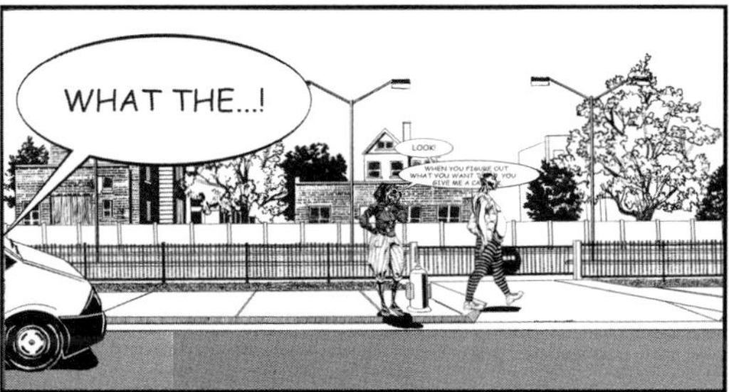
WHAT THE...!
LOOK!

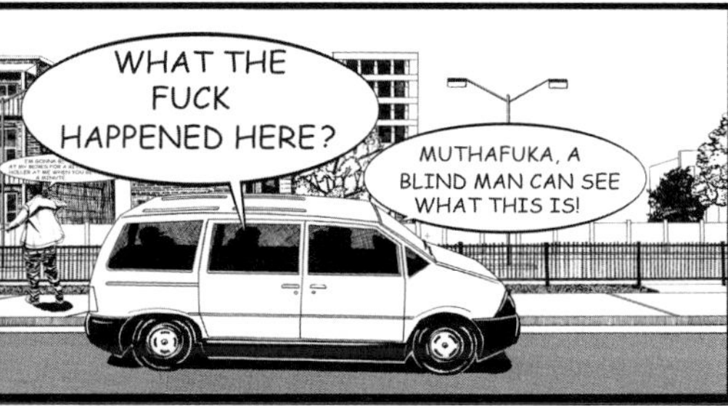
WHAT THE FUCK HAPPENED HERE?
MUTHAFUKA, A BLIND MAN CAN SEE WHAT THIS IS!

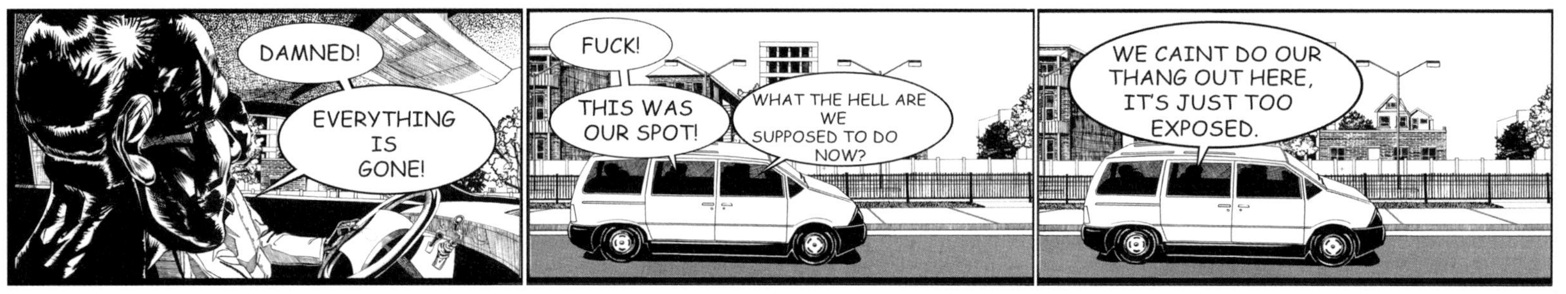
DAMNED!
EVERYTHING IS GONE!
FUCK!
THIS WAS OUR SPOT!
WHAT THE HELL ARE WE SUPPOSED TO DO NOW?
WE CAINT DO OUR THANG OUT HERE, IT'S JUST TOO EXPOSED.

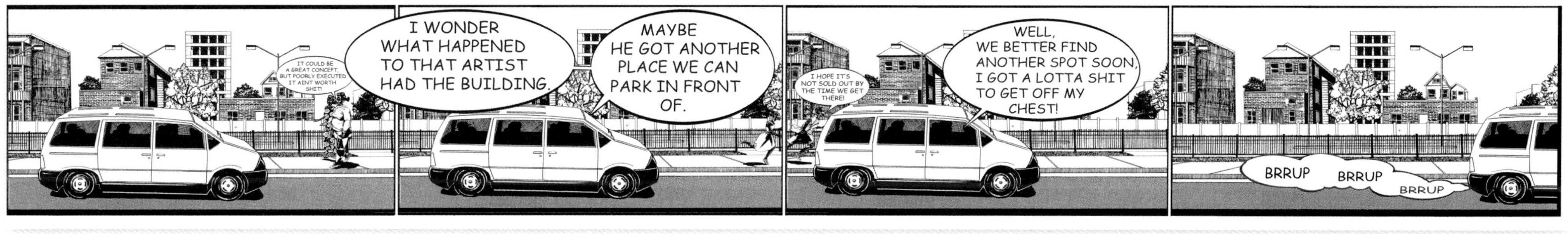
IT COULD BE A GREAT CONCEPT, BUT POORLY EXECUTED IT AINT WORTH SHIT!
I WONDER WHAT HAPPENED TO THAT ARTIST HAD THE BUILDING.
MAYBE HE GOT ANOTHER PLACE WE CAN PARK IN FRONT OF.
I HOPE IT'S NOT SOLD OUT BY THE TIME WE GET THERE!
WELL, WE BETTER FIND ANOTHER SPOT SOON, I GOT A LOTTA SHIT TO GET OFF MY CHEST!
BRRUP
BRRUP
BRRUP

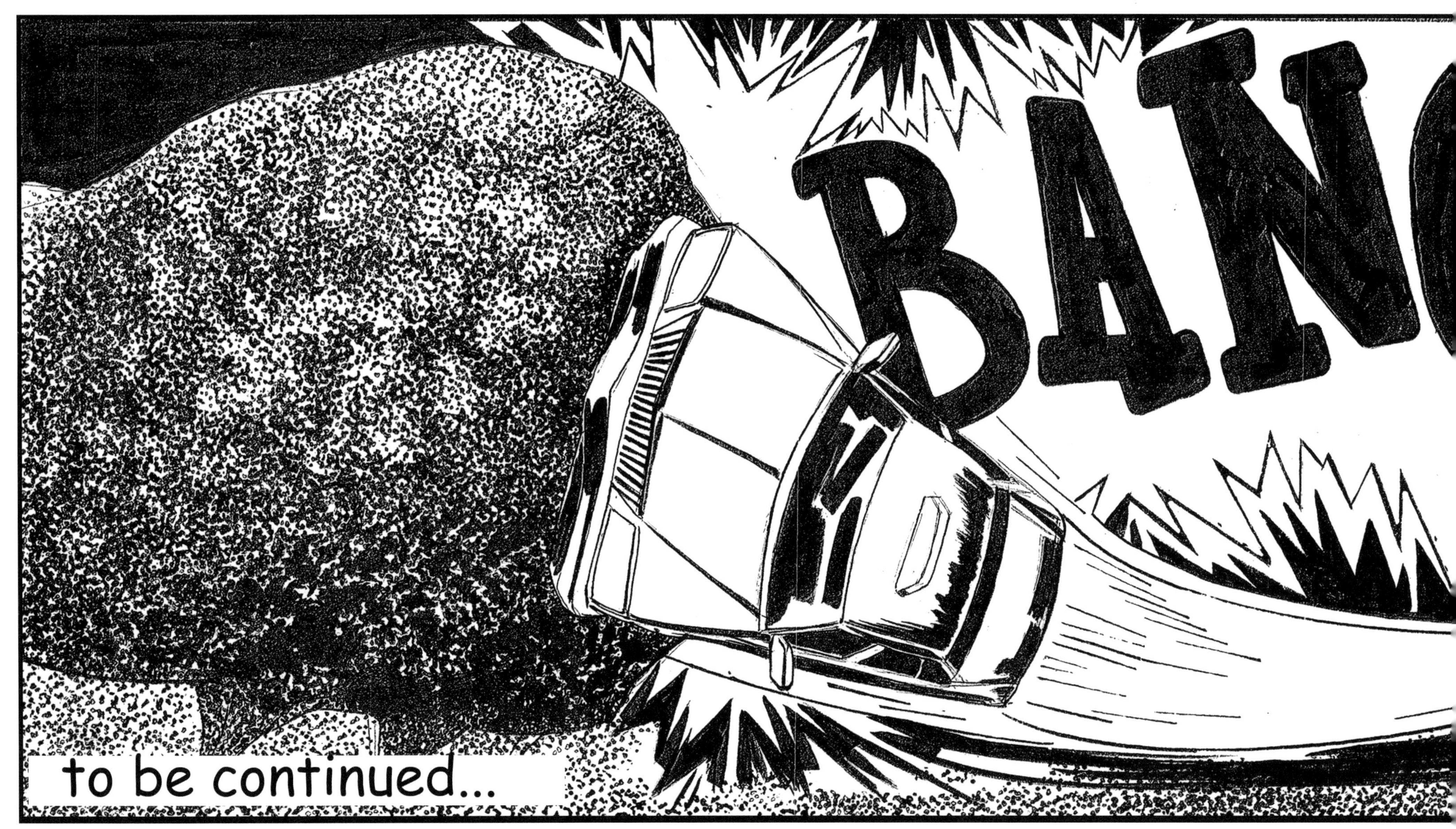
BAN
to be continued...

2018

RYTHM MASTR DAILY STRIP (RUNNERS)

UV-cured inkjet print on ten panels of translucent white Plexiglas

three panels 7 ½×40 in. (19×102 cm); three panels 7 ½×67 in. (19×169.5 cm); four panels 7 ½×93 ½ in. (19×238 cm); overall 7 ½×695 ¾ in. (19×1,767 cm)

Edition: 3

Numbered, titled, signed, and dated on studio label applied verso

Printed by Dr. Graphx, Chicago

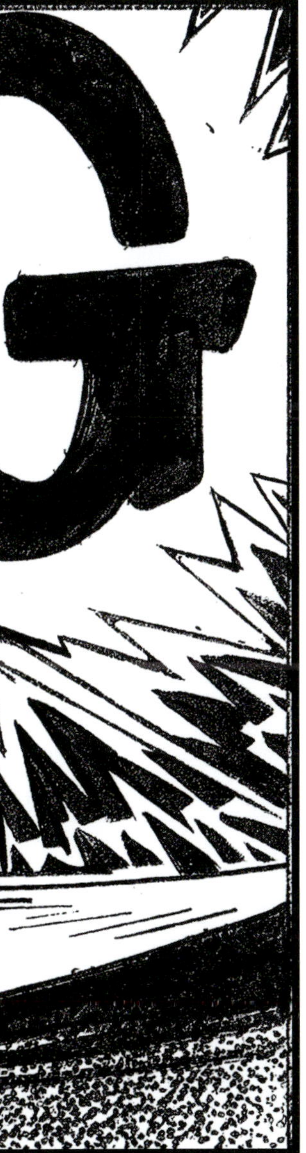

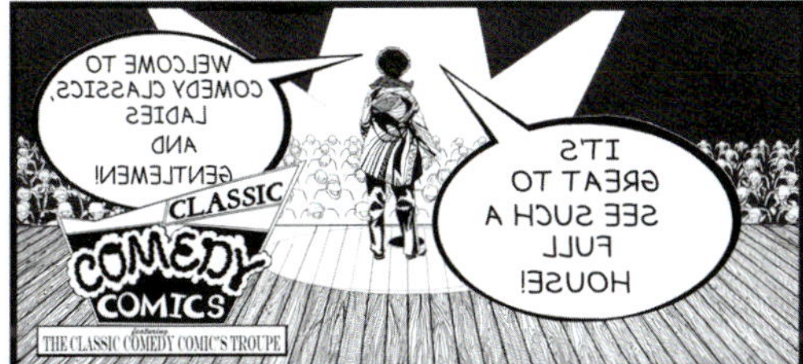

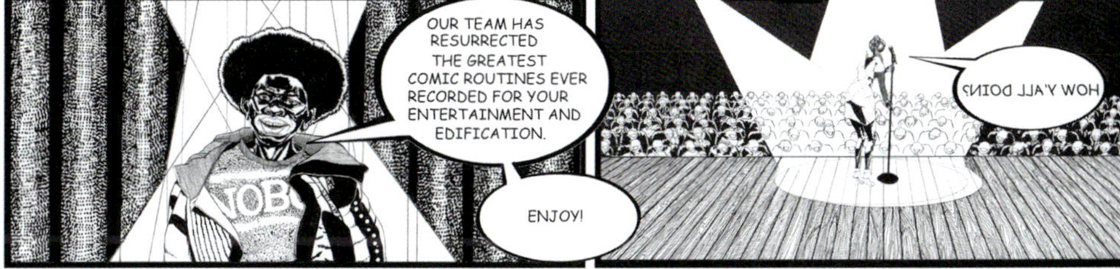

Almost two decades after *Rythm Mastr*'s debut at the Carnegie International, Marshall was invited back to Pittsburgh for the 2018/19 edition of the exhibition. The single strip created for the occasion mixes new storylines with heavily reworked parts from the original series. The Comedy Club part introduces the use of subverted speech balloons when the comedian is seen from behind. The opening at the 21st Century Gallery, where Marshall's 2016 painting *Untitled (Gallery)* is visible on the wall, is picketed by a mob, with one person holding a placard reading "Stop Running." (We soon learn that the "runners" reference the dangers people are frequently exposed to when they try to elude the police.) Other elements, such as streets becoming sentient and Oba and Boli flying over the city, are here reproposed and once again met by P-Van's skepticism. ("The other day I saw a man made out of iron flying through the air"; "You know, there's a lotta weird shit going on around here lately!")

Note: Marshall installed the piece to be experienced by walking back and forth. For a correct understanding of the narrative, readers should start reading from p. 213 backwards.

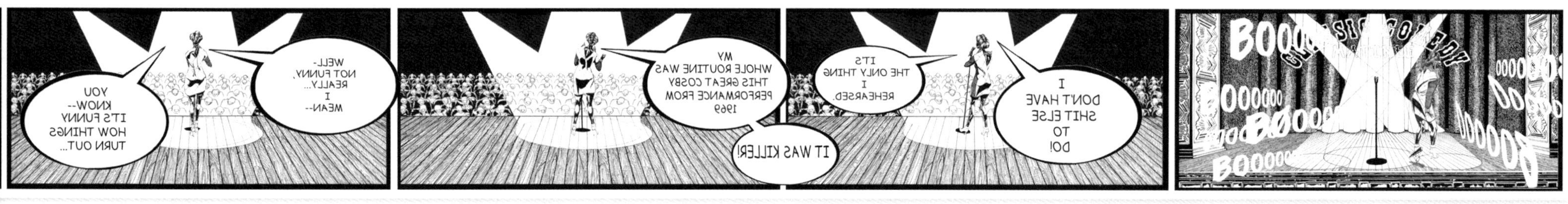
YOU KNOW-- IT'S FUNNY HOW THINGS TURN OUT...
WELL- NOT FUNNY, REALLY... I MEAN--
MY WHOLE ROUTINE WAS THIS GREAT COSBY PERFORMANCE FROM 1969
IT WAS KILLER!
IT'S THE ONLY THING I REHEARSED.
I DON'T HAVE SHIT ELSE TO DO!
BOOO
BOOOOOO
BOOOOO

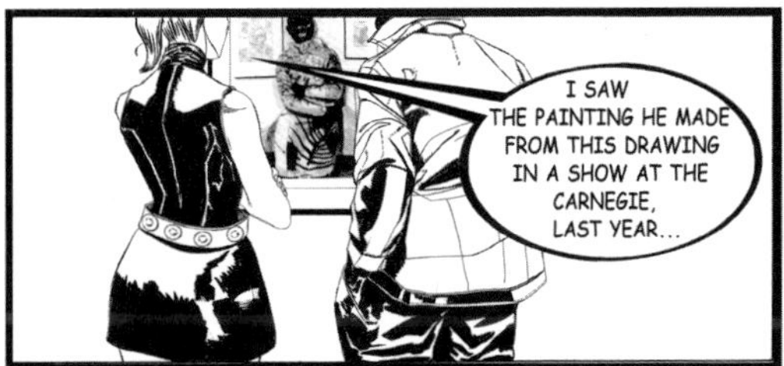
I SAW THE PAINTING HE MADE FROM THIS DRAWING IN A SHOW AT THE CARNEGIE, LAST YEAR...

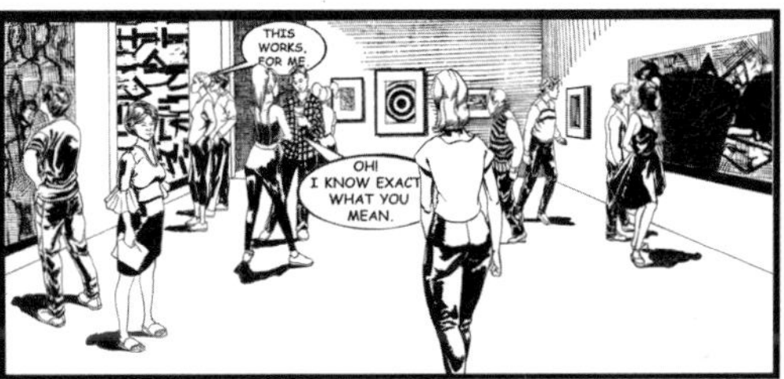
THIS WORKS, FOR ME.
OH! I KNOW EXACT WHAT YOU MEAN.

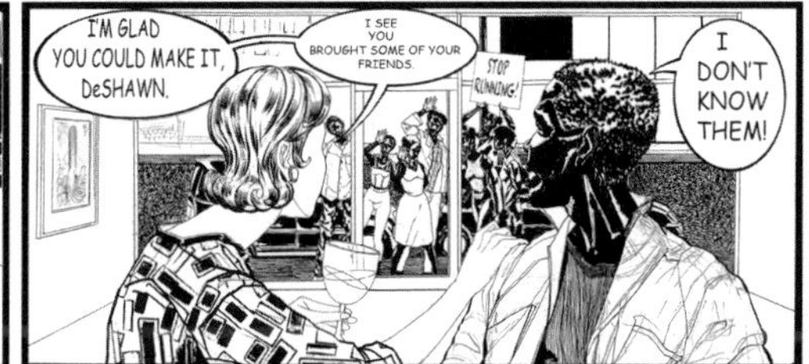
I'M GLAD YOU COULD MAKE IT, DeSHAWN.
I SEE YOU BROUGHT SOME OF YOUR FRIENDS.
STOP RUNNING!
I DON'T KNOW THEM!

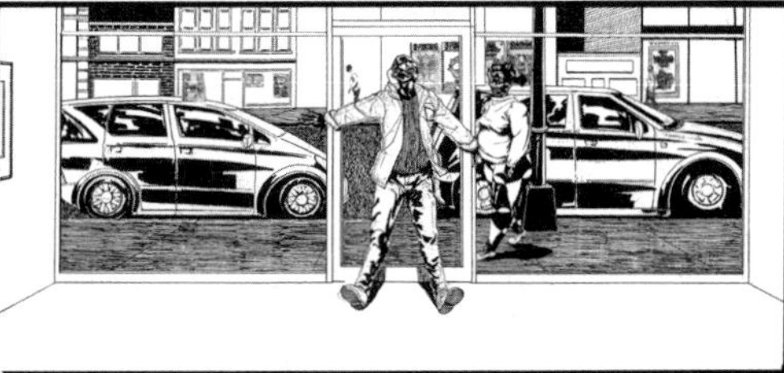

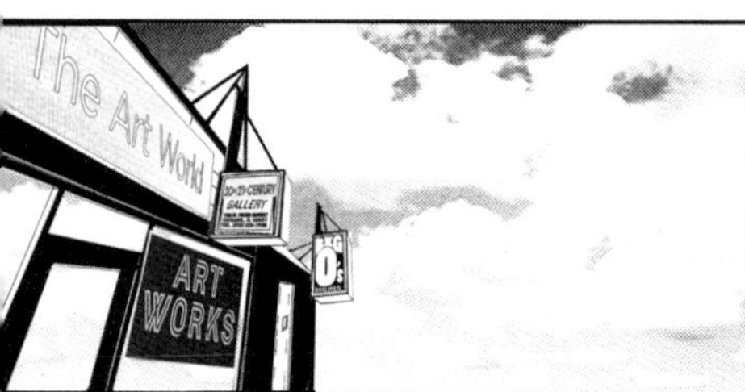
The Art World
ART WORKS

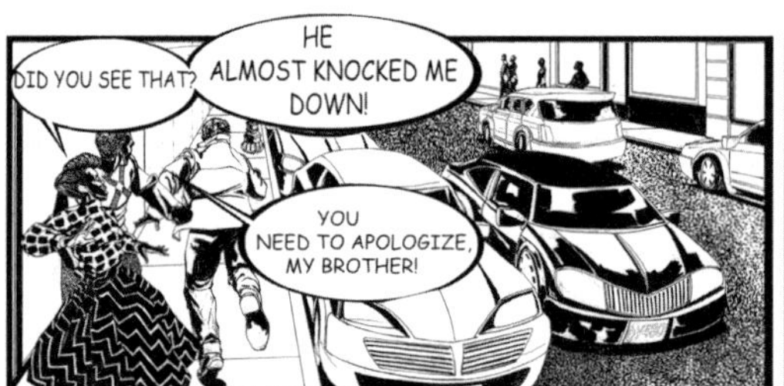
DID YOU SEE THAT?
HE ALMOST KNOCKED ME DOWN!
YOU NEED TO APOLOGIZE, MY BROTHER!

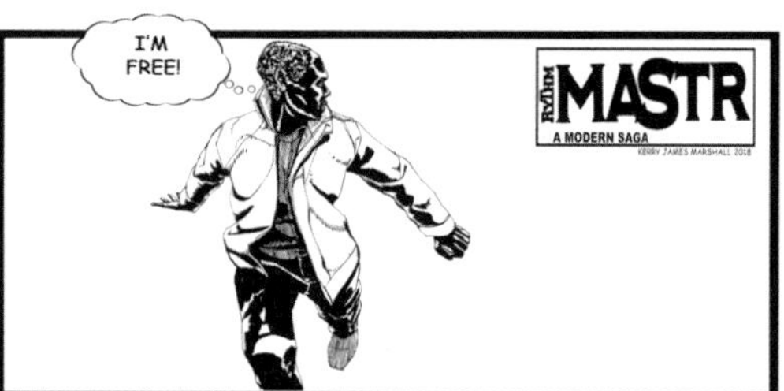
I'M FREE!
MASTR
A MODERN SAGA

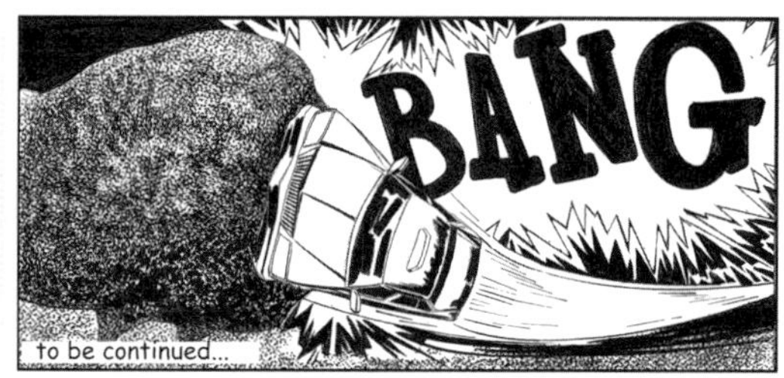
BANG
to be continued...

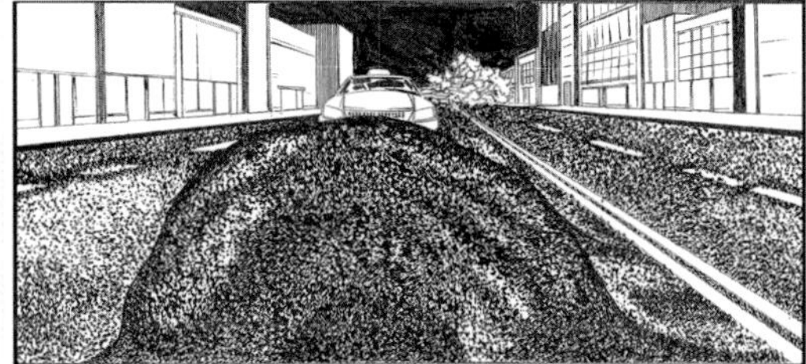

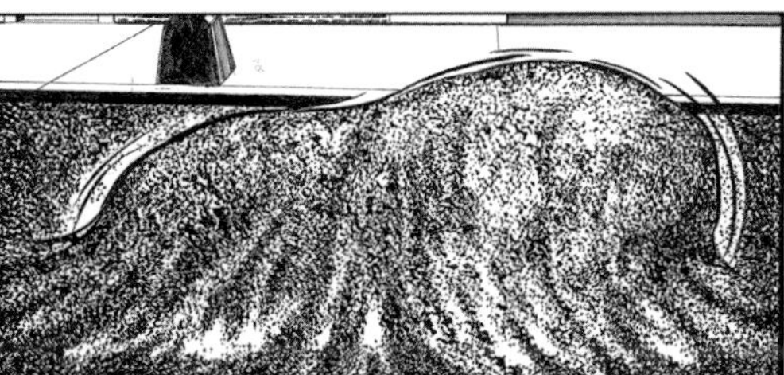

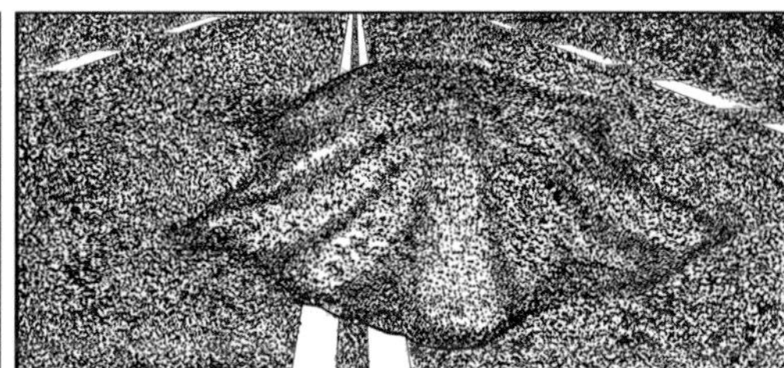

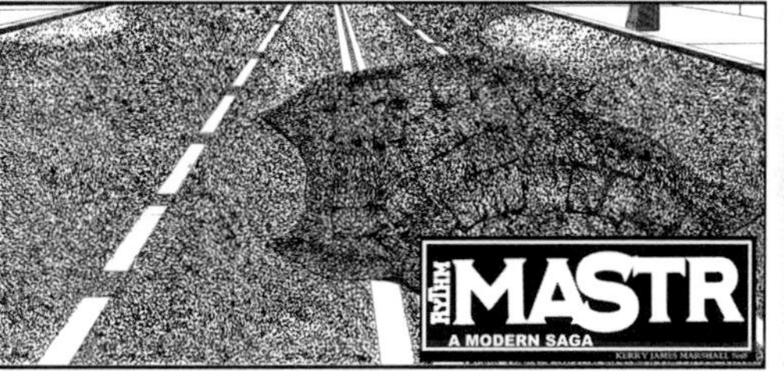

Rythm Mastr Daily Strip (Runners) **[2018]**

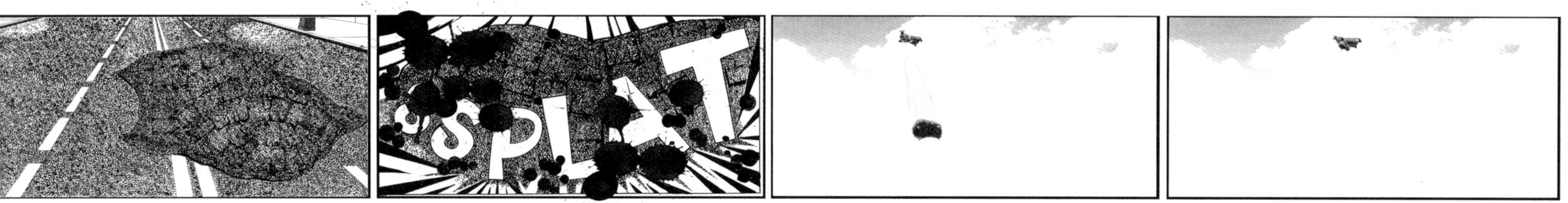
SPLAT

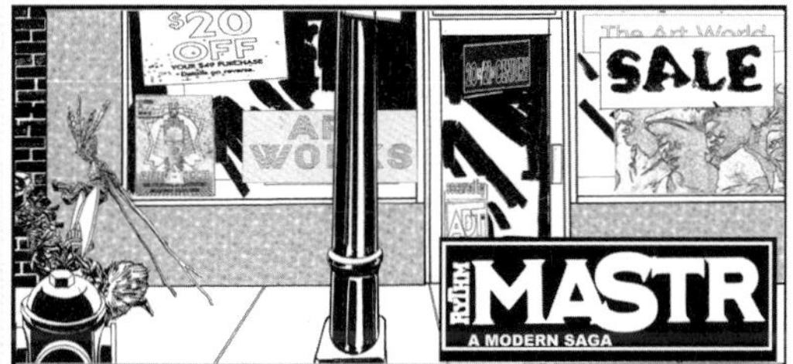

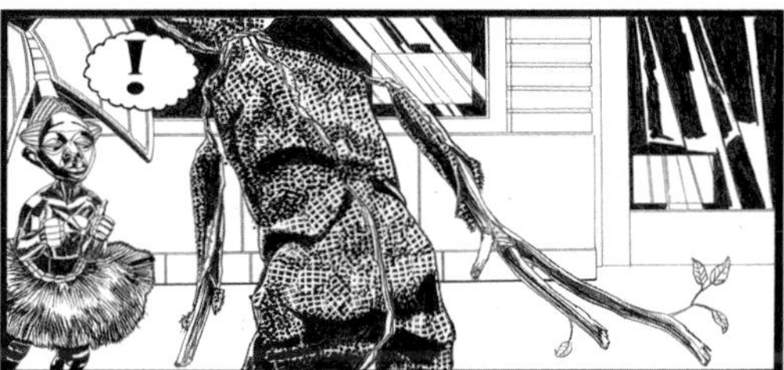

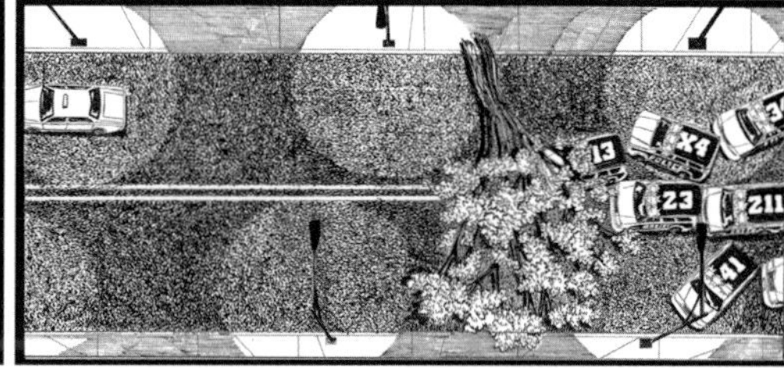

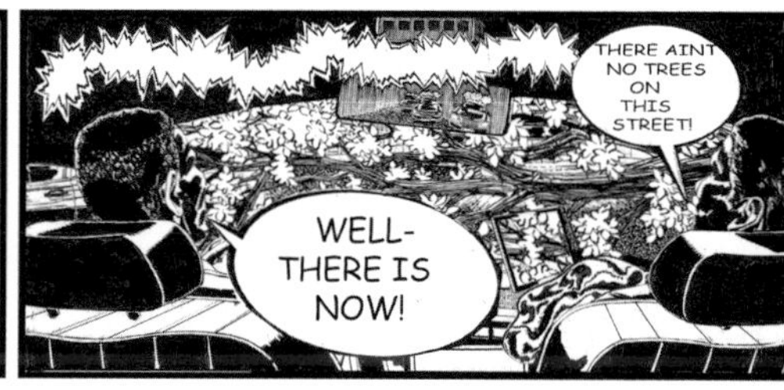

Rythm Mastr Daily Strip (Runners) **[2018]**

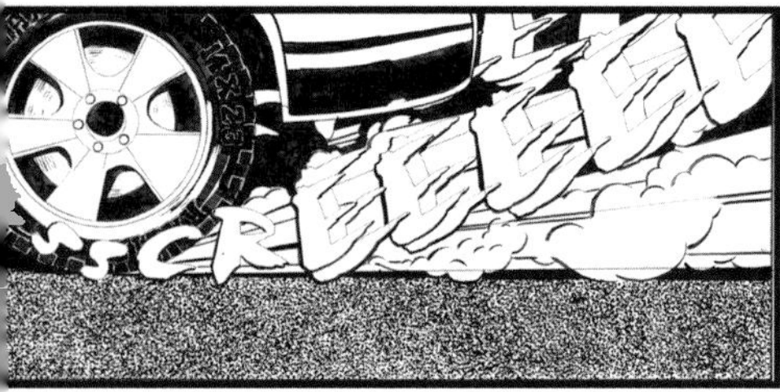

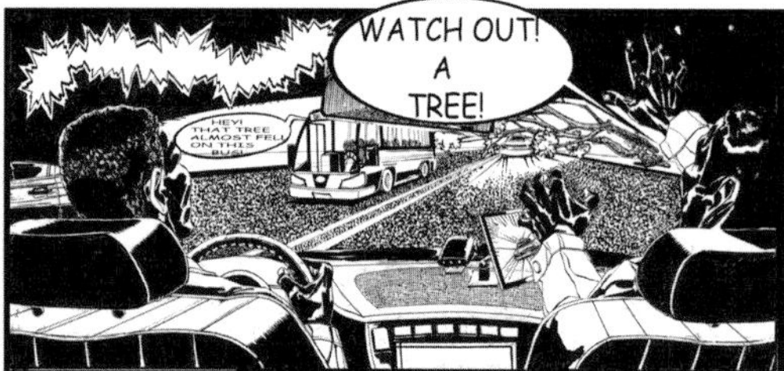
HEY! THAT TREE ALMOST FELL ON THIS BUS!
WATCH OUT! A TREE!

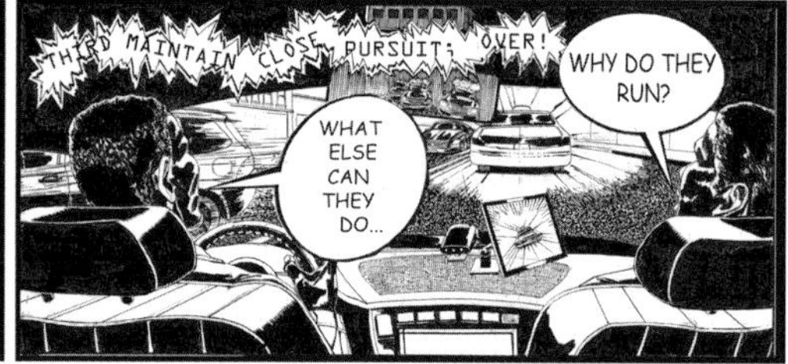
THIRD MAINTAIN CLOSE PURSUIT: OVER!
WHY DO THEY RUN?
WHAT ELSE CAN THEY DO...

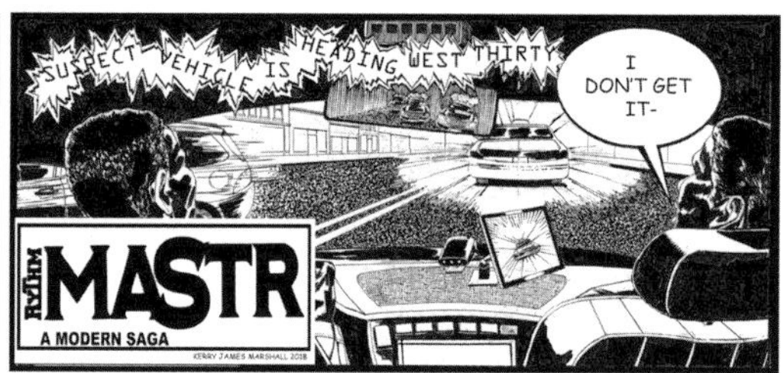
SUSPECT VEHICLE IS HEADING WEST THIRTY
I DON'T GET IT-
RYTHM MASTR
A MODERN SAGA
KERRY JAMES MARSHALL 2018

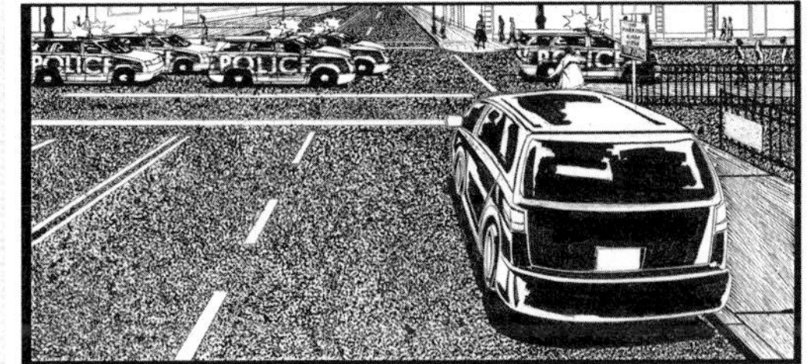

POLICE
POLICE

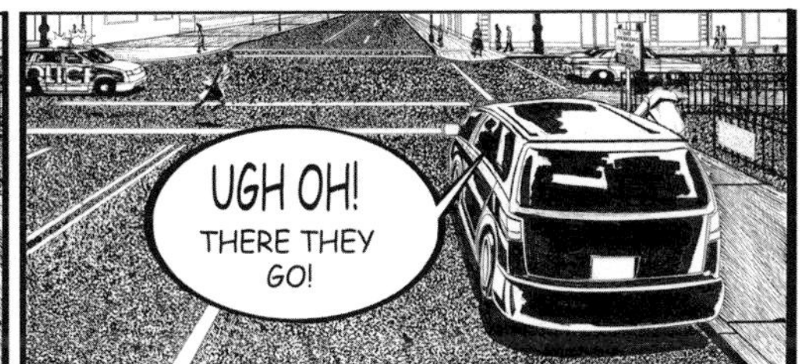

UGH OH!
THERE THEY GO!

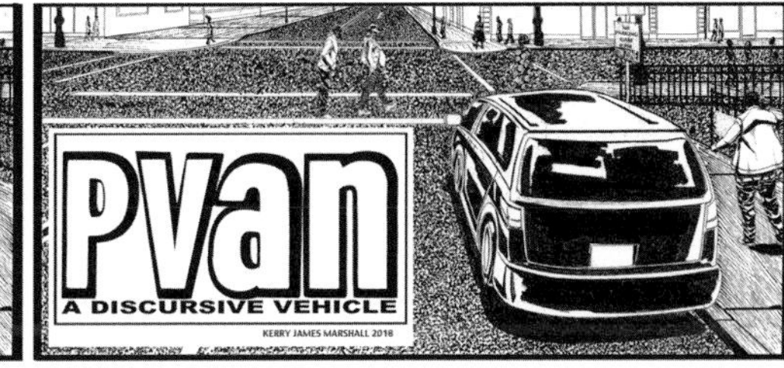

PVAN
A DISCURSIVE VEHICLE
KERRY JAMES MARSHALL 2018

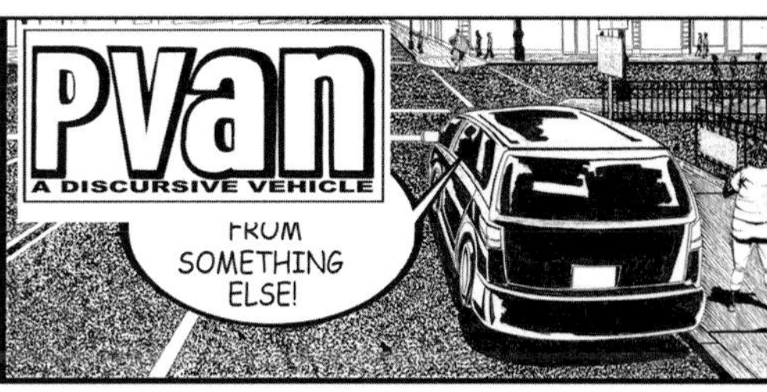

PVAN
A DISCURSIVE VEHICLE
FROM SOMETHING ELSE!

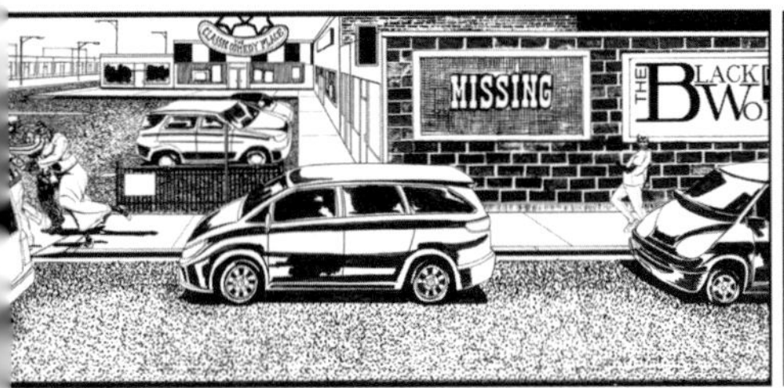
MISSING

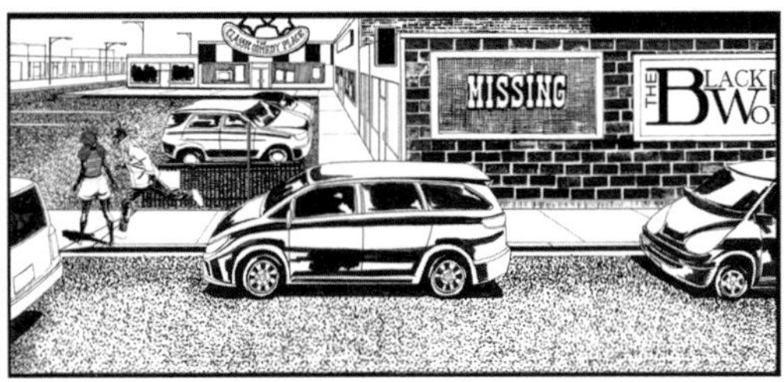
MISSING

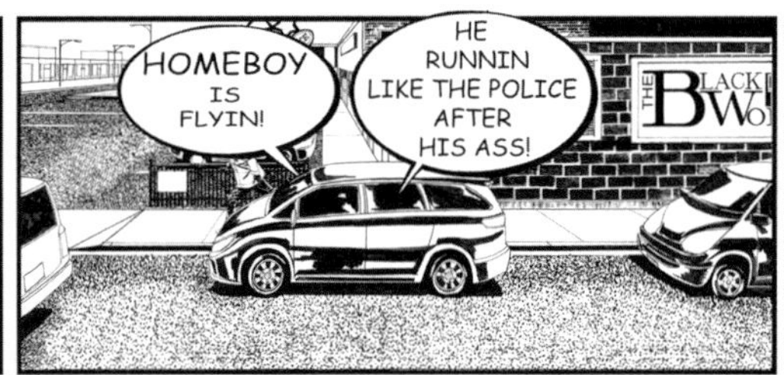
HOMEBOY IS FLYIN!
HE RUNNIN LIKE THE POLICE AFTER HIS ASS!

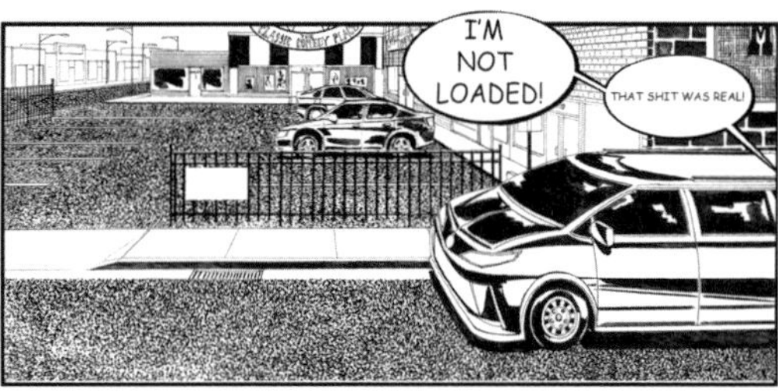
I'M NOT LOADED!
THAT SHIT WAS REAL!

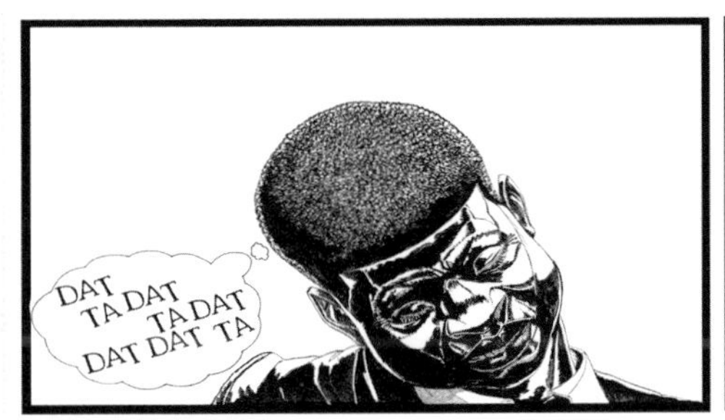

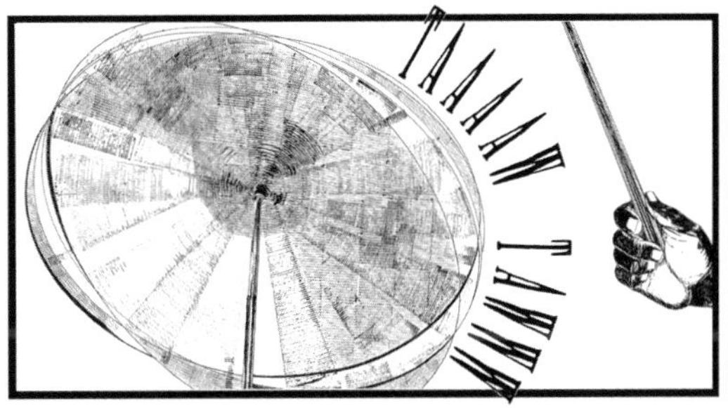

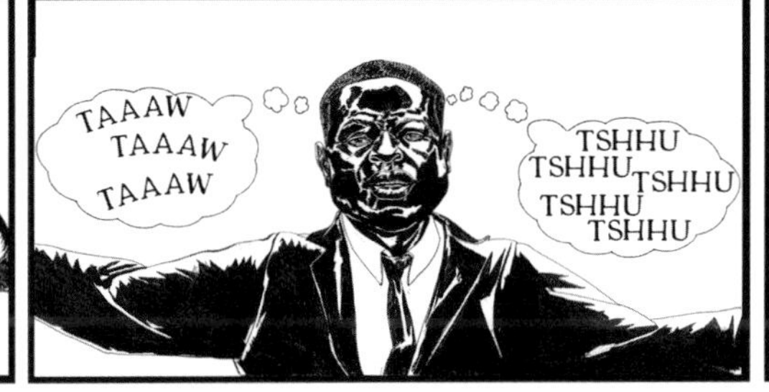

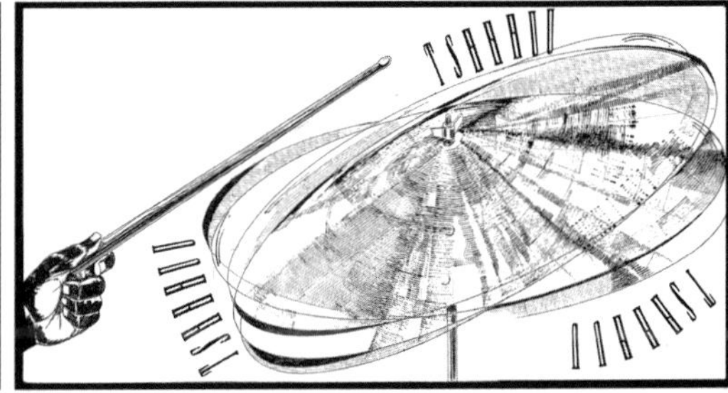

Rythm Mastr Daily Strip (Drum Solo) **[2021]**

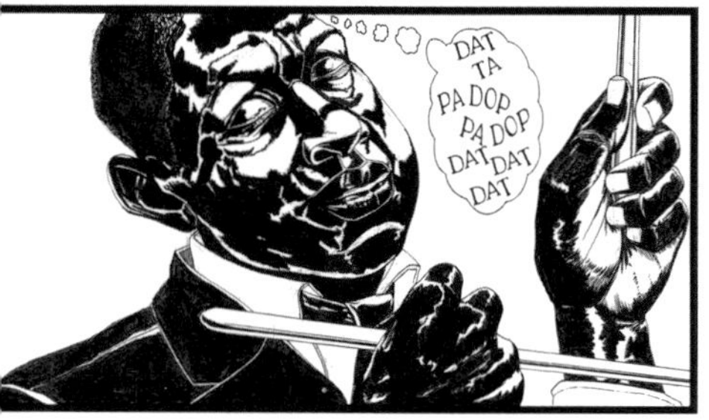
DAT
TA
PA DOP
PA DOP
DAT DAT
DAT

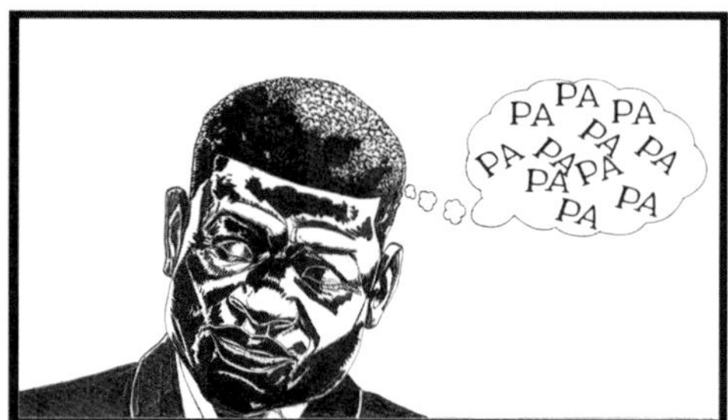
PA PA PA
PA PA PA PA
PA PA PA PA

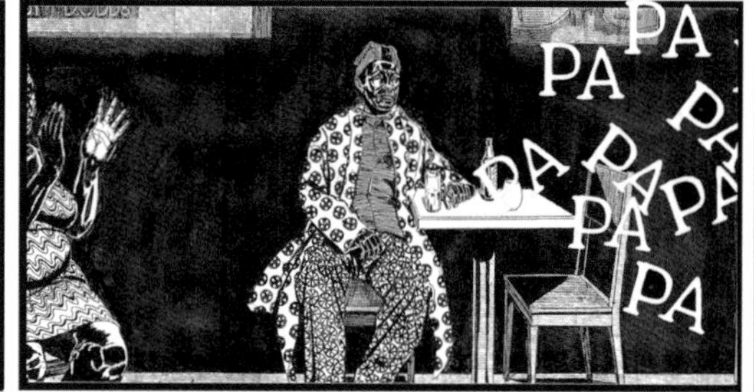
PA PA
PA PA PA PA PA PA
PA

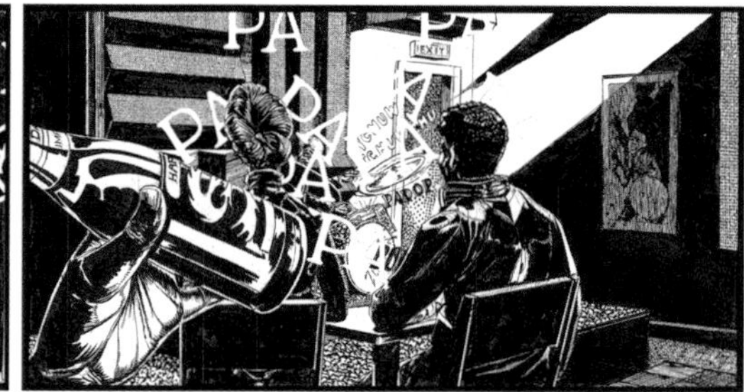
PA
EXIT
PADOP

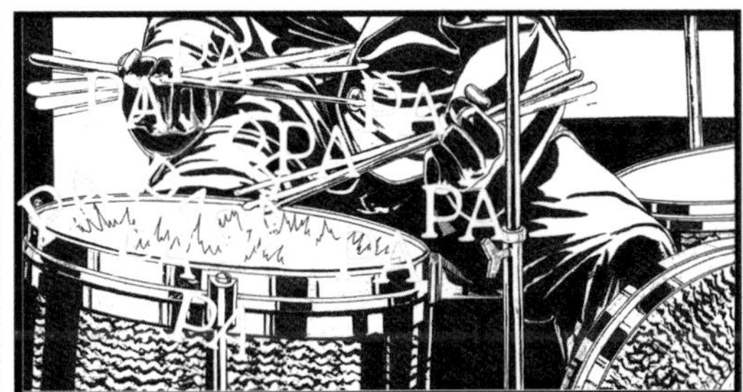

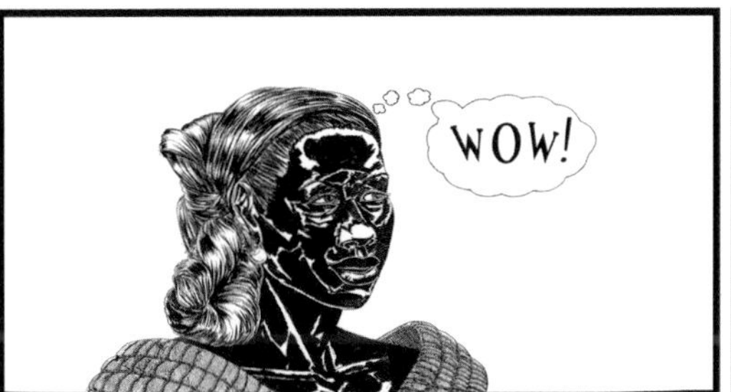

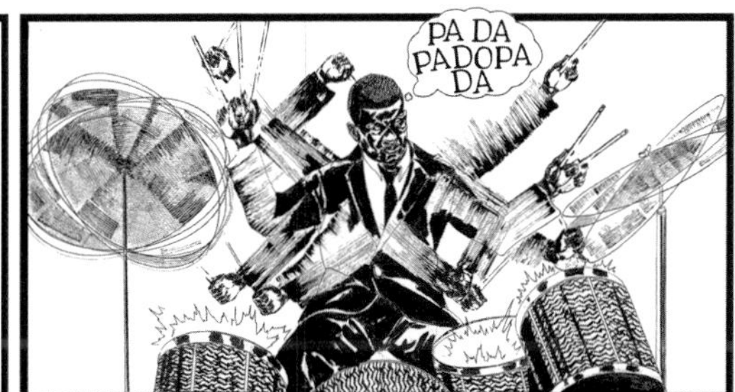

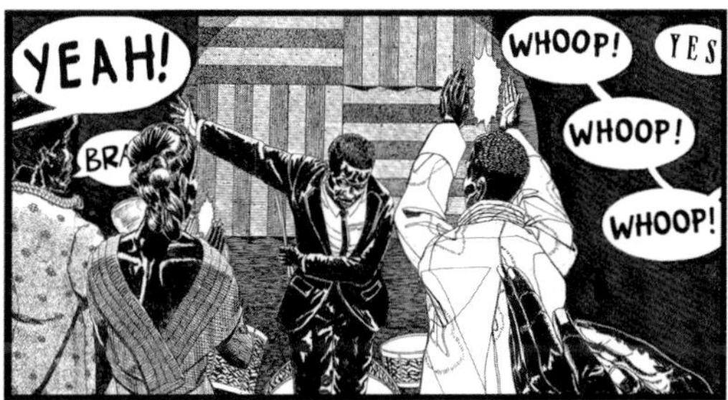

Rythm Mastr Daily Strip (Drum Solo) **[2021]**

2017–2022

DAILIES: EVERYTHING WILL BE ALRIGHT (SINGLE / LADIES)

UV-cured inkjet print on translucent white Plexiglas

23×31 in. (58.5×78.5 cm)

Edition: 5

Numbered, titled, signed, and dated on studio label applied verso

Printed by Alpha Graphics, Chicago

When asked to produce a limited edition, Marshall would often use the *Dailies*—especially *Everything Will Be Alright, I Just Know It Will*—as a starting point. Made with a commercial digital process called UV-cured printing, which can produce excellent results on every type of format, these multilingual prints do not represent a notable innovation to the overall narrative, except for the running characters in the diptych, later to be reprised in the *Rythm Mastr Daily Strip* of 2018. A fourth one, this time representing two women instead of the man-woman combo proposed so far, was designed around this time but only put into production five years later.

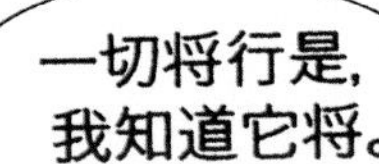

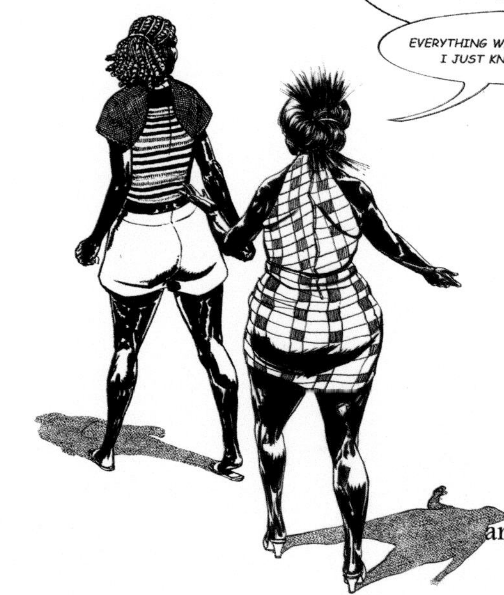

ames Marshall 2017

SELECTED BIBLIOGRAPHY

BOOKS AND EXHIBITION CATALOGUES

Alteveer, Ian, Helen Molesworth, Dieter Roelstraete, and Abigail Winograd. *Kerry James Marshall: Mastry*. New York: Skira Rizzoli, 2016.

Andress, Sarah, Shelly Bancroft, and Peter Nesbett, eds. *Letters to a Young Artist*. New York: Darte Publishing, 2006.

Bartels, Kathleen S., Kerry James Marshall, and Jeff Wall. *Kerry James Marshall*. Vancouver: Vancouver Art Gallery, 2010.

Cassel Oliver, Valerie, Kerry James Marshall, and Luc Tuymans, edited by Sarah Martin and Deborah Smith. *Kerry James Marshall: Along the Way*. London: Camden Art Centre, 2005.

Choon, Angela, Kerry James Marshall, and Robert Storr. *Kerry James Marshall: Look See*. New York: David Zwirner Books, 2014.

Clauß, Ingo, ed. *Comic in der Kunst/Comics in Art*. Heidelberg: Kehrer, 2013.

Cugini, Carla, ed. *Inside Out: Kerry James Marshall*. Cologne: Buchhandlung Walther König, 2018.

Fitzpatrick, Robert, Elizabeth A. T. Smith, Tricia Van Eck, and Stephanie Williams. *Kerry James Marshall: One True Thing, Meditations on Black Aesthetics*. Chicago: Museum of Contemporary Art, 2003.

Frankel, David S., ed. *Carnegie International 1999/2000*, vol. 1. Pittsburgh: Carnegie Museum of Art, 1999.

Gaines, Charles, Laurence Rassel, and Greg Tate, edited by Michele Robecchi. *Kerry James Marshall*. London: Phaidon, 2017.

Haq, Nav. *Kerry James Marshall: Painting and Other Stuff*. Brussels: Ludion, 2013.

Jafa, Arthur, Kerry James Marshall, and Terrie Sultan, edited by Eve Sinaiko. *Kerry James Marshall*. New York: Harry N. Abrams, 2000.

Marshall, Kerry James, András Pálffy, and Raél Jero Salley, edited by Tina Lipsky and Annette Südbeck. *Kerry James Marshall: Who's Afraid of Red, Black and Green*. Vienna: Secession, 2012.

Nadel, Dan, ed. *It's Life as I See It: Black Cartoonists in Chicago, 1940–1980*. Chicago: Museum of Contemporary Art, 2021.

Peeters, Wim, ed. *The Big Show*. Antwerp: Nieuw Internationaal Cultureel Centrum, 2002.

Schaffner, Ingrid, ed. *Carnegie International, 57th Edition: The Guide*. Pittsburgh: Carnegie Museum of Art, 2019.

Tallman, Susan. *Kerry James Marshall: The Complete Prints*. Brussels: Ludion, 2023.

Walker, Hamza, ed. *Kerry James Marshall: Mementos*. Chicago: The Renaissance Society, 1998.

MAGAZINES, JOURNALS, AND PERIODICALS

Applebroog, Ida, Cory Arcangel, Stephanie Burt, Julien Ceccaldi, Ian Cheng, Hillary Chute, Kerry James Marshall, Jim Shaw, Art Spiegelman, Fabrice Stroun, Jordan Wolfson, and Douglas Wolk. "Graphic Content: Art and Animation." *Artforum*, summer 2014.

Binlot, Ann. "Kerry James Marshall Created Comic Strip with Black Characters to Show 'It Can Be Done'." *Document Journal*, October 15, 2018.

Biro, Matthew. "Representing Blackness: Kerry James Marshall's Recent Work Re-thinks the Meaning of 'Black Art'." *Art Papers*, March–April 2004.

Ditmars, Hadani. "Kerry James Marshall on Painting, Politics, and P Diddy's Record-Breaking Purchase of His Work." *Art Newspaper*, June 3, 2018.

Gopnik, Blake. "Monumental Man." *Washington Post*, February 15, 2008.

Janssen, Kim. "Add Statue of Mussolini's Mutilated Body to Balbo Monument: Kerry James Marshall." *Chicago Tribune*, August 29, 2017.

MacMillan, Kyle. "Kerry James Marshall Changing the Narrative of Art History." *Chicago Sun Times*, April 20, 2016.

Marshall, Kerry James. "Artist's Project." *Esopus*, no. 14, spring 2010.

Marshall, Kerry James. "Marvel's *Black Panther*." *Artforum*, September 2016.

Reid, Calvin. "Interview with Kerry James Marshall." *Bomb*, winter, 1998.

Siegel, Katy. "1000 Words: Kerry James Marshall." *Artforum*, summer 2000.

Tani, Ellen Y. "The World of Groundbreaking Artist Kerry James Marshall." *Artsy*, April 20, 2016.

PHOTO CREDITS

Every effort has been made to contact copyright holders of photographs. Any copyright holders we have been unable to reach or to whom inaccurate acknowledgment has been made are invited to contact the publisher.

Accessed via the Family and Local History Department at the Carnegie Library of Pittsburgh: fig. 38; pp. 80–85.
A High Line Commission. Courtesy the artist, David Zwirner, London, and Friends of the High Line: fig. 45.
Birmingham Museum of Art: fig. 44.
Carnegie International, Pittsburgh. Photography Bryan Conley: fig. 55.
Carnegie Museum of Art: fig. 56.
Courtesy Esopus: pp. 178–183.
Courtesy Fondazione Prada, Milan. Photography Delfino Sisto Legnani and Alessandro Saletta – DSL Studio: fig. 60.
Courtesy Ludion Publishers: pp. 92–93.
Courtesy of the Greater Des Moines Public Art Foundation. Photography Jim Zeller: fig. 51.
Courtesy of the Wexner Center for the Arts at The Ohio State University. Photography Chet Hey: fig. 52.
Courtesy Rennie Collection, Vancouver. Photography Blaine Campbell: fig. 26.
Courtesy the artist and David Zwirner, London. Photography Jack Hems: fig. 50.
Courtesy the artist and David Zwirner, New York: figs. 39, 54; pp. 188–197.
Courtesy the artist and Jack Shainman, New York: figs. 1, 27, 37; pp. 151–153, 169–177.
Courtesy the artist, Jack Shainman Gallery, New York, and Koplin Gallery, Los Angeles: fig. 31.
Crystal Bridges Museum of American Art, Bentonville, Arkansas. Photography Vancouver Art Gallery: fig. 2.
Digital Image Museum Associates / LACMA / Art Resource NY, 2013: fig. 30.
Kerry James Marshall Studio: pp. 88–91, 95–139, 141, 143, 145, 155, 156, 158–163, 165, 167, 184–187, 198–221.
Los Angeles County Museum of Art: figs. 22–23.
Museum of Contemporary Art Chicago. Photography Joe Ziolkowski (fig. 6), Nathan Keay (fig. 61).
Museum of Modern Art, New York / Scala, Florence: pp. 147–149.
New York Magazine and Vox Media, LLC: fig. 58.
Philadelphia Museum of Art. Bridgeman Images: fig. 21.
Saint Louis Museum, transferred from the Richardson Memorial Library (inv. 32–34: 2019). Courtesy of the artist and Jack Shainman Gallery, New York: figs. 32, 34, 59, 62; pp. 64–79.

ACKNOWLEDGMENTS

I would like to thank Peter Ruyffelaere for giving me the opportunity to write this book and for his unconditional trust and support.

I would also like to thank Ruth Ruyffelaere for her enduring patience and all the hard work she put together in order to make this book possible.

A big thank you to Charles Miers, Margaret Rennolds Chace, Emily Ligniti, and everyone at Rizzoli who spent time on this project too.

I'm deeply grateful to Sara Harrison for the thoughtful copyediting job. And I'm indebted to Fabrice Stroun and Gino Udina for the time they took to read my manuscript and give their sage advice. Personal and/or professional support also came, at different stages of the process, from Francesca Bonazzoli, Emily Cushman, Kahil Elzabar, Alicia Loy Griffin, Charles R. Johnson, Melissa Larner, Balthazar Lovay, Senga Nengudi, Kate Nesin, Wim Peeters, Dieter Roelstraete, Lauren A. Schultz, Susan Tallman, Ellen Y. Tani, Emmy Waldan, and Cassandra Washington. Thank you all.

Finally, I would love to thank Kerry James Marshall, without whom this publication, and a lot of wonderful things, would not exist.

KERRY JAMES MARSHALL is an artist and professor. He taught painting at the School of Art and Design at the University of Illinois at Chicago (1993–2006) and has exhibited widely throughout Europe and the US since the late 1970s. Appointed to the Committee on the Arts and the Humanities in 2013, he was included in *Time*'s annual list of the world's 100 most influential people in 2017.

MICHELE ROBECCHI is a writer and curator based in London, where he is a commissioning editor at Phaidon. He is the author of *Mona Lisa to Marge: How the World's Greatest Artworks Entered Popular Culture* (2014) and *Portraits Unmasked: The Stories Behind the Faces* (2020).

First published in the United States of America in 2025 by
Rizzoli Electa, a Division of
Rizzoli International Publications, Inc.
49 West 27th Street
New York, NY 10001
rizzoliusa.com

Originally published in Belgium in 2025 by
Ludion Publishers
Weefstraat 26
9810 Nazareth, Belgium
ludion.be

Copyright © 2025, Kerry James Marshall
Copyright © 2025, Ludion Publishers and the author

All rights reserved. No part of this publication may be reproduced or transmitted in any form or by any means, electronic or mechanical, including photocopy, recording or any other information storage and retrieval system, without prior permission in writing from the publishers.

The publishers have made every effort to abide by all copyright legislation. Any copyright holders we have been unable to reach or to whom inaccurate acknowledgement has been made are invited to contact the publishers.

ISBN: 978-0-8478-3561-4
Library of Congress Control Number: 2025933325

2025 2026 2027 2028 / 10 9 8 7 6 5 4 3 2 1
Printed in Belgium

For Rizzoli Electa
PUBLISHER
Charles Miers
ASSOCIATE PUBLISHER
Margaret Rennolds Chace
EDITOR
Klaus Kirschbaum
ASSISTANT EDITOR
Emily Ligniti

For Ludion Publishers
PUBLISHER
Peter Ruyffelaere
COORDINATION AND IMAGE RESEARCH
Ruth Ruyffelaere

TEXT Michele Robecchi
GRAPHIC DESIGN Thijs Kestens, Armée de Verre Bookdesign
COPYEDITING Sara Harrison
PROOFREADING Sarah Auld

The authorized representative in the EU for product safety and compliance is Mondadori Libri S.p.A., Via Gian Battista Vico 42, Milan, Italy, 20123
mondadori.it

Visit us online
Instagram.com/RizzoliBooks
Facebook.com/RizzoliNewYork
Youtube.com/user/RizzoliNY

FSC
www.fsc.org
MIX
Paper | Supporting responsible forestry
FSC® C014767